ENERGY SECURITY

ENERGY SECURITY

Edited by

Dr. Parag Diwan

Dr. A.N. Sarkar

POWERING ENERGY...

PENTAGON ENERGY PRESS

ENERGY SECURITY

ISBN 978-81-8274-352-6

First Edition: 2009

First published in India by

PENTAGON ENERGY PRESS

An Imprint of

PENTAGON PRESS

206, Peacock Lane, Shahpur Jat,

New Delhi-110049

Phones: 011-64706243, 26491568

Telefax: 011-26490600

email: rajan@pentagon-press.com

website: www.pentagon-press.com

Printed at New Elegant Printers, New Delhi.

Preface

Energy Security: Definition

The International Energy Agency (IEA) defines energy security primarily in terms of stable supplies of oil and natural gas. A broader definition of energy security is the country's ability to optimize its energy resource portfolio and supply of energy services for the desired level of services that will sustain economic growth and poverty reduction. Energy security covers many concerns linking energy, economic growth, environment and geopolitics.

Energy Security: The Concept

The concept of energy security evolved from the major oil crisis of the 1970's when the OPEC oil embargo and the Iranian revolution threatened to cause price increases and quantity shortages for the United States. Since then, energy security has been viewed and perhaps co-terminus in terms of reliable and affordable access to oil by western countries that were dependent on oil imports for their energy needs. In today's context, energy security need is to be viewed at several levels: globally, to ensure adequacy of resources; regionally, to ensure that networking and trade can take place; at the country level, to ensure national security of supply; and at the consumer level, to ensure that consumer demand can be satisfied.

Energy security can be ensured by local adequacy—abundant and varied forms of indigenous energy resources. In the case of local shortages, which occur in most countries, energy security can be enhanced through the ability of the state or of market players, to draw on foreign energy resources and products that can be freely imported through ports or other transport channels and through cross-boundary energy grids (pipelines and electricity networks/ grids). Energy security can also be enhanced through energy conservation and efficiency measures. Reducing energy intensity reduces the dependence of the economy on energy consumption and imports. To achieve energy security requires first of all ensuring global energy adequacy—the existence of enough energy resources, or other prospects, to meet long-term world energy needs.

The traditional energy security elements—supply sources, demand centers, geopolitics and market structures—have been joined by additional considerations and their implicit ramifications. These include the interconnectedness of world economies and energy infrastructure systems, climate change concerns, technological innovation and increased pressure from a broader array of stakeholders. Oil has been a global commodity for many decades, delivered across borders via pipeline, by rail, by tanker trucks and ships. Natural gas is also increasingly becoming a global commodity. International pipelines transport natural gas from North Africa to Europe, from Russia to Europe, from Canada to the United States, from Bolivia to Brazil and eventually from Russia to Asian markets, while natural gas movements by LNG tankers also continue to grow. These emerging transport links offer opportunities for cooperation during energy emergencies, but also provide additional risks to economies that are so interdependent.

Energy Conservation and Efficiency

Energy conservation and energy efficiency are separate, but related concepts. Energy conservation is achieved when growth of energy consumption is reduced, measured in physical terms. Energy conservation is the result of several processes or developments, such as productivity increase or technological progress. On the other hand, energy efficiency is achieved when energy intensity in a specific product, process or area of production or consumption is reduced without affecting output, consumption or comfort levels. Promotion of energy efficiency contributes to energy conservation is therefore an integral part of energy conservation promotional policies leading to energy security.

Energy Security Summit Recommendations

The various recommendations emanated from the recently held Global Energy Security Summit at St. Petersburg, July 17, 2006, inter alia, as outlined below, provides the main operational framework of Global Energy Security Systems for universal adoption and application:

1. Energy is essential to improving the quality of life and opportunities in developed and developing nations. Therefore, ensuring sufficient, reliable and environmentally responsible supplies of energy at prices reflecting market fundamentals is a challenge for our countries and for mankind as a whole.
2. To tackle this overarching goal we have to deal with serious and linked challenges such as:
   - High and volatile oil prices;
   - growing demand for energy (estimated to rise by more than 50% by the year 2030, approximately 80% of which would still be met by fossil fuels, which are limited resources);
   - increasing import dependence in many countries;
   - enormous investment requirements along the entire energy chain;
   - the need to protect the environment and to tackle climate change;
   - the vulnerability of the critical energy infrastructure;
   - political instability, natural disasters and other threats

The International Energy Agency summarizes the issues of energy security facing the world as insufficient and secure supplies at affordable prices. The broad issues encompass the following:

- environmental harm caused by consuming too much fossil-fuel energy;
- the need to diversify production and consumption both by geographical location and fuel type; and
- the impact of rising oil and gas demand increasing the vulnerability of consumers to disruption and price shock. The IEA's principal concerns are environmental and economic.

Energy Demand-supply Balance and Resource-base

Global energy consumption is projected to grow by 57 percent between 2004 and 2030, according to the reference case projection from the International Energy Outlook 2007 released by the Energy Information Administration (EIA). The IEO-2007 shows the most rapid growth in energy demand for nations outside the Organization for Economic Cooperation and Development (OECD), especially in non-OECD Asia, where strong projected economic growth drives the increase in energy use.

Global energy demand will continue to grow despite the relatively high world oil and natural gas prices. However, rising oil prices will seriously dampen growth in demand for petroleum and other liquids fuels after 2015 and, as a result, will reduce their share of overall energy use from 38 percent in 2004 to a projected 34 percent in 2030. In contrast, the energy shares of natural gas, coal, and renewable energy sources are expected to grow over this period. Liquids consumption is still expected to grow strongly, reaching around 118 million barrels per day in 2030. The United States, China, and India together will account for nearly half of the projected growth in world liquids use.

India is both a major energy producer and consumer. India currently ranks as the world's eleventh greatest energy producer, accounting for about 2.4% of the world's total annual energy production, and as the world's sixth greatest energy consumer, accounting for about 3.3% of the world's total annual energy consumption. Despite its large annual energy production, India is a net energy importer, mostly due to the large imbalance between oil production and consumption.

Coal consumption, which grows an average annual rate of 2.2 percent, is the fastest-growing energy source worldwide. With oil and natural gas prices expected to continue rising, coal is an attractive fuel for nations with access to ample coal resources, especially in coal-rich countries like China, India, and the United States. These three countries combined account for 86 percent of the increment in world coal demand by 2030 in the reference case projection. India's has huge proven coal reserves, estimated (as of January 2005) at more than 90 billion tons, or about 10% of the world's total. Most of these reserves are relatively high ash bituminous coal and are located in the states of Bihar, West Bengal, Andhra Pradesh, Orissa, Jharkhand, Maharashtra and Madhya Pradesh. At the current level of production and consumption, India's coal reserves would last more than two hundred years. India is currently the third-largest coal-producing country in the world (behind China and the United States), and accounts for about 8.5% of the world's annual coal production. India is also currently the third-largest coal consuming country (behind the China and the United States), and accounts for nearly 9% of the world's total annual coal consumption. More than half of India's energy needs are met by coal, and about 70% of India's electricity generation is now fueled by coal.

India's proved oil reserves are currently estimated (as of January 2005) at about 5 billion barrels, or about 4.5% of the world total. Most of these reserves lie offshore near Mumbai and onshore in Assam state. However, exploration is still happening, and India's off-shore and on-shore basins may contain as much as 11 billion barrels. India presently ranks as the 25th greatest producer of crude oil, accounting for about 1% of the world's annual crude oil production. About 30% of India's energy needs are met by oil, and more than 60% of that oil is imported. A strong growth in oil demand has resulted in India's annual petroleum consumption increasing by more than 75% from what it was a decade ago, and petroleum consumption is projected to climb to about 3 million barrels per day by 2010. India is currently the world's sixth greatest oil consumer, accounting for about 2.9% of world's total annual petroleum consumption.

The country's annual crude oil production is peaked at about 32 million tonne as against the current peak demand of about 110 million tonne. In the current scenario, India's oil consumption by end of 2007 was expected to reach 136 million tone (MT), of which domestic production will be only 34 MT. The majority of India's roughly 5.4 billion barrels in oil reserves are located in the Bombay High, upper Assam, Cambay, and Krishna-Godavari. In terms of sector wise petroleum product consumption, transport accounts for 42% followed by domestic and industry with 24% and 24% respectively.

India's natural gas reserves are estimated (as of January 2005) at about 29-32 trillion cubic feet (tcf), or about 0.5% of the world total. Most of these reserves lie offshore northwest of Mumbai in the Arabian Sea and onshore in Gujarat state. Natural gas has experienced the fastest rate of increase of any fuel in India's primary energy supply; demand is growing at about 4.8% per year and is forecast to rise to 1.2 tcf per year by 2010 and 1.6 tcf per year by 2015. Natural gas accounts for about 8.9 per cent of energy consumption in the country. The current demand for natural gas is about 96 million cubic metre per day (mcmd) as against availability of 67 mcmd. By 2007, the demand was expected to be around 200 mcmd. Natural gas reserves are estimated at 660 billion cubic meters.

The all India installed capacity of electric power generating stations under utilities was 1,12,581 MW as on 31 May 2004, consisting of 28,860 MW-hydro, 77,931 MW - thermal and 2,720 MW- nuclear and 1,869 MW- wind (Ministry of Power). The gross generation of power in the year 2002-2003 stood at 531 billion units (kWh). India is presently the sixth-greatest electricity generating country and accounts for about 4% of the world's total annual electricity generation. India is also currently ranked sixth in annual electricity consumption, accounting for about 3.5% of the world's total annual electricity consumption. Overall, India's need for power is growing at a prodigious rate; annual electricity generation and consumption in India have increased by about 64% in the past decade, and its projected rate of increase (estimated at as much as 8-10% annually, through the year 2020) for electricity consumption is one of the highest in the world.

Nuclear Power contributes to about 2.4 per cent of electricity generated in India. India has ten nuclear power reactors at five nuclear power stations producing electricity. More nuclear reactors have also been approved for construction. Higher fossil fuel prices, energy security concerns, improved reactor designs, and environmental considerations are expected to improve prospects for nuclear power capacity in many parts of the world, and a number of countries are expected to build new nuclear power plants. World nuclear capacity is projected to raise from 368 gigawatts in 2004 to 481 gigawatts in 2030. Declines in nuclear capacity are projected only in OECD Europe, where several countries (including Germany and Belgium) have either plans or mandates to phase out nuclear power, and where some old reactors are expected to be discontinued. Currently, India has 17 nuclear power plants being operated by the Nuclear Power Corporation of India Limited (NPCIL) and the total installed nuclear power capacity is 4120 MWe.

India is endowed with a vast and viable hydro-potential, estimated at about 150,000 MW3 for power generation of which only 17% has been harnessed so far. Private participation in the hydro sector will be important to meet the target of an additional 45,000 MW of hydro capacity within the next ten years. It is assessed that exploitable potential at 60% load factor is 84,000 MW. Hydroelectric capacity represents about one-fourth of India's total installed capacity, and overall, India is currently ranked sixth-largest in the world in that category (accounting for about 3.7% of the world's installed hydroelectric generating capacity).

India has a vast potential for renewable energy sources, especially in areas such as solar power, biomass and wind power. The current installed capacity of renewable energy is around 92204 MW, constituting about 7.3 percent of India's total installed generation capacity. India is already the fourth largest in the world in terms of wind energy installations and we are seeing significant investment activity in this area. Technological breakthroughs for cost-effective photovoltaic technology could generate a quantum leap in the renewable energy sector since India is well endowed with solar insulation (average of 6 kwh/ sq.mt./day).

The country's final energy demand reached 165.3 MMBFOE (23.9 MTOE) in 2004. Oil consumption shared 52.3 percent, wherein bulk was used by the transport and industrial sectors. Meanwhile, biomass which shared 28.0 percent of the final demand and was used solely for non-power application reached 46.4 MMBFOE (6.7 MTOE). Electricity accounted for 15.9 percent, registering 26.2 MMBFOE (3.8 MTOE) of the final demand. Higher coal consumption, mostly by the cement industry, was recorded at 5.8 percent to 6.2 MMBFOE (0.9 MTOE). The total energy consumption of the residential sector in 2004 grew by 6.0 percent to 52.1 MMBFOE (7.5 MTOE). Biomass accounted for 67.0 percent of the total residential energy consumption. Demand for petroleum products, specifically liquefied petroleum gas (LPG) and kerosene used primarily for cooking declined by 5.9 percent due to fuel switching as an effect of soaring prices of these fuels. Household electricity consumption increased by 3.7 percent.

Final energy consumption of the sector increased to 39.2 MMBFOE (5.7 MTOE) in 2004. Oil and biomass were the major fuels of the sector accounting for average share of 38.1 percent and 23.3 percent, respectively. Used mainly by cement plants, coal demand increased by 5.7 percent to 6.2 MMBFOE (0.9 MTOE) in 2004. Electricity demand of the sector decreased by 1.2 percent to 8.9 MMBFOE (1.3 MTOE). Total energy consumption of the transport sector reached 57.2 MMBFOE (8.3 MTOE), registering an increase of 1.9 percent. Diesel registered the highest consumption at 31.4 MMBFOE (4.5 MTOE) representing 54.9 percent of the total sector's consumption. Road transport shared 80.3 percent in the total demand of the sector while the balance was shared by rail and air transport.

The National Energy Policy Perspectives

The Energy Policy of India is characterized by trade-offs between four major drivers:

- Rapidly growing economy, with a need for dependable and reliable supply of electricity, gas, and petroleum products;
- Increasing household incomes, with a need for affordable and adequate supply of electricity, and clean cooking fuel;
- Limited domestic reserves of fossil fuels, and the need to import a vast fraction of the gas, crude oil, and petroleum product requirements, and recently the need to import coal as well; and
- Indoor, urban and regional environmental impacts, necessitating the need for the adoption of cleaner fuels and cleaner technologies.

In recent years, these challenges have led to a major set of continuing reforms, restructuring and a focus on energy conservation and have led to a major set of continuing reforms and restructuring. The National Energy Policy of India comprises a set of measures involving that country's laws, treaties and agency directives. The energy policy of a sovereign nation, such as India, may include one or more of the following measures:

- A statement of national policy regarding energy planning, energy generation, transmission and usage.
- Legislation on commercial energy activities (trading, transport, storage, etc.).
- Legislation,affecting energy use, such as efficiency standards, emission standards.
- Instructions for state owned energy sector assets and organizations.
- Active participation in, co-ordination of and incentives for mineral fuels exploration and other energy-related research and development of fiscal policies related to energy products and services (taxes, exemptions, subsidies etc.).
- Energy security and international policy measures such as:
  - — International energy sector treaties and alliances,
  - — General international trade agreements,
  - — Special relations with energy-rich countries, including military presence.

A number of suggestions can be made on critical dimensions on energy security relating to questions of restructuring, rationalization and corresponding reforms in major sectoral activities. These include:

- The energy sector should be restructured and liberalized. Experts, for example, have recommended reforming the coal sector through deregulation, removing government control over the allocation of blocks and the approval process for coal mining, improving operational efficiency, strengthening coal distribution logistics, or focusing on future technology.
- The tax and pricing systems should be reformed, for example, by using relative rather than independent pricing of different kinds of fuels..
- Greater investment—especially through increased private participation—is one of the proposed solutions. Suggestions have

included providing incentives, the clarification of policy frameworks (in terms of energy pricing, market structure, cross-border investments, and import and exports of energy products) and the introduction of independent regulatory mechanisms.

- Experts emphasize that increased energy sector growth will require investment not only in exploration and production facilities, but also in distribution infrastructure: ports, railways, pipelines, and power transmission grids.
- There have also been calls for privatization—of everything from public sector undertakings to ports to pipelines—to bring in capital, technology, and skills.
- There has to be an increased focus on technological research. There have, in fact, been some improvements so far, for example, in clean-coal technology, better nuclear power generation, enhanced oil recovery programs, conversion of natural gas into liquid, coal-bed methane extraction, and heavy oil extraction.

The Committee set up by the Government of India has recently come out with the Integrated Energy Policy, which aims to bridge the prevailing gap in the demand and supply of energy in short, medium and long term perspective. Recognizing the role of both private and public sector participation in meeting the energy needs of the country, the policy strikes a right balance by stating that "wherever possible energy market should be competitive. However, competition alone has been shown to have its limitation in a number of areas of the energy sector and independent regulation becomes even more critical in such instances".

The broad approach of Integrated Energy Policy is summarized below:

(a) Till market matures in independent regulation across the energy streams is a necessity.
(b) Pricing and resource allocation to be determined by market forces under an effective and credible regulatory oversight.
(c) Transparent and targeted subsidies.
(d) Improved efficiencies across the energy chain.
(e) Policies that reflect externalities of energy consumption.
(f) Incentives/disincentives to regulate market and consumer behaviour.
(g) Management reforms to foster accountability and incentives for efficiency.

The broad vision behind the Energy Policy is to reliably meet the demand for energy services of all sectors at competitive prices. Further, lifeline energy needs of all households must be met even if that entails directed subsidies to vulnerable households. The demand must be met through safe, clean and convenient forms of energy at the least-cost in a technically efficient, economically viable and environmentally sustainable manner. Considering the shocks and disruptions that can be reasonably expected, assured supply of such energy and technologies at all times is essential to providing energy security for all. Meeting this vision requires that India pursues all available fuel options and forms of energy, both conventional and non-conventional. Further, India must seek to expand its energy resource base and seek new and emerging energy sources. Finally, and most importantly, India must pursue technologies that maximize energy efficiency, demand side management and conservation. Coal shall remain India's most important energy source till 2031-32 and possibly beyond.

Emerging Future Energy Issues

In recent years, a lot of attention is being paid to the issue of energy security. There are a number of concerns and fears associated to this, such as:

- Oil and other fossil fuel depletion (peak oil, etc.).
- Reliance on foreign sources of energy.
- Geopolitics (such as supporting dictatorships, rising terrorism, "stability" of nations that supply energy).
- Energy needs of poorer countries, and demands from advancing developing countries such as China and India.
- Economic efficiency versus population growth debate.
- Environmental issues, in particular climate change.
- Renewables and other alternative energy sources.
- Energy insecurity combined with other global issues risks fueling conflict, repeating past mistakes in history.

Access to energy is a crucial enabling condition for achieving sustainable development. Prudent energy policies and research can play an important role in steering both industrialized and developing countries onto more sustainable energy development paths. Specifically, they can strengthen the three pillars of sustainable development: the economy, by boosting productivity; social welfare, by improving living standards and enhancing safety and security; and the environment, by reducing indoor and outdoor pollution and remediating environmental degradation. The U.N. Human Development Index provides insight into this important correlation, showing that the increased use of energy and electricity is a prerequisite for continued economic development and improved quality of life, particularly for developing countries. Our challenge then becomes whether the world's economies can use energy more efficiently with reduced environmental impact, and diversify and expand energy production, while maintaining economic growth and prosperity. The International Chamber of Commerce is committed to the belief that business and industry, with its managerial, financial and technical expertise, along with governments, which must create stable and predictable investment conditions, can stimulate investment programmes that will achieve the common goal of sustainable access to energy.

Energy Priorities for Developing Countries

Achieving development goals in rural areas where poverty conditions are currently the greatest will require greater access and improved energy services as a means to reach education, health, water and other goals. In particular, expanding energy services is a means to generate increased employment and income generating opportunities—and is therefore a pre-requisite to increased value adding activities in rural areas. For the policy-maker, helping create a sustainable energy pathway will require broad societal consensus around the strategic choices of economic, environmental and social development. Depending on their current state of development and priorities, countries will likely pursue different paths towards a variety of sustainable development options. They will require different policy mixes, likely incorporating fiscal, regulatory and research and development efforts. Transparency, stakeholder involvement and institutional flexibility will be key ingredients of any set of decisions. Governments should therefore consider the following priority areas for energy policy and planning in developing countries in the world:

- Improving enabling frameworks in developing countries (open markets, rule of law, protection of property rights, energy supply and access).
- Enabling and encouraging technology innovation, dissemination, and co-operation, without technology constraints and trade barriers.
- Encouraging R&D on long-term technologies, such as clean fossil fuels, nuclear and renewable energy options.

- Examining whether an integrated approach to the provision of rural services, including energy in rural development and poverty reduction strategies through public financing that promotes services in a variety of areas (e.g.: water, health, education, energy and others), can improve affordability and sustainability.
- Supporting business models that provide a range of fuels and energy services through attention to both investment and consumer financing mechanisms to expand the role of the private sector in providing access to energy.
- Expanding electricity generation through centralized and decentralized systems using conventional or renewable energy based on the resources available domestically.
- Expanding access to modern and cleaner fuels, including liquefied petroleum gas, in rural areas through public-private collaboration to provide affordable alternatives to traditional fuel use for household and industry applications.
- Attending to the role of energy in peri-urban areas. The lack of energy services in rural areas directly contributes to migration to urban areas where inadequate energy services availability impacts urban and peri-urban poor populations. Energy services delivery programmes, including consumer financing options must be pursued to address this growing problem.

Strategic Oil Reserve and Storage Systems

Global Strategic Petroleum Reserves ("GSPR") refer to crude oil inventories (or stockpiles) held by the government of a particular country, as well as private industry, for the purpose of providing economic and national security during an energy crisis. According to the United States Energy Information Administration, approximately 4.1 billion barrels (650,000,000 m^3) of oil are held in strategic reserves, of which 1.4 billion is government-controlled. The remainder is held by private industry. At the moment the US Strategic Petroleum Reserve is one of the largest strategic reserves, with much of the remainder held by the other 26 members of the International Energy Agency. Recently, other non-IEA countries have begun creating their own strategic petroleum reserves, with China being the largest of these new reserves.

The Strategic Petroleum Reserve (SPR) is an emergency supply of federally-owned crude oil stored in deep underground salt caverns along the

Gulf Coast. The SPR is widely viewed as a useful asset for improving the nation's energy and economic security because it provides a potentially valuable buffer against short-term oil supply disruptions. Indeed, permanent authority to continue operation of the Reserve was among the uncontroversial provisions included in proposed national energy legislation in 2003. Within that context of broad support, debate has instead focused on: (a) how much oil should be stored in the SPR (b) what specific rules should govern future withdrawals and (c) what should the international community be doing in terms of establishing similar emergency reserves. In particular, there is disagreement about whether and when releases from the SPR should be used to dampen the macroeconomic impacts of high oil prices, even in the absence of an actual supply emergency. Questions have also been raised about recent government purchases to fill the SPR at a time when oil prices are high. India has begun the development of a strategic crude oil reserve sized at 37.4 million barrels, enough for two weeks of consumption. Petroleum stocks have been transferred from the Indian Oil Corporation (IndianOil) to the Oil Industry Development Board (OIDB). The OIDB then created the Indian Strategic Petroleum Reserves Ltd (ISPRL) to serve as the controlling government agency for the strategic reserve.

Energy security has become a growing concern for all the developing countries like India who are import dependent for its development energy needs. To ensure energy security at all times, the Government of India has decided to set up 5 million metric tones (MMT) strategic crude oil storages at various locations in the country [Mangalore (1.5 MMT), Vizag (1.0 MMT) and Padur near Udipi (2.5 MMT)]. This strategic storage would be in addition to the existing storages of crude oil and petroleum products with the oil companies and would provide an emergency response mechanism in case of short-term supply disruptions. The construction of the proposed strategic storage facilities is being managed by Indian Strategic Petroleum Reserves Limited (ISPRL), a Special Purpose Vehicle, owned by Oil Industry Development Board (OIDB).

Apart form developing adequate infrastructure towards building domestic capability for strategic oil and gas reserves there has to be a breakthrough in energy/power storage systems in a cost-effective and eco-friendly manner to help conservation and use efficiency. The principle devices successfully developed and used by different utilities in effective storage of various forms of energy include: Mechanical Energy Storage—Fly Wheels, Compressed Air Energy Storage, Pumped Hydroelectric Energy Storage,

Batteries, Thermal Energy Storage Systems, Superconducting Magnetic Energy Storage, Tidal Storage System etc. Efforts are underway to determine the cost-effectiveness and use efficiency of these energy storage devices.

Global Energy Markets and Interrelated Issues

Energy markets are currently going through a period of tremendous change. The deregulation of the electricity market is in full swing. The market price mechanism has replaced the old system of fixed rates. The new, free electricity market is marked by sharply fluctuating prices that may lead to unexpected and unfavorable price risks. The gas market is about to undergo the same deregulation process. The more traditional oil markets are volatile too, as has been witnessed over the past years. Besides economic fluctuations in the market, political and seasonal influences are both playing a major role in the price movements of energy markets.

While oil is essential to fuel economic growth, its supply is volatile, subject to short- term interruptions as well as longer-term lapses in the rate of supply development. Sustaining modest economic growth worldwide for the next several decades will require massive new investments in oil and gas internationally.

The world energy markets are inherently global, and no single country can exempt itself from the interdependencies of that market. Geographical differences in the location of supply and demand will continue to expand trade. Differences in resource ownership and access to capital and technology will require increasing cooperation between IOCs and NOCs. The consuming and producing countries share a mutual interest in this expansion, and in avoiding volatility. In fact, these interdependencies generate a web of mutual interests between producers and consumers, which can provide a basis for reducing the security problem. While there is no certainty that cooperation in expanding supplies over the next several decades will succeed, there is certainty that the cost of failing to do so will be enormous.

Energy Security and Future Sustainability

The 1970's oil shocks confronted the developing countries with a new set of energy security issues. Few of the oil importing countries had the necessary foreign exchange reserves to absorb price increases. Concerns about macroeconomic management and fiscal balance—national affordability—rose to the fore. Energy security was enhanced through reliance (sometimes an overreliance) on domestic resources, bilateral energy trading relationships with reliable nearby partners, and access to regional markets. However, vulnerability to significant price fluctuations remains a major energy security concern for both oil and gas exporting countries and net importers of energy products and services.

A second energy security preoccupation in developing countries is the ability to adapt and apply imported energy technologies to their local needs and manage them successfully. In the perception of many developing countries, failure to adapt and manage implies a continuing dependence on foreign technical know-how, a dependence that is usually interpreted as insecurity. Over time, lack of open and transparent markets and good governance also contributes to the degradation and disfunctionality of complex energy technologies. Failure to adapt technologies to local conditions also implies that energy service priorities will be determined on the basis of an exogenous energy technology that cannot meet affordability and the priority social needs of emerging market economies, especially in rural areas.

Third, developing countries have good reason to harbor concerns about the vulnerability of their energy infrastructure to disruption by natural or man-made events. The recent extensive losses of the electric transmission and distribution facilities of Orissa (cyclone) and Gujarat (earthquake) in India stand as a powerful testimony; floods can be equally damaging, and droughts threaten the viability of hydroelectric facilities. In addition, power stations, refineries, pipelines, and transmission lines are early targets in cases of domestic insurrection, civil war, and international conflict.

Finally, in developing countries that export hydrocarbon, the misuse and inequitable distribution of the rents from energy trade can itself be a driver of discontent, domestic instability, and violence, which are all threats to domestic energy markets, private investment flows, and infrastructure. Squandering valuable resource revenues may also result in disinvestment in the very energy production facilities that brought financial riches, ultimately threatening the pace and sustainability of domestic energy resource development.

Structural and Regulatory Reforms

Given the bleak current energy scenario and the future prospects, the Government of India has put in place several measures that it hopes would lead to an easing of the shortages in the country and a more even distribution of access to energy. Some key initiatives along these lines are listed below:

The oil and gas sector was one of the first sectors in which the

Government tried to introduce a much higher level of autonomy by allowing the public sec-tor enterprises to work as corporate entities with their own Boards of Directors that would man-age the companies at an arm's length distance from the Government. Private Sector participation in refineries was also introduced as a result of which the private sector body has a share of nearly 30% in India's refining capacities today. In the exploration and production areas, the Government has progressively refined its terms and conditions for sharing the benefits with the private sector under various rounds of the New Exploration Licensing Policies (NELP). The Government has also unbundled the functioning of erstwhile Oil Coordination Committee that was responsible for the complete supply planning and procurement of oil and gas in the country, into two entities—Petrofed which is a trade association for oil and gas and the Petroleum and Natural Gas Authority (PNAU) which is an independent regulator in the sector.

In the case of power sector, reforms were introduced in the early 1990's and, through a process of learning; India has finally reached a stage where it has enacted the Energy Conservation Act in 2001 and the Electricity Act in 2003. The Energy Conservation Act requires the establishment of a Bureau of Energy Efficiency (BEE) as a deemed statutory autonomous body that would work towards encouraging energy efficiency in the country. The broad objectives of BEE are to provide a policy framework and direction to national energy conservation and efficiency efforts and programs; to coordinate energy efficiency and conservation policies and programs and take it to the stakeholders; to establish systems and procedures to measure, monitor and verify energy efficiency results in individual sectors as well as at the macro level.

The Electricity Act, 2003: requires the functional unbundling of erstwhile vertically integrated state electricity boards and puts in lace regulatory commissions both at the federal and state level. These electricity regulatory commissions have significant powers and have the responsibility to determine not only the tariff structures in their areas of jurisdiction but also to satisfy quality of supply and service norms and create a competitive environment apart from several other functions. The coal sector, unfortunately, is one sector that has not made adequate progress on reforms.

Enhanced Private Sector Participation: Private sector interest in the oil and gas sector has built up and much more significantly than in the case of electricity sector because it got an early start and because distortions in the case of these sectors were not severe as in the case of electricity. Despite several efforts towards encouraging private sector participation in electricity generation and distribution the response from the private sector has been grossly inadequate. This has largely been because of the inability of the distribution business to generate adequate revenues to provide an adequate return or indeed comfort that the services would be paid for! Once again, learning from the past experiences and the need to quickly add significant capacities, the Government of India launched the Ultra Mega Power Project (UMPP) scheme that identified seven sites for setting up large-scale power plants with each site having a capacity of 4000 MW.

India and the "Petersburg Declaration"

India is almost completely in line with the core principles of the Petersburg action plan with a small differentiation in its approach to climate change and sustainable development. India is clearly pursuing aggressively the path of sustainable development which by itself has been well recognized both in the third and fourth Assessment Reports of IPCC (Intergovernmental Panel on Climate Change) as having strong linkages with climate change.

India is also strongly aligned with the principle of open, transparent and competitive markets with the exception of coal sector. Competitive bidding processes have been introduced in all segments of the other energy sectors. However, a key weak point comes to the fore when such processes run into disputes. What is required in such instances is to have strong and independent dispute resolutions mechanisms. The Government cannot assume onto itself this role - especially when a large part of the energy sector continues to be in the public sector. In a similar fashion while the dialogue between the Government and the various stakeholders in energy developments have increased substantially as compared to a decade ago, the challenge of informing and educating consumers of energy products and services still remains daunting. This is apparent both in the public consultations held by the Electricity Regulatory Commissions as well those that are part of the Environment Impact Assessment processes in the country. One key principle of the Petersburg declaration that needs focused attention, relates to the safeguarding of critical energy infrastructure. While it is easy to identify such critical infrastructures on a point basis, India has not undertaken any exercise to identify and prioritize critical points along its networks.

Energy and Climate Change

Energy security and climate protection are inextricably linked. To the extent that the consumption of fossil energies is rising worldwide, efforts to reduce in particular CO_2 emissions are necessary in order to avoid further increasing the already considerable burden on the environment. The question as what will happen in 2012 after the first commitment period of the Kyoto Protocol have ended is of global importance. It will be virtually impossible to prevent the impending climatic disaster without the cooperation of the US, Russia and the major emerging economies, especially India and China.

Faced with the huge challenge of meeting its rapidly increasing energy demand, India is focusing sharply on both energy efficiency improvements as well as tying up energy resources at the global level - either through purchases on the international markets or through equity investments in global assets. India would also be keenly interested in acquiring clean and efficient energy technologies. However, it would have to be extremely sensitive to the costs of such technologies. The Indian consumers, specially the very large percentage that today do not have an access to electricity, are extremely price sensitive and the Government would need to take into account not only the ability of such people to pay for energy services but also to its own ability to absorb the costs of energy subsidies. Energy subsidies, especially for the deserving, are provided by almost every country in the world—developed or developing.

- The option of using the clean development mechanism (CDM) also exists but has thus far been focused primarily on the "low hanging fruit". It would be interesting to look at the possibility of apply the public-private-partnership model to-wards the financing of clean technologies for a large scale energy production and consumption in the country.
- The Indian Government has already undertaken or planned for several policies and initiatives that encourage sustainable energy growth - both in terms of improved efficiency of use and in terms of its environmental implications. Several policies and measures have for example focused on improving energy efficiency, enhancing renewable and clean energy forms, bringing about power sector reforms, promoting clean coal technologies, promoting cleaner and less carbon intensive fuels for transport, and addressing environmental quality.
- The Indian Government has actively been pursuing a multi-pronged strategy for the promotion of renewable energy sources. Against a target of 3,075 MW, the country added 4,613 MW capacity based

on renewables during the Tenth Plan. During the Eleventh Plan period, the MNRE aims to have 10% of grid interactive power generation installed capacity and 4% of the electricity mix based on renewables. The study of alternative sources of fuels has become increasingly important in recent years.

Energy Sector: Need for Good Governance

With a population of around 1.1 billion, India is the world's second most populous country and ranks fifth in the world in terms of primary energy consumption, accounting for about 3.5 per cent of the world's commercial energy demand. With a GDP growth rate of around 8% during the Tenth Five Year Plan of the Government (2002-07), India is currently one of the fastest growing economies of the world. The future levels and patterns of energy use in India therefore have important implications—at the national level in terms of environmental impacts of energy use, issues of access and equity, and at the global level in terms of geopolitics of energy supply and GHG emissions related to the combustion of fossil fuels.

Beginning in February 2005, Chatham House, London and the Centre for Energy, Petroleum and Mineral Law Policy (CEPMLP) at Dundee University facilitated a dialogue between participants from government, national and international oil companies, NGOs and financial institutions from 23 developing and developed oil- and gas-producing countries. The conclusions of this dialogue have been supplemented with in-house research on international governance practices. The main conclusions of the project to March 2007, and the 40 general governance benchmarks for the petroleum sector comprised within this Report, are set out in *Good Governance of the National Petroleum Sector: The Chatham House Document*. This *Report* sets out the analysis and discussions on which these conclusions are based, and provides examples from country case studies and offers checklists and guidance for the petroleum sector policy- or strategy-maker. It is a 'living text 'for' good governance debate around the world, and will be revised to reflect future discussions and comments from petroleum sector stakeholders. Participants in the project were clear that, though principles might be universal, practice depends on the national context and the state of development of the sector. The report envisages promoting a greater awareness of the rich breadth of experience upon which producing countries can draw and provide a starting point for making practical improvements to governance systems.

Encyclopedia on Energy Security: Raison d'etre

Having provided a broad contour of the different elements, dimensions and issues concerning the larger question of energy security at local, country, regional, iner- & intra-regional, international and global context a clear need was felt to put together the relevant information on the theme in the shape of an Encyclopedia to benefit the academicians, scholars, research workers, planners, industries, politicians and the media to create general awareness, knowledge base and futuristic vision on Energy security and the interrelated issues surrounding it. Bearing in mind this core objective the Encyclopedia on "Energy Security" is brought out covering the following 6 chapters:

I. Energy Security: The Concept
II. Production, Demand and Supply Perspectives of Energy
III. Energy Policy
IV. Energy Storage Systems and Strategic Oil and Gas Reserves
V. Energy Risks Management
VI. Corporate Governance in Energy Security Management

The encyclopedia, inter alia covers a glossary of useful and appropriate technical terminologies in the wide-ranging areas of Energy security and allied disciplines. It includes broadly energy security as a concept, projecting energy security in the larger context of production and demand-supply management, national energy policies and its alignment with global energy security perspective, strategic energy reserve and storage systems to enlarge security options, energy risk management approaches and sharing of global experiences, and last but not the least the corporate governance issues to provide good governance to the corporate policy makers concerned with energy security at various levels.

The authors would feel gratified if this compilation is found to be useful to the readers and workers in the energy sector.

New Delhi
1 June 2008

Dr. Parag Diwan
Dr. A.N. Sarkar

Contents

Chapter 1

Energy Security: The Concept

Defining Energy Security

The International Energy Agency (IEA) defines energy security primarily in terms of stable supplies of oil and natural gas. However, this definition does not address the multidimensional nature of energy security for the developing world. ESMAP has redefined energy security to address the micro and macro level needs of developing countries as follows: *A country's ability to optimize its energy resource portfolio and supply of energy services for the desired level of services that will sustain economic growth and poverty reduction.* Energy security can also be defined in the following terms:

1. Enabling a certain percentage or number of countries to sustain the provisioning or availability of energy services for poverty reduction and economic growth.
2. Enabling a certain percentage or number of households, businesses and communities to meet their energy needs for consumptive, productive or socially productive uses.

Energy security is a broad umbrella term that covers many concerns linking energy, economic growth and political power (Energy Vision Update-CERA, 2006). The energy security perspective varies depending upon one's position in the value chain. Consumers and energy-intensive industries desire reasonably-priced energy on demand and worry about disruptions. Major oil producing countries consider security of revenue and of demand integral parts of any energy security discussion. Oil and gas companies consider access to new reserves, ability to develop new infrastructure, and stable investment regimes to be critical to ensuring energy security. Developing countries are concerned about the ability to pay for resources to drive their economies and fear balance of payment shocks. Power companies are concerned with the integrity of the entire network. Policymakers focus on the risks of supply disruption and the security of infrastructure due to terrorism, war or natural disaster. They also consider the volumes of security margins—the amount of excess capacity, strategic reserves, and infrastructure redundancy.

Throughout the value- chain, prices and supply diversity are critical components of energy security. In earlier periods, oil was used as a "weapon," and there is concern that natural gas could also be used to gain political leverage at some time in the future. The traditional elements of energy security include: supply sources, demand centres, geopolitics and market structures (and responsiveness of related institutions). In the energy crises of the 1970s, the primary focus for the Western industrial countries was on oil supply sources and geopolitics. These two elements were the underlying causes of energy security concerns, and the demand centres, market structures and new institutions created the solutions to the two energy crises that occurred. In fact, the creation of the International Energy Agency (IEA) was a direct response to the 1973-74 oil disruption by the then-dominant energy-consuming economies, and consequential major 'Oil-Shock' that followed.

The definition of energy security has changed over time. In the period post 1970's oil shocks, the definition of energy security related to the avoidance of oil supply risk resulting from potential disruptions of crude oil supply from the Middle-East. In this century, other factors that affect fuel supply stability and increase energy price have been added to the previous energy security definition. These factors include political conflicts, unexpected natural disasters, concern on terrorism, and energy-related environmental challenges.

The study conducted by IEA defines energy security as "the ability of an economy to guarantee the availability of energy resource supply in a sustainable and timely manner with the energy price being at a level that will not adversely affect the economic performance of the economy." Thus, there are several factors that can influence the 'security' of energy supply, such as: (1) the availability of fuel reserves, both domestically and by external suppliers; (2) the ability of an economy to acquire supply to meet projected energy demand; (3) the level of an economy's energy resource diversification and energy supplier diversification; (4) accessibility to fuel resources, in terms of the availability of related energy infrastructure and energy transportation infrastructure; and (5) geopolitical concerns surrounding resource acquisition. In terms of energy demand elasticity, an economy that is able to decouple economic growth with energy use—through energy efficiency and conservation– will have an advantage in terms of its energy security.

Following the above definition, there are 3 fundamental elements of energy security that need to be taken into account to evolve future energy security policy as also to ensure long-term sustainability.

(1) PHYSICAL energy security, the availability and accessibility of supply sources;

(2) ECONOMIC energy security, the affordability of resource acquisition and energy infrastructure development; and

(3) ENVIRONMENTAL SUSTAINABILITY, the sustainable development and use of energy resources that "meets the needs of the present without compromising the ability of future generations to meet their own needs".

The Evolution of Energy Security as a Concept

Background

The concept of energy security evolved from the major oil crisis of the 1970's when the OPEC oil embargo and the Iranian revolution threatened to cause price increases and quantity shortages for the United States. Since then energy security has been viewed in terms of reliable and affordable access to oil by western countries that were dependent on oil imports for their energy needs. As natural gas became more important in the energy mix, it was included in this thinking. However, energy security has still remained predominantly a western concept due to the dominance of OECD countries as consumers of the world oil and natural gas production as can be seen in Table 1.1. (http://www.esmap.org/filez/activity/228200762251 - Global Energy Security/Assessment.pdf)

Analytical Framework for understanding Energy Security

The definition of energy security implies that an analytical framework must examine the demand and supply side of the issue. The demand-side analysis includes the following factors:

Table 1.1: Share of OECD countries in Oil and Gas

	United States	*Europe & Eurasia*	*Asia-Pacific*	*Africa*
2003 daily oil consumption (share of total world consumption)	25.1	25.9	28.8	3.3%
Change in 2003 over 2002 consumption	1.9%	1.6%	4%	2.2%
2003 daily natural gas consumption (share of total world consumption)	24.3%	41.8%	13.3%	2.5%
Change in 2003 over 2002 consumption	-4.9%	3.6%	5.7%	8.3%

1. **Understanding the demand structure**: The demand for energy services is generated from four distinct user groups: households, communities, industrial and agricultural users. There is heterogeneity among each of these user groups in terms of their demand for energy services. The present consumption patterns of these groups, along with their projected demand must be studied to ensure adequate investments in capacity building to meet their needs. Demographic trends and their impact on the demand for energy services must be also be studied and documented.

2. **Ability and willingness of users to pay for services:** Utility companies in developing countries face financial constraints which prevent much needed investments in infrastructure upgrades and maintenance. This is in part, due to the amount of "theft" from the transmission infrastructure caused by illegal connections and customers that do not pay. Ensuring financial flows from customers is critical to sustaining the delivery energy services over the long term. It is therefore important to gauge the ability and willingness of users during the design and implementation of energy projects.

3. **Securing demand for energy services and incomes:** Viable energy services require users that are able to pay for those services. This implies that securing demand for services is linked to securing incomes at the user level to ensure affordability of services.

The Supply-side analysis, on the other had, includes the following factors:

1. **Macroeconomic indicators:** The ability of oil importing countries to provide a sustained level of energy services is dependant on their level of energy imports and their ability to pay for it. The recent oil price increases have impacted the economies of oil importing developing countries such as Madagascar, Rwanda and Uganda. For example, in Madagascar, the total value

of oil imports reached approximately US$213 million in 2001 from US$124 million in 1999. The effect of doubling of petroleum product prices on the already poor population (approximately 70 percent) has been severe. The price of gasoline, which increased 70 percent between April 1999 and October 2000, affects the transportation of all goods.

Kerosene used by the poor increased 65 percent and the cost of mass urban transportation increased by 100 percent in the same period. Certain developing countries such as India subsidize certain fuels such as LPG and kerosene to encourage consumption by the poorer sections of the population. An increase in international fuel prices increases the subsidy bill of the governments and affects the overall fiscal stability of the economy. Other macroeconomic factors which affect energy security by impacting the ability of countries to import fuels are the level of foreign exchange reserves and the exchange stability of its currency. An understanding of the various macroeconomic factors affecting energy security is thus important for effective policy making.

2. Geopolitical strategies: Thirty percent of the 2003 production of oil came from the Middle East. Approximately 63% of the world's proven oil resources and 40% of the world's proven natural gas resources are concentrated in the Persian Gulf in the Middle-East.

The geographic concentration of hydrocarbon resources has led to countries entering into bilateral or regional agreements to ensure stable supplies. For example, a study conducted by the Baker Institute at Rice University in 1999 stated that as China's oil import levels rise to levels above 2 million b/d, it will be increasingly difficult for China to meet its crude oil import requirements without concluding large, long-term contracts for the supply of oil. China has indicated intentions to deepen its oil trading relationships with Iraq or Iran, leading to fears that Beijing will form oil for arms, military client relationships with these nations. China's emergence as a major source of demand for hydrocarbons from the Persian Gulf is a source of concern for Japan which fears a "war for resources." It is thus, important to understand the geopolitical supply agreements that exist from each country's perspective to assess its level of energy security.

3. Institutional capacity: Developing countries can be categorized as net importers or net exporters of energy. Net exporting countries such as Chad, Algeria, Nigeria and Angola must have corporate and institutional structures in place to sustain gains from their energy exports, especially with the recent oil price increases. This is critical for their economies since they are heavily dependent on oil revenues. A robust institutional structure to invest the oil revenues to promote greater economic growth is therefore very important. Similarly, countries that might be net importers, but have refining and processing capabilities for exporting finished products, must have adequate institutional capacity to sustain revenues from these activities. It is important to understand these institutional capacities to formulate effective policies for enhancing energy security.

4. **Financial resources:** The total investment amount required for energy infrastructure over the next 25 years is projected to be $16 trillion. To provide the desired level of energy services for their populations, developing countries must be able to mobilize resources in the domestic and international capital markets. Attracting investment requires governments in developing countries to play an active role in promoting good governance and anticorruption measures.

5. **Environmental Impacts:** The rapid increase in energy use in countries like China and India is causing environmental problems such as smog and acid rain, which interfere with other economic sectors such as agriculture. Hence, expanding access to energy must be balanced with environmental considerations.

6. **Natural resource endowment & technological feasibility:** Understanding the energy endowments of each country such as hydrocarbon reserves, hydropower capacity, solar & wind energy capacities are important in assessing the ability of a country to domestically meets its energy requirements. It is equally important to analyze the investment outlays and required technologies to develop these resources which should be based on a framework consisting of (a) the premise that the level of energy services available to the people of any country is a function of the policies undertaken by the governments at the country level and (b) that the goal of every country's energy policy is to have a resource portfolio that is optimized against constraints that are country or region specific to enable a desired level of services.

Such a framework conceived by CERA can be translated into specific tasks which are outlined below:

Natural Resource Endowment and Technological Feasibility

Natural resource endowment & technological feasibility studies, inter alia, imply mapping the energy resource endowment of each country along with the economics of developing those resources. Factors affecting consumption of energy services for each user group (industrial, agricultural, community and households) may include:

- Current consumption levels
- Current expenditures on energy services
- Impacts of service disruption
- Securing demand for energy services
- Demand variations due to seasonal changes, transitioning economies, etc.
- Understanding the demand structure
- Ability and willingness of users to pay for services
- Demand side analysis
- Balance of payments
- Budgetary impacts of subsidies
- Foreign exchange reserves
- Macroeconomic factors
- Securing incomes among user groups to pay for services
- Ability of a country to attract domestic & int'l investment
- Financial factors
- Impact of expanding energy services
- Environmental sustainability
- Natural resource &technological endowment
- Geopolitical supply agreements
- Institutional capacity
- Supply side analysis

Ability of a country to optimize its energy resource portfolio and supply of energy services for the desired level of services that sustain economic growth & poverty reduction: the detailed framework conceived to optimize the energy resource portfolio and supply of energy services at desired level to sustain economic growth is outlined on next page. (UNDP - World Energy Assessment overview - 2004 update)-(1-A).

Geopolitical Dimension of Energy Security

Energy security issues have traditionally focused on crude oil supply

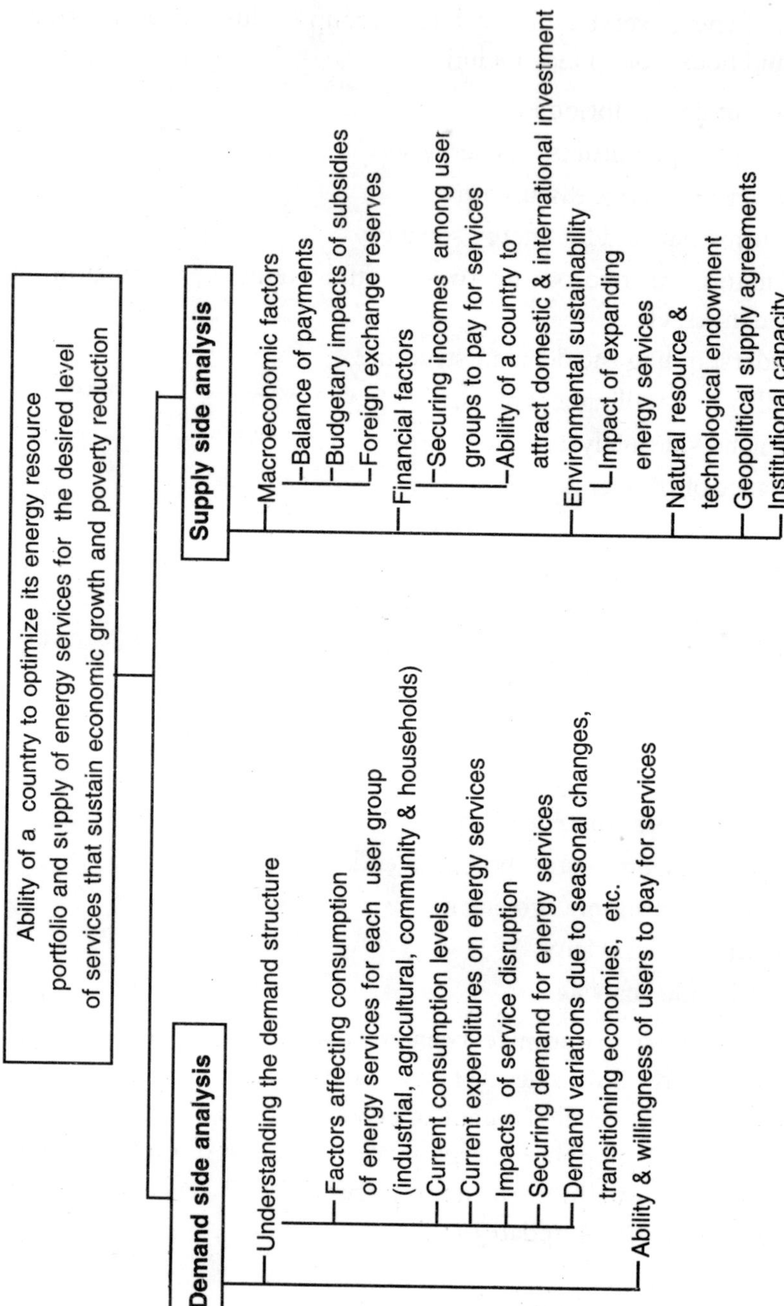

Exhibit 1.A: Country Optimisation Model for Energy Resources

Exhibit 1.A: *Contd.*

This framework can be translated into specific tasks which as outlined below:

Energy security-subcategories	*Tasks*
Macroeconomic factors	Measuring the import dependence of each country to understand its exposure to fuel price volatility
Demand & demographics	Understanding the demand function of each user group according to consumption patterns and the ability to pay for energy services.
Geopolitics and institutional capacity	Documenting existing geopolitical supply agreements.
	Analyzing changes in demand when economies are undergoing restructuring
	Corporate structure required to sustain energy imports or gains from energy exports
Financial feasibility	Documenting the ability of a country to attract domestic and international investment to expand energy infrastructure and service delivery
Environmental feasibility	Understanding the impacts of expanding access on the environment and the role of technology (e.g. improved devices such as cooking stoves, renewable energy generation) in mitigating these impacts
Natural resource endowment & technological feasibility	Mapping the energy resource endowment of each country and the economics of developing those resources

disruptions in the Middle-East. The instability of the Middle- East during the 1970s led to rising prices for more than a decade. After oil prices collapsed in the mid-1980s, followed by the end of the Cold War and the resolution of the 1990-91 crisis, the world passed into a decade of lower oil prices and overconfidence about energy security—and, indeed, security overall. But turmoil in the Middle East—accentuated by demographic pressures, generational change and the rise of extremism; by the threat to political order and infrastructure posed by terrorist organizations; by regional conflict; and by rising demand, market pressure and price spikes—all these have brought the issue centre stage again . Yet, over the past 30 years, all four elements of traditional energy security discussions have evolved. Oil and natural gas production occurs today in locations not anticipated 30 years ago.

The expansion of the European Union, the break-up of the Soviet Union and the economic explosion in the Asia Pacific region have meant major shifts in demand and supply and in geopolitics. Terrorist acts by small groups that are more concerned about disrupting economies than on controlling oil were not a consideration in the past. Now, every government must factor in the possibility of terrorist acts that could disrupt some part of the supply chain or systems that support the energy supply chain, including telecommunications. In the 1990s, natural gas became the "fuel of choice" for new power generating plants. Both globalization and the Internet revolution have also created interconnections in the supply chain that squeeze out inefficiencies and yet create new vulnerabilities for disruption. In this section of the report, we explore the major shifts in the world of energy between 1974 and 2005, beginning with oil—the original focus of energy security (Pronishka, 2007).

Energy security—the continuous availability of energy in varied forms, in sufficient quantities, and at reasonable prices—has many aspects. It means limited vulnerability to transient or longer disruptions of imported supplies. It also means the availability of local and imported resources to meet, over time and at reasonable prices, the growing demand for energy. Environmental challenges, liberalization and deregulation, and the growing dominance of market forces all have profound implications for energy security. These forces have introduced new elements into energy security, affecting the traditionally vital role of government. In the past, and especially since the early 1970s, energy security has been narrowly viewed as reduced dependence on oil consumption and imports, particularly in OECD and other major oil-importing countries. But changes in oil and other energy markets have altered that view. Suppliers have increased, as have proven reserves and stocks, and prices have become flexible and transparent, dictated by market forces rather than by cartel arrangements.

Global tensions as well as regional conflicts are lessening, and trade is flourishing and becoming freer. Suppliers have not imposed any oil sanctions since the early 1980s, nor have there been any real shortages anywhere in the world. Instead, the United Nations and other actors have applied sanctions to some oil suppliers, but without affecting world oil trade or creating shortages. All this points to the present availability of abundant oil supplies at all times, an availability that has been greatly enhanced thanks in large part to technological advances. Moreover, in today's market environment energy security is a shared issue for importing and exporting countries. Energy security can be ensured through local adequacy—abundant and varied forms of indigenous energy resources. But for countries that face local shortages, as most do, energy security can be enhanced through:

- The ability, of the state or of market players, to draw on foreign energy resources and products that can be freely imported through ports or other transport channels and through cross-boundary energy grids (pipelines and electricity networks). This is increasingly aided by energy treaties and charters and by investment and trade agreements.
- Adequate national (or regional) strategic reserves to address any transient interruption, shortages, or unpredictably high demand.
- Technological and financial resources and know-how to develop indigenous renewable energy sources and domestic power generating facilities to meet part of local energy requirements.
- Adequate attention to environmental challenges.
- Diversification of import sources and types of fuels.

Energy Security-Conservation Nexus

Energy security can also be greatly enhanced by energy conservation and efficiency measures, because reducing energy intensity will reduce the dependence of the economy on energy consumption and imports. But while all this is very encouraging, new threats to energy security have appeared in recent years. Regional shortages are becoming more acute, and the possibility of insecurity of supplies—due to disruption of trade and reduction in strategic reserves, as a result of conflicts or sabotage—still exists, although it is decreasing. All this points toward a need to strengthen global as well as regional and national energy security.

Adequate global energy supplies, for the world as a whole as well as for individual countries, are essential for sustainable development, proper functioning of the economy, and human well-being. Thus the continuous availability of energy—in the quantities and forms required by the economy and society—must be ensured and secured. Energy security—the continuous availability of energy in varied forms, in sufficient quantities, and at reasonable prices—has several aspects. It means limited vulnerability to transient or longer disruptions of imported supplies. It also means the availability of local and imported resources to meet growing demand over time and at reasonable prices.

Beginning in the early 1970s energy security was narrowly viewed as reduced dependence on oil consumption and imports, particularly in OECD and other major oil-importing countries. Since that time considerable changes in oil and other energy markets have altered the picture. Suppliers have increased, as have proven reserves and stocks, and prices have become flexible and transparent, dictated by market forces rather than by cartel arrangements. Global tensions and regional conflicts are lessening, and trade is flourishing and becoming freer. Suppliers have not imposed any oil sanctions since the early 1980s, nor have there been any real shortages anywhere in the world. Instead, the United Nations and other actors have applied sanctions to some oil suppliers, but without affecting world oil trade or creating shortages.

Regional Imbalance—A Potential Threat to Energy security

New threats to energy security have emerged in recent years. Regional shortages are becoming more acute, and the possibility of insecurity of supplies—due to disruption of trade and reduction in strategic reserves, as a result of conflicts or sabotage—persists, although it is decreasing. These situations point to a need to strengthen global as well as regional and national energy security. There is also a need for a strong plea, under the auspices of the World Trade Organization (WTO), to refrain from restrictions on trade in energy products on grounds of competition or differences in environmental or labour standards. Environmental challenges to sustainable development are gaining momentum and have profound implications for energy security, as do the current trends of liberalization, deregulation, and the growing dominance of market forces. These forces have introduced new elements into energy security, affecting the traditionally vital role of government. They also have consequences for medium-size companies and individual consumers, who may be tempted by cheap competitive prices and lack of information to sacrifice, sometimes temporarily, supply security.

Energy has always been important to humanity. But its importance is increasing each year. Interruptions of energy supply—even if brief—can cause serious financial, economic, and social losses. Some energy products and carriers have become absolutely essential for modern life and business. Interruption of electricity supply can cause major financial losses and create havoc in cities and urban centres. The absolute security of the energy supply, particularly electricity, is therefore critical. With the widespread use of computers and other voltage- and frequency-sensitive electronic equipment, the quality of supply has also become vital. In the electricity supply industry, a significant share of investment goes into reserve generating plants, standby equipment, and other redundant facilities needed to protect the continuity and quality of supply.

Energy Security Linked to Distribution and Supplies

Energy insecurity and shortages affect countries in two ways: they handicap productive activities, and they undermine consumer welfare. Energy insecurity discourages investors by threatening production and increasing costs. Shortages in electricity supplies (as in many developing countries) require more investment for on-site electricity production or standby supplies. For small investors, the cost of operation is increased, since electricity from private small-scale generation is more expensive than public national supplies. Electricity interruptions at home cause consumers great inconvenience, frustration, and loss of productivity, sometimes threatening their well-being. For any economy, an unreliable energy supply results in both short- and long-term costs. The costs are measured in terms of loss of welfare and production, and the adjustments that consumers facing unreliable fuel and electric power supplies undertake to mitigate their losses. Interruptions in supply may trigger loss of production, costs related to product spoilage, and damage to equipment. The extent of these direct economic costs depends on a host of factors, such as advance notification, duration of the interruption, and timing of the interruption, which relates to the time of day or season and to the prevailing market conditions and demand for the firm's output. These direct costs can be very high. In addition, the economy is affected indirectly because of the secondary costs that arise from the interdependence between one firm's output and another firm's input.

New dimensions and Challenges to Energy Security

Energy security needs to be investigated at several levels: globally, to ensure adequacy of resources; regionally, to ensure that networking and trade can take place; at the country level, to ensure national security of supply; and at the consumer level, to ensure that consumer demand can be satisfied (Khatib, 2007). At the country level, energy security is based on the availability of all energy consumption requirements at all times from indigenous sources or imports and from stocks. Normally in most countries, this is a state responsibility. However, markets in some OECD countries are increasingly shouldering part of this responsibility. To ensure energy security, projections, plans, and supply arrangements should look beyond short-term requirements to medium- and long-term demand as well. With the increasing deregulation and competition among private and independent suppliers, supply security at the consumer level can become more vulnerable and correspondingly more important in some cases. Consumer demand for energy services can be met by different suppliers competing to deliver different forms of energy at different prices, while the consumer remains unaware of the degree of supply security.

As explained above, environmental challenges deregulation, and market forces have introduced new players to the energy security scene. This chapter considers energy security at the national (and regional) level as well as consumer security in terms of energy services. In most countries these two levels of security are one and the same. But in some OECD countries, with markets and competition emerging at the consumer level, the two may diverge. The section also covers the geopolitical aspects of energy security as well as the limitations of the resource base and other factors that may affect long-term energy security. Of all energy sources, crude oil and its products are the most versatile, capable of meeting every requirement for energy use and services, particularly in transport. The other fossil fuels, coal and natural gas, are well suited for electricity production and such stationary uses as generation of heat and steam. Coal, increasingly used for electricity production, requires relatively expensive clean technologies, and treatment for liquefaction and gasification to make it more versatile. Natural gas also requires expensive infrastructure, and special treatment to make it useful for transport. Hydropower, newer renewable resources such as wind and photovoltaic, and nuclear energy have limited use beyond electricity production.

Given the versatility of crude oil and its products and the limitations of other energy sources, energy security depends more than anything else on the availability of crude oil in the required amounts (by ship or pipeline) to any importing country in the world. Thus, although energy security has to be interpreted more broadly than in the past, the uninterrupted supply of crude oil in the required amounts and at reasonable prices will continue to be the most important determinant of energy security. Uninterrupted supply—of oil and other forms of Energy—includes uninterrupted transit through third countries.

Pathways to Enhanced Energy Security

Energy security can be ensured by local adequacy—abundant and varied forms of indigenous energy resources. In the case of local shortages, which occur in most countries, energy security can be enhanced through: The ability, of the state or of market players, to draw on foreign energy resources and products that can be freely imported through ports or other transport channels and through cross boundary energy grids (pipelines and electricity networks).

- Adequate national (or regional) strategic reserves to address any transient interruption, shortages, or unpredictable surge in demand.
- Technological and financial resources and know-how to develop indigenous renewable sources and power generating facilities to meet part of local energy requirements.
- Adequate attention to environmental challenges.

Energy security can also be enhanced through energy conservation and efficiency measures. Reducing energy intensity will reduce the dependence of the economy on energy consumption and imports. To achieve energy security requires first of all ensuring global energy adequacy—the existence of enough energy resources, or other prospects, to meet long-term world energy needs. (www.ieej.or.jp/aperc)

Energy Adequacy

Although energy resources are examined in detail elsewhere in this volume, a quick review is provided here because energy security depends, to a great extent, on the availability of an adequate resource base. The resource base is the sum of reserves and resources. Reserves are occurrences (of all types and forms of hydrocarbon deposits, natural uranium, and thorium) that are known and economically recoverable with present technologies.

Resources are less certain, are not economically recoverable with present technologies, or are both. In the future, with advances in technology and geophysics, many of today's resources are likely to become reserves (McKelvey, 1972). In 1998, world consumption of primary energy totaled almost 355 exajoules, or 8,460 million tonnes of oil equivalent (Mtoe)—7,630 Mtoe of fossil fuels, 620 Mtoe of nuclear energy, and 210 Mtoe of hydropower. To this should be added around 47 exajoules (1,120 Mtoe) of biomass and other renewables, for a total of 402 exajoules (9,580 Mtoe). The huge resource base of fossil fuels, coal, water, sunshine and nuclear fuels will be adequate to meet such global requirements for decades to come.

Let us examine in brief the potentiality of these resources to meet the growing challenges of Energy Security.

Crude Oil

Proven oil reserves have increased steadily over the past 20 years, mainly because oil companies have expanded their estimates of the reserves in already discovered fields. This optimism stems from better knowledge of the fields, increased productivity, and advances in technology. New technologies have led to more accurate estimates of reserves through better seismic (three- and four-dimensional) exploration, have improved drilling techniques (such as horizontal and offshore drilling), and have increased recovery factors—the share of oil that can be recovered—from 30 percent to 40–50 percent (Campbell and Laherrere, 1998). Huge amount of untapped unconventional oil also exist, augmenting conventional oil reserves. Some 1.2 trillion barrels of heavy oil are found in the Orinoco oil belt in Venezuela. And the tar sands of Canada and oil shale deposits of the Russian Federation may contain 300 billion barrels of oil.

The U.S. Geological Survey assessed ultimate oil and gas reserves at the beginning of 1993 (IEA 1998; WEC, 1998). The results, which tally with the World Energy Council (WEC) and International Energy Agency (IEA) figures, point to ultimate conventional oil reserves of 2,300 billion barrels, with cumulative production until 1993 amounting to 700 billion barrels and unidentified reserves to 470 billion. No shortage of conventional liquid fuels is foreseen before 2020. Any deficiencies after that can be met by the ample reserves of unconventional oil.

Natural Gas

The U.S. Geological Survey also assessed ultimate natural gas reserves in 1993 (Masters, 1994). It estimated ultimate reserves at 11,448 trillion cubic feet

(11,214 exajoules, or 267 gigatonnes of oil equivalent [Gtoe]), with cumulative production until 1993 amounting to 1,750 trillion cubic feet (1,722 exajoules, or 41 Gtoe). Cumulative world gas production through the end of 1995 was only 17.1 percent of the U.S. Geological Survey's estimate of conventional gas reserves. Natural gas consumption is projected to grow 2.6 percent a year, mostly as a result of growth in electricity generation in non-OECD countries. Despite this growth, cumulative production is expected to be no more than 41 percent of the U.S. Geological Survey's estimate of conventional gas reserves by 2020. This points towards a resource base that is large enough to serve global requirements for natural gas well into the second half of the 21st century.

Coal

Coal is the world's most abundant fossil fuel, with reserves estimated at almost 1,000 billion tonnes, equivalent to 27,300 exajoules, or 650,000 Mtoe (WEC, 1998). At the present rate of production, these reserves should last for more than 220 years. Thus the resource base of coal is much larger than that of oil and gas. In addition, coal reserves are more evenly distributed across the world. And coal is cheap. Efforts are being made to reduce production costs and to apply clean coal technologies to reduce the environmental impact. Coal demand is forecast to grow at a rate slightly higher than global energy growth. Most of this growth will be for power generation in non-OECD countries, mostly in Asia. Although trade in coal is still low, it is likely to increase slowly over time. Long-term trends in direct coal utilization are difficult to predict because of the potential impact of climate change policies. Coal gasification and liquefaction will augment global oil and gas resources in the future.

Nuclear Energy

Although nuclear energy is sometimes grouped with fossil fuels, it relies on a different resource base. In 1998 nuclear energy production amounted to 2,350 terawatt-hours of electricity, replacing 620 Mtoe of other fuels. Uranium requirements amounted to 63,700 tonnes in 1997, against reasonably assured resources (reserves) of 3.4 million tonnes. Ultimately recoverable reserves amount to almost 17 million tonnes. Considering the relative stagnation in the growth of nuclear power, the enormous occurrences of low-grade uranium and the prospects for recycling nuclear fuels, such reserves will suffice for many decades.

Renewable

Renewable energy sources—especially hydroelectric power, biomass, and wind power, and geothermal energy— account for a growing share of world energy consumption. Today hydropower and biomass together contribute around 15 percent. Hydroelectric power contributes around 2,500 terawatt-hours of electricity a year, slightly more than nuclear power does. It replaces almost 675 Mtoe of fuels a year, although its direct contribution to primary energy consumption is only a third of this. But it has still more potential. Technically exploitable hydro resources could potentially produce more than 14,000 terawatt-hours of electricity a year, equivalent to the world's total electricity requirements in 1998 (WEC, 1998). For environmental and economic reasons, however, most of these resources will not be exploited. Still, hydropower will continue to develop. Hydropower is the most important among renewable energy sources. It is a clean, cheap source of energy, requiring only minimal running costs and with a conversion efficiency of almost 100 percent. Thus, its annual growth could exceed the growth of global energy demand, slightly improving hydropower's modest contribution towards meeting world requirements.

Renewable energy sources other than hydro are substantial. These take the form mainly of biomass. Traditional biomass includes fuelwood—the main source of biomass energy—dung, and crop and forest residues. Lack of statistics makes it difficult to accurately estimate the contribution of renewable to the world's primary energy consumption. But it is estimated that the world consumed around 1.20 Gtoe in 1998. About two-thirds of this was from fuelwood, and the remainder from crop residues and dung. Much of this contribution is sustainable from a supply standpoint. But the resulting energy services could be substantially increased by improving conversion efficiencies, which are typically very low.

The contribution of biomass to world energy consumption is expected to increase slightly. It is mainly used as an energy source in developing countries. While energy demand in these countries is steadily increasing, some of the demand is being met by switching from traditional to commercial energy sources. Biomass energy technology is rapidly advancing. Besides direct combustion, techniques for gasification, fermentation, and anaerobic digestion are all increasing the potential of biomass as a sustainable energy source. The viability of wind energy is increasing as well. Some 2,100 megawatts of new capacity was commissioned in 1998, pushing global wind generating capacity to 9,600 megawatts.

Wind power accounted for an estimated 21 terawatt-hours of electricity production in 1999. While that still amounts to only 0.15 percent of global electricity production, the competitiveness of wind power is improving and its growth potential is substantial. Use of geothermal energy for electricity generation is also increasing, with a present generating capacity of more than 8,300 megawatts.

Supply-side Security

Energy resources are not evenly distributed across the world. Oil in particular, and natural gas to a lesser extent, is concentrated in a few regions. The concentration of oil reserves in the Persian Gulf region has always caused concerns about continuity of supply. Most countries, particularly OECD countries, experienced oil shortages and high prices in the 1970s and early 1980s, with physical disruption in supply leading to economic disruption. Energy importers are anxious not to repeat such experiences.

The oil supply situation has improved significantly since then. OECD countries' share of the energy market is decreasing, while that of developing countries is increasing .This adds to the security of oil supplies because many developing countries are oil producers or have supply arrangements with producers. OECD countries, which accounted for 70 percent of the energy market in the 1970s, will see their market share fall to less than half by 2010.

Technological advance has allowed the discovery and development of new energy reserves and reduced the cost of supplies. It has also helped increase efficiency in energy use, loosening the historically tight link between economic development and energy consumption. Another major favourable development is the reduction in the sources of conflict that can affect global energy security. The cold war is over, and stability in the Middle-East, although still precarious, is improving, with the Arab-Israeli conflict moving towards resolution. However, some other global developments present both opportunities and new challenges to the energy sector. The policy emphasis on environmentally sustainable development, particularly in OECD countries, has important long-term implications for energy security; and the market liberalization taking place in most industrialized countries has reduced the state's role in energy security—and increased that of consumers.

Energy security is also important for energy producers and exporters. History shows that oil supply disruptions have negative effects on oil-exporting economies. As consumers in importing economies shift away from oil, the lower demand causes severe economic damage to the exporters. In addition, many oil-exporting countries have recently obtained stakes in downstream operations in importing countries. This involvement in OECD economies will contribute towards energy security, as supply disruptions could mean a loss of business opportunities for both oil exporters and importers.

Causes of supply disruption are not limited to disturbances in production facilities. Disruptions can also occur in the long supply chains, such as serious tanker accidents in the most heavily travelled zones—the Strait of Malacca, for example. Vulnerability to disruption may grow as energy supplies are increasingly delivered through grids (gas pipelines and extra-high-voltage transmission networks).

Some of these cross-national boundaries and are at least theoretically vulnerable to damage through sabotage and other political disturbances. Terrorist actions could damage liquefied natural gas (LNG) conversion and receiving stations and tankers. But such possibilities are remote. Most energy supplies are delivered under long-term contracts that commit governments to ensuring safe transit and security. Despite the favourable developments in the energy market, energy security continues to concern planners and strategists in most importing countries. Long-term energy security can be enhanced in several ways; namely through:

- Diversifying sources of supply and forms of energy used
- Encouraging international cooperation and agreements among energy-importing countries and between consumer and supplier countries, whether between governments or between companies.
- Investing in and transferring technology to developing countries. Enabling developing countries to develop more energy supplies will enhance the availability of global supplies. Helping these countries increase the efficiency of energy use and improve environmental management will have a similar effect.
- Enhancing and increasing national and regional strategic reserves of crude oil and its products.

Of all the forms of energy, crude oil and its products are still the most important for energy security, because of oil's versatility and because it is the optimal form of energy for the transport sector. Natural gas, because of its affordability and cleanliness, is gaining importance. Nuclear energy, despite its past promise, faces many difficulties. The security of all these energy forms, as well as coal, is discussed below. Energy intensity is also discussed, because improvements in this area could yield a wider range of benefits for energy security than could provide new sources of energy.

Security Concerns of Crude Oil Supply

Over the past 20 years many changes in the oil market have improved the overall security of the energy market. The world economy has become less dependent on oil, as most regions have diversified their energy sources. Oil constituted almost 46 percent of world commercial energy sources in 1973, compared with 40 percent now. There has also been diversification of supply. In the early 1970s the Organization of Petroleum Exporting Countries (OPEC) accounted for more than half the world's oil; today it provides only 42 percent. The world now has 80 oil-producing countries (although very few have the surge capacity needed in emergencies). The oil markets have become more like traditional commodity markets (with futures markets), transparent and able to respond quickly to changing circumstances. Big strides have been made in energy efficiency, gradually reducing the dependence of economic growth on increased oil consumption. (CERA, 2007).

Advances in technology have led to discoveries of more oil, reduced the cost of discoveries, and significantly improved the recovery rate, increasing the oil resource base to an estimated 2,300 trillion barrels. World trade has flourished in recent years. In 1998 it was three times that in 1980, and now accounts for 44 percent of global GDP, compared with 39 percent in 1980. Both energy exporters and importers benefit from trade. Most exporters are low-income countries that badly need oil income for development. Even with the increase in oil-producing countries, the fact remains that almost two-thirds of the world's oil resources are in the Middle-East, mostly in the Gulf region (the Islamic Republic of Iran, Iraq, Kuwait, Qatar, Saudi Arabia, and the United Arab Emirates). Although these six countries now account for only 27 percent of global crude oil supplies, they are expected to double their share to 52 percent in 2010. The Middle-East, particularly the Gulf region, has not been historically known for political stability and security. But as mentioned, the situation is improving.

OECD countries, which account for almost 80 percent of the world's economic activity and 63 percent of global oil consumption, are particularly dependent on oil imports. All OECD countries are expected to increase their dependence on oil imports over the next few years. Their oil imports, 56 percent of their energy requirements in 1996, are expected to rise to 76 percent in 2020.

Asia-Pacific countries' crude oil imports are expected to increase to 72 percent of their requirements in 2005 (up from 56 percent in 1993). The Middle East is expected to account for 92 percent of the region's imports, with the Gulf countries the main source of supply. The Gulf region is expected to supply 18 million barrels a day to Asia-Pacific countries in 2010, far more than its expected total supplies to Europe and the United States of 12 million barrels a day. That is why oil security, particularly for the major oil-importing countries, and the stability of the Gulf region have such importance to overall energy security and the world economy. This importance will only increase in the future.

Differences between regional requirements and regional supplies will be accentuated in the future. Nowhere will this be more serious than in Asia, particularly among the large oil-consuming countries—China, India, Japan, and the Republic of Korea. Competition for supplies may intensify during emergencies, creating a potential for severe strains among Asian powers. Shortages may tempt some of these countries to project political and even military power to ensure adequate oil supplies. Already some of them—as well as the United States—have increased their naval presence in the Asian and Indian oceans (Jaffe, 1998). And U.S efforts for cooperation and conflict resolution are linked to its military planning and presence in the Gulf region and key oil export sea routes (Kemp and Harkavy, 1997).

Threats to security in oil-exporting countries can be both internal and external. Continued supply from Saudi Arabia is the most important element of energy security. Saudi supplies, now more than 9 million barrels a day, will have to increase to 13–15 million barrels a day in 2010 to meet growing world demand and offset resource depletion in non-OPEC suppliers. By that time the United States will be importing more than 60 percent of its oil. Saudi Arabia has both the potential and the reserves to meet projected demand, but the expansion will call for investment resources from that country as well as the world financial community.

Over the past few decades the Gulf countries have proved to be stable; continued internal and external stability is crucial to energy security. Disruption of the Gulf oil flow would lead to a deep world-wide recession. This has been presented as one of the gravest threats imaginable to U.S. interests, short of physical attack (David, 1999). The cost of energy security goes beyond investing in redundant facilities and building pipelines, grids, and strategic reserves. Tremendous military expenditures—both visible and invisible—are required to head off any threats to the flow of oil, particularly from the Gulf countries. These costs cannot be easily computed or ascertained. The enormous expenditures on the 1990–91 Gulf-War, totalling several hundred billion dollars, were meant to ensure energy security for major oil importers and the world oil markets in general. The six Gulf Cooperation Council (GCC) states, which control nearly 45 percent of the world's recoverable oil resources, contributed more than $60 billion to the U.S.-led allied offensive to eject Iraqi forces from Kuwait in 1991 (AFP, 1998). The GCC countries' contribution in 1991 exceeded their oil export income in 1998 or 1999. The United States maintains a costly military and naval presence in strategic locations to ensure the uninterrupted flow of GCC oil exports to world markets.

Oil-stocks: Combating Supply Disruptions

Oil-stocks are usually held by oil companies for operational purposes, and by countries and state utilities to provide a cushion against unexpected surges in demand and possible disruptions in imports. Oil companies usually hold stocks that account for 55–65 days of consumption. International Energy Agency (IEA) members are required to hold emergency oil stocks equivalent to at least 90 days of net imports. The European Union requires its members—also IEA members—to hold stocks equivalent to at least 90 days of consumption. It is not easy to estimate oil stocks held by developing countries. Because of the cost, their stocks are relatively smaller than those of OECD countries, but can amount to 25–55 days of consumption, which is also typical for oil companies in these countries. Correspondingly, world oil stocks in 1997 were about 5,500 million barrels, equal to 70–80 days of average global consumption. With the continued growth of non-OECD oil consumption, oil stocks will function less effectively. Their size relative to the global oil market will decline, since most developing countries do not maintain emergency oil stocks (many cannot afford them). If this trend continues, vulnerability to sudden and substantial oil supply disruptions will increase.

Liberalization of Markets: Easing the Flow of Oil

Another aspect of security is the liberalization of energy markets in importing countries. Liberalization and deregulation, coupled with the development of oil futures and forwards markets, mean easier and more secure flow of oil from exporting to importing countries. Most oil producers are now inviting foreign companies to participate in oil development, which will significantly enhance the security of the oil market. And the strengthening of the World Trade Organization (WTO) will add further to the security of the energy market. Although security in terms of flows of oil and gas to importing countries is improving, the security of supply to consumers faces new challenges. Liberalization, the withdrawal of government responsibility for supply, and competition among private suppliers are creating challenges in securing reliable supply to individual consumers.

Security Aspects of Natural Gas Supply

Natural gas is slowly gaining importance in the energy market. Between 1987 and 1997 gas consumption increased from 1,756 giga cubic metres to 2,197, for an annual growth rate of 2.27 percent, compared with 1.47 percent for total primary commercial energy consumption. Over the period until 2020 natural gas demand is expected to grow still faster—at an annual rate of 2.6 percent, compared with 1.9 percent for oil. And natural gas supply, since it is starting from a much lower base than oil supply, is not expected to peak until well beyond 2020 (IEA, 1998).

Internationally traded natural gas accounted for 19 percent of gas consumption in 1997, compared with 44 percent for oil. So, just as for oil, though to a lesser extent, there is a mismatch between the location of gas supply and its consumption. Security of supply is therefore critical. But the physical characteristics of natural gas make ensuring security of supply for gas more complicated than for oil. Crude oil is an eminently fungible commodity, portable by ship, pipeline, road tanker, or even barrel. In contrast, gas requires expensive pipelines or LNG infrastructure. These delivery systems are relatively inflexible: pipelines cannot be moved or built overnight, and LNG, although somewhat portable, still requires an expensive receiving terminal.

Crude oil and, more important, refined oil products can be transported to any location that can receive a ship or road tanker. Moreover, gas is difficult to store in significant quantities. The energy content per unit of volume is much lower for gas than for oil. Gas is simply more difficult to handle than liquid. Its storage often depends on the suitability of geological structures, while oil tank farms can be built relatively easily and cheaply. All these factors mean that the solutions used to ensure security of oil supply (storage, diversification of supplies) do not apply as easily to gas. The gas supply system must be configured to give the required flexibility. Security of supply also involves reducing strategic risk, namely, the risk of a major disruption to supplies caused by, for example, political factors or major technical failure, such as the failure of a high-pressure pipeline. This is an extension of operational security, but of a different order of magnitude. Strategic risk is growing in parallel with the growing share of gas in meeting countries' primary energy requirements. It can be reduced through:

Interconnectivity—the degree of physical interconnection with other gas systems is an important factor in ensuring strategic security of supply. Interconnectivity is more than simply a guard against potential failure; it also encourages diversity of supply.

All sources of supply are unlikely to fail at the same time. Countries have often explicitly diversified supply by contracting with several countries. France, for example, buys gas from Algeria, the Netherlands, Norway, and Russia. In recent years there have been a number of spot LNG sales into Europe from LNG suppliers using spare capacity. Security of supply also entails guarding against long-term risk—ensuring that consuming countries can secure future and additional supplies as their existing supplies are depleted. This represents a challenge, as the bulk of the world's gas reserves are in areas that are far from current markets and also often have a high level of country risk. Some gas-importing countries, such as France, use long-term strategic storage to guard against significant disruption of supply. Such storage can be in depleted oil or gas fields, aquifers, salt caverns, or other geological structures.

Security of Coal Supply: Global Scene

Coal presents fewer challenges—other than environmental ones—to energy security than do oil and gas. It is abundant and more evenly distributed around the world than oil or gas. It is cheap, and costs are continuously being reduced by competition. Too many suppliers and the possibility of switching from one to another ensure supply security. The global ratio of coal reserves to production is 225 years; for OECD countries, it is even higher. Coal is still a local fuel, however. International trade in coal is limited, amounting to only 13 percent of production, a smaller share than for gas. The huge reserves of coal and their even distribution contribute to global energy security. Coal will continue to play a major part in ensuring the energy security of large energy consumers, particularly China (the largest coal consumer), the United States, and South Asia.

Over the next few decades the growth in demand for coal is expected to continue to be healthy, exceeding the growth in overall energy demand. Most of that growth will be for electricity generation, with coal consumption in the electricity sector expected to grow in all regions. But this is also the area where the main security challenge arises, because of the environmental effects of coal use—locally, regionally, and also possibly globally. Coal utilization is very inefficient, particularly in power generation, where its efficiency is less than 25 percent (Ecoal, 1998). The efficiency of oil and gas in electricity generation is at least 50 percent higher.

For coal to play its deserved role in global energy security, its many detrimental environmental impacts must be addressed. This will require not only clean coal technologies for new plants, but also rehabilitation and refurbishment of existing inefficient plants. And this must happen not only in industrialized countries, but also in developing countries, which are expected to account for most coal use and all this calls for technology transfer and huge investments.

Nuclear Energy and Energy Security

Nuclear energy could continue to add to the energy security of countries short of hydropower and indigenous fossil fuel resources, for several reasons. Uranium resources are widely distributed and abundant world-wide. Nuclear fuel is cheap: at the price of present long-term uranium supply contracts, the cost of natural uranium per kilowatt-hour is equivalent to an oil price of $0.35 per barrel, so several years' supply could be kept in reserve against possible future supply disruption at a low cost. And the cost of uranium contributes only about 2 percent to the cost of nuclear electricity generation, compared with 40–70 percent for fossil fuels in electricity generation, making the cost of nuclear electricity relatively insensitive to possible future increases in the uranium price. These considerations played a key part in the decisions of such economies as France, the Republic of Korea, Japan, and Taiwan (China) to launch major nuclear power programmes. In all likelihood, such considerations will also be important determinants in similar decisions by countries with a shortage of indigenous resources and a heavy reliance on imports. Moreover, the fact those nuclear power releases virtually no environmentally damaging emissions of carbon-dioxide, sulphur- di-oxide, and nitrogen oxide could make it an attractive option for many countries seeking technologies leading to reduced greenhouse gas emissions or abatement of local and regional pollution.

In the 1960s and 1970s, particularly after the first oil shock, nuclear power promised to be a viable solution for industrialized countries looking for energy security and cheap power. Largely as a result of investment decisions made in that period, nuclear power has grown to the point where it dominates electricity generation in several industrialized countries, providing about a sixth of global electricity in 1998. But the outlook for nuclear power is not bright. Most of the promise of nuclear energy has evaporated as a result of loss of investor and public confidence in the technology. There is likely to be growth in nuclear power in some Asian countries in the period to 2020 and modest expansion at the global level until 2010. But most projections show nuclear power accounting for a smaller share of global electricity generation in 2020 than today, and many show its absolute contribution staying the same or even shrinking. The loss of investor and public confidence in nuclear technology is due to concerns about costs, nuclear safety, radioactive waste disposal, and proliferation or diversion. Until these concerns are adequately dealt with, nuclear energy is unlikely to play an expanding role in enhancing global energy security.

The energy security benefits provided by nuclear power might even be diminished if there is another reactor accident involving substantial releases of radioactivity or a proliferation or diversion incident that could be plausibly linked in the public mind to nuclear power. Recognition that another major accident might not only diminish prospects for nuclear expansion but also trigger demands to shut down existing nuclear plants has catalyzed private sector-led efforts, under the auspices of the World Association of Nuclear Operators, to instill a culture of safety in the world's nuclear industry. This situation has also prompted an international effort, led by the International Atomic Energy Agency, to bolster national nuclear regulatory regimes.

This effort is embodied in the Convention on Nuclear Safety, adopted by the organization's members. The Nuclear Non-Proliferation Treaty and associated international safeguards and nuclear supplier agreements have been implemented to minimize the nuclear weapons link to nuclear power (Murray, 1995). To date, all but a few states (apart from the five nuclear weapons states recognized in the 1968 Non-Proliferation Treaty, these are India, Israel, and Pakistan) have committed themselves to putting all nuclear material, including the material used for uranium enrichment and reprocessing, indefinitely under safeguard of the International Atomic Energy Agency.

Recent events and concerns about the limitations of existing policies have led various experts to call for further efforts to weaken the nuclear weapons link to nuclear power. But because the risk of proliferation and diversion is not at the forefront of public concerns about nuclear power (and may not be until there is an incident), because national policies in this area differ widely, and because there is much disagreement in the technical community about the best approaches for minimizing this risk, there has been less action in this area than there has been in improving reactor safety. Increasing the authority and resources of the International Atomic Energy Agency for monitoring enrichment plants and spent fuel is the principal way immediately available to reduce the proliferation risks associated with existing uranium enrichment and fuel reprocessing capabilities.

In short, for the next couple of decades the prospects for enhancing energy security through expansion of nuclear power are not bright at the global level, although they are somewhat better in some Asian countries. In the longer term whether nuclear power can contribute to energy security depends not only on technical and economic considerations to be sorted out by the market, but also on the extent to which the public can be convinced that nuclear power is safe and that wastes can be disposed of safely. It also depends on whether the industry can avoid major accidents and proliferation and diversion incidents, and whether national and international policymakers and the technical community can reach consensus on what needs to be done to make nuclear energy technology widely acceptable.

Energy Intensity Aspects

One way to improve energy security in any country is by reducing its energy intensity—the amount of energy required to produce one unit of GDP. The rate of change in energy intensity reflects the overall improvement in energy efficiency as well as structural changes in the economy. Declining rates of energy intensity indicate that economic growth is less tightly linked to increases in energy use. Energy intensity has improved considerably in industrialized countries. In the United States over the past two centuries it has declined 1 percent a year on average. One unit of GDP now requires only a fifth of the primary energy required 200 years ago (IIASA and WEC, 1998). In the past 15 years energy intensity in the United States has improved 20 percent.

Energy intensity differs depending on the level of economic development. OECD countries generally have an energy intensity that is a fraction of that in developing countries. In 1996, the commercial energy intensity of middle-income developing countries was three times that of high-income countries.

This finding remains whether GDP is measured in market dollars or in purchasing power parity (PPP) terms. In most developing countries energy intensity is stagnant or even increasing because these countries are in the early take-off stages of industrialization, when energy-intensive industries and infrastructure are being established. Moreover, low-income developing countries usually show increasing commercial energy intensity because commercial energy sources are replacing non-commercial fuels. The prospects for lowering energy intensity are reduced in many developing countries by the proliferation of energy price subsidies and by the use of inefficient and outdated plants and equipment.

Generally, however, energy intensity in developing countries is similar to that in industrialized countries when they were at an earlier stage of development. Economic growth in developing countries has been relatively high in recent years, averaging 2.8 percent a year in the 1990s, compared with 2.1 percent for industrialized countries and 2.3 percent for the world. This trend is likely to continue. If this growth is matched by measures to conserve energy—such as phasing out subsidies and improving environmental awareness—energy security in developing countries is likely to continue to improve as well. Predicting the future of energy intensity is difficult, particularly for developing countries. In low-income countries energy intensity may increase in the next few years as these countries substitute commercial energy for traditional fuels. But for the world as a whole, energy intensity is likely to improve. Average improvements will range from 0.8 percent to 1.0 percent a year, depending on such factors as environmental awareness and energy prices (IIASA and WEC, 1998). If the world economy continues to grow at the expected average rate of 2.7 percent, energy demand growth will average 1.7–1.9 percent a year. That means that in 2020 global energy demand will be 45–51 percent higher than in 1998. This is a substantial increase. But without the expected efficiency improvements in global energy utilization, the demand could grow as much as 80 percent. The potential for efficiency improvements is high in many energy applications. Some of the most important progress in energy efficiency is that taking place in the conversion of energy to electricity. Modern combined cycle gas turbines burning natural gas have efficiencies approaching 60 percent, and efficiencies of 70 percent are within reach in the foreseeable future. Such efficiencies are more than double the average of 31 percent for the world stock of existing generating plants. As old plants are phased out and new, CCGT-type plants—or the traditional thermal generating plant firing coal at more than 40 percent efficiency—take over, considerable improvements in energy utilization will gradually occur. In addition, the increased use of electricity as an energy carrier world-wide will further improve energy efficiency. In some applications electricity is more efficient than other forms of energy, and its use is now growing 2.8–3.2 percent a year, a rate more than 50 percent higher than that for primary energy overall (Khatib, 1997). All this will significantly lower energy intensity and thus improve prospects for global energy security.

The Environment and Energy Security Relationship

The idea of sustainable development is gaining acceptance on the official level as well as among the public. Sustainable development demands environmental preservation. Energy production and utilization, particularly in the case of fossil fuels, can be major sources of environmental degradation. These detrimental environmental impacts have a direct bearing on the future of energy—in terms of fuels and the extent of their use—and on energy security. The United Nations Framework Convention on Climate Change, adopted at the Rio Earth Summit in 1992, and the Kyoto Protocol, signed by more than 160 countries in 1997, call for major reductions of greenhouse gas emissions, which are caused mainly by energy use. Fulfilling the commitments as agreed and at the schedules approved would greatly affect the use of energy resources and could compromise global economic progress. There is a large gap between the commitments and the means for implementation. Targets agreed upon by negotiators were not necessarily implemented by legislators or other policymakers. Implementation of such targets is hindered not only by cost but also by the need to maintain energy security. All indications are that fossil fuels will continue to dominate global energy resources for at least the first decades of the 21st century. Moreover, the demand for energy services will continue to increase. Most of the growth will be in developing countries, which can ill afford the high cost of containment measures. It is therefore essential to find means to contain energy-related emissions without compromising energy security.

The environmental effects of energy use occur at the local, regional, and global levels. Local effects consist primarily of heavy hydrocarbons and particulate matter (including sulphur flakes) that are deposited within hours and can travel up to 100 kilometres from the source. Regional effects include emissions and effluents, the most important of which are sulphur and nitrogen oxides, which are converted into acids; these acids, which last for a few days in the atmosphere, may travel up to a few thousand kilometres before being deposited, often after crossing boundaries. Global environmental impacts are exemplified by emissions of carbon dioxide and other gases (mainly methane) that have long residence times in the atmosphere. Local and regional impacts can be addressed by technologies. However, some of these technologies are expensive for developing countries, where growth in the use of low-quality coal will be particularly high. There are no easy answers in dealing with greenhouse gas emissions. Mitigation and sequestration measures are still to be developed. The most practical solution is to reduce the growth in fossil fuel use by increasing efficiency in energy utilization. Enhancing efficiency in energy use not only helps greatly to mitigate emissions; it also improves energy security. But for greater benefits for energy security, energy use should also be made more compatible with the aims of sustainable development through better containment of emissions. Such simple measures as washing coal will rid it of 20–50 percent of its sulphur. Advanced burners and scrubbers remove pollutants and effluent gases from smoke stacks and chimneys.

Fuel substitution is another effective measure. A modern CCGT power station, firing gas, will emit only 40 percent as much carbon dioxide as a traditional coal-fired thermal power station. The slow but persistent growth in the use of electricity as an energy carrier will also contribute towards energy security. Besides offering greater efficiency than other forms of energy in many applications, electricity concentrates emissions in a single remote location—the site of the power station—making them easier and cheaper to deal with.

Emerging Global Markets and Energy Security

Approaches to ensuring energy supply security in the 21st century should differ from past approaches that concentrated on oil substitution. Besides sustainable growth challenges, new approaches need to tackle the new energy security issues raised by market liberalization. The enhanced role of markets is tied closely to the process of globalization. Globalization, which is still gaining momentum, has encouraged competition and strengthened markets and regional and international trade, particularly for crude oil and oil products, natural gas, and energy services. Globalization is bringing new opportunities for energy security, such as better access to markets and services and the transfer of technologies that are helping to reduce the cost of energy exploration and expand proven reserves. International trade in energy resources and services is vital for energy security.

The creation of the World Trade Organization in 1995, built on the GATT, is the latest multilateral step towards creating an environment conducive to the exchange of goods and services. It will assist in trade liberalization and allow countries greater recourse to trade dispute settlement mechanisms. Foreign trade has grown more quickly than the world economy in recent years, a trend that is likely to continue. For developing countries, trade is growing faster than national income, reaching 50 percent of GDP, and a good share of that trade is in energy. The flow of information has become much easier and more transparent, increasing the resources and services available for trade and reducing prices. All this aids greatly in enhancing energy security. The introduction of a single market in Europe will lead to more competition in energy services and supply of cheaper electricity. Improvements in transport networks and technology are reducing the cost of energy trade. The liberalization of European gas and electricity markets will initiate major structural changes in European energy enterprises, increasing competition, improving economic performance, and contributing towards fuel diversification and greater energy security (EC, 1999).

In studying the influence of markets, there is a need to distinguish between OECD countries, where free markets prevail, and developing countries, where market liberalization is still at a very early stage. Security of supply is a public policy objective. But in free markets decisions are made by market players rather than by governments. Markets allow even small and medium-size consumers—as well as suppliers—a say in energy decisions. That requires redefining the political dimension of energy security.

Markets clearly produce benefits for consumers: trade, innovation, cost reduction, technological advances, and better allocation of resources. Moreover, unbundling the supply chain enhances transparency and allows tariffs to reflect real costs. Markets have also taught us a few lessons: they have proven that they can adjust more easily than governments to changing circumstances in the energy market and that it is costly to intervene against the market for an extended period.

Market liberalization is leaving much of the decision-making to consumers. Are the consumers capable of making the right choices? Or would they choose cheaper options (such as interruptible supply) even if that compromises their energy supply security? This possibility suggests a need for a government role. Moreover, liberalization will not necessarily cover the entire supply chain. Certain monopolies will remain in transmission and distribution. Governments therefore have a duty to protect consumers at the very end of the supply chain (retail consumers). In addition, the energy market may ignore the interests of other consumer classes, such as remote and isolated consumers. All this necessitates that government continue to be involved in the energy market to a certain extent in almost every country.

The argument applies particularly to the supply side. Energy development entails long-term, capital-intensive investments. Private investors may demand a higher rate of return in a liberalized market than in a government-controlled energy industry. In addition, markets usually look for short-term profits and may therefore forgo diversification of supplies, which is associated with high up-front investment and risk but long-term benefits.

Having said all that, there are several reasons to believe that regulatory reforms in the energy market that are aimed at enhancing competition would promote energy security. First, as discussed, reforms can lead to increased investment and trade in energy resources, which will, in turn, facilitate expansion of energy production, increase inter-fuel competition, and encourage the construction of trans-boundary energy delivery infrastructure, such as oil and gas pipelines. Second, the participation in downstream operations by firms from oil-exporting economies, and the participation in upstream operations by firms from oil-importing economies (all of which is facilitated by market liberalization), will be mutually beneficial and thus increase both exporters' and importers' interest in energy security.

In Asia deregulation and other energy sector liberalization will also promote accelerated growth in energy supplies and a greater sense of energy security. Third, regulatory reforms will enhance efficiency and effectiveness, even in the area of energy supply emergency response. The IEA's oil supply emergency systems place growing emphasis on drawdown of oil stocks compared with such measures as demand restraint. The release of oil stocks into the market is more market-oriented than government intervention to restrain demand. Thus, energy sector regulatory reforms could be compatible with or even enhance energy supply security. Governments, while withdrawing from energy investments themselves, need to create a positive climate for trade and investment. With increasing market liberalization, there is a growing need for governments to monitor private sector actors and deal with market failures. Certain investors might be looking for concentration through mergers and joint ventures, for example, which might conflict with government policy of promoting liberalization and fostering competition.

The World Energy Council (WEC) Safeguarding Energy Security

The World Energy Council (WEC, 2007) is the foremost multi-energy organization in the world today. WEC has Member Committees in over 90 countries, including most of the largest energy-producing and energy consuming countries. Established in 1923; the organization covers all types of energy, including coal, oil, natural gas, nuclear, hydro, and renewables, and is UN-accredited, nongovernmental, non-commercial and non-aligned. WEC is a UK-registered charity headquartered in London. WEC's Mission is "to promote the sustainable supply and use of energy for the greatest benefit of all people." WEC's objectives as they exist today are to promote the sustainable supply and use of energy for the greatest benefit of all people, by:

(a) Collating data about and undertaking and promoting research into the means of supplying and using energy having, short and long term, the greatest social benefit and the least harmful impact on the natural environment, and publishing or otherwise disseminating the useful results of such research;

(b) Undertaking actions, including but not limited to the holding of congresses, workshops and seminars, to facilitate such supply and use of energy; this includes the Triennial World Energy congress, a major energy industry event with 5,000+ delegates, comprehensive technical programmes, meetings, networking sessions and a major energy exhibition.

(c) Collaborating with other organizations in the energy sector with compatible goals. WEC's projects look at how current energy challenges can be tackled today, tomorrow and in the future. Global Studies: In depth studies highlighting the longer-term global implications of energy issues.

- Scenarios 2050: Policies to achieve sustainable energy supply and use;
- Energy and Climate Change: How effective climate change policies can shape sustainable energy development;
- Survey of Energy Resources—21st Edition: Comprehensive collection of global energy statistics.

Strengthening Global Alliances—Oil imports and Global Reserves

The U.S. influence on overall world markets is substantial in terms of production and consumption. The United States is the world's second largest natural gas producer and its third largest oil producer. The United States consumes over 25 percent of the oil produced worldwide, slightly more than half of which it imports. Nevertheless, because the price of our domestic and imported oil is determined by a world market, our energy security interests transcend the source of our physical energy supplies.

Larger Question of Improving Market Transparency

The United States must work with oil producers to improve the transparency, timeliness, and accuracy of the data that guide global oil markets. A lack of timely and accurate data relating to both oil production and inventory levels has contributed to the price volatility witnessed in 2000. Discussions among the major oil producers and consumer countries should be designed to improve the transparency, accuracy, and timeliness of data that guide the market. In turn, enhanced data quality and increased data transparency will improve market efficiency. Refocusing that dialogue beyond short-term market developments to long-term issues of world economic growth, improving data quality, and addressing energy infrastructure is needed to maintain a smooth flow of energy from the wellhead to the consumer (National Energy Policy, 2002).

The Role of Fossil Fuels in the Future Energy Mix

Likely fossil fuels will be the main energy driver at least for the next 3 decades to fulfill energy demand growth and support economic growth particularly in emerging economies. Strategy, required long-term policy, and appropriate policy instruments including its associated mechanisms to support the national program on decarburization need further to be established, otherwise within the next 3 decades fossil fuels will remain the dominant source of energy (Situmiang, 2007).

The goals of national energy security and environmental protection need to be reconciled, which requires strong and coordinated government action and public support. It needs firm action to steer the national energy system onto sustainable energy path while supporting national economic growth, with aims to enhance national energy security and mitigating CO2 emissions. To render low carbon emissions in energy path more firm efforts mainly on deployments and diffusions of environmentally sound technologies are really required (including development & transfer of technologies) in order to drive the energy system toward low carbon energy sources, low-carbon & carbon-free energy technologies, greater efficiency in energy production and distribution and in energy use.

Salient Items on Development and Transfer of Environmentally Sound Technologies (EST)

At least there are 3 salient items on development and transfer of Environmentally Sound Technologies (EST) that need to be pondered as a reference for our policy makers with a view towards covering important aspects such as: (i) strategy, mechanisms and required long-term policy for successful development & transfer of EST, (ii) proposed policy instruments to support the national program on decarbonization, (iii) innovative financing mechanisms for development & transfer of technology (UNEP, 2003).

So far, there have been 2 proposed mechanisms that had been raised under development and transfer of technology issues: under the convention and market-based. It seems difficult to reconcile these 2 mechanisms since each comes from fundamentally different approaches and perspectives. It can be noted further that there is a concern particularly from developing countries that implementation of development and transfer of technologies has not been realized as expected. The process has been slow even though in the beginning there has been option available pass through CDM project activities which has been expected as a viable mechanism. Financing and appropriate technology transfer mechanisms to support the development and transfer of technology are the main issues.

Thrust Areas of EST Applications

The need to curb the growth in fossil-energy demand, to improve national energy mix by geographic and fuel supply diversity and to reduce emissions in mitigating climate change is more urgent than before this linkages to energy security versus climate change.

The energy trajectory for reaching the national energy mix target needs to be strongly managed. Indonesia must maintain its economic growth rate of at least 7% a year to eradicate poverty and meets its economic and human development goals, accordingly sustainable growth of primary energy requirements must be maintained to deliver such economic growth.

The goals of national energy security and environmental protection need to be reconciled, which requires strong and coordinated government action and public support. It needs firm action to steer the national energy system onto sustainable energy path while supporting national economic growth, with aims to enhance national energy security and mitigating CO_2 emissions.

Drive the energy system toward low carbon energy sources, low-carbon and carbon-free energy technologies, greater efficiency in energy production and distribution and in energy use and proposed long-term policy and its policy instruments to support national energy policy & national program on decarbonization .

At least 2 important issues that need to be addressed for development and transfer of environmentally sound technologies to developing countries: (i) the need for long-term technology policy which includes associated strategic policy instruments and appropriate technology transfer mechanism to support the development and transfer of technology, and (ii) the need for innovative financing mechanisms.

Some Selected Policies such as: Power sector: enhancing the role of renewable energy, the role of nuclear power, carbon capture and storage; shifting towards new/other low-carbon and carbon-free energy technologies, improving energy efficiency (upstream to downstream activities); Industry and Manufacturing sector; Building sector; Transport (Mobility) sector; Customer Choices; Overcoming Hurdles to Government Action; etc., which need to be enhanced and established.

Climate Change

Climate change concerns also affect the perceptions of energy security. The objective of diversification of oil supplies has been replaced by the desire for diversification of *all* energy sources to meet energy security and environmental and reliability concerns. Although natural gas is referred to as "the fuel of choice," in fact, the emphasis should be on "choice." Many more fuel options are available today, compared to the 1970s. Wind power is competitive in some markets and subsidized in others. Photovoltaic cells have experienced an annual average growth rate of 43% over the past five years, resulting in total shipments of 1,195 megawatts in 2004. And nuclear power appears to be experiencing a renaissance.

Globally, four gigawatts (GW) of new nuclear plants have come online since January 1, 2005, and an additional 19 GW, representing 24 new nuclear power plants, are currently under construction. A number of US power companies and partners have taken initial steps to develop new nuclear reactors. These would be the first nuclear plant orders in the US for more than 25 years.

Bio-fuels Gaining Momentum

The transportation sector, the primary market for oil, is expanding its choices of fuels as well. The growth in hybrid vehicle sales and the push by several major automobile manufacturers to shift to hydrogen, indicate that the transport sector may well join the power sector with a broader selection of fuel options.

In many large cities in Asia, Europe and North America, public transport systems are fuelling buses with compressed natural gas and bio-fuels are gaining in popularity as well. Government incentives and regulations promoting ethanol and biodiesel are being stepped up around the world, as is research into biology and energy. A renewed interest in energy efficiency supports both energy security and climate change objectives. The tightness of energy markets can be relieved by reducing demand—through conservation and energy efficiency, or through the undesirable method of lower economic growth rates—or by increasing supplies. A combination of greater efficiency and additional supplies is required. However, the political will to focus on conservation has been lacking. Price signals may assist with energy efficiency. However, successful efforts will be short-lived unless consumers either believe that higher price levels will be sustained or there is a stronger market/political/ knowledge matrix to support conservation. The strong interest in carbon capture and storage (CCS) technology can also be linked to both energy security and climate change. Although the oil industry has led the way in CCS technology, it is of growing interest to the power sector. Building new coal-fired power plants that are based on integrated gas combined-cycle technology allows the operators to separate, capture and store streams of carbon dioxide. Because coal is both the most carbon-intensive and the most abundant fossil fuel, carbon capture and storage offers an attractive opportunity to keep coal in the fuel mix for energy security without releasing greenhouse gas emissions into the atmosphere.

Energy Security and Energy Conservation Nexus

The basic aim of energy security for a nation is to reduce its dependency on the imported energy sources for its economic growth. India will continue to experience an energy supply shortfall throughout the forecast period. This gap has widened since 1985, when the country became a net importer of coal. India has been unable to raise its oil production substantially in the 1990s. Rising oil demand of close to 10 percent per year has led to sizable oil import bills. In addition, the government subsidizes refined oil product prices, thus compounding the overall monetary loss to the government.

Imports of oil and coal have been increasing at rates of 7% and 16% per annum respectively during the period 1991–99. The dependence on energy imports is projected to increase in the future. Estimates indicate that oil imports will meet 75% of total oil consumption requirements and coal imports will meet 22% of total coal consumption requirements in 2006. The imports of gas and LNG (liquefied natural gas) are likely to increase in the coming years. This energy import dependence implies vulnerability to external price shocks and supply fluctuations, which threaten the energy security of the country.

Increasing dependence on oil imports means reliance on imports from the Middle-East, a region susceptible to disturbances and consequent disruptions of oil supplies. This calls for diversification of sources of oil imports. The need to deal with oil price fluctuations also necessitates measures to be taken to reduce the oil dependence of the economy, possibly through fiscal measures to reduce demand, and by developing alternatives to oil, such as natural gas and renewable energy.

Some of the strategies that can be used to meet future challenges to their energy security are:

- Building stockpiles
- Diversification of energy supply sources
- Increased capacity of fuel switching
- Demand restraint,
- Development of renewable energy sources.
- Energy efficiency
- Sustainable development

Although all these options are feasible, their implementation will take time. Also, for countries like India, reliance on stockpiles would tend to be slow because of resource constraints. Besides, the market is not sophisticated enough or the monitoring agencies experienced enough to predict the supply situation in time to take necessary action. Insufficient storage capacity is another cause for worry and needs to be augmented, if India has to increase its energy stockpile.

However, out of all these options, the simplest and the most easily attainable is reducing demand through persistent energy conservation efforts.

Energy Conservation and its Importance

Coal and other fossil fuels that have taken three million years to form are likely to be depleted soon. In the last two hundred years, we have consumed 60% of all resources. For sustainable development, we need to adopt energy efficiency measures. Today, 85% of primary energy comes from non-renewable and fossil sources (coal, oil, etc.). These reserves are continually diminishing with increasing consumption and will not exist for future generations (Fig. 1.1).

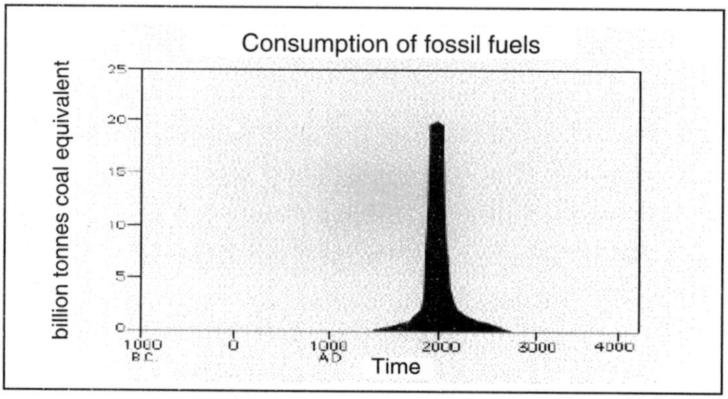

Figure 1.1: Dwindling Reserve of Oil with increasing consumption

What is Energy Conservation?

Energy Conservation and Energy Efficiency are separate, but related concepts. Energy conservation is achieved when growth of energy consumption is reduced, measured in physical terms. Energy Conservation can, therefore, is the result of several processes or developments, such as productivity increase or technological progress. On the other hand Energy efficiency is achieved when energy intensity in a specific product, process or area of production or consumption is reduced without affecting output, consumption or comfort levels. Promotion of energy efficiency will contribute to energy conservation and is therefore an integral part of energy conservation promotional policies.

Energy efficiency is often viewed as a resource option like coal, oil or natural gas. It provides additional economic value by preserving the resource base and reducing pollution. For example, replacing traditional light bulbs with Compact Fluorescent Lamps (CFLs) means you will use only 1/4th of the energy to light a room. Pollution levels also reduce by the same amount (refer Fig. 1.2). Incandescent Lamp60 WCompact fluorescent Lamp15 WEnergy

Energy Efficient Equipment uses less energy for same output and reduces CO_2 emissions

Incandescent Lamp
60W

Compact Fluorescent Lamp
15W

CO_2 Emission – 65 g/hr

CO_2 Emission – 16 g/hr

Figure 1.2: Energy Efficient Equipment

Efficient Equipment uses less energy for same output and reduces CO_2emissionsCO_2Emission –65 g/hr CO_2 Emission –16 g/hr.

Nature sets some basic limits on how efficiently energy can be used, but in most cases our products and manufacturing processes are still a long way from operating at this theoretical limit. Very simply, energy efficiency means using less energy to perform the same function.

Although, energy efficiency has been in practice ever since the first oil crisis in 1973, it has today assumed even more importance because of being the most cost-effective and reliable means of mitigating the global climatic change. Recognition of that potential has led to high expectations for the control of future CO_2 emissions through even more energy efficiency improvements than have occurred in the past. The industrial sector accounts for some 41 per cent of global primary energy demand and approximately the same share of CO_2 emissions. The benefits of Energy conservation for various players are given below:

Energy Efficiency Benefits Industry

- Reduced energy bills
- Increased Competitiveness
- Increased productivity

- Improved quality
- Increased profits

Nation

- Reduced energy imports
- Avoided costs can be used for poverty reduction
- Conservation of limited resources
- Improved energy security

Globe

- Reduced GHG and other emissions
- Maintains a sustainable environment

Energy Strategy for the Future

The energy strategy for the future could be classified into immediate, medium-term and long-term strategy. The various components of these strategies are listed below:

Immediate-term Strategy

- Rationalizing the tariff structure of various energy products.
- Optimum utilization of existing assets
- Efficiency in production systems and reduction in distribution losses, including those in traditional energy sources.

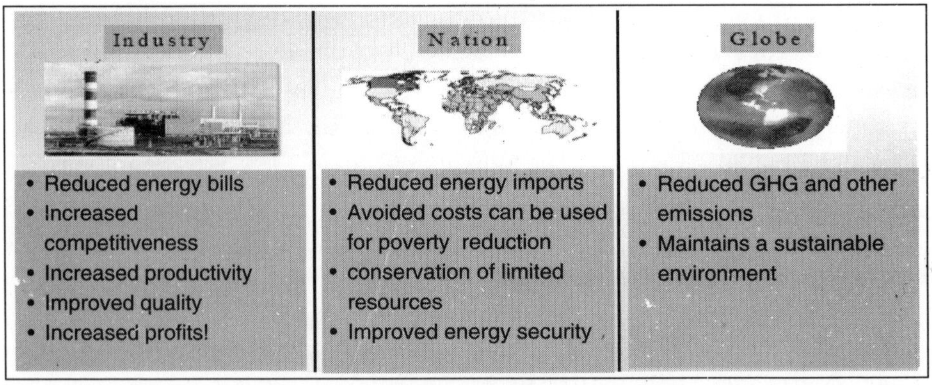

Figure 1.3: Energy Efficiency Benefits

- Promoting R&D, transfer and use of technologies and practices for environmentally sound energy systems, including new and renewable energy sources.

Medium-term Strategy

- Demand management through greater conservation of energy, optimum fuel mix, structural changes in the economy, an appropriate model mix in the transport sector, i.e. greater dependence on rail than on road for the movement of goods and passengers and a shift away from private modes to public modes for passenger transport; changes in design of different products to reduce the material intensity of those products, recycling, etc.
- There is need to shift to less energy-intensive modes of transport. This would include measures to improve the transport infrastructure viz. roads, better design of vehicles, use of compressed natural gas (CNG) and synthetic fuel, etc. Similarly, better urban planning would also reduce the demand for energy use in the transport sector.
- There is need to move away from non-renewable to renewable energy sources viz. solar, wind, biomass energy, etc.

Long-term Strategy

- Efficient generation of energy resources
  - Efficient production of coal, oil and natural gas
  - Reduction of natural gas flaring
- Improving energy infrastructure
  - Building new refineries
  - Creation of urban gas transmission and distribution network
  - Maximizing efficiency of rail transport of coal production.
  - Building new coal and gas fired power stations.
- Enhancing energy efficiency
  - Improving energy efficiency in accordance with national, socio-economic, and environmental priorities
  - Promoting of energy efficiency and emission standards
  - Labeling programmes for products and adoption of energy efficient technologies in large industries

- Deregulation and privatization of energy sector
  - Reducing cross subsidies on oil products and electricity tariffs
  - Decontrolling coal prices and making natural gas prices competitive
  - Privatization of oil, coal and power sectors for improved efficiency.
- Investment legislation to attract foreign investments.
  - Streamlining approval process for attracting private sector participation in power generation, transmission and distribution.

ENHANCING ENERGY SECURITY IN THE DEVELOPING WORLD

Reducing Vulnerability to External Shocks

Fuel and Source Diversity

Reducing vulnerability to external shocks through diversifying fuel types and sources is akin to the portfolio diversification well known to investors. Countries thus need to not only evaluate the security of individual supply chains, but also the riskiness of their energy supply portfolio against the vagaries of energy markets. Governments also need to avoid a false sense of security through ill-advised domestic ventures, such as maintaining inefficient local refineries based on imported oil feedstock in preference to rationalized fuel products procurement in regional markets. The contribution of new and renewable resources is also increasingly seen from an energy security perspective. Recent work extending modern portfolio theory to renewables shows that the reduction in risk through the introduction of a modest amount of renewables often outweighs the direct costs of even non-least-cost renewable sources. Significantly, these same analyses indicate that the optimal proportion of renewables is higher than current levels of deployment in many countries.

Moderating End-Use Energy Requirements

Increasing Supply- and Demand-Side Energy Efficiency

It is clear that the developing world will need to increase its energy consumption to meet economic and social development needs. Nevertheless, energy is typically produced, transported, and used inefficiently in both emerging and transition economies—with, for instance, ratios of gross energy use to economic output (energy/GDP) in some of the former Soviet republics being some 5–10 times higher than in Western Europe and Japan. Globally, it has been estimated that the developing countries could improve their energy efficiency by 10–30 percent, given the right set of policy and market incentives. Such "win-win" energy efficiency measures could reduce energy demand growth at no loss of useful energy services, and free up economic resources in the process. Moderating end-use energy requirement allows a higher proportion of needs to be secured through domestic and renewable sources; and the corresponding reductions in energy imports normally enhance energy security.

Reducing Energy Infrastructure Vulnerability

Distributed Energy

Centralized energy infrastructure efficiently exploits economies of scale in construction and operation, and when adequately designed and maintained, it has compiled an enviable record of technical reliability and environmental compliance. However, large-scale centralized facilities are also perceived to be vulnerable to large-scale catastrophe and loss. In addition, technological change is redefining the scale at which efficiency and economy can be captured—initially in the form of combined-cycle gas turbines, but in the longer term through efficient micro turbines, fuel cells, and sunlight-to-electricity converters as complements to large central facilities.- In parallel, these distributed energy resources provide inherent security advantages through their modularity and geographic diversity. The effect is similar to that overtaking mainframe computers and dedicated communication tie-ups; these are increasingly by-passed by distributed microcomputers linked by the Internet. In this connection, it is interesting to recall that the Internet itself was initially developed as a fault-tolerant, distributed network to provide highly secure communications.

Reducing Political and Social Divisions

Promoting Good Governance and Equitable Energy Sector Rent Distribution.

Mismanagement of energy resources and their uses is a contributor to impoverishment and inequity that breeds unrest and violence and ultimately threatens sustainable energy delivery. This vicious circle takes many forms, including draining of government resources for health, education, and welfare that go instead to subsidize inefficient parastatal energy monopolies; capture of benefits by urban elites at the expense of energy-poor rural or periurban populations, who also may be the hosts of disruptive energy resource extraction; and dissipation of energy-generated rents through corruption and diversion for private gains.

Interlinkages and Synergies

Although in some cases there are tradeoffs, in many cases there are clear synergies between the three principal themes of this paper. A number of the interlinkages have been alluded to earlier, but they warrant restatement and summary.

Between Climate Change and Economic Growth or Poverty

- In developing countries, where human activities are already close to the margin of tolerance for current variations in climate, the impacts of the projected changes are expected to be far reaching, adversely affecting the poorest of the poor. Changes in temperature could have a devastating impact on agricultural output, with attendant consequences for food security. Similarly, changes in precipitation patterns associated with climate change could adversely affect the availability and quality of water, especially in areas where scarcity is already a problem, or sea level rise could displace millions of people living in low-lying areas. Preparing for climate change, and indeed for current climate variability (for instance, storms, floods), is therefore inextricably linked to sustainable poverty reduction.
- Many technologies that represent appropriate means to provide energy services to the rural poor also provide climate change benefits. The toehold represented by these early markets can provide a basis for market expansion, cost reduction, and capacity building for sustainable energy technologies. In addition, the new distributed service delivery means can be provided by a greater number of enterprises, thus promoting competition, private sector entry, and income and employment creation.

- Off-grid renewables (such as wind and solar energy) are often the least-cost option for providing energy services to rural populations. Compared with more expensive options, such as grid extension to dispersed populations, they thus have financial advantages for both rural communities and central governments.
- Poverty reduction measures, such as the dissemination of improved biomass cook-stoves, reduce the time, effort, and expenditure devoted to household fuel supply; lessen exposure to indoor air pollution; mitigate GHG emissions associated with biomass combustion; and decrease pressures on carbon-fixing woodlands.
- Flows of investment and technology motivated by climate change (for example, through the CDM) provide economic surpluses in the form of carbon offset rents, air quality improvements, and other sustainable development benefits to the host partner countries.

Between Climate Change and Energy Security

- Energy efficiency gains, as part of a least-cost climate change abatement strategy, simultaneously reduce energy import requirements and enhance the entry of domestically based substitutes like renewables.
- Shifts to smaller-scale and distributed technologies can be an integral part of an energy security policy based on energy portfolio diversity.
- Many emerging and environmentally beneficial technologies are modular and naturally adapted to distributed energy markets. They enjoy inherent advantages in terms of lower vulnerability to natural and man-made disruptions, including those engendered by climate change itself (e.g., changed rainfall patterns that affect hydro availability and pumping demand or the potential for increased storm amplitude and frequency).

Between Economic Growth or Poverty and Energy Security

- Public resources are usually inadequate to finance the investments needed to meet the energy needs of the poor. Furthermore, the poor are usually the most vulnerable to the shocks provoked by energy market instabilities because energy already accounts for a high share of their meager cash income, and government social programs that benefit the poor tend to be cut back at times of fiscal stress.

- Lack of efficient energy services to fuel development, poor sector governance, the drain on public resources by poorly targeted energy subsidies, and support to loss-making monopoly energy enterprises are all part of a downward spiral that breeds domestic instability. The results may ultimately rebound as threats to domestic.
- Key parties needing to prepare include farmers, water supply and coastal zone managers, and urban planners, energy infrastructure and regional energy market integration. In hydrocarbon-rich developing economies, mismanagement and diversion of energy sector rents serve to exacerbate inequalities and domestic tensions.

The Action Agenda

The following action agenda for energy development assistance, based on the lessons of the World Bank Group's (WBG's) experience to date, is proposed to promote sustainable energy-related outcomes that will support the broader mission of poverty reduction.

Energy Access

A key need is to integrate rural and periurban modern energy access into the energy sector reform dialogue.

The private sector is the main engine for scaling up service provision, generating income in rural areas, attracting innovation, and promoting competition. Thus, as governments withdraw from the direct provision of energy services, it is critical to work toward removing barriers to entry while developing an enhanced environment for the private sector in providing energy solutions for the rural and peri-urban poor. Beyond this leveling of the playing field, evidence increasingly suggests that incentives will be required to motivate the private sector to invest in service provision to often remote and underdeveloped areas where the poor reside. Subsidies to enhance access should be well targeted at the poor and subsidize the capital costs of initial provision of service and not ongoing consumption and maintenance.

Productive/Social Uses

Energy assistance programs to the developing world need to be realigned around the theme of integrating energy services (with emphasis on lighting, motive power, telecommunications, heat supply, and modernized cooking) with income-generating and social uses to make the critical link to direct poverty reduction. This will imply expansion of energy applications identification efforts outside the energy sector and into other high-value social and productive sectors, such as education, health, water supply, communications, and agriculture/rural development.

Environment

Environmental concerns must be integrated into the energy sector reform dialogue. Despite the critical role of the private sector and civil society in minimizing the environmental impacts of energy production and use, governments must continue to play key roles by ensuring that appropriate environmental standards are set, monitored for compliance, and enforced through a combination of regulations, economic instruments (e.g. taxes and pollution charges), and market-based mechanisms. This will in turn require a strengthened environmental role for energy sector regulators, with concomitant needs for institutional strengthening and capacity building.

Technology Markets

The WBG is promoting market-pull and market aggregation mechanisms to facilitate market entry of new, more efficient, and less polluting technologies. Several support mechanisms being adopted in OECD countries (e.g., Renewable Portfolio Standards, Non-Fossil Fuel Obligations) offer alternatives to less sustainable practices in developing countries for promoting entry of new technologies.

Public-Private Partnerships

The WBG is expanding support for dedicated investment vehicles and new forms of public-private partnerships.

A number of promising new public-private investment vehicles have recently been launched (e.g., the Renewable Energy/Energy Efficiency Fund) and should be supported in order to demonstrate their full potential. Facilities such as the SDG mobilize both "hard" capital for investment and "soft" concessional funds from governments and foundations to finance needed business development and business advisory assistance.

Global Carbon Markets

The WBG is promoting the development of an efficient and equitable international carbon market to finance energy efficiency and renewable energy technologies in developing countries. In particular, there is a need to establish appropriate project certification and emissions verification rules for the CDM that are consistent with the requirements of assessing multiple installations of small-scale or distributed energy systems.

Players and Roles

The magnitude of the poverty and sustainable energy challenge requires bringing new skills and resources to bear from a variety of actors. Envisioned roles are outlined in Table 1.2.

Table 1.2: The WBG's Energy Business Lines

Players	*Emerging roles*
Governments	• Liberalizer of energy markets • Policymaker and regulator
Consultants and advisers	• Providers of technical expertise • Generators of knowledge
Consumers	• Greater say in the development of energy markets • Arbiters of energy service quality
Strategic investors	• Mobilizers of investment resources for private supply of energy services • key actors for developing competition in energy markets • Catalysts for developing domestic capital markets
Multilaterals and bilaterals	Focus on comparative advantages: • World Bank on sector policy reforms and macro/fiscal stability • Regional multilaterals on project lending • Bilaterals on supporting public interventions
NGOs	• Advocates for disadvantaged groups • Promoters of public policy issues • Supporters of alternative strategies for meeting energy policy objectives • Data gathering and empirical analysis
Equipment suppliers and entrepreneurs	• Technology innovators • Partners with strategic investors

Global Energy Security Challenges

The various recommendations emanated from the recently held Global Energy Security Summit at St. Petersburg, July 16, 2006 are outlined below; which, *inter alia*, provides the main operational framework of Global Energy Security Systems for universal adoption and application (http://eng8russia.ru/docs/u.html.) The resolutions arrives at in the summit will asfollows:

1. Energy is essential to improving the quality of life and opportunities in developed and developing nations. Therefore, ensuring sufficient, reliable and environmentally responsible supplies of energy at prices reflecting market fundamentals is a challenge for our countries and for mankind as a whole.

2. To tackle this overarching goal we have to deal with serious and linked challenges such as:

- high and volatile oil prices;
- growing demand for energy (estimated to rise by more than 50% by the year 2030, approximately 80% of which would still be met by fossil fuels, which are limited resources);
- increasing import dependence in many countries;
- enormous investment requirements along the entire energy chain;
- the need to protect the environment and to tackle climate change;
- the vulnerability of the critical energy infrastructure;
- political instability, natural disasters and other threats.

The global nature of these challenges and the growing interdependence between producing, consuming and transiting countries require strengthened partnership between all stakeholders to enhance global energy security. We agree that development of transparent, efficient and competitive global energy markets is the best way to achieve our objectives on this score. Governments and relevant international organizations also play an important role in addressing global energy challenges.

3. Neither global energy security, nor the Millennium Development Goals can be fully achieved without sustainable access to fuels for the 2.4 billion people and to electricity for the 1.6 billion people currently without such access in developing countries. They cannot be forgotten or marginalized.

Response of the International Community

4. Given political will, the international community can effectively

address three interrelated issues: energy security, economic growth and environmental protection (the "3Es"). Applying fair and competitive market-based responses to the global energy challenges will help preclude potentially disruptive actions affecting energy sources, supplies and transit, and create a secure basis for dynamic and sustainable development of our civilization over the long term.

5. G-8 Nations will pursue energy security through a comprehensive and concerted approach consistent with our common environmental goals. Last year in Gleneagles, we agreed to enhance our work under the Plan of Action for Climate Change, Clean Energy and Sustainable Development and resolved to take forward the dialogue on these issues whose results will be reported at the 2008 G8 Summit in Japan. We reaffirm this commitment.

G-8 Nations also reaffirm our commitment to the United Nations Framework Convention on Climate.

Change (UNFCCC) and to meet our shared multiple objectives of reducing greenhouse gas emissions, improving the global environment, enhancing energy security, and cutting air pollution in conjunction with our vigorous efforts to reduce energy poverty. G-8 Groups also agree to work to improve access to energy in developing countries.

Statement on Global Energy Security Principles

G-8 Nations resolved to undertake the following as the Global Energy Security Principles:

6. Recognizing the shared interest of energy producing and consuming countries in promoting global energy security, the Leaders of the G8, commit to:

- strong global economic growth, effective market access, and investment in all stages of the energy supply chain;
- open, transparent, efficient and competitive markets for energy production, supply, use, transmission and transit services as a key to global energy security;
- transparent, equitable, stable and effective legal and regulatory frameworks, including the obligation to uphold contracts, to generate sufficient, sustainable international investments upstream and downstream;

- enhanced dialogue on relevant stakeholders' perspectives on growing interdependence, security of supply and demand issues;
- diversification of energy supply and demand, energy sources, geographical and sectoral markets, transportation routes and means of transport;
- promotion of energy saving and energy efficiency measures through initiatives on both national and international levels;
- environmentally sound development and use of energy, and deployment and transfer of clean energy technologies which help to tackle climate change;
- promotion of transparency and good governance in the energy sector to discourage corruption;
- cooperative energy emergency response, including coordinated planning of strategic stocks;
- safeguarding critical energy infrastructure; and
- addressing the energy challenges for the poorest populations in developing countries.

7. Based on the above objectives, principles and approaches, G-8 Group will implement the common global energy security strategy through the following Plan of Action and invite other states, relevant international organizations and other stakeholders to join in these efforts.

CHAPTER 2

Energy Production, Demand and Supply Scenario

Projection of Global Energy Demand: IEA vs. IEO

The International Energy Agency (IEA, 2007) provides projections comparable with those in *IEO2007* in its *World Energy Outlook 2006*. Because IEA releases projections only for the years 2015 and 2030, two time periods are compared here—2004 to 2015 and 2015 to 2030. In the 2004 to 2015 projection period, both *IEO2007* and IEA expect world energy demand to increase by an average of 2.1 percent per year (Table 2.1). Not surprisingly, both outlooks project much faster growth in energy demand among the non-OECD nations than in the OECD, with non-OECD energy use growing three times as rapidly. There are, however, some regional differences. IEA's expectations for demand growth in OECD Asia, for instance, are much higher than those in *IEO2007*, and the projected 1.4-percent annual growth rate projected by IEA for the region exceeds the 1.3-percent rate in the *IEO2007* high economic growth case.

In the non-OECD regions, both outlooks have similar projections for growth in Europe and Eurasia. *IEO2007* projects 1.6-percent average annual growth in energy use between 2004 and 2015, and IEA projects 1.4-percent annual growth. IEA projects much slower growth than *IEO2007* over the 2004 to 2015 period for China and other non-OECD Asia, as well as for Africa and Central and South America. In each case, IEA's projected growth rates are lower than those in the *IEO2007* low economic growth case. On the other hand, IEA's projected 4.2-percent annual growth in Middle Eastern energy use over the same period is much higher than the projection of 3.1 percent per year in the *IEO2007* reference case and, in fact, exceeds the projected growth rate in the *IEO2007* high macroeconomic growth case.

In the later years of the projections, *IEO2007* and IEA generally agree, with worldwide energy demand growing by 1.5 percent per year between 2015 and 2030 in the *IEO2007* reference case and by 1.3 percent per year in the IEA projection (Table 2.1).

Table 2.1: Comparison of IEO2007 and IEA World Energy Consumption Growth Rates by Region, 2015-2030 (Average Annual Percent Growth)

Region	*IEO2007*			*IEA*
	Low Growth	*Reference*	*High Growth*	
OECD	0.6	0.9	1.2	1.2
North America	0.9	1.2	1.5	1.3
United States	0.7	1.0	1.3	1.2
Europe	0.3	0.5	0.8	0.8
Asia	0.7	1.0	1.3	1.4
Non-OECD	2.9	3.2	3.6	3.0
Europe and Eurasia	1.2	1.6	2.0	1.4
China	4.2	4.5	4.9	4.0
Other Non-OECD Asia	3.0	3.3	3.6	2.8
Middle East	2.7	3.1	3.4	4.2
Africa	2.8	3.1	3.4	2.1
Central and South America	2.8	3.1	3.4	2.4
Total World	1.8	2.1	2.4	2.1

Source: *IEO2007*: Energy Information Administration (EIA), System for the Analysis of Global Energy Markets (2007). IEA: International Energy Agency, *World Energy Outlook 2006* (Paris, France, November 2006), pp. 492-527.

Both outlooks anticipate similar regional growth over the 2015 to 2030 period. The largest regional difference between the two projections— and the only instance in which IEA regional growth projections fall outside the range defined by the *IEO2007* low and high macroeconomic growth cases—is for China. IEA anticipates that China's energy demand growth will slow to 2.0 percent per year for the final 15 years of the outlook, whereas the *IEO2007* reference case expects that China will maintain a 2.7-percent annual growth rate in energy demand through the end of the projection period. The IEA growth projection for energy use in China from 2015 to 2030 is lower than the *IEO2007* low macroeconomic growth case projection.

The projections vary not only with respect to levels of total energy demand but also with respect to the mix of primary energy inputs. In the 2004 to 2015 period, IEA expects slightly higher growth in fossil fuel use and slower growth in the use of non-fossil fuels than does *IEO2007* (Table 2.2).

Table 2.2: Comparison of IEO2007 and IEA World Energy Consumption Growth Rates by Fuel, 2004-2015 (Average Annual Percent Growth)

Region	*IEO2007*			*IEA*
	Low Growth	*Reference*	*High Growth*	
OECD	0.4	0.8	1.2	0.6
North America	0.6	1.1	1.5	0.8
United States	0.6	1.0	1.5	0.7
Europe	-0.1	0.3	0.6	0.4
Asia	0.4	0.8	1.2	0.6
Non-OECD	1.6	2.1	2.6	1.8
Europe and Eurasia	0.6	1.2	1.7	0.8
China	2.3	2.7	3.2	2.0
Other Non-OECD Asia	1.9	2.4	2.9	2.1
Middle East	1.3	1.7	2.2	2.1
Africa	1.3	1.8	2.2	1.8
Central and South America	1.4	1.8	2.3	2.0
Total World	1.1	1.5	2.0	1.3

Source: *IEO2007*: Energy Information Administration (EIA), System for the Analysis of Global Energy Markets (2007). IEA: International Energy Agency, *World Energy Outlook 2006* (Paris, France, November 2006), pp. 492-527.

For both renewables and nuclear power consumption, the growth rates projected by IEA are slower than those in the *IEO2007* low economic growth case. For renewables, the differences may be explained by the fact that IEA renewables projections include estimates for traditional, non-marketed biomass and the *IEO2007* projections do not. Traditional biomass is a substantial portion of the renewable energy base and is not expected, in most regions, to expand as nations migrate away from non-marketed to commercial energy use over the projection period—in contrast to hydroelectric power and other marketed renewable energy sources captured in the *IEO2007* projection.

For nuclear power, there are only small differences in projected growth rates between the *IEO2007* high macroeconomic growth and reference cases and no difference between the reference case and the low macroeconomic growth case. This is because the projections include only a limited number of plants, which are already planned or under construction, with expected completion dates before 2015 that analysts largely agree are achievable.

For the period from 2015 to 2030, *IEO2007* and IEA are largely in agreement. The only exception is nuclear power, for which the IEA growth projection falls below that in the *IEO2007* low macroeconomic growth case (Table 2.3).

Table 2.3: Comparison of IEO2007 and IEA World Energy Consumption Growth Rates by Fuel, 2015-2030 (Average Annual Percent Growth)

Fuel	*IEO2007*			*IEA*
	Low Growth	*Reference*	*High Growth*	
Liquids	1.2	1.5	1.9	1.7
Natural Gas	2.0	2.4	2.7	2.5
Coal	2.2	2.6	2.9	2.7
Nuclear	1.5	1.5	1.6	1.2
Renewable/Other	2.1	2.3	2.6	2.0
Total	1.8	2.1	2.4	2.1

Note: In the IEA projections, Renewable/Other includes traditional biomass.

Source: *IEO2007*: Energy Information Administration (EIA), System for the Analysis of Global Energy Markets (2007). IEA: International Energy Agency, *World Energy Outlook 2006* (Paris, France, November 2006), pp. 492-527.

IEA projects that nuclear power expansion will slow from the annual growth rate of 1.2 percent projected for relative to the 2004 to 2015 period to 0.4 percent for the 2015 to 2030 period. *IEO2007* projects increases in world nuclear power use averaging 1.3 percent per year from 2015 to 2030, compared with 1.5 percent per year from 2004 to 2015.

Comparisons with IEO-2006

The *IEO2007* outlook for total energy consumption in 2015 is largely the same as the outlook in *IEO2006*. In *IEO2007* total marketed energy consumption in 2015 is projected to be 559 quadrillion Btu, as compared with 563 quadrillion Btu in *IEO2006* (Table 2.4).

Table 2.4: Comparison of IEO2007 and IEO2006 Total World Energy Consumption, Reference Case, 2015 and 2030 (Quadrillion Btu)

Region	*2015*		*2030*		*Change in IEO2007*	
	IEO 2007	*IEO 2006*	*IEO 2007*	*IEO 2006*	*2015*	*2030*
OECD	265	270	298	309	-5	-11
North America	137	140	162	166	-3	-5
United States	112	114	131	134	-2	-3
Europe	86	87	89	95	-1	-5
Asia	42	43	47	48	-1	-1
Non-OECD	294	293	404	413	1	-9
Europe and Eurasia	59	63	72	79	-3	-7
China	97	92	145	139	5	6
India	22	23	32	33	-1	-1
Other Non-OECD Asia	36	35	50	52	1	-2
Middle-East	29	28	38	38	1	0
Africa	19	20	25	27	-1	-2
Central and South America	31	32	41	46	-1	-4
Total World	559	563	702	722	-4	-20

Source: *IEO2007*: Energy Information Administration (EIA), System for the Analysis of Global Energy Markets (2007). *IEA2006*: EIA, *International Energy Outlook 2006* DOE/EIA-0484 (2006) (Washington, DC, June 2006), Table A1, p. 83.

There are, however, some regional differences between the two *IEOs*. In *IEO2007*, total energy consumption for the OECD region in 2030 is about 5 quadrillion Btu lower than was projected in *IEO2006*. Most (3 quadrillion Btu) of the difference is attributed to lower demand in North America (largely, the United States), where the projection for average annual GDP growth from 2003 to 2015 is 0.2 percentage points lower in *IEO2007* than was projected in *IEO2006*. For the non-OECD region, the largest differences between the projections for 2015 in *IEO2007* and *IEO-2006* are found in two regions—China and non-OECD Europe and Eurasia. In *IEO2007*, China's projected total energy use in 2015 is 5 quadrillion Btu higher than projected in *IEO2006*. IEO2007 assumes much more rapid economic growth for China between 2003 and 2015 than was assumed in *IEO2006*—8.1 percent per year versus 7.0 percent per year. A 10-percent increase in China's GDP between 2003 and 2004 helped to spur a 20-percent increase in its energy use, a development that was not anticipated in the *IEO2006* projection, which was based on historical data series that ended in 2003.

For non-OECD Europe and Eurasia, the *IEO2007* reference case projects total energy consumption in 2015 that is 4 quadrillion Btu lower than projected in *IEO2006*. Nearly all of the difference resulted from a reassessment of energy demand in the region's industrial sector. For example, in the *IEO2006* reference case, demand for electric power in the industrial sector was projected to increase by an average of 4.3 percent per year from 2003 to 2015; in *IEO2007*, the corresponding projection is for a more moderate growth rate of 2.4 percent per year. EIA believes that the lower rate is more consistent with the annual increases seen in the region's industrial electricity consumption since 1998 (when industrial sector electricity use stopped declining after the fall of the Soviet Union and began to recover), which have averaged about 2.5 percent per year. The near-term differences between the *IEO2007* and *IEO2006* projections are carried through to 2030. The *IEO2007* reference case projection for total energy use worldwide in 2030 is 20 quadrillion Btu (about 3 percent) lower than the *IEO2006* projection. Again, the largest regional differences between the 2030 projections are for China and non-OECD Europe and Eurasia. In the *IEO2007* reference case, China's GDP is projected to increase at an average rate of 6.6 percent per year between 2003 and 2030, 0.6 percentage points higher than the GDP growth rate projected for China in *IEO2006*. As a result, the reference case projection for China's total energy use in 2030 is 6 quadrillion Btu (5 percent) higher in *IEO2007* than was projected in *IEO2006*. For non-OECD Europe and Eurasia, total projected energy consumption in 2030 is 7 quadrillion Btu lower in *IEO2007* than it was in *IEO2006*, largely as a result of EIA's reassessment of the potential for growth in the industrial sector.

Along with regional differences between the *IEO2007* and *IEO2006* projections, there are some differences between the two projections in the mix of energy resources expected to be consumed (Table 2.5).

The projections for worldwide consumption of petroleum and other liquids consumption are virtually the same throughout the projections, but there are pronounced differences in the other fuel outlooks. In *IEO2007*, the potential for nuclear power is viewed with more optimism than it was in *IEO2006*. As a result, the projection for nuclear power consumption in 2015 is 5 percent higher in *IEO2007* than in *IEO2006*, and the difference between the two projections increases to 14 percent in 2030.

With the higher projection for nuclear power in the *IEO2007* reference case, projections for consumption of natural gas and renewables in the electric

Table 2.5: Comparison of IEO2007 and IEO2006 World Energy Consumption by Fuel, Reference Case, 2015 and 2030 (Quadrillion Btu)

Region	*2015*		*2030*		*Change in IEO2007*	
	IEO 2007	*IEO 2006*	*IEO 2007*	*IEO 2006*	*2015*	*2030*
Liquids	198	199	239	239	-2	0
Natural Gas	134	140	170	190	-6	-19
Coal	152	144	199	196	7	4
Nuclear	33	31	40	35	2	5
Renewable/Other	43	48	53	61	-5	-8
Total	559	563	702	722	-4	-20

Source: *IEO2007*: Energy Information Administration (EIA), System for the Analysis of Global Energy Markets (2007). *IEA2006*: EIA, *International Energy Outlook 2006* DOE/EIA-0484 (2006) (Washington, DC, June 2006), Table A2, p. 84-85.

power sector are lower throughout the period from 2004 to 2030. The impact on renewable energy sources is larger: total renewable energy use is 12 percent lower in 2015 and 14 percent lower in 2030 in the *IEO2007* projections than in *IEO2006*. The difference is somewhat inflated, however, because consumption of biofuels in the *IEO2007* projections is included with petroleum and other liquids consumption, whereas it was included with renewable energy consumption in *IEO2006*. Removing the transportation biofuels portion of renewable energy consumption from the *IEO2006* projections reduces the difference to about 10 percent in both 2015 and 2030.

IEA Projections of Global Energy Demand

The International Energy Agency (IEA, 2007) summarizes the issues of energy security facing the world as insufficient and secure supplies at affordable prices. The broad issues encompass the following:

- environmental harm caused by consuming too much fossil-fuel energy:
- the need to diversify production and consumption both by geographical location and fuel type.
- the impact of rising oil and gas demand increasing the vulnerability of consumers to disruption and price shock. The IEA's principal concerns are environmental and economic.

Other observers of the world energy scene have raised concomitant political risks in the following manner:

- heightened competition over depleting energy sources
- the new scramble for Africa's oil and gas
- the security of supplies from the Middle-East and instability of their governments' dependency on "petrodollars"
- the future of Iraq, with the second largest world oil reserves
- energy-rich countries using energy supply and price as a political weapon

Despite national differences f approach, the trend in European Union countries in recent years has been to open up their gas and electricity utilities to competition, promoting cheaper gas and electricity.

World Energy Use Projected to Grow 57 Percent between 2004 and 2030

World marketed energy consumption is projected to grow by 57 percent between 2004 and 2030, according to the reference case projection from the International Energy Outlook 2007 (IEO, 2007) released today by the Energy Information Administration (EIA). The IEO2007 shows the most rapid growth in energy demand for nations outside the Organization for Economic Cooperation and Development (OECD), especially in non-OECD Asia.

Global energy demand grows despite the relatively high world oil and natural gas prices in the reference case. However, rising oil prices dampen growth in demand for petroleum and other liquids fuels after 2015 and, as a result, reducing their share of overall energy use from 38 percent in 2004 to a projected 34 percent in 2030. In contrast, the energy shares of natural gas, coal, and renewable energy sources are expected to grow over this period (Fig. 2.1). Liquids consumption is still expected to grow strongly, however, reaching 118 million barrels per day in 2030. The United States, China, and India together account for nearly half of the projected growth in world liquids use.

To meet the increment in world liquids demand in the IEO2007 reference case, supply in 2030 is projected to be 35 million barrels oil equivalent per day higher than the 2004 level of 83 million barrels per day (Fig. 2.1). Conventional resources account for about 27 million barrels per day of this increase, with a projected 21 million barrels per day increase in production by members of the Organization of Petroleum Exporting Countries (OPEC) and 6 million barrels per day increase in non-OPEC countries. Production from unconventional

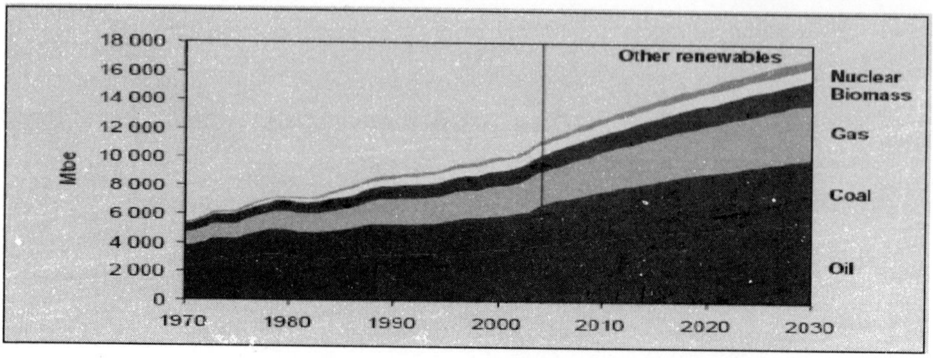

Figure 2.1: Global Energy Demand Outlook-2030

resources (including biofuels, coal-to-liquids (CTL) and gas-to-liquids) increases by nearly 8 million barrels per day and accounts for nearly 9 percent of total world liquids supply in 2030 (Fig. 2.1).

Other report highlights include the following projection of energy supply vis-a-vis demand (Table 2.6).

Table 2.6: Energy Supply and Demand Projections

Item	*2004*		*2010*		*2020*		*2004-2020 Growth Rate (%)*
	Million KLOE	*%*	*Million KLOE*	*%*	*Million KLOE*	*%*	
Total Supply	129.1	100	147.2	100	173.9	100	2.1
Indigenous	12.2	9	39.5	27	45.6	26	18.3
Imported	116.9	91	107.7	73	128.3	74	0.5
Coal	43.5	34	44.2	30	64.3	37	2.9
Petroleum	63.5	49	63.8	43	56.3	32	-0.5
Natural Gas	0.8	1	0.7	0	0.7	0	-1.2
LNG	9.9	8	18.2	12	29.0	17	7.9
Pumped Storage Hydro	1.0	1	1.0	1	0.9	1	-0.6
Nuclear Power	9.8	8	14.3	10	12.0	7	1.3
Renewable Energy	0.6	0	5.0	3	10.7	6	17.4
Domestic Consumption	107.6	100	123.9	100	146.3	100	2.1
Coal	10.8	10	130.0	11	15.9	11	2.1
Petroleum	42.2	39	41.8	34	36.8	25	-0.5
Natural Gas	2.4	2	3.0	2	3.3	2	1.9
Electricity	51.5	48	61.1	49	79.5	54	2.9
Renewable Energy	0.6	1	5.0	4	10.7	7	17.4

Source: IEO, Paris, 2007.

- Coal consumption, which grows an average annual rate of 2.2 percent, is the fastest-growing energy source worldwide in the IEO2007 reference case projection, which assumes that existing laws and policies remain in effect through 2030 notwithstanding concerns related to the rising level of energy-related greenhouse gas emissions. World coal consumption increased sharply from 2003 to 2004, largely because of a 17-percent increase—on a British thermal unit (Btu) basis—in non-OECD Asia (mainly China and India). With oil and natural gas prices expected to continue rising, coal is an attractive fuel for nations with access to ample coal resources, especially in coal-rich countries like China, India, and the United States. These three countries combined account for 86 percent of the increment in world coal demand by 2030 in the reference case projection.
- Higher fossil fuel prices, energy security concerns, improved reactor designs, and environmental considerations are expected to improve prospects for nuclear power capacity in many parts of the world, and a number of countries are expected to build new nuclear power plants. World nuclear capacity is projected to raise from 368 gigawatts in 2004 to 481 gigawatts in 2030. Declines in nuclear capacity are projected only in OECD Europe, where several countries (including Germany and Belgium) have either plans or mandates to phase out nuclear power, and where some old reactors are expected to be retired and not replaced.
- In the IEO2007 reference case, which does not include specific policies to limit greenhouse gas emissions, energy-related carbon dioxide emissions are projected to rise from 26.9 billion metric tons in 2004 to 33.9 billion metric tons in 2015 and 42.9 billion metric tons in 2030. From 2003 to 2004, carbon dioxide emissions from the non-OECD countries grew by almost 10 percent, while emissions in the OECD countries grew by less than 2 percent. The result of the large increase in non-OECD emissions was that 2004 marked the first time in history that emissions from the non-OECD exceeded those from the OECD countries (Table 2.7). Further, because of the expectation that non-OECD countries will rely on fossil fuels to supply much of their future energy demand growth, carbon dioxide emissions from the non-OECD countries in 2030 are projected to exceed those from the OECD by 57 percent.

Table 2.7: India Primary Energy Requirements Scenario

Year	Scenario 7 % Growth Per-Year (Million TOE)					
	Hydro	*Nuclear*	*Coal*	*Oil*	*Gas*	*TPES*
2003-04	7	5	167	119	29	327
	(2.1%)	(1.5%)	(51.1%)	(36.4%)	(8.9)	(100%)
2006-07	9	7	200	124	35	375
2011-12	15	15	253	151	49	483
2016-17	19	29	322	188	67	625
2021-22	24	54	393	234	92	797
2026-27	34	79	517	294	127	1051
2031-32	43	115	641	370	175	1344
	(3.2%)	(8.6%)	(47.7%)	(27.5%)	(13%)	(100%)
Growth Rates 2032 (%)	6.7	12.2	4.9	4.1	7	5.2

Source: Pradeep Chaturvedi, Chairman, Safety & Quality Forum, Institute of Engineers, India; "An integrated policy for India": Page-32, Table 1:Draft Report of the Expert Committee on Integrated Energy Policy—Planning Commission, Government of India, December 2005; World Energy in 2006, WEC.

Overall Production and Consumption

India is both a major energy producer and consumer. India currently ranks as the world's eleventh greatest energy producer, accounting for about 2.4% of the world's total annual energy production, and as the world's sixth greatest energy consumer, accounting for about 3.3% of the world's total annual energy consumption. Despite its large annual energy production, India is a net energy importer, mostly due to the large imbalance between oil production and consumption. An historical summary of India's Total Primary Energy Production (TPEP) and Consumption (TPEC) is shown in Table 2.8.

Table 2.8: India's TPEP and TPEC, 1993-2003 (in Quads)

	1993	*1994*	*1995*	*1996*	*1997*	*1998*	*1999*	*2000*	*2001*	*2002*	*2003*
TPEP	7.49	8.00	9.48	8.75	9.17	9.37	9.58	9.83	10.23	9.99	10.15
TPEC	9.24	9.97	11.49	11.14	11.76	12.17	12.74	13.50	13.85	13.79	14.03

Note: 1 Quad = 1 quadrillion Btu.
Source: DOE/EIA.

Petroleum

India's proved oil reserves are currently estimated (as of January 2005) at about 5 billion barrels, or about 4.5% of the world total. Most of these reserves lie offshore near Mumbai and onshore in Assam state. However, exploration is still happening, and India's off-shore and on-shore basins may contain as much as 11 billion barrels. India presently ranks as the 25th greatest producer of crude oil, accounting for about 1% of the world's annual crude oil production. About 30% of India's energy needs are met by oil, and more than 60% of that oil is imported. A strong growth in oil demand has resulted in India's annual petroleum consumption increasing by more than 75% from what it was a decade ago, and petroleum consumption is projected to climb to about 3 million barrels per day by 2010. India is currently the world's sixth greatest oil consumer, accounting for about 2.9% of world's total annual petroleum consumption. An historical summary of petroleum production and consumption in India is shown in Table 2.9.

Table 2.9: Petroleum Production and Consumption in India, 1993-2003 (in thousands of barrels per day)

	1993	*1994*	*1995*	*1996*	*1997*	*1998*	*1999*	*2000*	*2001*	*2002*	*2003*
Production (total)*	578	651	770	751	780	761	765	770	782	813	815
Production (Crude Oil only)	534	590	703	651	675	661	653	646	642	665	660
Consumption	1,311	1,413	1,575	1,681	1,765	1,844	2,031	2,127	2,184	2,263	2,320

* includes crude oil, natural gas plant liquids, other liquids, and refinery processing gain.
Source: DOE/EIA.

Natural Gas

India's natural gas reserves are currently estimated (as of January 2005) at about 29-32 trillion cubic feet (tcf), or about 0.5% of the world total. Most of these reserves lie offshore northwest of Mumbai in the Arabian Sea and onshore in Gujarat state. India does not yet rank in the top 20 of the world's greatest natural gas consumers, but that will soon change. Natural gas has experienced the fastest rate of increase of any fuel in India's primary energy supply; demand is growing at about 4.8% per year and is forecast to rise to 1.2 tcf per year by 2010 and 1.6 tcf per year by 2015. An historical summary of natural gas production and consumption in India is shown in Table 2.10.

Table 2.10: Dry Natural Gas Production and Consumption in India, 1993-2003 (in tcf)

	1993	1994	1995	1996	1997	1998	1999	2000	2001	2002	2003
Production	0.53	0.59	0.63	0.70	0.72	0.76	0.75	0.79	0.85	0.88	0.96
Consumption	0.53	0.59	0.63	0.70	0.72	0.76	0.75	0.79	0.85	0.88	0.96

Note: "dry" gas means gas with condensates removed.
Source: DOE/EIA.

Coal

India's has huge proven coal reserves, estimated (as of January 2005) at more than 90 billion tons, or about 10% of the world's total. Most of these reserves are relatively high ash bituminous coal and are located in Bihar, West Bengal, and Madhya Pradesh states. At the current level of production and consumption, India's coal reserves would last more than two hundred years. India is currently the third-largest coal-producing country in the world (behind China and the United States), and accounts for about 8.5% of the world's annual coal production. India is also currently the third-largest coal consuming country (behind the China and the United States), and accounts for nearly 9% of the world's total annual coal consumption. More than half of India's energy needs are met by coal, and about 70% of India's electricity generation is now fueled by coal. The annual demand for coal has been steadily increasing over the past decade, and is now nearly 50% greater than it was a decade ago. Even though India is able to satisfy most of its country's coal demand through domestic production, less than 5% of its reserves is coking coal used by the steel industry. As a result, India's steel industry imports coking coal, mainly from Australia and New Zealand, to meet about 25% of its annual needs. An historical summary of coal production and consumption in India is shown in Table 2.11.

Electricity

India is presently the sixth-greatest electricity generating country and accounts for about 4% of the world's total annual electricity generation. India is also currently ranked sixth in annual electricity consumption, accounting for about 3.5% of the world's total annual electricity consumption. Overall, India's need for power is growing at a prodigious rate; annual electricity generation and consumption in India have increased by about 64% in the past decade, and its projected rate of increase (estimated at as much as 8-10% annually, through the year 2020) for electricity consumption is one of the

Table 2.11: Coal Production and Consumption in India, 1996-2005 (in millions of short tons)

	1996	*1997*	*1998*	*1999*	*2000*	*2001*	*2002*	*2003*	*2004*	*2005*
Production	295.56	311.96	323.63	319.93	326.58	337.94	352.60	367.29	389.20	412.95
Anthracite	n/a	n/a	n/a	n/a	n/a	n/a	n/a	n/a	n/a	n/a
Bituminous	273.41	289.32	300.40	296.51	304.10	313.69	327.79	341.27	361.24	382.61
Lignite	22.15	22.64	22.23	23.42	22.48	24.25	24.81	26.02	27.96	24.34
Consumption	332.2	358.5	362.9	375.4	406.1	413.6	430.6	430.6	N/A	N/A

n/a—not applicable.

N/A—not available.

Note: components may not add to total due to rounding.

Source: Government of India, Ministry of Coal & Mines.

Table 2.12: Electricity Generation and Consumption in India, 1995-2005 (in billions of kilowatt-hours)

Year	*1995*	*1996*	*1997*	*1998*	*1999*	*2000*	*2001*	*2002*	*2003*	*2004*	*2005*
Net Generation	396.0	412.6	441.1	470.7	504.3	529.1	548.0	563.5	556.8	558.33	587.37
hydroelectric	71.9	68.2	73.9	82.2	79.9	73.7	73.0	63.5	68.5	73.77	84.50
nuclear	6.5	7.4	10.4	10.6	11.4	14.1	18.2	17.8	16.4	17.77	16.84
geo/solar/wind/biomass	0.5	0.8	0.9	1.0	2.3	2.9	3.9	4.1	4.2	n/a	n/a
conventional thermal	317.2	336.1	355.8	376.8	410.7	438.5	453.0	478.2	467.7	466.82	486.03
Net Consumption	369.8	385.2	411.6	439.0	470.1	493.4	510.9	525.4	519.0	n/a	n/a
Imports	1.7	1.6	1.6	1.5	1.4	1.5	1.5	1.5	1.4	1.4	1.4
Exports	0.1	0.1	0.1	0.2	0.3	0.2	0.3	0.2	0.2	0.2	0.2

n/a—not applicable.

Note: generation components may not add to total due to rounding.

Source: DOE/EIA and Government of India.

highest in the world. An historical summary of electricity generation and consumption in India is shown in Table 2.12.

India is currently ranked fifth in the world in terms of total installed electricity generating capacity, and accounts for about 3.5% of the world total. Hydroelectric capacity represents about one-fourth of India's total installed capacity, and overall, India is currently ranked sixth-largest in the world in that category (accounting for about 3.7% of the world's installed hydroelectric generating capacity). There is a large amount of hydroelectric capacity in construction and planning stages, and in particular, hydropower development in the Brahmaputra river basin in eastern India is expected to result in six large power plants, which will add nearly 30,000 megawatts (MWe) of generating capacity. The largest of these will be the 11,000 MWe Dihang Upper project, which, when completed in about 2012, would become the world's third-largest power plant. An historical summary of installed electricity generating capacity in India is shown in Table 2.13.

Table 2.13: Installed Electricity Generation Capacity in India (in thousands of megawatts)

	1997	*2002*	*2003*	*2004*	*2005*
Hydroelectric	21.65	26.26	26.76	29.50	30.94
Nuclear	2.22	2.72	2.72	2.72	2.77
Geothermal/Solar/ Wind/Biomass	1.27	1.51	1.74	1.87	3.81
Conventional Thermal	59.64	74.55	76.65	77.97	80.90
Total Capacity	85.79	105.05	107.88	112.06	118.42

Note: components may not add to total due to rounding.
Source: Government of India.

Carbon Emissions Information

Lowering energy intensity of GDP growth through higher energy efficiency is key to meeting India's energy challenge and ensuring its energy security. India's energy intensity vis-à-vis GDP growth has been falling and is about half what is used to be in early 70s. Energy consumption, per unit of GDP in purchasing power parity terms is only 0.19 kilogram oil equivalent per dollar as compared to 0.21 of the world average. But there is a still room for improvement and can be brought down further significantly with current commercially available technologies.

Despite of a reasonable growth in GDP and dependence on fossil fuels to meet the Energy needs of India, carbon dioxide emission per capita in India is still low, i.e., around 1 tonne against the world average of about 4 tonnes and of about 19 tonnes in case of some developed countries (According to IEA). A historical summary of CO_2 emissions from fossil fuel use in India is shown in Table 2.14.

Table 2.14: Fossil Fuel-related CO_2 Emissions in India, 1990-2002

Component	*1990*	*1995*	*1998*	*1999*	*2000*	*2001*	*2002*	*% change 1990-2002*
CO_2/TPES (t CO_2 per Tj)	38.87	42.88	43.77	44.29	45.00	44.90	45.10	16.0%
CO_2/GDP (kg CO_2 per 1995US$)	2.16	2.23	2.09	2.06	2.07	1.99	1.97	-8.8%
CO_2/GDP (kg CO_2 per 1995 US$ PPP)	0.45	0.47	0.44	0.43	0.43	0.42	0.41	-8.9%
CO_2/Population (t CO_2 per capita)	0.70	0.85	0.90	0.93	0.96	0.95	0.97	38.6%

Source: Planning Commission, GOI.

A composite position of Primary energy & electricity resources, exploiting fossil fuels, nuclear and renewable sources are illustrated in Table 2.15.

Assumptions for Potential Calculations are as given below:

Fossil Fuels

1. Complete Source is used for calculating electricity potential with a thermal efficiency of 0.36.
2. Calorific Values: Coal: 4,200 kcal/kg, Hydrocarbon: 10,200 kcal/kg.
3. Ministry of Petroleum and Natural Gas has set strategic goals for the next two decades (2001-2020) of 'doubling reserve accretion' to 12 BT (Oil + Oil equivalent gas) and "improving recovery factor' to the order of 40%. Considering the fact that exploration is a dynamic process and India is one of the les explored countries, reference assumes that cumulative availability of hydrocarbons up to 2052 will be 12 BT.

Table 2.15: Primary Energy and Electricity Resources

	Amount	*Thermal energy*			*Electricity potential*
		EJ	*TWh*	*GWYr*	*GWe-Yr*
Fossil					
Coal	38 -BT	667	185,279	21,151	7,614
Hydrocarbon	12 -BT	511	141,946	16,204	5,833
Non-Fossil					
Nuclear					
Uranium-Metal	61,000-T				
In PHWRs		28.9	7,992	913	328
In Fast-breeders		3,699	1,027,616	117,308	42,231
Thorium-Metal	2,25,000-T				
In Breeders		13,622	3,783,886	431,950	155,502
Renewable					
Hydro	150-GWe	6.0	1,679	192	69
Non-conventional renewable	100-GWe	2.9	803	92	33

Source: Planning Commission, GOI.

Non-Fossil Fuels

Thermal energy is the equivalent fossil energy required to produce electricity with a thermal efficiency of 0.36.

Nuclear

1. PHWR burn-up = 6,700 MWd/T of U-oxide, thermal efficiency 0.29
2. It has been assumed that complete fission of 1kg of fissile material gives 1000 MWd of thermal energy. Fast reactor thermal efficiency is assumed to be 42%. Fast breeders can use 60% of the Uranium. This is an indicative number. Actual value will be determined as one proceeds with the programme and gets some experience. Even if it is half of this value the scenario presented does not change.
3. Breeders can use 60% Thorium with thermal efficiency 42%. At this stage, types of reactors wherein thorium will be used are yet to be decided. These numbers are only indicative.

Hydro

1. Name-plate capacity is 150 GWe.
2. Estimated hydro-potential of 600 billion kWh and name-plate capacity of 150,000 MWe gives a capacity factor of 0.46.

Non-conventional Renewable

1. Includes: Wind 45 GWe, Small Hydro 15 GWe, Biomass Power/ Co-generation 19.5 GWe and Waste to Energy 1.7 GWe etc.
2. Capacity factor of 0.33 has been assumed for potential calculations.

Demographic Demand and Oil Prices

World annual average per capita or 'demographic' oil demand increased, regularly but erratically, through the 1970s (from about 4.7 barrels/capita/year in 1970) to attain a peak of a little more than 5.5 barrels/capita/year (bcy) in 1979. Since that time, the demographic rate 'bottomed' in the low oil price period of 1986-99, and of late slowly started to increase again. Table 2.16 shows how demographic demand has varied since 1979:

Table 2.16: Demographic Demand and Oil Price through 1979-2003

Year	*1979*	*1985*	*1990*	*1995*	*2003*
World population Millions*	4342	4810	5236	5640	6300
World oil demand Daily average Mbd**	65.9	58.3	66.7	69.5	78
Demographic demand Barrels/capita	5.53	4.42	4.64	4.49	4.52
Year oil price range in 2003 dollars/ barrel §	53-103	45-52	21-39	19-25	25-45•

Sources: *Population data/ UN Population Information Network (PIN). **Year average oil demand BP Statistical Review, OECD IEA. § Year oil price data/ Platts Oilgram, OPEC Bulletin, 'Oil Economists Handbook' Elsevier Press Dollar purchasing parity correction utilising price deflator of California Energy Commission 'Delphi Series' and OECD data. •Estimated price range for 2003.

Impact of Oil Shocks on Demographic Demand

The term 'oil shock' can have many meanings, but here we utilize what would be the essential element of the term—very large price changes in a short period of time. On this base, there have been at least 4 'oil shocks' since 1973, that is 3 upward price shocks (1973-74, 1979-1981 and 1998-1999), and 1 downward price shock (1985-86). None of these price shocks had an immediate and large impact on demographic demand. The only 'price elastic' response that can be attributed to oil shocks would be the consistent, and large cumulative falls in demographic oil demand through 1980-85, with the demand rate of 4.42 bcy in 1985 being the lowest in the entire 1979-2003 period. Troubling yet further any supposed 'price elastic' response or trigger for this fall is the fact that demographic demand had begun to fall by 1977-78.

Three essential points have to be mentioned. In the 1973-79 period, after a 295% oil price rise in nominal terms through 1973-74, there was almost no effective reduction in the demographic demand rate. The price rise impact through 1973-74 can be called a 'pause', rather than a major inflexion or change of trend. After 1979-81, with oil prices briefly attaining $103-per-barrel (in dollars of 2003) in that period, the decline in the demographic rate began to accelerate. What is most notable, however, is that the demographic rate continued to fall after prices had fallen well below the highs of the 1979-81 periods. As the table above shows, the 1995 demographic rate was almost unchanged from that of 1985, but oil prices had been more than halved in real terms. Perhaps most important to note is the third point: since 1999, and the 'price shock' of 1998-99 (about 230% price rise in nominal terms), the demographic demand rate has continued to rise, if only slowly.

The Real Impact of Higher Oil Prices: Global Economic Growth

The real impact of higher oil prices, certainly up to the range of about $60/barrel, is to increase economic growth at the global, or composite worldwide level. This is the main reason why demographic oil demand in the 1975-79 period, with the barrel oil price in the range of about $40-$65 in 2003 dollars, was significantly higher than it is today. It should be clearly understood that if the demographic rate in 2003 was the same as 1979, then world oil demand in 2003 was predicted to be 95.4 Million barrels per day. Relative to real demand at this time (about 78 Mbd) the additional capacity needed would be close to two times Saudi exports, more than three times Russia's export offer, or well above 5 times Venezuela's current export capacity. There is no certainty at all that the world oil supply would meet this demand.

Higher oil prices operate to stimulate first the world economy, outside the OECD countries, and then lead to increased growth inside the OECD. This is through the income or revenue effect on oil exporter countries, and then on metals, minerals and agro commodity exporter countries, most of them Low Income (GNP per capita below $400/year). Almost all such countries have very high marginal propensity to consume. That is any increase in revenues, due to prices of their export products increasing in line with the oil price, is very rapidly spent on purchasing manufactured goods and services of all kinds. In the 1973-81 period, in which oil price rises before inflation were of 405%, the New Industrial Countries (NICs) of that period—notably Taiwan, South Korea and Singapore—experienced very large and rapid increases in solvent demand for their export goods. The NICs as a group or bloc of economies rapidly expanded their oil imports and increased their oil consumption as prices increased in 1974-81, because demand for their export goods had increased, due to the global economic impacts of higher oil and 'real resource' prices. This has very strong implication for oil demand of today's emerging and giant NICs with large populations and immense internal markets—China, India, Brazil, Pakistan and Iran. For the much smaller NICs of the 1975-85 periods their oil import trends through 1974-81 show dramatic growth only slightly impacted by the major price rises of the period. In general terms (Table 2.17) the NICs Taiwan, South Korea and Singapore increased their oil demand by about 60% to 80% in volume terms in this period of a 405% increase in nominal prices.

Table 2.17: Asian Tiger Export Demand Driven Adjustment to Oil-Shock

(Oil Consumption Thousand barrels/day)

	1975	*1976*	*1977*	*1978*	*1979*	*1980*	*1981*	
Singapore	141	165	165	170	183	181	208	Increase 1975-81 : 47.5%
South Korea	278	310	371	426	480	475	497	Increase 1975-81 : 78.8%
Taiwan ROC	214	271	304	353	358	388	359	Increase 1975-81 : 67.8%

Source: BP Statistical Review of World Energy, various editions.

Future Perspectives

Cheap Oil is seen by the decision-making elite in the richer nations as the 'passport to economic growth'. This is a pure fantasy. Only 'extreme' oil prices (probably above $75-$100/barrel) will abort or cancel the global economy expansionary impacts of higher oil prices

Since about 1995 'demand shock' has begun to operate in the world economy for a number of economic, social or 'secular' and technical reasons, leading to considerably higher underlying growth rates of world oil demand. Current 'trend growth rates' for world energy and world oil demand are about 2.25% for oil and about 2.5% for energy on an annual basis. Cheap oil and energy remains the essential base of conventional economic development and social progress anyplace in the world. This in turn is a powerful motor for continued and strong demand growth for fossil energy, worldwide. Upward potential for personal consumption of fossil fuels is essentially unlimited in this context.

Conventional or classic economic growth is enabled and facilitated at the world or 'composite' level by rising oil prices to high price levels. This also underpins, or even increases world demand for fossil energy supplies, indicating that concerted international action is needed to plan for the effects of persistent underestimates of real demand growth trends.

Key Imperatives for India

To meet its large and growing energy needs, there are certain key imperatives for the Indian energy sector:

Private Sector Investment needs to Complement Public Sector

Reliability of energy supply and its cost will be key determinants of both, economic growth and social upliftment. Achieving this will require significant investment—of capital as well as of capabilities. Private sector will necessarily need to complement the public sector in both areas. The Government policies continue to lay emphasis on enabling a higher level of private sector participation. Sector reforms are aimed at attracting private investment and efficiency, through different forms of competitive markets. A large part of the power sector, for example, will become contestable by 2008, opening up a USD 5 bn market. Overall, the investment needed in the Indian energy sector is to the tune of USD 120 to 150 bn over the next five years.

To encourage private investment, clarity and stability in policy framework is essential. For example, clarity in matters related to pricing of energy products, the market structure and Government incentives and subsidy administration are important to minimize the risks of investment. Some clarity has emerged, for example, in areas such as oil & gas pricing where the price determination process has been set out.

Encourage Market Mechanisms with a Credible and Independent Regulatory Oversight

The benefits of market mechanisms in bringing in production and resource allocation efficiencies are needed. Market mechanisms will also encourage investments as it will tend to minimize the regulatory risks.

However, the market mechanisms have to be introduced gradually as supply side situation improves. Currently, with the huge deficit in energy products, market mechanisms are likely to get abused if not managed to some degree by an independent regulatory oversight. For example, the regulator for the power sector has been in place for a while. While tight regulation was adopted in the initial years, now we are seeing market mechanisms being used. For example, the case of long-term generation tariffs being determined through a competitive bidding process and the development of a short-term market for power.

Reduce Vulnerability to Price and Supply Shocks

The Indian energy basket is weighted towards coal (51%) and oil (36%). From a long term energy security perspective, it is necessary to diversify the energy basket. For example, if the known coal reserves are expected to exhaust in about 40 years, it would be a challenge to replace 51 percent of the energy basket. Diversification would mean increasing the share of Natural Gas, Nuclear and Hydro energy apart from a strategic thrust towards renewable energy. The other issue is vulnerability to price shocks. Vulnerability to price shocks are addressed by diversifying the fuel basket, enhancing domestic production of energy and in initiatives such as taking equity positions in energy resources abroad. We are seeing a positive trend in all these areas. Nuclear, natural gas and hydro power are getting the required impetus. Domestic production is being enhanced with initiatives on private participation and Indian companies have begun to take equity positions in international energy resources including oil & gas and coal.

Bringing in Efficiency and Enhancing Capacity in Energy Transport Infrastructure

In India, there is a high degree of inter-regional disparity in terms of energy sources and the growth centers. Significant initiatives are underway to enable investment in ports and railway infrastructure to move coal, pipelines and storage network for oil and gas, and transmission network for electricity.

Enhanced transmission capacity will also enable exploitation of the Himalayan hydro resources in Himachal Pradesh, Uttaranchal and the North Eastern states, as also in Nepal and Bhutan. For this purpose, private participation in energy transport sector is actively being promoted. Private investment in ports, dedicated freight corridors, pipelines and power transmission has already begun to take place.

Tariff Reform and Power Sector Reform

This is one of the most difficult and important area as far as the energy sector is concerned. Prices of electricity and some of the other energy products are highly distorted thereby promoting inefficient end-use and sometimes even inefficient energy choices. For example, power, kerosene and domestic gas are highly subsidized. There have been various policy measures to address this and to some degree of success. However, the challenge is in implementation and bringing in the required political will to address this issue. Power sector reform on the distribution front is another key area where progress has been slow. High network losses largely due to theft and pilferage have left the power sector cash strapped. While some states have done well on the distribution reform front, in others private sector participation in the form of franchising is being now tried as a potential solution.

Provide Government Support for Energy Efficiency

The Government needs to create a policy framework that provides incentives for energy efficiency. This could, for example, mean providing incentives in urban areas for mass transport systems and promoting R&D in energy efficiency. The environment should encourage energy efficiency companies to come up and operate profitably. In parallel, India is also emerging as a significantly active market in terms of Clean Development Mechanism (CDM) projects being conceptualized and registered with the Executive Board (EB). The growing awareness of the CDM benefits would make this an important area for investments in the Indian energy sector. CDM should also give the necessary fillip for energy efficiency measures in India.

The Government of India is recognizing the importance of private sector participation, and independent regulation in the energy sector. The future holds a lot of opportunities for international and domestic private participation.

The majority of India's energy requirement is met by coal; which is largely mined in the Eastern and the Central regions of the country. In 2005-06, the total coal production in the country was around 405.2 MMT (advanced estimates) and majority of it catered to the core sectors of power, steel and cement.

Inspite of various policy initiatives to diversify the fuel mix, it is becoming increasingly evident that coal will continue to play a major role in sustaining the growth momentum of India. Based on estimates, the consumption of coal is projected to rise by nearly 40 percent over the next five years and set to almost double by 2019-20. However, in the recent past, the country's coal sector has come under pressure due to its inability to meet demand, both planned and unplanned, of the user industries. As per the government's own estimates, production will lag behind demand by about 100 MMT as of 2011-12 and by 250 MMT by 2019-20.

The Indian Opportunity

The recognition of private investment requirements and acknowledgement for the need to improve operational efficiency provides immense investment opportunities in coal and related sectors. Participation of the private sector in captive mining, across different user industries, is an immediate investment opportunity. Thirty eight coal fields with mineable coal reserves in excess of 2,800 million tonnes15 have been identified and are in the process of being allocated for captive mining. This may imply a total capital requirement of around USD 1.5-2 billion. However, it should be remembered that deposits, which are on the surface and are easily extractable, may have already been largely explored. In future agencies would need to address increasingly difficult terrain and search coal at greater depths using more sophisticated technology; thus requiring more capital investments and a larger scale of operations. Apart from coal production, there have also been investments in other parts of the value chain such as coal washeries. There is a need to issue new regulations which support a free market, allow the formation of joint ventures or other alliances, and encourage the development of shared infrastructure such as dedicated rail lines and power transmission networks.

To achieve these goals, the Government will have to overcome strong opposition from political and business interests within the sector. Being a related sector, seaports that receive shipments of coal, railroads, etc would require USD 40-50 billion in investments for harmonious capacity expansion in capacity. The government's plan to invest USD 2 billion to increase capacity and remove bottlenecks at existing major ports is much lower compared to an estimated actual requirement of USD 30 billion. Similarly, a total USD 15-20 billion is required towards creation of new freight corridors and integrating them with existing rail operations. Oil comprises about 36 per cent of India's primary energy consumption at present, and driven by India's overall economic growth, it is expected to grow both in absolute and percentage terms. The growth in demand is projected to catapult the overall demand to 196 MMT in 2011-12 and 250 MMT in 2024-25. The growing demand-supply gap has led the Indian government to open up exploration and production to private participants through NELP and develop a more holistic strategy for acquisition of equity oil abroad.

Key Issues Facing the Oil Sector

The following are the major issues faced by the Oil sector:

- ***Absence of statutory framework in the upstream industry***: India has significantly shied away from structural regulation; regulations in India being more focused towards use of standards in the areas of health, safety and environment, and certain critical aspects of operations and pricing. The scope of the proposed legislation, through the recently drafted Petroleum Regulatory Board Bill, is confined to the downstream industry—while the upstream industry is still governed under a policy framework by the Directorate General of Hydrocarbons. Notable is the absence of any statutory framework in the upstream sector.

- ***Incidence of cross subsidy due to social obligations***: Till recently the subsidy burden on LPG, SKO and diesel were allocated to the national oil companies; but the incidence has been spread out across to the private sector. Although this phenomenon is likely to remain due to social obligations of the Government, a more transparent procedure for the allocation of subsidies would boost investor confidence further.

Policy and Regulatory Framework

The current upstream regulation is provided by Director General of Hydrocarbons (DGH) primarily on technical aspects than on pricing front. The midstream and downstream sectors are largely unregulated. However, downstream regulation is proposed to be introduced with the passing of the PNGRB bill.

Over the past five to six years, the trend has been towards opening up the sector for greater investment, setting up an independent regulator to monitor post production activities, and enabling a transition from an administered to a market driven mechanism. This also includes de-controlling

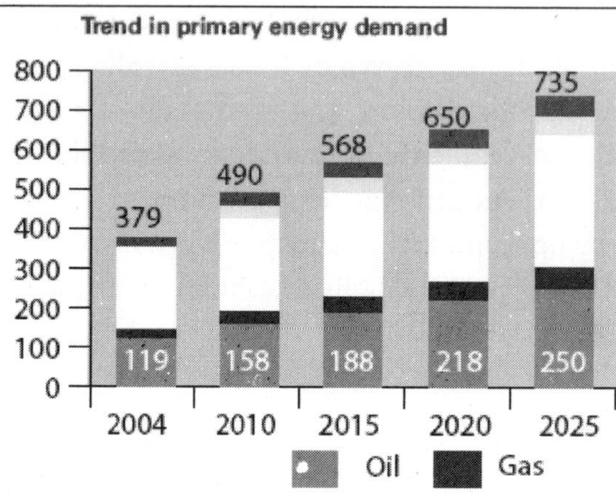

- Demand for oils expected to grow form 119 MTOE from 2004 to 250 MTDE during 2025 at annual growth of 3.6 per cent.
- During the same period domestic production from existing developed reserves expected to grow at approximately 2.5 per cent.
- The gap in demand and output will catapult India to one of the largest consumers of crude oil along with China. The 2 countries will account for 35 per cent of the world's incremental energy demand.

Source: BP and EIA.

Figure 2.2: India's Energy Mix and Outlook for Oil

of most of the petroleum products and allowing private sector companies to market them at the market determined prices. Another significant trend in oil and gas regulation in India, and one which is likely to continue, is the opening up of the sector to private and foreign participation. A 100 percent Foreign Direct Investment is allowed in exploration, creation of pipeline infrastructure, refining and in downstream retailing. A 100 percent FDI in retailing is allowed subject to minimum investment of USD 445 million in midstream or upstream sector. Combined with the attractiveness of the Indian market in the oil sector, this is likely to bring forth significant investments in the future.

On the pricing front, the government-appointed committee on pricing and taxation of petroleum products has recommended that the oil companies should shift from an 'import parity based pricing' to a 'trade based pricing'. It has also suggested the reduction in custom duties on petrol and diesel from 10 per cent to 7.5 per cent and the shifting of excise duty from an ad-valorem levy to a specific levy. The oil marketing companies are expected to benefit from the current Union Budget proposal of lowering excise duty on vehicle fuels from 8 percent to 6 percent. This is expected to reduce the losses of oil marketing companies that are currently selling both petrol and diesel at discounted state-determined prices.

The India Opportunity for Self-Reliance

Investments under NELP

To increase investment in the upstream side, the Ministry of Petroleum & Natural Gas (MoPNG) has introduced a transparent bidding process for allocation of oil and gas blocks. Six rounds of competitive bidding under the Government policy, named New Exploration Licensing Policy (NELP), have already been done, around 185 blocks were awarded and reserves estimated at 700 MMT2 of oil and gas have been discovered. However, the recent rounds of NELP bidding are still dominated by public sector. To bring new technologies and international practices into the oil and gas exploration sector, the government is keen on greater foreign participation under NELP process. In NELP-VI, the latest round, a total of 65 blocks including shallow water, deepwater and on-land blocks were put on offer. NELP-VI was a success with 165 bids being received from both domestic and international companies for exploration rights. Going forward, Directorate General of Hydrocarbons has indicated that 70-80 blocks, including those in un-explored states, will be made available in NELP-VII.

Destination India as Refining-hub

India's key advantages for developing itself as an export refining hub includes cost competitiveness and location advantage. India has significant lower cash operating costs on account of cheaper power and labor costs. The capital costs are also lower by as much as 25 to 50 percent over other Asian counterparts.

Geographically, India is strategically located en route of Middle East crude for East Asian and Pacific-rim markets. In fact, India possesses surplus refining capacity and has already turned into a net exporter of products. Certain areas of the country have been already demarcated for the development of export-oriented refineries and dialogues are underway between MoPNG and some oil companies on implementation of the strategy; which also includes building supporting infrastructure for enabling exports.

By 2010, the expected worldwide deficit in refining capacity would be around 112 MTPA because of shutting down of some of the smaller refineries in developed economies. Smaller refineries in North America and Europe are finding it uneconomical to invest in cleaner fuels because of high compliance cost and cleaner fuel norms. In Japan and Australia, oil majors have rationalized their refining assets because they are becoming uneconomical to

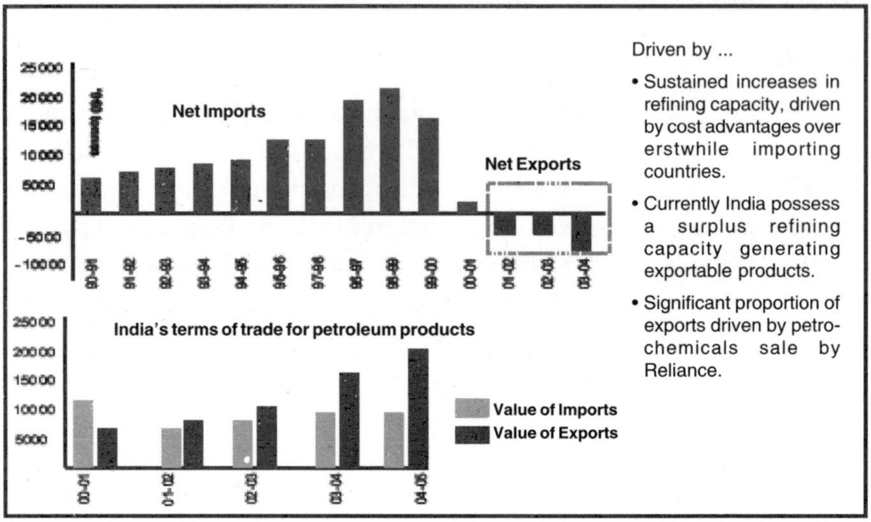

Figure 2.3: India's Petroleum Exports on the Rise since 2001

operate. On the domestic supply side, India's current refining capacity stands at around 143 MMT. The domestic refining companies have planned capacity additions to the tune of 90 to 100 MMTPA in the next 4 to 5 years. This large scale commissioning of capacities, when viewed against the expected demand of 196 MMT, suggests that India's petroleum product exports are slated to rise from the current 17 percent of fuel processed in the country. It is expected that RIL's (Reliance Industries Limited) refinery expansion of 580,000 bpd at Jamnagar would be only to supply to export markets in Europe and North America.

Another development has been the receipt of foreign direct investment (FDI) in a public sector refinery for the first time. Hindustan Petroleum Corporation Limited (HPCL) has entered into a partnership with Mittal Investments for setting up the refinery-cum-petrochemical complex at Bhatinda in Punjab. This development might be viewed as the first step towards greater involvement by international oil firms in Greenfield projects.

Increased Investment in Fuel Quality Upgradation

Prompted by stringent fuel specifications in the developing countries and the domestic "Auto Fuel Policy" which mandate Euro IV norms by 2010, significant investments have been planned for upgrading existing refineries. In order to hedge against variation in crude supplies and achieve cost-competitiveness by accommodating cheaper quality crude, it has become essential to upgrade the refineries to more complex configurations. Indian Oil Corporation Limited has planned investments of INR 60 billion towards upgradation of its Gujarat refinery, INR 140 billion for installation of a naphtha unit at its Panipat plant and INR 30 billion for its Haldia refinery. Similar investments have been planned by HPCL and Bharat Petroleum Corporation Limited (BPCL) for their Vishakapatnam and Mumbai refineries, respectively.

Building Strategic Petroleum Reserve through Public Private Partnership

Taking into account the oil security concern, the Government has decided to set up strategic crude oil storage at various locations in the country.

India, China and SE Asia

Strategic storage would be in addition to the existing storage of crude oil and petroleum products with the oil companies and would provide an emergency response mechanism whenever there are any short-term supply disruptions. Additionally, the government is also exploring the possibility of increasing the oil stockpile in the country through various innovative schemes such as leasing of storage space to international oil trading companies and building of additional storage terminals through the concessions route.

Acquisition of Overseas Oil Assets

MoPNG has conceived a more coordinated approach towards acquisition of overseas oil assets through joint forays, bilateral engagements with other countries to benefit from each others strengths in areas of technology transfers, R&D, safety and training, as well as multilateral engagements such as the Asian Round Tables, International Energy Forum etc. Recently India has signed an MoU with China for joint bidding of hydrocarbon blocks.

Competition in the Downstream (retail and institutional) Segment

As per Petroleum Regulatory Board ('PRB') Bill, all upcoming pipelines would have mandatory open access. Creation of open access capacity would drive competition in the retail and the institutional segment. In anticipation of competition, major oil firms are expanding their retail network and forming alliances with a host of product and services companies to offer non-fuel products and services as part of their overall proposition. On the institutional

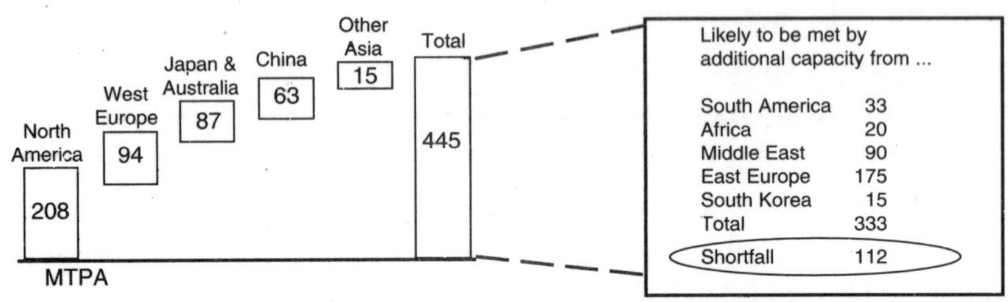

• North America and Europe	• Cleaner fuel norms • High compliance cost	• Smaller refineries in the region and finding uneconomical to invest for cleaner fuels. 70 (out of 375) refineries in North America and Europe are small with capacity less than 2.5 mtpa
• India, China and SE Asia*	• Reduced tariff protection due to liberalisation • Greater stringent fuel norms call for additional Investments	• Inefficient refineries are closing down 16 mtpa of sub-scale capacity has closed down in China during the last two years Another 21 refineries (–9 mtpa) are facing closure in the Shandong province
• Japan and Australia	• Old, inefficient assets are becoming uneconomical	• Oil majors have rationalized their refining assets in Australia & Japan Shell has dosed Cycle Refinery, Australia In Japan,9 mtpa of refining capacity is expected to be rationalised in next 2 years

Figure 2.4: Supply Defeict and Consolidation in Refinery Sector Throws up Opportunity for Indian Exports

segment, incumbents are focusing on profitable segments for subsidized products like LPG (commercial & non-domestic) as well as on specialty products like Hexane.

When compared to mature natural gas (NG) based economies like Japan, Korea, and the United States, India is a relatively new entrant. However, the increasing significance of the fuel in the Indian context can be gauged from the fact that, by 2025, the country is expected to rival both China and Japan in having the largest NG demand in Asia. Demand in each of these countries is expected to be in the range of 350 MMSCMD.

The significant potential for NG demand, especially in the context of India's projected GDP growth above 8 percent, is being driven by the following key factors:

- The share of natural gas in India's energy basket is only around 9 percent as compared to the world average of around 24 percent. More than 50 percent of NG volume goes to sectors where it is a substitute to petroleum products and the rest goes to the power sector where it substitutes coal. In this context, NG volume in the country will partly be driven as a substitute to petroleum products because it is cheaper and cleaner. In addition, reforms in the power sector would also encourage NG to be used as a cleaner substitute to coal in the long term. The share of NG in the fuel mix is expected to go up from the present 8.8 percent levels to 22 percent in 2031-32.

- Per capita consumption of NG in India is currently amongst the lowest in the world; being at 29 cu m as compared to a world average of around 538 cu m.
- Demand for NG (at more than 120 mmscmd) in the country has far outstripped supply (about 75 mmscmd), and there has an increasing trend towards emergence of new NG demand as well as conversion from existing fuels to NG.

Key Issues

India's gas supply issues are different from that of oil, mainly because domestic onshore and offshore gas has been contributing to meet more than 90 percent of demand so far. Except for the LNG terminals at Hazira and Dahej, all other gas requirements are being met through domestic sources only. However, existing onshore and offshore fields have been facing a declining trend in production and are unlikely to contribute to growth in supply. It is projected that production in 2015 may be less than 50 percent of current production. The identification of new sources of gas supply would be critical to sustaining the demand for gas in the country.

Domestic Reserves/Production will not be Sufficient

While there have been new finds of about 70 Bcm a year in the last decade, unattractive market prices have contributed to production not increasing correspondingly. However, significant shortfall will mean that one way or the other these reserves will have to start getting utilized. Significant incentives are being offered by the government through its NELP programs to attract greater investment in this area.

Cross-border Gas Pipelines Facing Uncertainty, but Attracting Interest

While initiatives related to cross-border NG pipelines with Iran,

Pakistan, Myanmar, Turkmenistan, etc. have been under discussion for quite some time, the political environment and international climate has been unfavorable, thus delaying these projects indefinitely. As LNG becomes even more expensive, the importance of these sources is increasingly being recognized. Interestingly, globally, transnational gas pipelines have rarely faced disruptions in supply once they have been put into use. Hence, this may be a good sign for India despite the political sensitivities involved.

Inability to take International Prices

Due to the distinctive nature of the Indian market, current international prices cannot be passed through to major NG user's viz. power and fertilizer sectors (which constitute over 70 percent of demand). These customers had traditionally been buying gas at administered prices of less than USD 3 per MMBtu upto a couple of years ago. However, due to existing plant efficiencies being significantly impacted by shortages in the recent past, gas is being purchased even at USD 6 per MMBtu. In the power sector, focus has temporarily shifted away from new gas-based capacity to coal-based capacity addition. Other industrial customers may still prefer gas because of the high prices of Naphtha, FO or LPG.

Policy and Regulatory Framework

Over the past six years, the trend in natural gas regulation has been towards opening up the sector for greater investment, setting up an independent regulator to monitor post production activities, and enabling a transition from the administered control regime to a market driven mechanism. Significant regulatory issues which will impact the gas sector in India include:

Petroleum and Natural Gas Regulatory Board Act, 2006 (PNGRB Act, 2006)

The Act envisages setting up a Petroleum and Natural Gas Regulatory Board to regulate the refining, processing, storage, transportation and distribution, marketing and sale of petroleum, petroleum products and natural gas; excluding production of crude oil and natural gas. The objective of the board is to protect the interests of consumers and entities engaged in specified activities relating to petroleum, petroleum products and natural gas, to ensure uninterrupted and adequate supply of petroleum, petroleum products and natural gas in all parts of the country and to promote competitive markets in India.

Policy for Development of Natural Gas Pipelines and City or Local Natural Gas Distribution Networks

The objective of the policy is to promote investments from public as well as private sector in natural gas pipelines and city or local natural gas distribution networks, to facilitate open access for all players to the pipeline network on a non-discriminatory basis, to promote competition among entities and to protect the end consumer. A Gas Advisory Board (GAB) will be set up to promote and develop the gas pipeline network in India

Gas Linkage Committee

The Gas Linkage Committee (GLC) was established to manage the allocation of gas to eligible customers. This was linked with the administered price mechanism which depressed domestic gas prices for certain sectors. However, new fields under the National NELP are already exempt from the purview of the GLC and can trade at market prices.

Infrastructure Status for Gas Pipelines

Development of gas pipelines and related storage has been granted 'Infrastructure Status'. While this would translate into a number of benefits for companies planning on developing gas transmission pipelines, it could also allow for lower gas transmission tariffs if part of these benefits are passed on to the end consumer. While some quarters expect the LNG import sector to be also given infrastructure status in the interest of increasing economical gas sourcing options for the country, the same has not happened yet.

Foreign Direct Investment in NG Sector

Foreign Direct Investment of 100 percent is allowed in the exploration, pipeline infrastructure, LNG and trading segments; subject to approval. Combined with the attractiveness of the Indian market in the NG sector, this is likely to bring forth significant investments in the future. The integrated LNG policy is currently under discussion and is likely to be put in place soon.

Importance given to Nuclear Energy

The importance accorded to nuclear energy by the Government of India can be gauged from the following:

- Indian government's willingness to co-operate and enter into civilian nuclear agreements with countries like U.S., France and Russia, despite internal opposition to opening up of its still-guarded nuclear reactors to international scrutiny.
- Deal with Russian Federation for setting up of 1000 MWe LightWater Reactors (LWR's) under IAEA safeguards.
- Aggressive targets on the nuclear closed fuel cycle based three-stage nuclear power programme, where Bharatiya Nabhikiya Vidyut Nigam Limited (BHAVINI) has been setup for the construction of its first Fast Breeder Reactor (FBR) by 2010.
- Nuclear power plant capacity targets as envisaged by the Department of Atomic Energy (DAE) are given below:
  — 10,280MWe by 11th Five year plan
  — 20,000 MWe by 2020
  — 50,000 MWe by 2030
  — 250,000 MWe of nuclear power by 2050

India's Nuclear Power Programme

Three-stage Indian Nuclear Programme

The importance of nuclear energy was recognized in the 1940s itself by Dr.H.Bhabha who envisaged a three–stage nuclear power programme with the aim of utilizing the thorium potential of India. The closed nuclear fuel cycle has been the core strategy of the Indian Nuclear Power Programme being followed by the Department of Atomic Energy, Government of India. The first stage of Nuclear Power Programme comprising setting up of Pressurized Heavy Water Reactors (PHWRs) is already in commercial domain.

- India has achieved considerable expertise in its first stage of nuclear power programme and about 10GWe of nuclear installed capacity is possible from indigenous uranium.
- Budgetary allocation for uranium exploration, including drilling, has been continuously increasing in recent years.

Nuclear Energy

Inviting domestic and foreign private sector firms to participate in uranium exploration activities in India

The second stage of Nuclear Power Programme comprising setting up of Fast Breeder Reactors (FBRs) backed up by reprocessing plants and plutonium-based fuel fabrication plants is in the technology demonstration stage.

- Energy potential of natural uranium can be increased to about 300GWe in the second stage through FBRs, which utilize plutonium obtained from the recycled spent fuel of the first stage along with thorium as blanket to produce U-233.
- FBRs of 4000MW each will be built every year from 2021. The third stage of the Nuclear Power Programme requires a large capacity of FBRs to be built up.
- Research on the third stage is in progress with a 300MWe Advanced Heavy Water Reactor (AHWR) developed by Bhabha Atomic Research Center (BARC) to expedite transition to thorium based system.
- Research on other advanced technologies like Compact High Temperature Reactor (CHTR), Accelerator Driven Systems (ADS) and indigenously built Tokomaks, as part of the nuclear fusion research programme, are in full swing at BARC. However, completing this ambitious three-stage plan successfully will require heavy investments and considerable development is required before the thorium cycle can be commercialized. The Government of India has been supporting all the investments required by the three-sage Nuclear Power Programme, with the ultimate goal of realizing energy security.

Nuclear Power Projects in India: Planned and Under Operation

Currently, India has 17 nuclear power plants being operated by the Nuclear Power Corporation of India Limited (NPCIL) and the total installed nuclear power capacity is 4120MWe. The Kaiga-3, 220MWe plant achieved criticality on 26th February, 2007. Given below are the plans of nuclear power plant capacity addition in India by DAE.

- New capacity addition of 2660MWe to be under commercial operation by December 2008.

— Under Construction: 3 PHWRs (3 × 220MWe) and 2 LWRs (2 × 1000MWe)

- New capacity addition of 6800MW to be under commercial operation by 2012.

— LWRs (4*1000MWe) (Jaitapur, Maharashtra and Kundakulam, Tamil Nadu)

— PHWRs (4*700MWe) (Kakrapar, Gujarat and Rawatbhata, Rajasthan)

Capital costs of nuclear power plants based on PHWR technology are in the range of INR 6 to 7 Crores per MW with a corresponding design life of more than 40 years. Gestation period for setting up of nuclear power plants in India has improved over years and is around 5 years with the current technology. Nuclear power competes economically with coal based plants at load centre generation of around 1000 Km from the pit head coal mines. Current power tariffs from some of the atomic power stations of NPCIL are in the range of INR 1.75 to 2.80 per unit, depending on the life of the reactor.

CHAPTER 3

Energy Security Policy

Energy Policy of India

The Energy Policy of India is characterized by trade-offs between four major drivers:

- Rapidly growing economy, with a need for dependable and reliable supply of electricity, gas, and petroleum products;
- Increasing household incomes, with a need for affordable and adequate supply of electricity, and clean cooking fuels;
- Limited domestic reserves of fossil fuels, and the need to import a vast fraction of the gas, crude oil, and petroleum product requirements, and recently the need to import coal as well; and
- Indoor, urban and regional environmental impacts, necessitating adoption of cleaner fuels and cleaner technologies.

In recent years, these challenges have led to a major set of continuing reforms, restructuring and a focus on energy conservation. These trade-offs are often difficult to achieve. For example, the supply of adequate, yet affordable electricity generated and used cleanly is a continuing challenge because expansion of supply, and doption of cleaner technologies, especially renewable energy, often means that this electricity is too expensive for many Indians, particularly in rural areas. In recent years, these challenges have led to a major set of continuing reforms and restructuring.

Policy Framework

Energy policy is the manner a given entity (often governmental) has decided to address issues of energy development including energy production, distribution and consumption. The attributes of energy policy may include: legislation, international treaties, incentives to investment, guidelines for energy conservation, taxation and other public policy techniques. A long-term energy policy perspective is provided by the Integrated Energy Policy Report 2006 which provides policy guidance on energy-sector growth (Planning Commission, 2006).

Measures used to Produce an Energy Policy

A national energy policy comprises a set of measures involving that country's laws, treaties and agency directives. The energy policy of a sovereign nation may include one or more of the following measures:

- A statement of national policy regarding energy planning, energy generation, transmission and usage.
- Legislation on commercial energy activities (trading, transport, storage, etc.)
- Legislation affecting energy use, such as efficiency standards, emission standards
- Instructions for state owned energy sector assets and organizations
- Active participation in, co-ordination of and incentives for mineral fuels exploration and other energy-related research and development of fiscal policies related to energy products and services (taxes, exemptions, subsidies etc.).
- Energy security and international policy measures such as:
  - International energy sector treaties and alliances,
  - General international trade agreements,
  - Special relations with energy-rich countries, including military presence

Frequently, the dominant issue of energy policy is the risk of supply-demand mismatch. Current energy policies also address environmental issues. Some governments state explicit energy policy, but, declared or not, each government practices some type of energy policy.

Factors Governing Energy Policy

There are a number of elements that are naturally contained in a national energy policy, regardless of which of the above measures was used to arrive at the resultant policy. The chief elements intrinsic to formulation of an energy policy are:

- What is the extent of energy self-sufficiency for this nation (i.e. India)?
- Where from future energy sources will derive?
- How future energy will be consumed (e.g. among sectors)?
- What fraction of the population will be acceptable to endure energy poverty?
- What are the goals for future energy intensity, ratio of energy consumed to GDP?
- What is the reliability standard for distribution reliability?
- What environmental externalities are acceptable and are forecast?
- What form of "portable energy" is forecast (e.g. sources of fuel for motor vehicles)?
- How will energy efficient hardware (e.g. hybrid vehicles, household appliances) be encouraged?
- How can the national policy drive province, state and municipal functions?
- What specific mechanisms (e.g. taxes, incentives, manufacturing standards) are in place to implement the total policy?

Energy Security—An Indian Perspective

It is interesting to note the growing convergence of views in Political, Diplomatic, Business and Government circles for a coherent policy and actions towards the national goal of Energy Security. Globally, the popular sources of energy, namely Coal, Oil, Gas and Nuclear have been in use over the past decades, and are expected to be in use in the future as well. The sources of renewable energy are gradually entering into commercial domain (http://mea.gov.in/disarmament/dm13apr00.htm). Hydro-energy has been in use over the centuries and is expected to continue to be a major source in future also. Non-conventional sources like wind, bio-mass are contributing their mite, but may not command a bigger mind-share in energy security considerations, in the immediate future.

Internationally, we are being exposed the Geo-political and Commercial measures being taken by countries like the USA, China and Japan in securing long-term access to sources of energy and these measures have sensitized all of us, connected to the Indian Energy Business, to proactively examine the issue of our energy security in al its dimensions.

The dimensions of energy security can broadly be enumerated as follows:

1. Current sources of energy and current level of access to these sources
2. Technological measures to increase national access to sources of energy
3. Structural measures to increase national access to sources of energy
4. Demand management to reduce the wasteful usage of energy
5. Strategic management of Energy security

Current Sources of Energy and Current Level of Access to these Sources

- Coal: India has proven reserves exceeding 85 Billion tonnes. Coal provides app. 56% of all our energy needs. Our current coal consumption is to the tune of 0.35 Billion annually.
- Oil: India currently produces 1/3rd of its needs for oil and imports the rest. The vision shown in spreading the wings by OVL in securing assured access to oilfields outside the country is commendable and needs to be supported to the hilt. However, reliance on imported oil continues be a major unhedged variable in the energy security matrix.
- Gas: Gas had been a poor cousin to oil as recently as ten years ago. Ironically, it seems that Enron, through the Dhabol project, introduced the idea of LNG terminals. Through the visionary measures such as the NELP, as well as identification of LNG as a viable long-term source of Natural Gas, the scenario for gas availability has substantially brightened.
- Nuclear: On account of national security considerations, NPCIL is solely mandated for generating nuclear power in the country. Given the established technological competence in the country, and the Thorium and Uranium reserves, it is estimated that 30000 MW of electric power can be generated, as against current generation of about 2000 MW.

Technological Measures to Increase National Access to Sources of Energy

- Super-critical cycles, which are an internationally proven technology, are being implemented in the country, for the first time by NTPC. Usage of this technology could be mandated as an increasing percentage of total generation, to help increase the usage efficiency.
- Integrated coal gasification technology, implemented in a 6.2 MW module by BHEL, and now being planned for execution in a 100 MW module, needs to be implemented within a defined timeframe. This measure shall catapult India ahead over other major users of coal energy.
- Schemes for accessing the reserves of coal-bed methane are under consideration, jointly by ONGC, backed with Russian technology, and CIL. These measures shall hopefully yield as source of energy as useful as NG.
- R&M schemes designed to improve the PLF and fuel efficiency of old generating and process plants, rely on known and proven technologies. However the implementation on the ground has been somewhat slow, on account of structural issues.
- Measures such as Bharat III norms for engines for automobiles, have resulted reducing emissions, better fuel dispensing systems, more silent automobiles and in general a lower specific consumption.

Structural Measures to Increase National Access to Sources of Energy

- All of us have seen the penetration of telecom networks and mortgage housing in the country in the last 10 years. It can be seen that these miracles have been wrought by an enlightened regulatory framework, largely in-house entrepreneurs and a benign tax structure. Measures such as open access to all consumers, tax-breaks for interest payments towards principal repayment for energy mining and converting assets and coherent regulation at central and state levels, can increase national investment and thereby access.
- Measures such as free power subtract heavily from responsible behavior on part of all entities in the energy value chain. Intelligent redirection of subsidies is needed to reduce wastage and improve the climate for investment.

DEMAND MANAGEMENT TO REDUCE THE WASTEFUL USAGE OF ENERGY

- Country-wide implementation of measures such as Time-of-day pricing of power, would reduce the investment needs to cater for peak demand, as well as improve the generation efficiencies.
- Energy efficiency measures touched earlier would reduce specific fuel consumption.

STRATEGIC MANAGEMENT OF ENERGY SECURITY

- Today the country has a professional working as a National Security Adviser, integrating all dimensions and presenting a coherent view to the top leadership of the country.
- Integration of State level and central level laws impacting the energy sector is the need of the hour.
- The country has a vibrant public and private sector. Let us work out Public-Private partnerships to harness local resources, technologies, innovativeness and above all locally available capital to sculpt a secure future for our generation and for generations of Indians to come.

The Search for an Energy Strategy

Tanvi Madan (2006), in his detailed "Brookings Energy Policy Studies—an Energy Security Series for India"—made an in-depth analysis of the energy security options and corresponding energy security policy to support these options on a national priority perspective. To-date, India has developed a cluster of energy policies rather than an overarching energy strategy. Ideology, politics, and processes have complicated the country's quest for energy. Attempts at integrating energy policies have been hindered by separate entities overseeing each type of energy source, as well as by stove-piped policymaking on related issues of foreign affairs, economics, and the environment. And the realities of domestic politics and socioeconomic concerns have curbed policymakers' willingness to make tough, yet necessary, choices. Now at a critical juncture, India's policymakers are increasingly aware of the need for an effective and diversified energy strategy—or at least an integrated set of policies to balance foreign policy, economic, environmental, and social issues with the rising demand for energy. While there is little consensus over how best to proceed, there is no doubt that India's need for oil and other forms of energy will continue to grow. Meeting this need will have a decisive impact on the country's actions not just in the energy sector, but in its efforts to achieve its broader strategic goals at home and abroad.

This policy study focuses on India's need for oil and how this demand fits within its broader set of energy policies as outlined below in 3 segments:

Part 1: surveys the country's overall energy demand-supply situation, the "energy security" debate in the country, and the issues, actors, processes, and politics involved in energy policy and decision-making.

Part 2: focuses on India's search for oil, including its supply-side policies, such as efforts toward domestic E&P, acquisition of upstream assets abroad, supply and fuel diversification, and the development of strategic oil stocks. It also examines India's demand-side policies, including regulatory, price and tax reform, fuel conservation, and efficiency measures.

Part 3: The concluding section offers observations about India's likely actions in the energy sector at home and abroad and suggests further areas for research.

A number of key findings resulted from this study include:

- India is likely to continue to have a set of separate energy policies formulated by different entities rather than an overarching energy strategy. Integration of these policies will likely improve over time.
- Reform of India's energy sector will continue—but at a slow pace. Implementing policies will be harder than formulating them.
- India's energy-related actions in the global arena will reflect its current foreign policy path of "enlightened self-interest" and maintaining diverse options. It will be cooperative or competitive, as suits its interests—in acquiring assets or pursuing partners—when it thinks it needs to be. However, India would much rather cooperate than compete.
- India would be more inclined to cooperate with the international community (rather than focusing on a particular country or region) in the energy sphere if it were given a seat at the decision-making table. Global players should find a way to bring India into the International Energy Agency (IEA) or at least find a place for it in an "energy half-way house" en route to full membership.
- For the foreseeable future, however, India will hesitate to rely completely on global markets. As a consequence, its country-by-

country energy diplomacy and purchase of overseas assets will continue. However, its energy interests are not likely to trump the country's larger strategic goals.

- India's energy interests are also likely to factor into its military strategy and behavior in the future. For example, India might be willing to take on a greater share of the international security burden related to protecting oil and gas supply lines.

The Government's Other Considerations

Strategic Issues

Today, India's foreign policy is following what the current prime minister calls a path of "enlightened self-interest." India is forming partnerships—though not alliances—with multiple countries. In a variation on the Palmerstonian axiom, India's policy seems to be "no permanent allies; lots of good friends." The country is forming these relationships to serve a number of different interests, including energy security. But each partnership is designed to attain the goal of a strong, respected, independent India that can shape its environment (globally as well as regionally) and protect its core interests. However, India has conflicting interests that may indeed clash in the future. While it is engaging in more aggressive oil diplomacy with a few countries, considering more acquisitions of oil and gas assets abroad, and thinking about participating in the construction of a number of pipelines, these attempts are not played out in a vacuum. They occur in the context of India's developing strategic relationships with a number of other countries, including the United States that might view some of these other "energy relationships" with concern.

A good example of this clash is the proposed Iran-Pakistan-India gas pipeline, which has been discussed for over a decade and a half. Over the last few years the proposal has taken on new momentum, but the budding U.S.-India strategic partnership complicates any Indian decision to participate. While the United States did not ask India to choose between the pipeline and their bilateral relationship, it has made its views on the former quite clear. India is also likely to run into conflicts of interest with the United States when considering potential energy suppliers like Myanmar, Sudan, and Venezuela. While India is loath to act under pressure in each of these cases, before acting on its energy security imperatives, the country will have to consider its other strategic interests.

Fiscal Considerations

Political, socioeconomic, and energy imperatives, in turn, have to be balanced with fiscal requirements. A case in point is the pricing of petroleum products (like LPG, kerosene, diesel, and petrol). Whether out of genuine concern for large sections of society or out of fear that voters will make them feel their pain—or both—India's decision-makers have chosen to keep petroleum product prices low, as mentioned above. Following are some of the glaring examples:

- Between September 7, 2002 and September 7, 2005 the price of Dubai crude rose almost 111 percent.
- The retail price of regular gasoline in the United States, during the same period, increased 124 percent; in India, the retail price of petrol rose only 49 percent.84 In India, the true cost of international price increases is borne largely by the public sector oil companies, which absorb the losses and by the government, which bails them out. With private interests now permitted limited participation in the energy sector, they also assume a share of the burden.
- Recently, the Petroleum Secretary indicated that state-owned oil marketing companies (OMCs) were losing $51 million a day. The state-owned Indian Oil Company (IOC)—India's largest downstream company—announced that it lost nearly $270 million in April 2006 alone because it could not pass on high prices. Subsidies also create a burden, though the government has substantially reduced expenditures on them over the years. Central government subsidies on petroleum products are still equivalent to 2.5 percent of the government's fiscal deficit. In the last fiscal year, the Ministry of Petroleum and Natural Gas estimates that the state-owned oil companies have subsidized $8.7 billion in petroleum products. With cross-ownership, even the upstream companies absorb subsidy burdens.

The Oil and Natural Gas Corporation (ONGC) absorbed about $2.5 billion worth of them in 2005–06.

The government bails out state-owned OMCs when they suffer under recoveries due to retail price controls. It does so by issuing them oil bonds, which they can liquidate to ensure that losses are limited (or absent) on the companies' balance sheets. In 2005–06 these oil bonds were equivalent to almost 4 percent of the fiscal deficit. So even if the effects of high global oil prices do not show up at the gas pump, in inflation statistics, or on the companies' balance sheets, they are contributing to the country's fiscal deficit. This is true of its trade deficit as well. In 2005–06 India spent $38.8 billion to import crude oil, up from $25.9 billion the previous year. Its import bill for crude oil and petroleum products constituted almost a third of India's total import bill and contributes significantly to India's persisting trade deficit, which stood at $51.5 billion.

Environmental Factors

India's powerful environmental groups are deeply rooted in its society and have strong ties to various international environmental movements. Environmentalism has recently gone mainstream amid visible signs of increasing pollution in many Indian cities, growing numbers of cases of respiratory illnesses, shrinking forest cover, and reports that India's carbon dioxide emissions have been increasing "alarmingly." India's president has warned of immense environmental problems if China and India maintain their dependence on fossil fuels.

Policy-making

There are well over a dozen organized agencies, institutions, and sectors that can affect decisions related to energy policy in India. Some of these groups are within the government, which is not monolithic and has many voices on energy policy; some are outside it. The number is growing rapidly, as the private sector plays a larger role in energy decisions and as environmental and political groups expand their influence. Given below is an overview of the actors involved.

Role of Central Ministries in Energy Policy

This section describes the significant roles played by several central Ministries of Government of India for ensuring energy security in an integrated manner.

Department of Atomic Energy

This independent department has all matters related to atomic energy under its purview, and is responsible for designing, commissioning, constructing, and operating nuclear power plants.

Ministry of Coal

This ministry is "responsible for development and exploitation of coal and lignite reserves in India." It sets the "policies and strategies" for the sector and has administrative control of Coal India Ltd., a state-owned corporation, and its eight subsidiaries, which together control most coal mining in the country.

Ministry of Petroleum and Natural Gas (MPNG)

The purview of this Ministry includes exploration and production of oil and natural gas; refining, distribution, and marketing of petroleum products; and the conservation, import, and export of oil and natural gas. It also has administrative control of the state-owned oil and gas companies—including those of ONGC, IOC, GAIL and OIL. The Directorate General of Hydrocarbons (DGH), which could be described as the regulator of the upstream sector, also falls under this ministry, as does the Oil Industry Development Board (OIDB), which provides financial assistance (in the form of loans and grants) to the industry. The central government provides the funds that OIDB distributes from the cess (a term for tax) that is collected from firms producing oil domestically. The Petroleum Planning and Analysis Cell (PPAC, formerly the Oil Coordination Committee) within the Ministry administers subsidies, and is responsible for analysis and forecasting related to the oil sector. The MPNG tends to be the most coveted of the energy-related ministries among potential ministerial candidates. Some analysts say that this is because it is a high-profile posting; others simply refer to it as a "party fundraising machine."

Ministry of Non-conventional Energy Sources (MNES)

This ministry is responsible for the policies for all non-conventional energy sources including wind, solar, small hydro, biogas, and biomass. It is the first of its kind in the world, a fact many of its officials like to highlight. However, it is probably also the most neglected of the energy ministries.

Ministry of Power

It has responsibility for policy and planning related to power projects and for enacting laws related to thermal and hydroelectric power generation, transmission, and distribution.

Other Central Ministries

A number of other related ministries have authority touches on energy related decisions. The more directly related agencies are the Ministry of Heavy Industries and Public Enterprises and the Ministry of Commerce and Industry. Also involved are the Ministry of Finance, the Ministry of External Affairs (MEA), the Ministry of Environment and Forests, the Ministry of Railways, the Ministry of Shipping, the Ministry of Road Transport and Highways, the Ministry of Water Resources, and the Ministry of Science and Technology.

The Planning Commission

Planning Commission operates as the government's think tank, conducting research and analysis and laying-out plans, policies and targets. The Commission's Power and Energy Division is responsible for the energy sector. The Planning Commission also coordinates plans with the chief ministers of India's states (together they compose the National Development Council). In addition, the Commission has a number of advisers and consultants.

The role and clout of these ministries and the Planning Commission vary over time, depending on who leads them, how close that person is to the prime minister or the governing party's coalition's leaders, and the personal interests of the prime minister. Decisions emanating from these entities stem from a number of the imperatives mentioned above, but they also depend on other factors like the political parties the minister belongs to the personalities associated and the processes involved.

State Level Planning

India's constitution divides responsibilities between the federal and state governments according to three lists:

- The Union List provides the issues the federal government takes care of;
- The State List provides those for which the state governments is responsible; and
- The Concurrent List provides those for which both have shared responsibility.

For example, the Union List includes "atomic energy and mineral resources necessary for its production regulation and development of oilfields and mineral oil resources; petroleum and petroleum products; other liquids and substances declared by Parliament by law to be dangerously inflammable" and "regulation of mines and mineral development to the extent to which such regulation and development under the control of the Union is declared by Parliament by law to be expedient in the public." Power, however, falls under the Concurrent List.

Beyond the responsibilities that the Constitution directly assigns them, there are other reasons the states play a role in energy policy. While major energy resources are subjects of the center, their development can have an impact on issues that fall under one of the other lists. Forests, for example, come under the Concurrent List and agriculture falls under the State List—both of which can be affected by policies made by the MNES. Additionally, some Indian states own energy firms, like the Gujarat State Petroleum Corporation, which dominates exploration and production in the oil and gas sectors in the state of Gujarat, and is also the parent company of gas transporter Gujarat State Petronet Ltd., which has a network of pipelines across the state.

Coordination Aspects

India's diversified official decision-making does have some advantages—including more and different inputs as well as cheerleaders for each energy source, ensuring that none are totally neglected—but it comes at a cost. The cross-cutting nature of energy issues and the various entities' responsibilities mean that there is always a need for coordination—among the ministries (and departments) responsible for energy-related issues, as well as between the center and the states. This obligation even extends to ministries that normally would not be considered energy related. At higher levels of government there are processes and mechanisms in place. Issues of crosscutting impact are brought up in Cabinet Committee discussions, where the concerned ministries have representation. This setting is the venue for coordinating policies and resolving conflicts. The government can also constitute Committees of Secretaries that bring together the senior-most bureaucrats from ministries involved in certain issues. The Planning Commission also offers a venue for coordination. However, one senior official, lamenting the lack of an integrated approach, indicated that he did not think that the Commission was the ideal forum for coordination.

Energy Division conducts the prep work and policy analyses for the

Energy Coordination Committee (ECC). Just as the ECC represents an opportunity for coordination at a higher level, some have also suggested the creation of an inter-ministerial task force at the joint secretary level—possibly coordinated by an additional secretary from the Power Ministry. But these suggestions seem to have been shelved for now. Because implementation has been a problem; the planning commission also suggested that the prime minister create a body that would "operationalize" the policies being developed.

The Companies' Role

Two decades ago, a list of the companies involved in the Indian energy sphere (especially in oil) would have been quite short and dominated by the public sector. Today, as a result of the reentry and rise of the private sector, it is much larger and still growing.

State-Owned Companies

Estimates are that Indian state-owned companies own and operate 75 percent of India's energy assets and infrastructure. The level of government ownership varies across these companies; as does their profitability, quality of leadership, management and function. The latter used to be much more clear-cut, particularly when it came to the national oil companies (NOCs); it was easy to categorize them as upstream, midstream, and downstream. Increasingly, a number of NOCs have been transitioning to become integrated companies.

The major state-owned oil and gas companies include the Oil and Natural Corporation (ONGC), its subsidiary ONGC Videsh Ltd., Oil India Limited (OIL), Gas Authority of India Limited (GAIL), Indian Oil Corporation Limited (IOC), Bharat Petroleum Corporation Limited (BPCL), and Hindustan Petroleum Corporation Limited (HPCL). Major state-owned non-oil and gas companies include Coal India Limited (CIL) and its subsidiaries operate almost all the mines in the country. The Nuclear Power Corporation of India Limited (NPCIL) constructs and operates all of India's civilian nuclear reactors. The National Thermal Power Corporation Limited (NTPC) is the state-owned thermal power generating company that operates coal and gas-based power plants. The National Hydroelectric Power Corporation Limited develops hydroelectric power projects.

Relations between the Government and State-Owned Companies

A government official noted that the government "provides general direction" to the state owned companies. Though experts believe that there have been positive changes in government-company relations, there is some concern (even among a group of experts appointed by the government) that these changes have been too "incremental." Government interference has lessened and the companies have become more independent. But the government's influence is still unmistakable. It can be seen in personnel appointments and extensions, as well as in price setting and production targets, among other things.

State-owned companies in India are under the administrative control of designated ministries. The oil and gas companies, for example, come under the MPNG. All state-owned companies are not created equal, nor are they treated equally. Of the many state-owned oil and gas companies, four—BPCL, HPCL, IOC, ONGC—have been designated *navratnas* (literally this term means nine precious stones). This gives these companies a little more financial and operational autonomy than other PSUs enjoy in their ability to form joint ventures, strategic alliances, and subsidiaries; in the amount of capital expenditure they can incur; in ensuring that each has an audit committee; and in the composition of their board of directors.

Personnel

The boards of the companies have both independent and government directors. Since the government is the main promoter, it typically can nominate

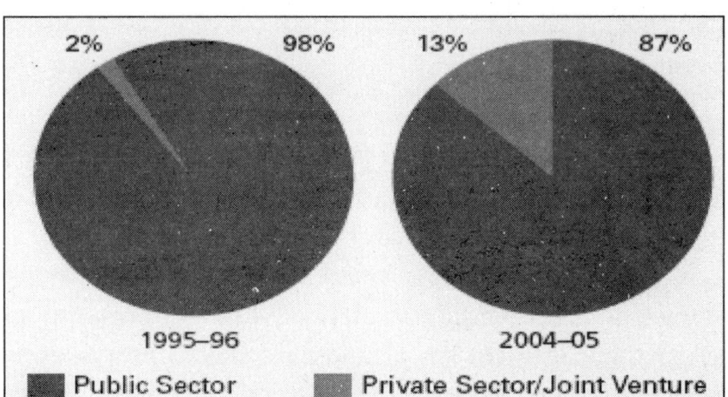

Source: Ministry of Petroleum and Natural Gas, India (petroleum.nic.in/petstat.pdf)

Figure 3.1: Domestic Oil Production by Sector

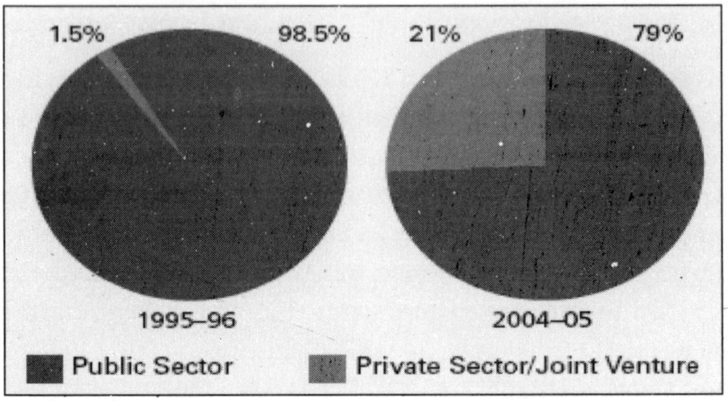

Source: Ministry of Petroleum and Natural Gas, India (petroleum.nic.in/petstat.pdf)

Figure 3.2: Domestic Natural Gas Production by Sector

two persons on the board, although this can vary. The government also has a role in approving the other directors of the board. These so-called independent directors are eminent persons or professionals appointed by the cabinet from a list put forward by the Public Enterprise Selection Board (PESB). Assessments indicate that this has made for "quicker decision-making," brought in a fresh outlook, motivated employees, and improved overall performance in a number of these companies. But there is widespread criticism that the boards of these companies are not truly empowered and that appointments are politically motivated. Critics contend that the government role in their appointment means that even the independent directors are independent in name only. The government also has the dominant role in appointing the management of state-owned companies. Those appointing personnel have to take into account not just the recommendations of the PESB and the preferences of the minister concerned, but often also politics, regional, and union sentiment.

Processes

There has also been concern (including by a government-appointed committee) that the government continues to interfere in the day-to-day affairs of companies, particularly in purchasing decisions, and this gives rise to accusations of corruption and delays. The government persists in controlling most management travel, and a number of proposals—even from the *navratnas*—still require approval. It also conducts quarterly performance reviews of the companies.

Production Targets and Pricing

The government also plays a role in determining prices and production targets. Production targets for all *navratna* NOCs, for example, are set annually through MoUs between the MPNG and the companies. The government also affects the pricing of products produced by the PSUs. Some companies are affected more adversely—for example, companies marketing petroleum products, which sometimes lament that they get the short end of the stick (while the upstream companies suffer less from the burden of subsidies and artificially low prices). These OMCs—like IOC, HPCL, and BPCL—sometimes have to sell their products below cost. This year, for the first time, these companies reported losses in the first quarter as a result of the government holding retail prices artificially low despite increasing global crude oil prices. While the government attempted to offer them some aid, differences between the Finance and P&NG Ministries over what was acceptable delayed the process.

Benefits

Companies also derive benefits from their association with the government, as many private sector players will be quick to point out. Therefore they may not want to totally disavow their association, even if it sometimes seems as if leadership is straining at the leash. Robert Manning, in fact, has called the relationship between the energy bureaucracy and the state-owned companies "mutually reinforcing." The government exercises control. The companies get preferential treatment and still operate in a closed market. Even when markets are cracked open a bit, the state-owned companies find it easier to absorb losses because of government support. For example, in the downstream oil sector, private companies like Reliance Industries Limited (RIL) and Essar—which priced their products at the high end of government limits to avoid losses—have seen their market share fall since the end of December 2005. However, state-owned companies have been able to sustain lower prices and gain market share. As mentioned above, the government issues oil bonds to the state-owned oil companies to rescue their balance sheets from these losses.

Private Energy Companies

A number of private energy companies operate in India today. In the oil and gas sector, these include the Indian companies Essar Oil Limited (EOL),

Reliance Industries Limited (RIL) and Videocon Industries. Foreign companies operating in the oil and gas sector include the BG Group, BP, Cairn Energy Limited, and Royal Dutch Shell. Private energy companies operating in India, especially in the mid- and downstream oil sector, continue to face the challenge of certain unfavorable government policies. Nonetheless, their role across the energy sector is increasing. While some companies have tried and given up on the energy sector, others are rediscovering it. Recent figures indicate that private sector or public-private joint ventures control about 13 percent of oil production and more than one-fifth of natural gas production. In 2004-05, the private sector owned a quarter of the installed refinery capacity. They also marketed 15.2 percent of petroleum products; in 1990-91 their market share was nil.

In general, the government is giving private companies a warmer welcome, and they are becoming savvier players. Recently private firms demanded financial support from the government. Both RIL and Essar asked for oil bonds like the ones PSUs receive from the MPNG to support the burden placed on their retailing operations. In the past, RIL has also demanded a discount on the crude supplied to them by state-owned upstream companies, similar to discounts benefiting the downstream PSUs. But these companies continue to tread cautiously and are careful to maintain good relations with both the central and state governments. They still require licenses from the government or approval for their development plans in the E&P sector.

A Strategic Approach: Way Forward

India do not have an overarching energy strategy—instead it has a number of disparate policies. Because many politicians and analysts use the terms "strategy" and "policy" interchangeably, it is not always an obvious distinction. Separate vision statements have emerged from the different energy-related ministries and departments. The Hydrocarbon Vision: 2025 report, for example, focused exclusively on oil and gas. Even within Ministries, the emphasis tends to be on specific and limited polices rather than a long-term, integrated strategy.

While there continues to be debate about whether an overarching strategy is necessary, India's decision-makers recognize that—at the very least—the country's disparate energy policies need to be integrated. This notion has proved problematic so far. There has been little indication of how policies should be prioritized, no plan for funding them, and often a gap between policymaking and implementation.

Despite these incongruities, there does seem to be a dominant policy trend toward diversification of sources, suppliers, pricing, and technologies. Diversification is also evident in the number and variety of proposals to increase energy security for India. At its most basic level, policy diversification offers India more options, not just in terms of energy security, but in foreign policy as well. Pursuing multiple tracks also helps ensure that India is not affected by area-specific shocks.

Today, India is attempting to close the gap between the demand and supply of oil through what one observer has called "a series of measures." On the supply side, this includes encouraging domestic exploration and production, acquiring upstream assets abroad, oil diplomacy, fuel diversification, maintaining strategic oil stocks, and regulatory reform. On the demand side, this comprises regulatory reform, rationalizing prices and taxes, fuel substitution, and conservation and efficiency measures.

Supply-Side Policies

Ironically, India's supply-side oil policies are decidedly Churchillian. Churchill's thoughts on oil—"on no one quality, on no one process, on no one country, on no one route and on no one field must we be dependent. Safety and certainty in oil lie in variety and variety alone"—are shared in India. The rider in India's case is "on no one fuel must we be dependent." And Indian policymakers have taken a number of steps to try to ensure that India achieves each of those goals.

Domestic Exploration and Production (E&P) Scenario

As noted above, India's domestic oil production figures have been dismal and unable to keep up with demand. ONGC, India's largest producer, has decreased production over the last few years. While its profits have grown, it failed to meet its production targets during 2005–06, falling short by 8 percent. There was a major disruption last year due to a fire at the offshore Bombay High field, which accounts for a significant portion of ONGC's production. The shortfall had to be made up through increased imports. With ONGC accounting for three-fourths of India's domestic crude output, its poor domestic production performance has had a significant impact.

ONGC has also had a poor record of discoveries of late. The discoveries it has made do little more than replace the existing fields that have been going offline.159 Former petroleum minister Aiyar even mocked ONGC for being unable to find new fields while others, like Cairn Energy, have made discoveries. He accused ONGC of focusing more on foreign activities than domestic ones (a criticism often leveled at him as well). Critics from other quarters have stated that ONGC's ventures into retail and other services have also taken away from its core business of E&P, which is suffering from lack of attention and resources. ONGC's discovery-to-exploration record from 2000 to 2005 stood at 42 percent, while others, like RIL and Cairn, had far better records of 71 percent and 80 percent, respectively. But even their discoveries have been few and far between. In addition, a number of areas that could hold potential reserves have not been explored. As of 1999, only six of India's twenty-six sedimentary basins had been explored in depth. The government has tried to increase domestic exploration and production through at least three different policies designed to:

- Encourage investment,
- Strengthen the NOCs, and
- Improve recovery.

Encourage Investment

In 1997–98, India's NDA coalition government realized that the state-owned companies did not have sufficient technological or financial resources, as banks are often unwilling to finance exploration ventures in India. Private investors—both foreign and domestic—were also put off by the operating restrictions in India's oil and gas sector.

Accordingly, the government instituted the New Exploration Licensing Policy (NELP) to encourage investment in the E&P sector. Since then five licensing rounds have been completed and a sixth is underway. The Directorate General of Hydrocarbons—the *de facto* upstream regulator—monitors implementation of the policy.

NELP aims to fast track the government's system for awarding oil and gas exploration licenses and to provide greater transparency. In theory, it provides equal treatment to public and private sector companies, paying market-driven prices for the crude they produce. It also provides tariff concessions for companies. NELP does not require that proposed energy projects include state participation or a minimum investment commitment.

Once the government announces a licensing round, they accept bids for six months. To attract foreign companies and funding, petroleum ministers routinely go on international road shows. For the current round (February–

September 2006), the minister or ministry officials have visited Australia, Canada, Dubai, Malaysia, the United Kingdom, and the United States. Their pitch can sometimes be exaggerated—a former minister admitted to an audience of former diplomats that his referring to the Bay of Bengal as South Asia's North Sea in a briefing to foreign investors was "hype." It takes two to four months to announce the winners after the bidding is closed. It then takes about two months to negotiate and finalize production sharing contracts with the winning companies or consortiums. A company is given a specific period of time to explore a block. If a discovery is not made within the specified time frame, either the company has to file for an extension or the block reverts back to the government, which can then put it up for sale again. If a company does not make promised investments, the Directorate General of Hydrocarbons can also recommend to the Ministry of Petroleum and Natural Gas that the company be asked to surrender its blocks, as happened recently with RIL and ONGC.

NELP has been seen as a way of bringing in much-needed technology, skill, and capital to the E&P sector. Initial interest was limited partly due to bad timing—oil prices were low at the time and demand was slow. There were also delays due to the still complex bureaucratic process and a lack of clarity on the tax structure. MPNG delayed announcing tax incentives. When it did make an announcement, the Ministry could not get the Income Tax Department to approve some of the tax features in time (including equalizing corporate tax with the NOCs' rate, which was 10 percent lower).

NELP has attracted greater attention recently. Three years ago under the offer of twenty four blocks for NELP-IV, the government received forty-six bids; last year, under NELPV offering twenty blocks, there were sixty-nine bids; and in the round ending in September 2006 that offered fifty-five blocks, there were 165 bids. Cairn Energy's 2005 discovery of oil in the Mangala field in Rajasthan (which is expected to be producing by the end of 2007) as well as the spike in oil prices has sparked somewhat more interest. The number of private (particularly foreign) participants in bidding has especially increased in the recent rounds. Of the sixty-six companies bidding in the sixth round, thirty-five are foreign.

While a greater number of companies want to participate, progress has been limited. In the current round, despite government expectations, with a few exceptions, the oil majors stayed away. Of the 165 bids in NELP-VI, 110 came from the public sector. Potential foreign investors do not perceive India as having much oil; they have preferred to put their money into safer bets. This appears to be true of Indian companies as well—in fact, the NOCs seem to be increasingly focused abroad, where they consider returns to be better.

Furthermore, there have been delays in awarding contracts and little or poor seismic data available. Delays in gaining required approvals from other departments like the Ministry of Environment and Forests have also frustrated the participants. Regulatory procedures are still unclear and concerns remain that despite its best intentions, the Indian government is loath to give up total control. The majors thus have stayed away (except for BP), though smaller independent companies have continued to take part in the bidding process.

Private players are concerned about political changes and how they might affect their interests. There is also a perception that state-owned companies still get preferential treatment and better acreages. This was the case initially, at least, when state-owned companies were awarded what were considered the best blocks and the rights to more than 60 percent of all the blocks offered in the second, third, and fourth rounds. On the other hand, they were not offered some of the concessions and terms that private participants were given and state-owned companies had to sell their oil at a much lower rate at home than on the global market. Some analysts argue that state-owned companies' success in bidding rounds might owe in part to their knowledge of how the system works. This has, in fact, led to a number of private companies submitting joint bids with the NOCs and in the fourth and

Fifth rounds, 25 and 39 percent respectively of the blocks were awarded to such consortiums. The government meanwhile is learning along the way—in the recent round, it obtained environmental clearances in advance for the blocks being offered. It is also considering an open acreage policy, which would make blocks available year-round outside the NELP framework.

Strengthen the National Oil Companies (NOCs)

While the navratna NOCs have tended to generate profits, some consider them inefficient and uncompetitive. There are indications that these NOCs need improved exploration technology, better management, and the ability to meet global benchmarks for efficiency. Some have suggested that if the Government reduced its role (by setting up a holding company to manage its interest), this could strengthen the NOCs and allow them to attract better talent and make better alliances. The companies have been losing talent to the private sector due to uncompetitive salaries and benefits. The administrative ministries recognize this problem, though reform on this front has been slow—

to the extent that the 45,000 officers in the oil public sector undertakings (PSUs) have threatened to go on strike because of their compensation. This state of affairs is partly a result of the nature of the Indian system—even if one Ministry (the MPNG in this case) recognizes the problem, it is the Department of Public Enterprises (in the Ministry of Heavy Industries) that has to agree to a hike in salaries. Although there tends to be political agreement on the need to reform the state-owned companies, the main political parties disagree about how to achieve reform.

Improved Recovery

There is also a push to get better recovery from existing fields. ONGC, for example, is aiming to improve its recovery factor from 28 percent to 40 percent. There are plans for greater investment, including $2 billion in fourteen oilfields as part of an Enhanced Oil Recovery program. OIL plans both to develop discovered fields faster and increase recovery from existing fields and has set higher targets for the future. Increased domestic exploration and production alone, however, are unlikely to quench India's "thirst-for-oil". A former petroleum minister acknowledged that even if more oil is found, India will likely find further use for it; therefore, the country would have to continue to look abroad for additional sources.

Acquisition of Upstream Assets Abroad

There is increasing concern about India's susceptibility to volatile international oil prices because of its dependence on foreign oil. But the solution proposed by a number of decision makers and experts—and being implemented by Indian NOCs—also seems to lie abroad in stakes in overseas E&P companies and equity in oil and gas blocks. There is some debate about the wisdom of this policy. Some decision makers consider equity oil cheaper and therefore "worthwhile" to acquire. They believe that equity oil abroad will "ensure cheap and reliable oil supply" and they point to OVL getting equity oil at $10 to $14 a barrel. The NOCs have ambitious plans—OVL has set a long-term target of producing 60 million tons of oil a year from overseas properties by 2025. ONGC aims to double its reserves by 2020, with 20 million tons coming from OVL, which has spent about $4.5 Billion abroad. These targets have already been pushed back from those set in 2004, when the aim was to produce 20 million tons by 2010.

Future Strategy

Setbacks do not seem to have dissuaded Indian companies; they have changed and adapted. The NOCs have taken a few steps to be more competitive. OVL was formed as an ONGC subsidiary in 1996 to focus on acquiring and developing overseas assets. Late last year, the government decided to form a comparable unit under OIL, with similar financial powers. The NOCs have also formed partnerships with other domestic and foreign companies, both public and private. In December, 2004 IOC-OIL formed a consortium, in which OIL acts as operator. In July 2005 ONGC and Mittal decided to jointly pursue oil and gas projects (exploration, development, and production-related activities) in Central Asia and Africa. With Mittal having a presence in Malaysia, Indonesia, CIS, and Angola, this partnership offered some advantages. In December 2005 RIL and CNOOC agreed to explore for oil in Africa together. And in January 2006 Shell Exploration and ONGC signed an MoU. In January 2006 Chinese and Indian NOCs also agreed to bid jointly for stakes in companies and blocks as part of a larger set of cooperative energy agreements signed by India and China. There also seems to be a clearer interest in cooperating on India's part. China might eventually decide that it is better to partner with the oil majors. Even within India, many considered the MoU merely a pet project of the petroleum minister at the time, and therefore not apt to generate much activity.

The state-owned companies are learning to cope with the challenges of dealing with local politics, leaders, and social groups who want to have a say in how they develop these ventures. As part of this process, the NOCs are developing new projects in host countries—OIL, for example, runs an E&P consultancy service in Nigeria, helping companies—including local ones—evaluate and submit bids (though this service has recently run into trouble). OVL is taking up refinery upgrades and pipeline contracts in Sudan, and private company RIL has decided to take a 30 percent stake in a refinery construction project in Yemen.

Private Indian companies are getting into the act as well and are organizing themselves accordingly. Reports indicate that RIL has created a twenty-person group that will search for potential investment assets in Nigeria, Congo, Cameroon, Mauritania, Namibia, Ivory Coast, Gabon, Sierra Leone, Guinea Bissau, and Angola. The company tends to create local subsidiaries for its international operations to minimize friction and manage more efficiently. RIL is also being careful not to compete directly with

ONGC—part of the reason might be that they do not want to run up against government interests, especially since most of their refinery output still goes to the state-owned OMCs. The government clearly sees the acquisition of upstream assets abroad as a priority and realizes that better integration on its part is needed.

Cooperative Dialogues and Agreements

India has signed cooperative agreements or memorandums, or discussed energy partnerships with a number of countries including Japan, South Korea, 220 Romania, the Gulf Cooperation Council, the Association for South-East Asian Nations, the South Asian Association for Regional Cooperation, BIMSTEC, and Australia. The usefulness of some of these discussions has been questioned. The Memorandum of Cooperation signed in Romania, for example, agreed on the need to increase energy productivity and prevent pollution, seemingly self-evident points.

India has also started broader energy dialogues with both the EU and the United States. After the fifth Hague summit, India and the EU established a panel to discuss energy issues, with working groups to discuss coal and conversion of coal-related technologies, energy efficiency and renewables, and energy associations including India's participation in ITER. India and the United States started an energy dialogue in May 2005; it had five working groups including one that will focus on oil and gas.

In Central Asia, India is looking toward purchasing assets and participating in pipeline projects. In the long-term, it is also seeking to acquire oil from the BTC pipeline through the Suez Canal or the Israeli Ashkelon-Eilat pipeline. Earlier this year, the Indian prime minister visited Uzbekistan, following a trip to India last year by the Uzbek president. Two of the seven memorandums they signed were energy related. The two countries agreed to form a joint working group on hydrocarbons. GAIL will explore the possibility of constructing LPG factories, gas pipelines, and gas processing facilities in Uzbekistan. Kazakhstan is also a country of great interest to India.

Fuel Diversification Strategy

The government has been looking at fuel diversification as another way to meet India's energy needs—not just in terms of replacing oil, but also to satisfy additional demand. Despite the possibilities for a fuel diversification "solution," fossil fuels are projected to continue to be dominant sources of energy. Even if nuclear and renewable sources meet optimistic projections, they are not expected to contribute more than 15-17 percent of the country's energy supply by 2031–32. However, by 2050, technological advances are expected to make nuclear and solar major contributors of energy.

Natural Gas

The MPNG's Hydrocarbon Vision: 2025 report indicated that natural gas should be India's preferred source of energy. To encourage investment in domestic exploration and production, natural gas blocks are being offered as part of NELP. In total, 70 bcm of reserves are said to have been discovered through NELP. However, despite development efforts, domestic production alone is unlikely to meet demand in the country. So to increase and improve imports, India intends to add LNG terminals, encourage pipelines, acquire assets abroad, and conduct aggressive "gas diplomacy." There continue to be problems that could inhibit the greater availability and consequently the use of natural gas. Existing producing fields in the country are expected to witness a declining trend in production. In terms of India's efforts to acquire natural gas from abroad, questions of logistics, politics, cost-effectiveness, and security issues have continued to dog proposed pipelines. India has experienced setbacks in its quest for LNG abroad as well.

Coal

Given the country's large coal reserves, the government has been trying to encourage more efficient mining and greater coal production. However, estimates indicate that reserves will be exhausted in forty years if there is a 5 percent growth rate in production. At the current rate of consumption, proven reserves will be exhausted in eighty years. Importing coal is more expensive than using domestic coal and requires additional investment in ports and railroads, which would raise the cost of power generation.

Most officials recognize the biggest problem for the coal sector, though few will admit it publicly: CIL's monopoly. The company is considered inefficient (production costs are estimated at 50 percent higher than in leading countries), with too many employees (it is the second largest employer in the world), strong unionization, too few funds, and low productivity. The company lacks the technical (and sometimes financial) capacity to mine efficiently and access coal in deeper areas.

Nuclear Energy

The government is moving ahead with various plans to increase the country's capacity to produce nuclear energy. Currently, eight nuclear reactors are under construction, with a total capacity of 3420 MW. Earlier this year, eight more reactors (which would have a total capacity of 6800 MW) were cleared for construction. The recent nuclear "deal" between President Bush and Prime Minister Manmohan Singh—which would allow the sale or transfer of nuclear technology, equipment, and materials for India's civilian nuclear program—brought to the fore the potential for nuclear energy in India. On the basis of this prospect and subsequent international cooperation, the prime minister doubled the nuclear energy production target to 40,000 MW.

But nuclear energy may not prove to be the fix that some purport it to be. India has limited quantities of uranium (only enough to produce 10,000 MW), and reactors using thorium—of which India has large reserves—are probably still decades away. Officials acknowledge that it is going to take a while for nuclear energy to make a significant impact in India. Nuclear energy also involves a number of waste disposal and safety issues that have not been fully thought through. Finally, relative to other sources, nuclear energy remains an expensive proposition.

Hydro Sources

Because of high initial set-up costs and risks, the government is providing financial support to some development projects in hydroelectricity generation. It is trying to attract private sector investment, and is considering a proposal that would put state-owned companies in charge of projects until they are approved. The projects would then be transferred to private companies or operated in a joint venture with them. The government is also trying to rationalize tariffs, accurately assess completion costs, and provide investment incentives. Yet problems persist with this energy source as well. The World Bank and other funders have become reluctant to fund hydroelectric projects. Project clearances take time and involve land acquisition and dealings with state governments, which have their own agendas. There has also been opposition on environmental and social grounds, as these projects can displace large numbers of people.

Non-conventional Sources

With limited proven oil and gas reserves, rising oil prices, depleting coal deposits, increasing greenhouse gas emissions, an endangered ecosystem, and significant amounts of nuclear energy still years away, and the government has been encouraging the development of nonconventional energy sources. In the long-run, these sources are considered cleaner and more viable than fossil fuels and their external costs are less extensive. Given below is a brief look at some of the options in this sector:

Biodiesel

The government has supported establishment of a $10 million biodiesel production facility in Mysore that aims to produce 10 million liters a year (from jatropha and other oil seeds). It is estimated that India has 50 million hectares of wasteland and 34 million hectares of protected forest areas that could be used to cultivate such crops. There is talk of producing about 100,000 MW of power from biodiesel.

Solar Energy

India is considered to have the largest decentralized solar energy program in the world. With estimates of about 300 clear sunny days annually, this program is considered to have vast potential.

Wind Energy

By 2004 India was the fifth largest producer of wind energy, with 95 percent of the investment coming from the private sector. The total installed capacity was 3595 MW. By 2007, it is estimated that an additional 3,000 MW of additional capacity of wind energy will be installed. The Planning Commission estimates that India has the potential for grid-connected wind capacity of around 20,000 MW.

Others Sources

The government is also looking to encourage energy development from tides, biomass, and hydrogen.

As the Planning Commission has said, it would require a "more visionary plan" for India to get more than a modest energy contribution from non-conventional sources. Data on these sources and evaluation of their potential are not up to speed. But there are significant problems to overcome. Biodiesel and biomass projects divert much-needed water (as well as fertilizer, the production of which in turn requires natural gas). Solar energy remains expensive. As for wind energy, there are limited regions in the country where wind speeds allow effective harnessing of this resource. There are also logistical issues and trade-offs that will have to be weighed by planners, producers, and users. The development of almost all non-conventional energy sources requires land, which is limited in India. This gives rise to food security concerns in addition to potential environmental problems.

Strategic Oil Stocks

To hedge against short-term supply disruption, India is considering the establishment of a strategic petroleum reserve (SPR). The country has stored oil for some time now. Reports indicate that India's current reserves offer a cushion of twelve to thirteen days. In addition, India has access to thirty-five to forty days of refined products. Indian oil companies are required to maintain these crude oil reserves and petroleum products. As a precautionary measure, in anticipation of a crisis or a substantial price hike, they sometimes also buy up additional oil supplies. For example, in June 2004, Indian downstream companies bought 25 million barrels reportedly for such purposes. The downstream companies were also formerly required to maintain "military stock levels" to supply the military.

The original proposal for creating an SPR was put forward in 1998. But the government took the next few years "studying the issue," and only made an announcement about the SPR in 2003, when the Iraq war had created a renewed sense of urgency. While the Indian Planning Commission suggested a reserve that would store ninety days of the country's oil imports, the government decided that the reserve would hold 5 million metric tons p.a. (mmtpa) or fifteen days of the country's oil imports. India has been seeking advice on the construction and operation of SPRs from countries like Japan and the United States. Indian officials also met with IEA officials to discuss IEA aid and ideas about coordinating the use of such stocks.

In 2004, Indian Oil established the Indian Strategic Petroleum Reserves Ltd (ISPR) to take the project forward (its equity has since been transferred to the OIDB) and build and operate the reserve. However, there have been delays. When this project was initially announced, the minister in charge said it would take two years (until 2006) to construct the SPR. Now the plan is to begin constructing the reserve in July 2007 and have it operating by 2011–12.

Regulatory Reforms

In 2002, the NDA government of India proposed a Petroleum Regulatory Board Bill that called for the creation of an independent regulator for the downstream petroleum sector. There was skepticism about how independent such a regulator would really be, not least because the bill contained clauses indicating that the government could "give direction," a rather all encompassing term, if this were in the public interest. Concerns also surfaced about the government influencing the appointment of members of this board, whose functions are outlined very loosely. A Parliamentary Standing Committee suggested amendments, including limiting the government's ability to give direction only in cases of war and natural calamities and extending the regulation to the gas sector as well. The bill, however, went nowhere. Late last year, the UPA government reintroduced the bill as the expanded Petroleum and

Natural Gas Regulatory Board Bill to incorporate a number of changes. The bill was passed in March 2006, and contains provisions to regulate the refining, processing, storage, transportation, distribution, marketing, and sale of petroleum and natural gas products. The board was expected to be in place by September but has not yet been constituted. However, it was not structured to have authority to regulate the upstream sector, a fact that is highly criticized because a number of the companies involved are integrated or on their way to becoming integrated. Taking it a step further, there have been recommendations to establish one regulating agency for the entire energy sector. On the flip side are those who call for separate regulation—even for the gas and oil sectors. There also continue to be questions about the board's independence, and whether it will have any teeth when it comes to the issue of pricing.

Demand-Side Policies

Demand-side management has taken a backseat to supply-side management in India—in terms of official attention, resources, and even media coverage. Given below are typical instances of a few of the related areas in which the government has formulated policies. While this section does not take a more detailed look at the policy initiatives related to R&D and education, it should be noted that the government has been trying to promote them to encourage fuel substitution and efficiency measures.

Price Reforms

There is a realization that price reform is necessary—both to lessen the burden on state-owned oil companies and the central exchequer, as well as to change consumer behavior. Time and again the prime minister has talked of the need to pursue a "rational pricing policy." It has been suggested that subsidies be removed altogether, but many feel that a more realistic solution would be to implement a targeted and transparent subsidy system. Analysts have indicated that what is required is a set of comprehensive, transparent steps to price reform. While it has not undertaken a comprehensive approach, the government has been taking small steps toward reform as suggested by various committees and reports. A former MPNG official noted that over the last few years, governments have created an environment in which tough price decisions can be taken.

For years, there was an administered price mechanism (APM) in place that determined prices for petroleum products. In 2002, to rationalize oil and gas prices, the NDA government dismantled the APM (with the Congress party supporting the move). The government also reduced—but did not eliminate—subsidies for LPG and kerosene. As a result, even though crude oil prices increased by over 90 percent between April 2002 and April 2005, subsidies on petroleum products were reduced by 68 percent. However, there continued to be a price ceiling and the retail price of petrol at the pump only increased 43 percent during that period.

The APM thus is yet to be fully been dismantled and the shift to a market-based pricing system is incomplete. Prices are based on the principle of import parity (the government announced recently that they would shift to the trade parity principle), but in reality the government continues to set retail prices.

In October, 2006, the government set up the Rangarajan Committee, a panel of experts that makes recommendations on fuel pricing and taxation policy. The head of the committee called for the government to stay "at arm's length from price determination." Its report, released in February, 2007 called for greater freedom for OMCs to set prices for their products and subsidization of kerosene based on the economic situation of the consumer. The Committee recommended substantially increasing the price of LPG, with complete removal of the subsidy in the future. It added that the government should cease asking its upstream companies to bear a direct portion of the subsidy burden. It recommended funding subsidies through levies that the upstream companies are already required to pay to the Oil Industry Development Board and from the Government's budget. It further suggested that a uniform freight charge be discontinued—currently this charge on petroleum products is the same across India, regardless of the distance transported. Very few of these recommendations have been implemented amidst criticism that they would make for a more profitable industry, but would not address underlying problems.

Recently, the petroleum minister announced that the government would allow the OMCs to hike petroleum product prices if crude oil prices rose above $73 a barrel. The regulatory board appointed under the Petroleum and Natural Gas Regulatory Board Act would—if the Act were implemented—"formulate and regulate the pricing mechanism and ensure competitive structure of this sector." The OMCs are hoping that the board involves itself in pricing issues. However, the Act gives the regulator monitoring authority, but not price setting authority.

Fuel Taxation

One third of the Indian government's tax income is estimated to come from petroleum products. In addition, states also tax these products at differing rates. Estimates indicate that levies and taxes on petroleum products—including state taxes, custom duties, and excise levies—constitute more than half the price the Indian consumer pays for them. The government benefits, at least financially, from increases in the price of petroleum products since taxation is based on a percentage of the basic value. Critics argue that it is these high taxes—more than price hikes reflecting the higher cost of crude oil—that cause inflation.

When the federal government is denounced for higher prices at the pump, it asks states to cut their taxes to minimize the burden on the consumer. When the MPNG raises the price of petroleum products, it also often negotiates with the Finance Ministry to reduce central taxes to minimize the effect of the price hike. (Because it affects revenue in a less direct way, there are those who contend that the government prefers issuing oil bonds to the OMCs over reducing taxes.) Sometimes the Finance Ministry also decreases customs duty when global crude oil prices increase. Over the years, there have been cuts on taxes and duties on some petroleum products (WTO commitments have required some of these). In the 2005–06 Union budget, the government announced custom duty cuts for crude (from 10 to 5 percent) and petroleum products (from 15 to 20 percent down to 10 percent).

Cooperation among Laboratories, Academic Institutions and the Automobile Industry

There have been some attempts to encourage the availability and use of biofuels—especially biodiesel and ethanol. States like Chhattisgarh have announced that they intend to become biofuel self-reliant by 2015, and are encouraging the cultivation of jatropha in all districts. While India is the world's fourth largest producer of ethanol and the largest user of imported ethanol from Brazil, the ethanol is often used for purposes more profitable than fuel. Inspired by Brazil's success, however, the Indian government is looking anew at ethanol to alleviate the demand pressure on oil. Among other things, it is encouraging investment in ethanol production plants. ONGC, for example, is currently setting up an ethanol refinery, in which it has offered equity to Petrobras. Furthermore; a five percent ethanol blend has been used in about a third of Indian states since 2004, and the government recently announced that starting in October 2006, all refiners will have to produce such a blend. If the program is successful, it might increase this requirement to a ten percent blend in 2007.

Another proposal being considered is to blend diesel with 20 percent biodiesel. The Indian Railways has already been using a 5 percent biodiesel blend. The government has also been trying to encourage the use of LNG and has discussed customs duty exemptions on LNG imports.

The judiciary has played a role in increasing fuel substitution, for example, by mandating the use of CNG (initially by 2001—in the case of public transportation in Delhi—and later applied to a larger set of cities). Egged on by the Supreme Court, which was acting on the filing of public interest litigation, Delhi replaced its entire fleet of diesel buses with CNG buses in 2002. Today, all public transportation in Delhi is required to run on CNG. The Energy Information Administration estimates that this has replaced about a quarter of a million gallons of diesel and gasoline.

Apart from substituting transportation fuels, the Electricity Act 2003 tried to accelerate the development of power generation from non-conventional sources (and away from the increased use of petroleum products to produce power). States are requiring power distributors to purchase power generated from renewable sources. Karnataka requires 5–10 percent generation from renewable sources; Maharashtra, Orissa, and Gujarat (which has required 2 percent since 2004–05, increasing 0.5 percent a year) have also joined the bandwagon.

Conservation and Efficiency

The Planning Commission's Vision: 2020 on Energy and the Environment (Planning Commission, 2006) emphasized that future growth should be as "resource-efficient and environmentally benign" as possible. Looking ahead, it said that more efficient use of energy is a major necessity. Some estimates indicate that by 2031-32, efficiency measures by end users could reduce India's overall energy requirements by 5.3 percent. Increased efficiency in the transport sector—through mass transport, better use of vehicles, and better fuel efficiency—could reduce needs by another 4.2 percent. Official estimates indicate an even higher potential energy savings of 20 percent countrywide.

The Indian president has listed conservation as one of the key foundations on which to base India's energy security, stating that security cannot be achieved unless the minimum possible energy is used and India cuts down on energy losses. The head of one of India's main business confederations has estimated that India could shave more than $2 billion off its oil import bill if it cut consumption by 7 percent. India's tenth Five Year Plan set a target for 13 percent savings through efficiency, though it did not lay out which sectors should achieve these savings. It also called for benchmarking the Indian hydrocarbon sector's efficiency against that of other countries. A number of efficiency efforts and initiatives have been concentrated in the power sector. Realizing that the transportation sector is going to continue to depend on petroleum products for the near future, the Planning Commission has called for efficiency on the oil demand side through use of more efficient automobiles, availability of increased public transport, electrification of railways (to move away from diesel), and encouragement of the use of biodiesel and coal-to-liquid efforts.

In theory, the Petroleum Conservation Research Association (PCRA) under the Petroleum Ministry is responsible for conservation issues related to petroleum products. The PCRA's role is supposed to include creating awareness, promoting the use of efficient equipment and vehicles, and supporting R&D efforts. The Bureau of Energy Efficiency under the Ministry of Power has been given the responsibility of coordinating overall efficiency efforts, but so far it has been neglected.

There has been some movement on this front. Authorities are working toward phasing out older vehicles in cities like Delhi and requiring Bharat-III emission standards (which are also more fuel efficient) in at least eleven cities, which were to have upgraded to Bharat-III by April 2005 and Bharat-

IV five years after that. By 2005, Bharat-II standards were required to have been adopted for cars, light commercial vehicles, and bus and trucks across the country. There have been some delays. The government has announced that starting in 2010, Euro-II equivalent norms (Bharat-II) would be implemented in the entire country and Euro-III norms (or their equivalent) in select cities. The government has also announced cuts in excise on small cars.

The government has also directed its oil companies to produce and market higher grade lubricants and encouraged state-owned refineries to upgrade facilities to make their use of petroleum products more efficient and to minimize losses in the production of those products. The PCRA, along with the NOCs, has also been conducting annual Oil Conservation Weeks since 1991, which have now become Oil and Gas Conservation Fortnights. These are used to acknowledge companies' conservation and efficiency improvement efforts and to create awareness about related issues.

Conservation and efficiency efforts have already paid some dividends. Petrol and diesel consumption growth has slowed (Between 1980–81 and 2003–04, the petrol consumption growth rate stood at 7.4 percent a year, while that of diesel was 5.7 percent a year. Between years 2000–05, petrol consumption grew at the rate of 6.9 percent and diesel at 3.1 percent annually). These improvements have been attributed to better roads and more efficient vehicles. India is reaching outside its borders for help with improving energy efficiency. It has, for example, joined the U.S.-led Clean Development Initiative with China, South Korea, Japan, and Australia. One of the initiative's major areas of emphasis is energy efficiency.

India's Future Energy Security Policy Challenges

In a world characterized by both rapid change and uncertainty, India has to make the best use of available resources and opportunities to promote the well-being of its people. India's interests demand a stable, quiet environment in which it can concentrate on economic and social modernization and technological development. A country's desire for peace and rapid development, however, cannot by itself be a guarantee of its security and prosperity. India is pursuing a pioneering model of modernization via democracy—a model that holds important lessons for both India and other developing countries. It is a model that provides for grassroots participation in governance and development and whose openness, transparency and free avenues for expression are in accord with India's historical character as a benign, assimilative civilization (IAGS, 2004).

In a world in which rapid economic growth has usually been set in motion through political autocracy, India presents itself as a commendable democratic model of modernization. Even as Indian voters have regularly thrown out politicians who became too big for their boots, India has quietly moved from being an emblem of poverty to being a knowledge-driven nation threatening to steal high-tech jobs from the West.

India demonstrates that democratic politics and market economics can blend nicely for developing nations and that they need not follow the model set by South Korea, Taiwan, Thailand and other states which first achieved impressive economic growth under authoritarian rule before moving to democracy under pressure from their burgeoning middle classes. Autocratic rule is addictive and, as exemplified by Singapore, a transferal to a fully-fledged democracy can at times be difficult to achieve. Another lesson is that democracy takes roots through self-choice, not through imposition from outside.

Democracy also makes India's political future less uncertain in comparison to states that practice autocratic politics. For example, the question many ask is whether China will continue to grow economically and militarily in a linear fashion. That question arises from a basic contradiction in the two paths China is committed to pursuing: political autocracy and market capitalism. If China manages to resolve that contradiction, it could emerge as a peer competitor to the United States. The other possibility is that the paths of political autocracy and market capitalism are not reconcilable and that at some point they will collide, as they did in Indonesia, with negative consequences. If they do collide, the next question is whether China will be able to handle and manage the adverse fallout in a way that preserves its unity and rising strength. No one, however, is raising such questions about India.

Whether India will assume a global role commensurate with its size depends on a host of factors, including its leadership quality, strategic vision, and continued pursuit of growth-boosting policies, control of corruption, spread of education, political stability and internal cohesion. A key determinant of India's future will be its ability to meet its spiralling energy needs. Despite that challenge, India appears set on a rising economic path. Although democracy remains India's biggest asset, populist electoral considerations have prompted federal and state governments to ignore hard choices and seek soft options. An example is the way the unchecked influx of millions of illegal immigrants from Bangladesh has been allowed to strain the already-fragile ethnic balance in several parts of India's diverse North-East and exacerbates the internal security challenges there. More broadly, to help sustain its pride as the world's largest democracy, India has to demonstrate that fair elections bring not just new governments but also good, clean, national interest-focused Governance. Having disproved that its inherited social values are a barrier to rapid economic growth, India can now show that those values do not promote a lack of accountability, or a tolerance of political corruption, or even an aversion to hard decisions. It is against this background that India's energy-security challenges need to be seen (Challeney, 2007).

Policy Incentives to Establish Renewable Energy Power Projects

Policy Incentives

The policy incentives announced by the MNES to promote RE power projects include the following:

- No clearance is required from the Central Electricity Authority for power generation projects up to 1,000 million rupees.
- A tax holiday is allowed for RE power generation projects.
- A consolidated rate of customs duty has been made applicable for all items imported for a project under the "project imports" scheme, irrespective of the nature of the goods imported and their customs classification.
- Customs duty concessions are available for RE parts and equipment, including machinery required for renovation and modernization of power plants.
- The excise duty on a number of capital goods and instruments in the RE sector has been reduced or exempted.
- To encourage investment by private and public sector companies in renewable energy electricity generation, the MNES has issued guidelines to the states, which require the relevant state electricity boards, (SEB) to ensure the following:
    1. **Wheeling.** Each SEB is required to undertake to transmit on their grid power generated by an RE power project, and make such power available to the producer for captive use or to a third party within the state at a uniform wheeling (distribution)

charge of 2 percent of the energy fed to the grid, irrespective of the distance from the generating station. The third party must be a "high tension" consumer of the SEB, unless this stipulation is relaxed specifically by the SEB.

2. **Banking.** The SEB is required to permit the electricity generated to be banked for a period of up to one year.
3. **Sale of power.** The SEB is required to purchase electricity offered by the producer at a minimum rate of INR 2.25 per unit, with no restriction on the time or quantity of electricity supplied for sale. This rate is to be reviewed every year and will be linked to standard criteria such as the wholesale price index. Producers also have the option to sell the electricity they generate to third parties within the state at a rate to be mutually agreed upon.
4. **Exemption from duty.** Consumption of electricity generated by producers is exempt from the electricity duty.
5. **Sales tax benefits** are available to producers that own their project.
6. **Income tax benefits**, such as accelerated depreciation, are available to RE power projects.
7. **Concessions** given to industrial units in underdeveloped areas are provided, such as exemption from taxes and duties, capital subsidies, etc.
8. **Infrastructure facilities** such as access roads, water supply, cranes, power during construction period, etc., are provided, as is done with industrial estates.

1. Specific Fiscal Incentives

The largest number of proposals for CDM projects in India relate to biomass/cogeneration projects and wind-power projects. Accordingly, following is a brief list of fiscal incentives that will be available to such projects.

1. Biomass/Cogeneration Projects

- An 80 percent depreciation may be claimed in the first year for specified equipment required for cogeneration systems.
- A five-year income tax holiday with a 30 percent exemption for power generation projects with power purchase agreements.

- A customs duty leviable for RE projects of less than 50-MW capacity (under the "project import" scheme) is 20 percent ad valorem.
- Sales tax exemption is available in certain states.
- Banking, wheeling, and third-party sales benefits.

2. *Wind-power Projects*

- An 80 percent depreciation may be claimed in the first year for specified equipment required for wind-power projects.
- Income tax holiday,
- Concessional import duty on specified wind turbine parts.
- Sales tax, excise duty relief.
- Nine states have introduced specific policies to encourage such projects.
- Banking, wheeling, and third-party sales benefits.

CDM Project Opportunities

Investors will prefer CDM projects that satisfy three basic criteria:

1. High possibility of approval by the government.
2. Low transactions costs.
3. Significant reduction potential.

Energy Sector Priorities

Despite a slow start, the GoI is now actively trying to access GEF funds. This is partly because some of the activities have a high overlap with the developmental objectives of the government. The GoI has identified the following project ideas in accordance with its development objectives.

- Removal of implementation barriers of biomass-based power generation.
- Strategy for removing barriers in achieving industrial energy efficiency.
- Carbon reduction through grid-interactive PV power generation.
- Energy conservation through technological upgradation of steel rerolling mills.
- Solar PV diesel hybrid systems for decentralized village electrification.

- Cogeneration in cement plants.
- Carbon emission reduction in power plants.
- Decentralized rural electrification through biomass and solar energy through private participation.
- Switching to non-petroleum fuels, electricity-powered and hybrid engines in transport sector.
- Demand-side management in basic material and construction industry.
- Improving efficiency of rural agriculture pumpsets.
- Energy conservation in paper industry.

As the above list shows, the priority options for the GoI are efficient technologies in power generation, centralized and decentralized renewable energy options, and energy efficiency in steel and paper industries. The text submitted by India on flexible mechanisms states that no forestry sector projects will be allowed. Preference will be given to projects in the renewable sector and those with a focus on energy efficiency improvements. Projects that improve the quality of life of the very poor from the environmental standpoint and promote state-of the art, environmentally sound technology will be sought. The energy sector mitigation options identified above were ranked by policy makers on the basis of:

- Cost of mitigation.
- Feasibility of the option.
- Environmental and other benefits.
- Consonance with the overall development priorities of the country

Priority CDM Projects

Based on the above information, the following projects could be proposed for CDM in India.

Power Generation

1. Coal power plant using IGCC (integrated gasification combined cycle)
2. Coal power plant using PFBC (pulverized fluidized bed combustion)
3. Renovation and modernization of power plants

Renewables

1. Wind-based power generations (grid connected)
2. Solar-thermal energy for power generation (grid connected)
3. Wind pumps for agriculture

Industrial Efficiency

1. Direct reduction processes in iron and steel industry
2. Continuous pulp digesters in pulp and paper industry
3. Demand-side management: efficient motors

Power Generation

India currently has an installed power generation capacity of about 87481 MW, which is insufficient to meet the demands of the country. The demand for power has been growing at the rate of 9 per cent a year and is likely to accelerate because of the economic liberalization policies of the GoI. TERI estimates the power demand in India will be 385000 MW by the year 2020, requiring 380 billion dollars of investment in the power sector alone. Of the total generation capacity of the nation, 71% is based on coal. With proven reserves of about 70 billion tonnes and estimated reserves of about 200 billion tonnes, coal will continue to be the dominant fuel for power generation in the country. Hence introduction of cleaner technologies for coal utilization is one of the sustainable objectives of the nation. The proposed options for power generation are:

1. Coal power plant using IGCC
2. Coal power plant using PFBC
3. Renovation and modernization of power plants

Coal Power Plant using PFBC

PFBC is a clean and efficient technology for coal-based power generation. In this technology, the conventional combustion chamber of the gas turbine is replaced by a pressurized fluidized bed combustor. The products of combustion pass through a hot gas cleanup system before entering the turbine, thereby reducing the amount of CO_2 emitted through combustion. The CO_2 reduction from a per unit of power supplied at bus bar using PFBC, over the conventional technology is 0.18 kg. Replacing a conventional plant of 500 MW capacity with a PFBC plant will result in CO_2 emission reduction of 0.58

million tonnes a year. The national mitigation potential for this technological option has been calculated at 8.166 million tonnes of CO_2 annually.

As PFBC technology has a high capital cost, the cost of production is marginally higher than that from a conventional power plant. But savings in coal compensate for the higher costs. The technology results in considerably lower emissions of SO_2 and NO. The technology therefore has a good potential both from a commercial and an environmental perspective.

Coal Power Plant using IGCC

IGCC is one of the technologies being explored to improve the efficiency of power generation and reduce the environmental burden. A coal gasification combined cycle technology centres around two elements:

1. A gasification plant that converts the fuel into a combustible gas and purifies the gas.
2. A combined cycle power plant which produces synthetic gas that fuels a gas turbine whose hot exhaust gases are used to generate steam to drive a steam turbine.

The efficiency of the IGCC is the product of the gasification system efficiency and the combined cycle efficiency. The auxiliary power consumption in oxygen blown gasifier is much higher than air blown gasifier and other pulverized coal plants. It is approximately 20% of the gross output. The air separation plant is very energy intensive because of the cryogenic process involved for the production of oxygen. However, the net efficiency of this technology is significantly higher because of the higher calorific value of the synthetic gas produced. For the second-generation technologies, net efficiencies are expected to be in the range of 45%-50%.

The current capacity of thermal power plants (existing and sanctioned) is 12647 MW, and the GoI has cleared another 16898.5 MW capacity for implementation. These plants are expected to have a net efficiency of 36% whereas the state-of-the-art IGCC plants have net efficiencies of 46%. Estimates based on above efficiency levels indicate that an IGCC plant will result in CO_2 emission reductions of 0.25 kg/kWh. Replacing a conventional plant of 500 MW capacity with an IGCC plant will result in CO_2 emission reduction of 0.69 million tonnes. Assuming that IGCC would be adopted for 10% of the capacity sanctioned, 1690 MW, the total potential for emission reduction using IGCC will be 2.33 million tonnes of CO_2.

The proposed IGCC power plant will reduce emissions of SO_2, NOx, and SPM (suspended particulate matter). It will also reduce solid waste disposal by nearly 70% compared to direct coal-fired plants. An IGCC plant consumes is 0.46 kg of coal for one unit of power generated as opposed to conventional plant's consumption of 0.60 kg/kWh. This reduces energy use and resource spent on producing and transporting coal. The demonstration of this technology will reduce its implementation cost. The planned activities are expected to advance the financial, technological, and economic viability of the technology, creating distribution channels for manufacturing and engineering activities related to gasification technology, advanced gas turbines, and other IGCC/power-related activities.

Renovation and Modernization of Power Plants

With increasing demand for power, the state-of the art power plants can possibly meet all the requirements but the constraint is the extremely high cost resulting from the high capital cost. Many old and inefficient power plants that contribute to the grid could be upgraded to work efficiently. For a developing country like India, where there is a shortage of financing for additions to capacity and a large number of inefficient and old plants still in operation, renovation and modernization can greatly help improve efficiency, as this just entails a replacement of parts of the plant. Most of the small plants running on coal in India operate below 30% efficiency. Increasing the efficiency could lead to huge amounts of reductions in the emission of CO_2 from this sector. But renovation and modernization has been very slow in the country mainly due to paucity of funds. The proposed project looks into the renovation and modernization of existing old inefficient power plants in the country and will result in reductions in the emissions of SO_2, NOx, and SPM. The project would reduce coal consumption which in turn would greatly reduce CO_2 emissions.

Integrated Energy Policy: The Concept

Energy is a vital input into production and this means that if India is to move to the higher growth rate that is now feasible, we must ensure reliable availability of energy, particularly electric power and petroleum products, at internationally competitive prices. We cannot hope to compete effectively in world markets unless these critical energy inputs are available in adequate quantities and at appropriate prices.

The present energy scenario is not satisfactory. The power supply position prevailing in the country is characterized by persistent shortages and unreliability and also high prices for industrial consumer. There is also concern about the position regarding petroleum products. India depends to the extent of 70 percent on imported oil, and this naturally raises issues about energy security. These concerns have been exacerbated by recent movements in international oil prices. Electricity is domestically produced but its supply depends upon availability of coal, exploitation of hydro power sources and the scope for expanding nuclear power, and there are constraints affecting each source. Achieving an efficient configuration of the various forms of energy requires consistency in the policies governing each sector and consistency in the pricing of different types of energy. There is also a need for clarity in the direction in which we wish to move in aspects like energy security, research and development, addressing environmental concerns, energy conservation, etc. To address these issues in an integrated manner, the Prime Minister had directed that the Planning Commission should constitute an Expert Committee to undertake a comprehensive review and to make recommendation for policy on this basis. The Report of the Expert Committee provides a broad overarching framework for guiding the policies governing the production and use of different forms of energy from various sources. It makes specific recommendations on a very large range of issues. The report is a valuable input into policy making and will help shape our energy policy in the 11th Plan. Early implementation of the recommendations in the report would contribute substantially to putting the economy on a sustainable higher growth path.

Integrated Energy Policy: The Broad Framework

India faces formidable challenges in meeting its energy needs and in providing adequate energy of desired quality in various forms in a sustainable manner and at competitive prices. India needs to sustain an 8%—10% economic growth rate over the next 25 years in order to eradicate poverty and meet its human development goals. To deliver a sustained growth rate of 8% through 2031-32 and to meet the lifeline energy needs of all citizens, India needs, at the very least, to increase its primary energy supply by 3 to 4 times and, its electricity generation capacity/supply by 5 to 6 times of their 2003-04 levels. With 2003-04 as the base, India's commercial energy supply would need to grow from 5.2% to 6.1% per annum while its total primary energy supply would need to grow at 4.3% to 5.1% annually. By 2031-32 power generation capacity must increase to nearly 8, 00,000 MW from the current capacity of around 1,60,000 MW inclusive of all captive plants. Similarly, requirement of coal, the dominant fuel in India's energy mix will need to expand to over 2 billion tonnes/annum based on domestic quality of coal. Meeting the energy challenge is of fundamental importance to India's economic growth imperatives and its efforts to raise its level of human development. The broad vision behind the energy policy is to reliably meet the demand for energy services of all sectors at competitive prices. Further, lifeline energy needs of all households must be met even if that entails directed subsidies to vulnerable households. The demand must be met through safe, clean and convenient forms of energy at the least cost in a technically efficient, economically viable and environmentally sustainable manner (Planning Commission, 2006).

Considering the shocks and disruptions that can be reasonably expected, assured supply of such energy and technologies at all times is essential to providing energy security for all. Meeting this vision requires that India pursues all available fuel options and forms of energy, both conventional and non-conventional.

Further, India must seek to expand its energy resource base and seek new and emerging energy sources. Finally, and most importantly, India must pursue technologies that maximize energy efficiency, demand side management and conservation. Coal shall remain India's most important energy source till 2031-32 and possibly beyond. Thus, India must seek clean coal combustion technologies and, given the growing demand for coal, also pursue new coal extraction technologies such as *in-situ* gasification to tap its vast coal reserves that are difficult to extract economically using conventional technologies. The approach of the Committee is directed to realizing a cost-effective energy system. For this the following are needed (Planning Commission, 2006):

(i) Wherever possible, energy markets should be competitive. However, competition alone has been shown to have its limitations in a number of areas of the energy sector and independent regulation becomes even more critical in such instances.

(ii) Pricing and resource allocations that are determined by market forces under an effective and credible regulatory oversight.

(iii) Transparent and targeted subsidies

(iv) Improved efficiencies across the energy chain

(v) Policies that reflect externalities of energy consumption

(vi) Policies that rely on incentives/disincentives to regulate market and consumer behaviour

(vii) Policies that is implementable

(viii) Management reforms that create accountability and incentives for efficiency

A competitive market without any entry barriers is theoretically the most efficient way to realise optimal fuel and technology choices for extraction, conversion, transportation, distribution and end use of energy. The tax structure and regulation across energy sub-sectors should be consistent and institutional arrangements should provide a level playing field to all players. Social objectives should ideally be met through direct transfers. Environmental externalities should be treated uniformly and internalised. A consistent application of "polluter pays" principle may be made to attain environmental objectives at least-cost where prescribed environmental norms are either not applied consistently or not being adhered to. An energy market with the above features would minimise market distortions and maximise efficiency gains. An integrated energy policy is needed to ensure that energy costs and availability do not constrain India's economic growth and competitiveness. While the medium to long-term challenges of ensuring competitive energy markets are formidable, the immediate problems of acute power shortages, adequate supply of good coal, gas shortages, and concerns of States rich in coal and hydro resources require immediate policy action. The Committee recommendations address immediate as well as the medium to long-term issues. Key, high priority recommendations are summarised below:

(i) **Ensuring Adequate Supply of Coal with Consistent Quality:** Coal accounts for over 50% of India's commercial energy consumption and about 78% of domestic coal production is dedicated to power generation. This dominance of coal in India's energy mix is not likely to change till 2031-32. Since prices were de-controlled, the sector has become profitable primarily as a result of price increases and the rising share of open cast production. India would need to augment domestic production and encourage thermal coal imports to meet its energy needs. The Committee has concluded that along the western and southern coasts of India imported coal is more cost competitive compared to domestic coal and further, imported coal is far more cost competitive compared to imported gas at these coastal locations. Such a cost advantage of imported coal over imported gas is likely to continue for some time in the future. Thus:

Domestic coal production should be stepped up by allotting coal blocks to central and state public sector units and captive mines of notified end users. Coal blocks held by Coal India Limited (CIL) that cannot be brought into production by 2016-17, either directly or through joint ventures, should be made available to other eligible candidates for development and for bringing into production by 2011-12.

At the same time the needed infrastructure must be created to facilitate thermal coal imports. This will facilitate coastal power generation capacity based on imported thermal coal. Imports of thermal coal will also put competitive pressure on the domestic coal industry to be more efficient.

A system of pricing coal on its gross calorific value must replace the current system of pricing coal on the basis of broad bands of its useful heat value.

- Coal companies must be asked to conform to international practice of preparing coal prior to its sale.
- Washed coal must become the norm and use of unwashed coal should become the exception.
- The current system of coal linkages should be replaced by long-term coal supply agreements with strict
- Penalties for not meeting contracted supplies, quality and offtake commitments.
- Coal must be brought under independent regulation to improve exploitation and allocation of available resources, and to regulate e-auctions and coal prices and to enable a competitive coal market to take shape.
- By the end of 2007-08 the quantity of coal sold through e-auction must reach 20% of domestic production.
- Ideally, the Coal Mines (Nationalisation) Act, 1973, should be amended to facilitate: (a) private participation in coal mining for purposes other than those specified in the Act, and (b) offering of future coal blocks to potential entrepreneurs. A consensus should be built on the need to reform this Act.

(ii) **Addressing Concern of Resource Rich States:** Both coal and hydro resources are concentrated in a few states. Increasingly states are becoming more assertive in demanding higher share of benefits that their local energy resources provide to the country as a whole. Even though these are national resources and should not be rendered uncompetitive because of such demands, it is conceivable that mechanisms can be put in place that results in resource rich states reaping more equitable benefits. Allowing resource rich States a share in the profits of the enterprise tapping such local resources through what is called a "carried equity interest" and further allowing the state or its residents an opportunity to invest in such projects on equal terms and appropriately revising the royalty rate etc. are possible solutions to removing hurdles in exploiting these domestic sources of primary energy. The NDC must take up this issue immediately in respect of coal and hydro resources. Over the longer term, a National Policy on Domestic Natural Resources should be formulated and enacted through the Parliament.

(iii) **Ensuring Availability of Gas for Power Generation:** There is a total generation capacity of 12,604 MW based on gas and liquid fuels. Bulk of it is base loaded under combined cycle operation. However, gas supplies have been restricted and the overall utilisation remains at only 54.5%. A significant part of this capacity was realised under the earlier liquid fuel policy while the rest has been built based on unenforceable fuel supply agreements that would have been unbankable in any other environment.

While requiring that no new gas capacity be built without firm and bankable gas supply agreements, effort should be made to allocate available domestic gas supplies to the fertiliser, petrochemicals, transport and power sectors at prices that are regulated to yield a fair return to domestic gas producers. Such a practice should be enforced till a better demand-supply balance emerges and domestic gas production achieves some of the potential that is often cited. A more competitive market can then function.

(iv) **Power Sector Reforms:** These must focus on controlling the aggregate technical and commercial losses of the state transmission and distribution utilities. This is essential to creating a financially robust power sector in each state. Only financially healthy state power distribution utilities can sustain the growing generation and transmission of Central Power Sector. PSUs and State Power Sector Utilities (SPSUs) and provide the needed comfort on payment security to attract private investment in the power sector at internationally competitive tariffs.

Committee Recommendations

- To control AT&C losses, the Committee recommends that the existing Accelerated Power Development and Reform Programme (APDRP) be restructured to ensure energy flow auditing at the distribution transformer level through automated meter reading, a Geographical Information System (GIS) mapping of the network and consumers and the separation of feeders for agricultural pumps. Investment in developing a Management Information System (MIS) that can support a full energy audit for each distribution transformer is essential for reduction in AT&C losses. This will also fix accountability and provide a baseline which is an essential prerequisite to management reform and/or privatisation. The revised APDRP will provide incentives to State Electricity Boards (SEBs) that are linked to performance outcomes and will also include incentives to staff for reduction in AT&C losses.

- The Committee also recommends that the liberal captive and group captive regime foreseen under the Electricity Act 2003 be realised on the ground. India's liberal captive regime will not only derive economic benefits from the availability of distributed generation but will also set competitive wheeling charges to supply power to group captive consumers. This will pave the way for open access to distribution networks. It will also facilitate private generation that limits its interface with the host utility to the use of the distribution network for a fee and thus can be realised even before AT&C losses are reduced.
- To achieve these objectives, the Committee feels that it is essential to separate the cost of the pure wires business (carriage) from the energy business (content) in both transmission and distribution at different voltages. The Electricity Act 2003 recognises such separation for the transmission sub-segment.
- Separation of content from carriage in the distribution sub-segment, however, is considered only as a means to the provision of open access. The wires business within the distribution sub-segment is also a natural monopoly and must be regulated. Further, introduction of Availability Based Tariffs (ABT) for the intra-state sales and the upgrading of State Load Despatch Centres to the technological level of Regional Load Despatch Centres should be realised.
- Open access is resisted by incumbents as they fear that all the high value paying customers would go away and they would be left with small and subsidized agricultural and domestic customers. Since these customers have strong political constituencies, it may be

difficult to raise their tariffs when needed and the incumbent utilities would not remain viable for long. These concerns can be taken care of if the cross-subsidy surcharge, wheeling charge and back-up charge are set properly. However, if these are set too high, open access could be effectively thwarted. These charges need to be periodically revised and independently regulated.

- A robust and efficient inter-state and intra-state transmission system with adequate surplus capacity that is capable of transferring power from surplus regions to deficit regions is a must for ensuring optimal operation of the system.
- Rehabilitation of existing thermal stations could raise capacity at leastcost in the short-run. Similarly rehabilitation of hydro stations could yield much needed peak capacity at negligible cost. Both these steps must be taken up urgently.

(v) Reduction in Cost of Power: In terms of purchasing power parity, power tariffs in India for industry, commerce and large households are among the highest in the world. It is important to reduce the cost of power to increase both the competitiveness of the Indian economy and also to increase consumer welfare. A number of measures are suggested for this.

- The Government Policy should ensure that all generation and transmission projects should be competitively built on the basis of tariff-based bidding. Public Sector Undertakings shall also be encouraged to participate in such bids even though the tariff policy allows them a 5 year window wherein projects undertaken by the public sector need not be bid competitively.
- In cases where tariff continues to be determined on the basis of costs and norms, regulators may either adopt a return on equity approach or return on capital approach, whichever is considered better in the interest of consumers. In deciding the level of return provided, the regulator should *interalia* take into account the return available on long-term government bonds and reasonable risk premiums associated with equity investments.
- The current practice of state regulators not allowing state public sector power utilities the same returns as the central public sector utilities should be strongly opposed in the interest of strengthening fair competition which alone will bring down prices in the long-run. Similarly differential payment security structures for Central Power Sector PSUs and the private sector should be abolished.

- Consumer prices for electricity are currently set by State Electricity Regulatory Commissions on cost plus basis. Regulators should set multi-year tariffs and differentiate them by time of day.
- Government should seed the capital markets to develop market-based instruments that effectively extend the tenure of debt available to power projects to, perhaps, 20 years. This will reduce the capacity charge in the earlier years and spread it more evenly over the life of the project.
- Unit sizes should be standardized and global tenders invited for a number of units to get substantial bulk discount.
- Distribution should be bid out on the basis of a distribution margin or paid for by a regulated distribution charge determined on a cost plus basis including a profit mark up similar to that paid for generation as suggested above.

(vi) **Rationalisation of Fuel Prices:** Relative prices play the most important role in choice of technology, fuel and energy form. They are thus the most vital aspect of an Integrated Energy Policy that promotes efficient fuel choices and facilitates appropriate substitution. In a competitive set up, the marginal use value of different fuels, which are substitutes, should be equal at a given place and time so that the prices of different fuels at different places do not differ by more than the cost of transporting the fuels. The resulting inter-fuel choices will then be economically efficient. Further:

Prices of different fuels should not be set independently of each other.

As a general rule, all commercial primary energy sources must be priced at trade parity prices at the point of sale, namely the Free-on-Board (FOB) price for products for which the country is a net exporter and Cost, Insurance and Freight (CIF) price for which it is a net importer. The price of a product for which the country is self-sufficient in a competitive market with many suppliers and buyers would fluctuate between the two depending upon the ease of import/ export and reliability of supplies.

In a situation with a monopoly supplier with exportable surplus at import parity price, the price would be in between the two depending on the price elasticity of domestic demand. This principle is extremely relevant for the petroleum sector wherein bulk of the crude oil is imported and India has become a net exporter of petroleum products.

To cushion domestic prices against short-term volatility of prices on the international market (FOB or CIF) domestic prices can be set on the basis of median prices over the previous month or a three month period. The petroleum and natural gas sector is, once again, devoid of any competition and independent oversight of either upstream or downstream activities. On the upstream side, Directorate General Hydrocarbons (DGH), an arm of the Ministry, oversees allocation and exploitation of oil & gas reserves and enforces profit sharing with exploration & production companies. The current arrangement needs to be strengthened and made independent. On the downstream side, despite the dismantling of the Administered Price Mechanism, the GOI continues to control the pricing of automotive fuels, LPG, large part of domestic natural gas and PDS kerosene. There is no real competition in the sector other than in some peripheral products such as lubricants, despite the presence of a large domestic private player in refining and the likely emergence of other private players in this field. In fact, the prevailing pricing and taxation policies and the market structure provide significant protection to the private refineries. The result is that India's refining capacity exceeds the demand by 18% already. There is an urgent need to have an independent regulator for both upstream and downstream sectors. The notification of the Petroleum & Natural Gas Regulatory Board Act, 2006, is thus welcome.

In the petroleum sector, full price competition at the refinery gate and the retail level would lead to trade parity prices as described above. Thus instead of administering prices, full price competition should be introduced.

Coal prices should ideally be left to the market and trading of coal, nationally and internationally, should be free. Only a competitive free market can do an efficient job of price determination. A competitive market requires that there are multiple producers and that there are no entry barriers to new producers or to importers. Pending the creation of such a competitive market, independent regulation of coal prices becomes essential.

Apart from CIL's virtual monopoly in coal supply, coal prices cannot be determined in a competitive market open to all users as long as the largest coal consuming sector, i.e. power, has coal cost as a pass through. However, since other users of coal are numerous and consume substantial quantities of coal, a strategy for competitive price discovery is possible. The Committee recommended as follows:

- High quality coking and non-coking coal which is exportable may be sold at export parity prices as determined by import price at the nearest port minus 15%. This practise is currently being adopted for supply of good quality coking coal to the steel industry.

- 20% of the production may be sold through e-auction. Quantities to be sold through e-auction from different mines must be determined annually with a monthly mine-wise schedule to be independently monitored and enforced by a coal regulator.
- Remaining coal should be sold under long-term Fuel Supply and Transport Agreements (FSTAs). Regulated utilities should be allowed upto 100% of their certified requirements through FSTAs. Other bulk consumers could be allowed partial FSTAs based on coal availability. Any shortfalls should be met through eauction supplies or imports.
- Pithead price of coal under FSTAs should be revised annually by a coal regulator on a basis that *inter-alia* takes into account prices obtained through e-auction, FOB price of imported coal (both adjusted for quality) and production cost, inclusive of return based on efficiency standards.
- Coal prices may be made fully variable based on Gross Calorific Value (GCV) and other quality parameters.

Natural Gas is not an easily tradable commodity. Making gas tradable requires significant investments in pipelines or, alternatively, in liquefaction, cryogenic shipping and regasification. Comparing local gas prices to spot LNG prices in the international market is grossly misleading. Again, linking gas prices to crude price movements is also misleading. Long-term supply contracts such as those in Europe are more representative of natural gas prices. Natural gas price can be determined through competition among different producers where multiple sources and a competitive supply-demand balance exist. As long as there is shortage of gas in the country and the two major users of gas, namely fertiliser and power, work in a regulated cost plus environment, a competitive market determined price would be highly distorted. Such distortions would get further amplified by the prevailing regime of fertilizer subsidies & power sector subsidies and cross subsidies. In such a situation price of domestic gas and its allocation should be independently regulated on a cost plus basis including reasonable returns.

Another option could be to price gas on a net-back basis. If gas becomes a key component in India's energy mix, it is pointed out that beyond the level of gas consumption in the fertilizer, petrochemical, automotive and domestic sectors, gas must compete with coal as the key alternative for power generation. This implies that the cost of generating peak or base electricity using gas cannot exceed the cost of peak or base electricity from coal, the cheapest alternative. A competitive coal market is thus important for setting a proper price of natural gas on a net-back basis. An alternative for gas producers is to export gas, in which case the domestic gas price could be the net realization of the domestic natural gas producer after investing and getting a return on the investment needed to make the natural gas tradable across borders in either a trans-border pipeline or through liquefaction and shipping facilities. For the foreseeable future, domestic gas supplies to both the fertilizer and the power sector, that together account for about 80% of the current gas usage, would need to be allocated based on availability and charged at regulated price that reflects cost of production and a reasonable profit.

Central and State taxes on commercial energy supplies need to be rationalized to yield optimal fuel choices and investment decisions. Relative prices of fuels can be distorted if taxes and subsidies are not equivalent across fuels. This equivalence should be in effective calorie terms. In other words they should be such that producer and consumer choices as to which fuel and which technology to use are not affected by the taxes and subsidies. Socio-economic benefits such as employment generation and positive impact on energy security may support differential taxes on alternate fuels.

Environmental taxes and subsidies, however, are levied precisely to affect choices. Differential taxes can be justified here if they appropriately reflect environmental externalities. A consistent application of the "polluter pays" principle or "consumer-pays" principle should be made to attain environmental objectives at least cost where prescribed environmental norms are either not applied consistently or not being adhered to.

(vii) Energy Efficiency and Demand Side Management: Lowering the energy intensity of GDP growth through higher energy efficiency is important for meeting India's energy challenge and ensuring its energy security. The energy intensity of India's growth has been falling and is about half of what it used to be in the early seventies. Currently, we consume 0.16 kg of oil equivalent (kgoe) per dollar of GDP expressed in purchasing power parity terms. India's energy intensity is lower than the 0.23 kgoe of China, 0.22 kgoe of the US and a World average of 0.21 kgoe. India's energy intensity is even marginally lower than that of Germany & OECD at 0.17 kgoe. However, Denmark at 0.13 kgoe, UK at 0.14 kgoe and Brazil & Japan at 0.15 kgoe are ahead of India. These figures and many sectoral studies confirm that there is room to improve and energy intensity can be brought down significantly in India with current commercially available technologies. Lowering energy intensity through higher efficiency is equivalent to creating a virtual source of untapped domestic energy. It may be noted that a unit of energy saved by a user is greater than a unit produced, as it saves on production losses as well as transport, transmission and distribution losses. Thus a "Negawatt", produced by a reduction of energy need has more value than a Megawatt generated.

The Committee feels that with an aggressive pursuit of energy efficiency and conservation, it is possible to reduce India's energy intensity by up to 25% from current levels. Efficiency can be increased in energy extraction, conversion, transportation, as well as in consumption. Further, the same level of output or service can be obtained by alternate means requiring less energy. The major areas where efficiency in energy use can make a substantial impact are mining, electricity generation, electricity transmission, electricity distribution, water pumping, industrial production processes, haulage, mass transport, building design, construction, heating, ventilation, air conditioning, lighting and household appliances. As the Indian economy opens up to international competition, it will have to become more energy efficient. This is well demonstrated by India's steel and cement industry. However, the Committee recommends the following policies for raising energy efficiency. Some of these policies can be implemented through voluntary targets undertaken by industry associations as opposed to external dictates and enforcement.

- Merge Petroleum Conservation Research Association (PCRA) with Bureau of Energy Efficiency (BEE). The merged entity should be an autonomous statutory body under the Energy Conservation Act, be independent of all the energy ministries and be funded by the Central Government. It must:
- Force the pace of improvement in energy efficiency of energy using appliances, equipment and vehicles, and create "golden carrot" incentives in the form of substantial rewards to the firm which first commercialises equipment that exceeds a prescribed energy efficiency target.
- Enforce truthful labelling on equipment, and impose major financial penalties if the equipment fails to deliver stated efficiencies.
- Establish benchmarks of energy consumption for all energy intensive sectors
- Disseminate information, support training and reward best

practices with national level honours in energy efficiency and energy conservation.

- Increase the gross efficiency in power generation from the current average of 30.5% to 34%. All new plants should adopt technologies that improve their gross efficiency from the prevailing 36% to at least 38-40%.
- Require a least-cost planning approach to provide a level playing field, to Negawatts and Megawatts so that regulators permit the same return on the investment needed to save a watt as to supply an additional watt.
- Promote minimum life cycle cost purchase instead of minimum initial cost procurement by the government and the public sector.
- Promote urban mass transport, energy efficient vehicles and freight movement by railways through scheduled freight trains with guaranteed, safe and timely deliveries. Enforce minimum fuel efficiency standards for all vehicles.
- Institute specialisations in energy efficiency/conservation in technical colleges and commence certification of such experts.

(viii) Augmenting of Resources for Increased Energy Security: India's energy resources can be augmented by exploration to find more coal, oil and gas, or by recovering a higher percentage of the in-place reserves. Developing the thorium cycle for nuclear power and exploiting non-conventional energy, especially solar power, offer possibilities for India's energy independence beyond 2050.

At a growth rate of 5% in domestic production, currently extractable coal resources will be exhausted in about 45 years. However, only about 45% of the potential coal bearing area has currently been covered by regional surveys. It is also felt that both regional as well as detailed drilling can be made more comprehensive. Several possible options are recommended:

Covering all coal bearing areas with comprehensive regional and detailed drilling could make a significant difference to the estimated life of India's coal reserves.

India's extractable coal resources could be augmented through **in situ** coal gasification which makes use of those coal deposits which are at greater depth and cannot be extracted economically by conventional methods.

Extracting coal bed methane before and during mining could augment the country's energy resources.

Enhanced oil recovery and incremental oil recovery technologies could improve the proportion of in-place reserves that could be economically recovered from abandoned/depleted fields.

Isolated deposits of all hydrocarbons including coal may be tapped economically through sub leases to the private sector.

(ix) Using Energy Abroad: In case India can access cheap natural gas overseas under long-term (25-30 years) arrangements, it should consider setting up captive fertiliser and/or gas liquefaction facilities in such countries. This would essentially augment energy availability for India.

(x) Role of Nuclear and Hydro-Power: Even if India succeeds in exploiting its full hydro potential of 1,50,000 MW, the contribution of hydro energy to the energy mix will only be around 1.9-2.2%. It is clarified that hydro share in the primary energy mix comes out lower because of the way oil equivalence of hydro electricity is calculated. A hydroelectric plant converts a unit of primary energy in the form of potential energy to almost one unit of electricity. The fossil fuel route or the nuclear route needs almost 3 units of a primary energy source to produce the same unit of electricity. Thus while hydro's share in primary energy mix is lower than that of nuclear, the kWh produced from hydro is higher. Similarly, even if a 20-fold increase takes place in India's nuclear power capacity by 2031-32, the contribution of nuclear energy to India's energy mix is also, at best, expected to be 4.0-6.4%. If the recent agreement with the US translates into a removal of sanctions by the nuclear suppliers' group, possibilities of imports of nuclear fuels as well as power plants should be actively considered so that nuclear development takes place at a faster pace.

Nuclear energy theoretically offers India the most potent means to long-term energy security. India has to succeed in realizing the three-stage development process described in the main report and thereby tap its vast thorium resource to become truly energy independent beyond 2050. Continuing support to the three-stage development of India's nuclear potential is essential. Though its contribution to energy requirement is limited, hydroelectricity's flexibility and suitability to meet peak demand makes it valuable. Moreover, the development of hydropower, especially storage schemes, is critical for India as our per capita water storage is the lowest among other comparable countries. Creating such storages is critical to India's water security, flood control and drought control. The environmental concerns and the problem of resettlement and rehabilitation of project affected people (PAPs) can and must be satisfactorily handled. The PAPs should benefit from the project as much as other beneficiaries.

(xi) Role of Renewables: From a longer-term perspective and keeping in mind the need to maximally develop domestic supply options as well as the need to diversify energy sources, renewable remains important to India's energy sector. It would not be out of place to mention that solar power could be an important player in India attaining energy independence in the long-run. With a concerted push and a 40-fold increase in their contribution to primary energy, renewables may account for only 5 to 6% of India's energy mix by 2031-32. While this figure appears small, the distributed nature of renewables can provide many socio-economic benefits. Subsidies for renewables may be justified on several grounds. A renewable energy source may be environmentally friendly. It may be locally available thereby making it possible to supply energy earlier than in a centralized system. Grid connected renewables could improve the quality of supply and provide system benefits by generating energy at the ends of the grid where otherwise supply would have been lax. Further, renewables may provide employment and livelihood to the poor. However, the subsidies should be given for a well-defined period or up to a well-defined limit.

The Committee recommends that for promoting renewables, incentives should be linked to outcomes (energy generated) and not just outlays (capacity installed). Even when a capital subsidy is needed, it should be linked to outcomes. For example, capital subsidy could also be given in the form of a Tradable Tax Rebate Certificate (TTRC) that could be based on actual energy generated. The rebate claim would become payable depending upon the amount of electricity/energy certified as having been actually supplied.

Power Regulators must create alternative incentive structures such as mandated feed-in-laws or differential tariffs to encourage utilities to integrate wind, small hydro, cogeneration etc. into their systems.

An annual renewable energy report should be published providing details of actual performance of different renewable technologies at the state and national levels. This should include actual energy supplied from different renewable options, availability, actual costs, operating and maintenance problems etc. It should also report on social benefits, employment created, and women's participation and empowerment.

Policies for promoting specific alternatives are suggested in the main text. These include fuel wood plantations, bio-gas plants, wood gasifier based power plants, solar thermal, solar water heaters, solar photovoltaics, bio-diesel and ethanol.

It is also recommended that the Indian Renewable Energy Development Agency Ltd (IREDA) be converted into a national refinancing institution on the lines of NABARD/National Housing Bank (NHB) for the renewable energy sector. IREDA's own equity base can be expanded by the financial institutions of the country instead of continuing the current system of GOI support.

(xii) Ensuring Energy Security: India's energy security, at its broadest level, is primarily about ensuring the continuous availability of commercial energy at competitive prices to support its economic growth and meet the lifeline energy needs of its households with safe, clean and convenient forms of energy even if that entails directed subsidies. Reducing energy requirements and increasing efficiency are two very important measures to increase energy security. However, it is also necessary to recognise that India's growing dependence on energy imports exposes its energy needs to external price shocks. Hence, domestic energy resources must be expanded. For India it is not a question of choosing among alternate domestic energy resources but exploiting all available domestic energy resources to the maximum as long as they are competitive. The Committee, however, felt that obtaining equity oil, coal and gas abroad do not represent adequate strategies for enhancing energy security beyond diversifying supply sources. In contrast, pipelines for importing gas do enhance security of supply if the supplying country makes a major investment in the pipeline. The most critical elements of our energy security, however, remain the measures suggested herein to increase efficiency, reduce requirements and augment the domestic energy resource base. Ensuring energy security requires dealing with various risks. The threat to energy security arises not just from of availability of imported energy, but also from possible disruptions or shortfalls in domestic production.

Supply risks from domestic sources, such as from a strike in CIL or the Railways, also need to be addressed. Even if there is no disruption of supply, there can be the market risk of a sudden increase in energy price. Even when the country has adequate energy resources, technical failures may disrupt the supply of energy to some people. Generators could fail, transmission lines may trip or oil pipelines may spring a leak. One needs to provide security against such technical risks. Risks can be reduced by lowering the requirement of energy by increasing efficiency in production and use; by substituting imported fuels with domestic fuels; by diversifying fuel choices (gas, ethanol, or emulsion tar sands etc.) and supply sources; and by expanding the domestic energy resource base. Risks can also be dealt with by increasing the ability to withstand supply shocks through creation of strategic reserves, the ability to import energy and face market risk by building hard currency reserves and by providing redundancy to address technical risks. In this regard, the following is recommended:

Maintain a reserve, equivalent to 90 days of oil imports for strategic-cum-buffer stock purposes and/or buy options for emergency supplies from neighbouring large storages such as those available in Singapore.

(xiii) Research and Development (R&D) in the energy sector is critical to augment our energy resources, to meet our long-term energy needs and to promote energy efficiency. Such R&D would go a long way in raising our energy security and delivering energy independence over the long-term. R&D requires sustained and continued support over a long period of time. Energy related R&D has not been allotted the resources that it needs. India needs to substantially augment the resources made available for energy related R&D and to allocate these strategically. To take an innovative idea to its commercial application involves many steps. Basic research leading to a fundamental breakthrough may open up possibilities of applications. R&D is needed to develop conceptual breakthroughs and prove their feasibility. This needs to be followed up by a working, laboratory scale model. Projects that show economic potential could then be scaled up as pilot projects, while keeping in mind cost reductions that could be achieved through better engineering and mass production. Demonstrations of such projects, economic assessments and further R&D to make the new technology acceptable and attractive to customers could follow, before finally leading to commercialization and diffusion. Some key policy initiatives relevant to energy related R&D is detailed below:

A National Energy Fund (NEF) should be set-up to finance energy R&D. Our expenditure on R&D excepting for atomic energy, which as of today provides less than 3 percent of our total electrical energy supply, is miniscule compared to what industry and governments spend in developed countries. In the latter, firms generally spend more than 2 percent of their turnover for R&D. The total expenditure on R&D in 2004-05 was INR 610 crores for Atomic Energy and INR 70 crores for Ministry of Power, Coal and Non-Conventional Energy Sources. Even at one-tenth of the rate at which firms in developed countries spend on R&D, i.e. 0.2% of the turnover of all energy firms whose turnover exceeds INR 100 crores a year, we end up with INR 1000 to INR 1200 crores per year which will increase overtime. We should be spending much more than this on R&D. Much of R&D can be considered a public good. It is thus better financed by the Government. Initially an allocation of INR 1000 crores should be made for energy R&D excluding atomic energy. To begin with, individuals, academic research institutions, consulting firms, private and public sector enterprise, should all compete for this fund. Firms may also be encouraged to enhance their expenditure on R&D through tax incentives.

- The resources devoted to research in different areas depend on the economic importance of that particular area, the availability of technology and the likelihood of success. The latter changes with time as new developments in science and technology take place and uncertainties reduce.
- The NEF should support energy policy modeling activities in a number of institutions on a long-term basis. The different modelers should be brought together periodically in a forum to address specific policy issues.
- A number of technology missions should be mounted for developing near commercial technologies and rolling out new technologies in a time bound manner. These include coal technologies (where India should focus) for efficiency improvement; in-situ gasification; IGCC and carbon sequestration; solar technologies covering solarthermal and photovoltaics; bio-fuels such as bio-diesel and ethanol; bio-mass plantation and wood gasification, and community based bio-gas plants.
- Coordinated research and development in all stages of the innovation chain to reach a targeted goal (such as that in place in the departments of atomic energy and space research) should be used to develop more efficient industrial plant, machinery and processes, efficient appliances, hybrid cars, super batteries, nuclear technologies related to thorium and fusion, gas hydrates, and hydrogen production, storage, transport and distribution.
- The NEF could provide R&D funding in support of applications, innovative new ideas, fundamental research etc. to researchers in different institutions, universities, organisations and even individuals working independently.

- A number of academic institutions should be developed as centres of excellence in energy research.

(xiv) Household Energy Security—Electricity and Clean Fuels for All: One of the toughest challenges is to provide electricity and clean fuels to all, particularly rural populations given their poor paying capacity, the limited availability of local resources for clean cooking energy, and the size of the country and its population. The considerable effort spent on gathering biomass and cow-dung and then preparing them for use is not priced into the cost of such energy. These fuels create smoke and indoor air pollution, are inconvenient to use, and adversely affect the health of people, particularly women and children. Yet, given the fact that women and girls carry most of the burden of the drudgery and also bear the brunt of indoor air pollution, the urgency to meet the challenge should be high. Such steps are needed for our broader need to achieve universal primary education for girls, promote gender equality and empower women. Easy availability of a certain amount of clean energy that is required to maintain life should be considered as a basic necessity. Energy security at the individual level implies ensuring supply of such a lifeline energy need. India cannot be energy secure if her people remain without secure supply of energy for lifeline needs. Ensuring this would require targeted subsidies as many households would be unable to pay for safe, clean and convenient commercial energy to meet lifeline needs. This requires:

Electrification of All Households: The government has announced its commitment to ensure this by 2009-10.

Provision of Cooking Energy: We may set a goal to provide clean cooking energy such as LPG, NG, biogas or kerosene to all within 10 years. It may be noted that the requirement of cooking energy does not increase indefinitely with income. Thus the total amount of LPG required for providing cooking energy to 1.5 billion persons is around 55 Mtoe.

Other Sources: We may provide fuel wood plantations within one kilometre of all habitations. Those who do not have access or cannot afford even subsidised clean fuels, rely on gathering wood. Neighbourhood plantations can ease their burden and the time taken to gather and transport wood.

(xv) An Enabling Environment for Competitive Efficiency: Apart from pricing policies, an environment that allows multiple players in each element of the energy value chain to compete on transparent and equal terms is essential to realising efficiency gains within the energy sector. Currently the sector is dominated by large Public Sector Companies and some sub-sectors have natural monopoly characteristics potentially offering economies of scale. Given this ground reality, independent & informed regulation becomes essential to realising competitive efficiency. Such regulation can play an important role to see that competitive markets develop and mature. Such regulation must in the very least ensure that:

The regulatory responsibility/functions of the State are separated from the Ministries that control the Public Sector Units dominating the energy sector; and

Till effective competitive markets emerge, independent regulators should fix prices or price caps to mimic competitive markets based on principles summarised in para (v) above. Even when competitive markets emerge, the regulators' role will continue to remain important.

(xvi) Climate Change Concerns: Concern vis-a-vis the threat of climate change has been an important issue in formulating the energy policy. Even though India is not required to contain its GHG emissions, as a signatory to the UN Framework Convention on Climate Change and a country which has acceded to the Kyoto Protocol,

India has been very active in proposing Clean Development Mechanism (CDM) projects. By May, 2006, a total of 297 projects had been approved by India with approximately 240 million tones of CO_2 reduction. Also, since the impact on the country's poor, due to climate change, could be serious, this report has suggested a number of initiatives that will reduce the green house gas intensity of the economy by as much as one third. These are:

Energy efficiency in all sectors—Emphasis on mass transport—Active policy on renewable energy including bio-fuels and fuel plantations:

—Accelerated development of nuclear and hydro-electricity

—Technology Missions for clean coal technologies

—Focussed R&D on many climate friendly technologies

The broad policy framework and the thrust of development suggested here need to be made more specific. To this end once the policy framework is accepted, detailed roadmaps of development should be chalked out and specific policy measures for implementation drafted.

With the recommendations of the Committee, India can meet her energy requirements in an efficient, cost effective way and be on a path of sustainable energy security.

National Electricity Policy

The Government of India decided and notified the National Electricity Policy in February, 2005 (Ministry of Power, 2005). The policy aims at accelerated development of power sector, providing supply of electricity to all areas and protecting interests of consumers and other stakeholders.

Objectives of the Policy are:

- Access to Electricity—Available for all households in next five years
- Availability of Power—Demand to be fully met by 2012. Energy and peaking shortages to be overcome and spinning reserve to be available
- Supply of Reliable and Quality Power of specified standards in an efficient manner and at reasonable rates
- Per capita availability of electricity to be increased to over 1000 units by 2012
- Minimum lifeline consumption of 1 unit/household/day as a merit good by year 2012
- Financial Turnaround and Commercial Viability of Electricity Sector
- Protection of consumers' interests

The Policy prescribes development of Rural Electrification Distribution backbone, village electrification and household electrification to achieve the target of completing household electrification in next five years, financial support in terms of capital subsidy to States for rural electrification and special preference to Dalit Bastis, Tribal Areas and other weaker sections for rural electrification. REC is to be the nodal agency for rural electrification at Central Government level.

The Policy emphasizes on:

(i) Creation of adequate generation capacity with a spinning reserve of at least 5% by 2012 with availability of installed capacity at 85%.

(ii) Full development of hydro potential. Provision of long tenor finance for these projects.

(iii) Choice of fuel for thermal generation to be based on economics of generation and supply of electricity.

(iv) Nuclear Power is an established source of energy to meet the base load demand. Share of nuclear power in the overall capacity profile will need to be increased significantly.

(v) Development of National Grid.

(vi) Cost of recovery of service from consumers at tariff reflecting efficient costs to ensure financial viability of the sector.

(vii) Provision of support to lifeline consumers (households below poverty line having consumption of 30 units per month) in terms of tariffs.

(viii) Availability based tariff (ABT) to be extended to State level for better grid discipline through economic signaling.

(ix) Special emphasis on time bound reduction of transmission and distribution losses.

(x) Measures to promote competition aimed at consumer benefits.

(xi) Reliability and quality of power supply to be monitored by State Electricity Regulatory Commissions.

(xii) Exploitation of non-conventional energy sources such as small hydro, solar, biomass and wind for additional power generation capacity. Required encouragement through suitable promotional measures.

(xiii) Emphasis on achieving higher efficiency levels of generating plants through necessary renovation and modernization.

(xiv) Central Government to facilitate the continued development of national grid. Central Transmission Utility and State Transmission Utility to undertake coordinated planning and development.

(xv) Transmission capacity to have redundancy level and margins as per international standards.

(xvi) Adequate transitional financial support for reforming power utilities. Encouragement for private sector participation in distribution.

(xvii) The State Regulatory Commissions to put in place independent third party meter testing arrangement.

(xviii) Support for adoption of IT system for ensuring correct billing to consumers.

(xix) Speedy implementation of stringent measures against theft of electricity.

(xx) Full emphasis on augmentation of R&D base. Mission approach for identified priorities areas.

(xxi) Demand side management through energy conservation measures. Labels regarding energy efficiency to be displayed on appliances. Efficient agricultural pumpsets and efficient lighting technologies to be promoted. Appropriate tariff structure for managing the peak load.

(xxii) Special attention for developing training infrastructure in the field of regulation, trading and power market.

(xxiii) For giving boost to renewable and non-conventional energy sources, a prescribed percentage of power, as specified by State Regulatory Commissions, to be purchased from such sources of energy at the earliest.

(xxiv) Necessary regulations and appointing Ombudsman for redressal of consumers' grievances to be in place in six months.

Electricity Tariff Policy

The Government of India notified the Electricity Tariff Policy in January, 2006. The objectives of the Policy are:

(a) Ensure availability of electricity to consumers at reasonable and competitive rates;

(b) Ensure financial viability of the sector and attract investments;

(c) Promote transparency, consistency and predictability in regulatory approaches across jurisdictions and minimize perceptions of regulatory risks; and

(d) Promote competition, efficiency in operations and improvement in quality of supply.

All future requirement of power needs to be procured competitively by distribution licensees except in cases of expansion of existing projects or where there is a State controlled / owned company as an identified developer. Even for Public Sector projects, tariff of all new generation and transmission projects needs to be decided on the basis of competitive bidding after a period of five years.

It gives the framework for performance based cost of service regulation in respect of aspects common to generation, transmission as well as distribution.

(i) Rate of return to be notified by the Central Commission for generation and transmission. The rate of return notified for transmission would be adopted by State Electricity Regulatory Commissions (SERCs) for distribution also with appropriate modification to take care of higher risks involved in the distribution. For uniformity a common approach to be evolved by the Forum of Regulators (FOR) for rate of return in distribution.

(ii) The depreciation rates for generation and transmission to be notified by the Central Electricity Regulatory Commission (CERC). These rates are to be adopted by SERCs also for distribution with suitable modification as evolved by the FOR.

(iii) Same rates of depreciation would be applicable both for tariff as well as accounting purposes.

It emphasizes the need of keeping duties like electricity duty at reasonable level for making electricity available at reasonable prices along with the following measures:.

- Multi-year tariff framework to be adopted for tariff to be determined from April 1, 2006
- Suitable performance norms of operations with incentives and disincentives along with appropriate arrangement for sharing the gains of efficient operations with the consumers
- The CERC to notify operating norms for generation and transmission in consultation with the CEA Operating norms for distribution to be notified by the SERCs based upon uniform approach as evolved by the FOR.
- It gives essential features of commercial arrangements for harnessing surplus power available from captive generators.
- Future requirements of energy from non-conventional sources to be procured as far as possible through competitive bidding process to bring down the costs.

In line with the National Electricity Policy (NEP, 2005), National Tariff framework for transmission is to be implemented by April 1, 2006 to ensure sharing of the total transmission cost among the users in proportion to their respective utilization of the system within the overall framework of the following modalities:

- Private investment in transmission to be invited through competitive process for making transmission asset available according to laid down operational norms.
- Insistence on making electricity available for 24 hours particularly for those consumers who are willing to pay tariff which reflects efficient costs in accordance with the NEP.
- Emphasis on giving subsidy in transparent and targeted manner.
- Cross subsidies for different consumers to be brought within the range of + 20% of average of the supply by the end of the year 2010-2011.
- Tariff fixation to ensure sustainable use of ground water resources. At the same time there is a stipulation for supporting poor category consumers.
- The cross subsidy surcharge to be computed in a way so that open access becomes a reality. The policy gives unambiguous methodology.

Recent Reforms in the Coal Sector

In India, the annual coal production is about 400 million tonnes as in the year 2006-07. More than 90% of coal production is non-coking coal. In the non-coking category, more than 80% of coal is consumed by the Indian Power Sector. Dependence of Indian Power Sector on imported coal is rather marginal – about 11 million tonnes in 2005-06 and the likely import during 2006-07 was projected at about 16 million tonnes. Coal production has been primarily in the hands of the Central Government owned coal companies. Recently, it has been decided to allot a number of coal blocks to power plant producers for the purpose of captive coal mining. Coal blocks have been allotted and are being allotted to generating companies under the Central Government, State Governments generating companies and also to private sector. Almost 20 billion tonnes of coal reserves have been identified by the Ministry of Coal to be allocated to various power producing companies. This initiative would have far-reaching positive impact in transforming the present structure of the Indian coal industry and market. This development also has the potential of bringing new technologies, establishing performance benchmarks, improving productivity not only in the coal mines allotted to power producers, but also among the Government owned coal companies. Their performance level has already started showing significant improvement.

Merchant Power Plants

In order to introduce and increase the extent of competition in the electricity market, Ministry of Power, Government of India has recently announced a scheme of Merchant Power plants.

(i) For quite some time a need has been felt for setting up of Merchant Power Plants to facilitate development of electricity market. Unlike traditional utilities, Merchant Power Plants compete for customers and absorb the full market risk. There are no guarantees that they will have a minimum off-take of their output. They must respond to market needs. Typically the risk of a Merchant Power Plant is carried on the balance sheet of the promoter. Merchant Power Plants can provide the additional generating reserves that India needs now and will need in the future. They are a modern, market-based answer—at least in part—to energy challenges faced by the country.

(ii) Merchant Power Plants are a product of the restructuring of the electricity industry. In the past, utilities owned their own generating facilities or contracted with an independent power producer (IPP) to buy electrical output on a long-term basis. Merchant Power Plants fill different niches in the market; some provide steady supplies to a power grid, while others fire up only when demand is highest and meet peak loads. Merchant power plants operating competitively help assure that power is produced with efficiency and supplied to locations where it is needed most.

(iii) Considering the redundancies that are being provided in the grid to promote open access in transmission and open access in distribution in coming years, it would be reasonable to expect that merchant power plants each of capacities of 1,000 MW and below could be accommodated for being able to access transmission availability for wheeling of power to customers which are generally not pre-determined. By the year 2012, it is expected that inter-regional transmission capacity in the National Grid would rise to about 37,000 MW. Besides, intra-transmission capacities are also being augmented with required redundancies to take care of such short-term needs of transmission of power across the country from one region to another and within the region. Merchant Power Plants would be expected to have dedicated lines upto the nearest regional/national grid system.

(iv) Merchant Power Plants would be provided coal linkage for capacity of any of the plant upto 1,000 MW. Merchant Power Plants may be provided coal blocks also as captive mines for capacity of any of this plant in the range of 500–1000 MW.

Rural Electrification Policy

The Government of India notified a comprehensive Rural Electrification Policy in August, 2006. The Policy aims at;

(a) Provision of access to electricity to all households by year 2009;

(b) Quality and reliable power supply at reasonable rates;

(c) Minimum lifeline consumption of 1 unit per household per day as a merit good by year 2012.

It is relevant to mention that 56% of rural households, according to Census 2001, do not have access to electricity and the number of such households is as high as 78 millions. The balances 44% of households, which have access, because of inadequacy of power, have to suffer power supply disruption of as many as 10-16 hours a day. For Indian Power Sector, therefore, access to electricity for rural India has acquired top-most priority.

The Salient Features of the Policy are given below

(a) Grid connectivity is the normal way of electrification of villages. For villages/habitations where grid connectivity is not feasible or not cost effective, off-grid solutions based on standalone systems are envisaged.

(b) State Governments are required to prepare and notify rural electrification plans within six months which will indicate the electrification delivery mechanisms so as to provide access to electricity to all households and electrification of all villages and hamlets.

(c) Ministry of Power will put in place a coordination mechanism for identifying villages to be covered in different schemes.

(d) District Committees are to be set up to ensure involvement of local community in rural electrification. Adequate representation of women in these Committees is to be ensured.

(e) Least cost option is to be adopted for rural electrification after taking into account full life cycle cost and explicit as well as implicit subsidies.

(f) Emphasis has been given on development of economic load to make the business of rural supply economically viable.

(g) RGGVY already mandates franchisee for the projects financed under the scheme. System of franchisees is to be introduced in other areas not covered under RGGVY also in phased manner to ensure revenue sustainability of the rural supply.

(h) Benefit of capital subsidy given to the rural electrification projects is to be fully passed on to the consumers.

(i) Annuity based approach has to be adopted for provision of capital subsidy to the decentralized generation system in order to ensure efficient operation and maintenance.

(j) Programmes for encouraging energy efficient equipments specially irrigation pump sets have to be taken up.

(k) The definition of rural area as laid down in Article 243 of the Constitution is being adopted for the purpose of the Electricity Act also.

(l) The tariff for sale of electricity by the standalone systems is to be decided by the competitive market forces. However, the benefit of financial assistance/ capital subsidy received from the Government is to be fully passed on to the consumers according to the guidelines made by the Appropriate Commission.

Policy Framework—Energy Conservation Act, 2001

With the background of high energy saving potential and its benefits, bridging the gap between demand and supply, reducing environmental emissions through energy saving, and to effectively overcome the barrier, the Government of India has enacted the Energy Conservation Act – 2001. The Act provides the much-needed legal framework and institutional arrangement for embarking on an energy efficiency drive.

Under the provisions of the Act, Bureau of Energy Efficiency has been established with effect from 1st March 2002 by merging erstwhile Energy Management Centre of Ministry of Power. The Bureau would be responsible for implementation of policy programmes and coordination of implementation of energy conservation activities.

Important features of the Energy Conservation Act are:

Standards and Labeling

Standards and Labeling (S&L) has been identified as a key activity for energy efficiency improvement. The S&L program, when in place would ensure that only energy efficient equipment and appliance would be made available to the consumers.

The main provision of EC act on Standards and Labeling are:

- Evolve minimum energy consumption and performance standards for notified equipment and appliances.
- Prohibit manufacture, sale and import of such equipment, which does not conform to the standards.
- Introduce a mandatory labeling scheme for notified equipment appliances to enable consumers to make informed choices.
- Disseminate information on the benefits to consumers.

Designated Consumers

The main provisions of the EC Act on designated consumers are:

- The government would notify energy intensive industries and other establishments as designated consumers;
- Schedule to the Act provides list of designated consumers which covered basically energy intensive industries, Railways, Port Trust, Transport Sector, Power Stations, Transmission & Distribution Companies and Commercial buildings or establishments;
- The designated consumer to get an energy audit conducted by an accredited energy auditor;
- Energy managers with prescribed qualification are required to be appointed or designated by the designated consumers;
- Designated consumers would comply with norms and standards of energy consumption as prescribed by the central government.

Certification of Energy Managers and Accreditation of Energy Auditing Firms

The main activities in this regard as envisaged in the Act are:

A cadre of professionally qualified energy managers and auditors with expertise in policy analysis, project management, financing and implementation of energy efficiency projects would be developed through Certification and Accreditation programme. BEE is to design training modules, and conduct a National level examination for certification of energy managers and energy auditors.

Energy Conservation Building Codes

The main provisions of the EC Act on Energy Conservation Building Codes are:

- The BEE would prepare guidelines for Energy Conservation Building Codes (ECBC);
- These would be notified to suit local climate conditions or other compelling factors by the respective states for commercial buildings erected after the rules relating to energy conservation building codes have been notified. In addition, these buildings should have a connected load of 500 kW or contract demand of 600 kVA and above and are intended to be used for commercial purposes;
- Energy audit of specific designated commercial building consumers would also be prescribed.

Central Energy Conservation Fund

The EC Act provisions in this case are:

The fund would be set up at the centre to develop the delivery mechanism for large-scale adoption of energy efficiency services such as performance contracting and promotion of energy service companies. The fund is expected to give a thrust to R & D and demonstration in order to boost market penetration of efficient equipment and appliances. It would support the creation of facilities for testing and development and to promote consumer awareness.

Bureau of Energy Efficiency (BEE)

The mission of Bureau of Energy Efficiency is to institutionalize energy efficiency services, enable delivery mechanisms in the country and provide leadership to energy efficiency in all sectors of economy. The primary objective would be to reduce energy intensity in the Indian Economy.

The general superintendence, directions and management of the affairs of the Bureau is vested in the Governing Council with 26 members. The Council is headed by Union Minister of Power and consists of members represented by Secretaries of various line Ministries, the CEOs of technical agencies under the Ministries, members representing equipment and appliance manufacturers, industry, architects, consumers and five power regions representing the states. The Director General of the Bureau shall be the ex-officio member-secretary of the Council.

The BEE will be initially supported by the Central Government by way of grants through budget, it will, however, in a period of 5-7 years become self-sufficient. It would be authorized to collect appropriate fee in discharge of its functions assigned to it. The BEE will also use the Central Energy Conservation Fund and other funds raised from various sources for innovative financing of energy efficiency projects in order to promote energy efficient investment.

Role of Bureau of Energy Efficiency (BEE)

The role of BEE would be to prepare standards and labels of appliances and equipment, develop a list of designated consumers, specify certification and accreditation procedure, prepare building codes, maintain Central EC fund and undertake promotional activities in co-ordination with center and state level agencies. The role would include development of Energy Service Companies (ESCOs), transforming the market for energy efficiency and create awareness through measures including clearing house.

Role of Central and State Governments

The following role of Central and State Government is envisaged in the Act:

> **Central**—to notify rules and regulations under various provisions of the Act, provide initial financial assistance to BEE and EC fund, Coordinate with various State Governments for notification, enforcement, penalties and adjudication.
>
> **State**—to amend energy conservation building codes to suit the regional and local climatic condition, to designate state level agency to coordinate, regulate and enforce provisions of the Act and constitute a State Energy Conservation Fund for promotion of energy efficiency.

Enforcement through Self-Regulation

EC Act would require inspection of only two items. The following procedure of self-regulation is proposed to be adopted for verifying areas that require inspection of only two items that require inspection:

§ The certification of energy consumption norms and standards of production process by the Accredited Energy Auditors is a way to enforce effective energy efficiency in Designated Consumers.

§ For energy performance and standards, manufacturer's declared values would be checked in Accredited Laboratories by drawing sample from market. Any manufacturer or consumer or consumer association can challenge the values of the other manufacturer and bring to the notice of BEE. BEE can recognize for challenge testing in disputed cases as a measure for self-regulation.

Penalties and Adjudication

§ Penalty for each offence under the Act would be in monetary terms i.e. Rs. 10,000 for each offence and Rs. 1,000 for each day for continued non-compliance.

§ The initial phase of 5 years would be promotional and creating infrastructure for Implementation of Act. No penalties would be effective during this phase.

§ The power to adjudicate has been vested with state Electricity Regulatory Commission which shall appoint any one of its member to be an adjudicating officer for holding an enquiry in connection with the penalty imposed.

CHAPTER 4

Energy Storage System and Strategic Reserve of Oil and Gas

Introduction

The efficient use of energy requires the use of storage systems that permit a proper matching of demand for electricity with generating capacity without excessive investment in generating capacity. The basic problem is that demand for energy varies with day of the week, time of the day, season and weather conditions. There must be enough generating capacity to match peak demand, and ideally, production and demand ought to be matched at all times. Certain types of generating equipment can be shut down or restored quickly, for example, small gas turbines have a low response time and the sluice gates of hydroelectric power stations can be operated fairly rapidly. However, large fossil fuel or nuclear power stations are not amenable to frequent shutdowns. Moreover, they are at their most efficient level when run at a fairly constant power output. It is therefore, advantageous for generating boards or authorities to run their large stations continuously and to find some means by which the excess power they generate when demand is low can be stored for use during peak load conditions.

Energy storage is also of relevance to in the field of power production from natural sources - solar, wind, waves, tides, etc. a number of these sources suffer from a common disadvantage in that they are intermittent. If these sources are ever to be used as first choice power units, then they must be linked to efficient systems of storing energy during periods of peak production in order to make energy available during barren times.

Energy storage usually involves conversion. In the absence of practical system for the direct storage of electricity, storage is accomplished by conversion of electricity into some other form of energy, which can be re-converted to electricity as needed. Some energy is usually lost in the process of conversion or storage. Energy storage systems currently in use include: battery, flywheels, compressed air, chemical energy systems and pumped storage (pumped hydro).

Why Energy Storage?

We need energy—electrical or thermal—but in most cases not where or when it is available. Energy storage technologies are a strategic and necessary component for the efficient utilization of renewable energy sources and energy conservation. There is a great technical potential to substitute for burning fossil fuels by using stored heat that would otherwise be wasted and using renewable generation resources. These energy sources can be used more effectively through the addition of short and long term energy storage. Thermal and electrical energy storage systems enable greater and more efficient use of these fluctuating energy sources by matching the energy supply with demand. Thermal energy storage can also be used for cooling to reduce or eliminate the demand for electricity, including the most expensive electrical energy that is generated during periods of peak power demand.

Importance of Energy Storage System (ESS)

The following are conceived to be some merits of an Energy Storage System:

- Thrust for Renewable Energy sources
- Variable outputs
- Energy Buffering
- Importance in the present context
- Importance of new technologies and devices in Energy Sector

Types of ESS

Energy Storage systems can be broadly categorized into 4 groups:

- Mechanical Energy Storage
- Magnetic Energy Storage
- Thermal Energy Storage
- Chemical Energy Storage

A brief Operational Principle of each of the above category of Energy Storage system is explained below.

Mechanical Energy Storage: Fly Wheels

Flywheel

The flywheel is one of the important means of storing energy. When the generating equipment is producing electricity, some could be used to drive a motor, which in turn rotate the mass—a flywheel. When electricity is no longer being produced, the rotary kinetic energy stored in the flywheel could 'take over' and drive the generator to produce electricity. However, they would have to be extremely large to handle the storage for an electric utility.

The importance of energy storage devices has been increased due to the demand of using energy more efficiently as peoples are getting more concerned about the resource or environmental problems. For example, the surplus energy from windmill electricity generation should be stored to somewhere; otherwise, the energy will be just wasted.

Flywheel energy storage systems are one of energy storage devices. They are nothing but rechargeable batteries. They store energy mechanically in the flywheel rotor by rotating the rotor while as chemical batteries stores energy electrically. When we want to use the stored energy in the rotor, a generator is used to convert mechanical energy to electrical energy.

Since the flywheel system is a very efficient energy storage device, it can be used for various applications. Hybrid electric vehicles could be one example of flywheel applications. Hybrid vehicles contain a power unit such as internal combustion engines and electric motors and an energy storage unit such as flywheels or chemical batteries. When vehicles are cruising at a constant speed like 60 mph, relying on only internal combustion engines can be sufficiently efficient way. However, when we need to accelerate vehicles, internal combustion engines tend to use more fuel than needed. Therefore, if we use both internal combustion engine power and auxiliary power from flywheels or chemical batteries, we can save considerable amount of energy to get to a certain speed. Currently, chemical batteries are usually used for hybrid vehicles; however, flywheel systems can substitute chemical batteries. Flywheel systems are not sensitive to temperature since they are operating in a vacuum containment. Therefore, the hybrid vehicle with flywheel systems can run without any problem at very cold or hot areas. And, flywheel systems can store more energy per system weight compared to chemical batteries, which enables the hybrid vehicle to have more space and less weight while performing same as the hybrid vehicle with large size of chemical batteries (Bernard et al, 2003).

Compressed Air Energy Storage

Compressed Air Energy Storage (CAES) refers to the compression of air to be used later as energy source. At utility scale, it can be stored during periods of low energy demand (off-peak), for use in meeting periods of higher demand (peak load). Alternatively it can be used to power tools, or even vehicles.

Compressed air energy storage can be done adiabatically, diabatically, or isothermally:

With Adiabatic storage, the heat that appears during compression is also stored (usually in a separate container from the air to avoid loss to the air tank walls, and to reduce the air volume required), then returned to the air when the air is sent from storage to be expanded in the turbine to power a generator. This is a subject of ongoing study, but no utility scale plants of this type have been built. Round trip energy storage efficiency is expected to be 70%. Heat can be stored in a solid such as concrete or stone, or more likely in a fluid such as hot oil (up to 300C) or a molten-salt (600C).

With Diabatic storage, the extra heat is removed from the air with intercoolers following compression (thus approaching isothermal compression), and is dissipated into the atmosphere as waste. Upon removal from storage, the air must be re-heated (usually in a natural gas fired burner for utility grade storage or with a heated metal mass for large Uninterruptable Power Supplies) prior to expansion in the turbine to power a generator. The heat discarded in the intercoolers degrades efficiency, but the system is simpler than the adiabatic one, and thus far is the only system which has been implemented commercially. The Mclntosh CAES plant requires 0.69kWh of electricity and 1.17kWh of gas for each 1.0kWh of electrical output (a non-CAES natural gas plant can be up to 60% efficient therefore uses 1.67kWh of gas per kWh generated). Isothermal compression and expansion (which attempts constant temperature operation by atmospheric heat exchange) during compression and expansion is not practical for power levels above a few watts, due to the large heat exchangers required.

Compression is done with an electrically powered turbo-compressor. Expansion is done with a turbo 'expander' which drives an electrical generator air engine (generator) to produce electricity.

Air is stored in mass quantity in underground in a cavern created by solution mining (salt is dissolved away) or an abandoned mine. Plants are designed to operate on a daily cycle, charging at night and discharging during the day. Compressed air energy storage can also be used to describe technology on a smaller scale such as exploited by air cars or wind farms in steel or carbon-fiber tanks (Fig. 4.1).

Pumped Storage Hydroelectricityis a method of storing and producing electricity to supply high peak demands by moving water between reservoirs at different elevations. At times of low electrical demand, excess generation capacity is used to pump water into the higher reservoir. When there is higher demand, water is released back into the lower reservoir through a turbine, generating electricity. Reversible turbine/generator assemblies act as pump and turbine (usually a Francis turbine design). Some facilities use abandoned

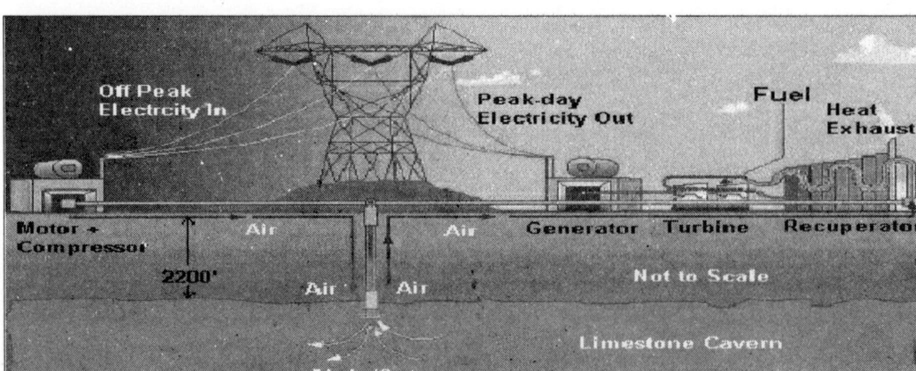

Figure 4.1: Compressed Air Energy Storage

mines as the lower reservoir, but many use the height difference between two natural bodies of water or artificial reservoirs. Pure pumped-storage plants just shift the water between reservoirs, but combined pump-storage plants also generate their own electricity like conventional hydroelectric plants through natural stream-flow. Plants that do not use pumped-storage are referred to as conventional hydroelectric plants; conventional hydroelectric plants that have significant storage capacity may be able to play a similar role in the electrical grid as pumped storage, by deferring output until needed.

The first use of pumped storage was in the 1890s in Italy and Switzerland. In the 1930s reversible hydroelectric turbines became available. These turbines could operate as both turbine-generators and in reverse as electric motor driven pumps. The latest in large-scale engineering technology are variable speed machines for greater efficiency. These machines generate in synchronization with the network frequency, but operate asynchronously (independent of the network frequency) as motor-pumps.

A new use for pumped storage is to level the fluctuating output of intermittent power sources. The pumped storage absorbs load at times of high output and low demand, while providing additional peak capacity. In certain jurisdictions, electricity prices may be close to zero or occasionally negative (Ontario in early September, 2006), indicating there is more generation than load available to absorb it; although at present this is rarely due to wind alone, increased wind generation may increase the likelihood of such occurrences. It is particularly likely that pumped storage will become especially important as a balance for very large scale photovoltaic generation.

In 2000 the United States had 19.5 GW of pumped storage capacity, accounting for 2.5% of baseload generating capacity. PHS generated (net) - 5.5 GWh of energy because more energy is consumed in pumping than is generated; losses occur due to water evaporation, electric turbine/pump efficiency, and friction.

In 1999 the EU had 32 GW capacity of pumped storage out of a total of 188 GW of hydropower and representing 5.5% of total electrical capacity in the EU.

Electrochemical Storage

Recently, a new class of reversible electrochemical energy storage systems have been developed that use: (a) the capacitance associated with charging and discharging of the electrical double layer at the electrode-electrolyte interface and are hence called electrical double-layer capacitors (EDLCs), and (b) the pseudo-capacitance with electro-sorption or surface redox reactions which are referred as pseudo capacitors. While EDLCs with capacities of many tens of farads per gram of the electrode material have been achieved employing high surface-area carbon powders, fibres, or felts, much higher capacitance values are accomplished with pseudo capacitors employing certain high surface-area oxides or conducting polymers. These electrochemical capacitors are being envisaged for several applications to complement the storage batteries. This article provides a brief introduction to scientific fundamentals and technological applications of electrochemical super capacitors. It is also stressed that there is a substantial scope for technology development in this newly emerging area, where materials science and polymer technology will have a pivotal role in conjunction with electrochemistry (Shukla et al, 2000).

Battery

A battery is two or more electrochemical cells connected in series which store chemical energy and make it available as electrical energy. Common usage has evolved to include a single electrical cell in the definition. There are many types of electrochemical cells, including galvanic cells, electrolytic cells, fuel cells, flow cells, and voltaic piles. A battery's characteristics may vary due to many factors including internal chemistry, current drain, and temperature (http://en.wikipedia.org/wiki/Battery_(electricity).

Types of Batteries

- Small Capacities
- Lead-Acid Batteries
  - — They use a chemical reaction to do work on charge and produce a voltage between their output terminals.
  - — Energy density is 0.6 MJ/Kg.
  - — Efficiency of the cell is only 15%
  - — Large Scale

One common division of batteries distinguishes two types: primary (disposable) and secondary (rechargeable). Primary batteries are designed to be used once only because they use up their chemicals in an effectively irreversible reaction. Secondary batteries can be recharged because the chemical reactions they use are reversible; they are recharged by running a charging current through the battery, but in the opposite direction of the discharge current. Secondary, also called rechargeable batteries can be charged and discharged many times before wearing out. After wearing out some batteries can be recycled. Fuel Cell

A fuel cell is a device in which the energy of an electrochemical reaction is converted into electrical energy with a continuous supply of reactants in a galvanic cell (http://en.wikipedia.org/wiki/Fuel_cell). A fuel cell differs in concept from a battery in that a continuous supply of reactants is made available to the two electrodes of the cell. Fuel (normally hydrogen) is supplied to one electrode and an oxidant, usually oxygen or air, is supplied to the other. The fuel and the oxidant then combine in the form of ions to produce electricity. Unlike a battery, a fuel cell does not run down; it operates as long as fuel and an oxidant are supplied continuously from outside the cell.

The two electrodes of a fuel cell are of opposite charges and are separated by an electrolyte, a substance that allows charged particles (ions) to pass through it. Fuel is made available to the anode (positive), and an oxidant is fed to the cathode (negative). In a hydrogen cell, hydrogen is made available to the anode, while air is supplied to the cathode. The anode of the hydrogen fuel cell strips electrons from the hydrogen atoms thus producing electron-deficient hydrogen atoms i.e. positively charged hydrogen ions. The electrons move from the anode through the external part of the electric circuit to the cathode, creating an electric current that can be tapped to provide power. The positively charged hydrogen ions meanwhile pass through the electrolyte to the cathode. There the electrons that passed through the external part of the circuit recombine with the hydrogen ions to produce hydrogen. Oxygen (from the air) reacts with the recombined hydrogen to produce water. Water produced at the cathode is removed continuously to avoid flooding the cell.

Types of Fuel Cells

Classified on the basis of operating conditions and various electrolytes used as given below:

- Alkaline fuel cells (AFC)
- Polymer electrolyte membrane (PEM)
- Phosphoric acid fuel cells (PAFC)
- Molten carbonate fuel cells (MCFC)
- Solid oxide fuel cells (SOFC)
- Regenerative fuel cells

Advantages of Fuel Cells

- No green house gases
- Not much political dependence

More operating time.

Energy Storage Technology

Advanced technologies for energy storage that are under active development include processes that are mechanical (flywheels, pneumatic), electrochemical (advanced batteries, reversible fuel cells, hydrogen, ultracapacitors), and purely electrical (superconducting magnetic storage). Energy storage devices are added to the utility grid to improve productivity, increase reliability or defer equipment upgrades. Energy storage devices must be charged and recharged with electricity generated elsewhere. Because the storage efficiency (output compared to input energy) is less than 100%, on a kilowatt-per-kilowatt basis, energy storage does not directly decrease CO_2 production. The exception to this rule is the use of advanced energy storage in conjunction with intermittent renewable energy sources, such as photovoltaics and wind that produce no direct CO_2. Energy storage allows these intermittent resources to be dispatchable.

Energy-storage devices do positively affect CO_2 production on an industrial output basis by providing high-quality power, maximizing industrial productivity. New battery technologies, including sodium sulfur and flow batteries, significantly improve the energy and power densities for stationary battery storage as compared to traditional flooded lead-acid batteries.

System Concepts

Stationary applications: The efficiency of a typical steam-power plant falls from about 38% at peak load to 28%-31% at night. Utilities and customers could store electrical energy at off-peak times, allowing power plants to operate near peak efficiency. The stored energy could be used during high-demand periods displacing low-efficiency peaking generators. CO_2 emissions would be reduced if the efficiency of the energy storage were greater than 85%. Energy storage also can be used to alleviate the pressure on highly loaded components in the grid (transmission lines, transformers, etc.) These components are typically only loaded heavily for a small portion of the day.

The storage system would be placed downstream from the heavily loaded component. This would reduce electrical losses of overloaded systems. Equipment upgrades also would be postponed, allowing the most efficient use of capital by utility companies. For intermittent renewable, advanced energy storage technology would improve their applicability.

Power quality: The operation of modern, computerized manufacturing depends directly on the quality of power the plant receives. Any voltage sag or momentary interruption can trip off a manufacturing line and electronic equipment. Industries that are particularly sensitive are semiconductor manufacturing, plastics and paper manufacturing, electronic retailers, and financial services such as banking, stock brokerages, and credit card-processing centers. If an interruption occurs that disrupts these processes, product is often lost, plant cleanup can be required, equipment can be damaged, and transactions can be lost. Any loss must be made up decreasing the overall efficiency of the operation, thereby increasing the amount of CO_2 production required for each unit of output. Energy-storage value is usually measured economically with the cost of power-quality losses, which is estimated in excess of $1.5 B/year in the United States alone. Industry is also installing energy-storage systems to purchase relatively cheap off-peak power for use during on-peak times. This use dovetails very nicely with the utilities' interest in minimizing the load on highly loaded sections of the electric grid. Many energy-storage systems offer multiple benefits. The system provides power-quality protection for the plant's pollution-control equipment, preventing an environmental release in the event of a loss of power. The system carries the critical plant loads while an orderly shutdown occurs. The battery system also in discharged daily during the afternoon peak (and recharged nightly), reducing the plant's energy costs.

Representative Technologies

For utilities, the most mature storage technology is pumped hydro; however, it requires topography with significant differences in elevation, so it's only practical in certain locations. Compressed-air energy storage uses off-peak electricity to force air into underground caverns or dedicated tanks, and releases the air to drive turbines to generate on-peak electricity; this, too, is location specific. Batteries, both conventional and advanced, are commonly used for energy-storage systems. Advanced flowing electrolyte batteries offer the promise of longer lifetimes and easier scalability to large, multi-MW systems. Superconducting magnetic energy storage is largely focused on high-power, short-duration applications such as power quality and transmission system stability. Ultracapacitors have very high power density but currently have relatively low total energy capacity and are also applicable for high-power, short-duration applications. Flywheels are now commercially viable in power quality and UPS applications, and emerging for high power, high-energy applications.

System Components

Each energy-storage system consists of four major components: the storage device (battery, flywheel, etc.); a power-conversion system; a control system for the storage system, possibly tied in with a utility SCADA (Supervisory Control And Data Acquisition: http://www.ncs.gov/library/tech_bulletins/2004/tib_04-1.pdf) system or industrial facility control system; and interconnection hardware connecting the storage system to the grid. All common energy-storage devices are DC devices (battery) or produce a varying output (flywheels) requiring a power conversion system to connect it to the AC grid. The control system must manage the charging and discharging of the system, monitor the state of health of the various components and interface with the local environment at a minimum to receive on/off signals. Interconnection hardware allows for the safe connection between the storage system and the local grid.

Thermal Energy Storage

Description

Thermal energy storage systems cool a storage medium and then use that cold medium to cool air at a later point in time. Using thermal storage can reduce the size and initial cost of cooling systems, lower energy costs, and reduce maintenance costs. If electricity costs more during the day than at night, thermal storage systems can reduce utility bills further. Systems can be sized to eliminate compressor energy use during periods when electricity is most expensive, but most systems are designed to simply augment mechanical cooling in order to limit peak demand. The latter type of system can be considerably smaller than the former.

Two forms of TES systems are currently used. The first system uses a material that changes phase, most commonly water and ice. The second type just changes the temperature of a material, most commonly water.

Applications: TES may be economical if one or more of the following conditions exist:

- High utility demand costs
- Utility time-of-use rates (some utilities charge more for energy use during peak periods of day and less during off-peak periods)
- High daily load variations
- Short duration loads
- Infrequent or cyclical loads
- Capacity of cooling equipment has trouble handling peak loads
- Rebates are available for load shifting to avoid peak demand
- Effective applications of thermal energy storage include:
- Electrical power use management by shifting the cooling load to off-peak hours and reducing peak load
- Reducing required capacity of building and process cooling systems, or helping existing cooling equipment to handle an increased load

Water Storage System

Water storage systems (http://www.oasisdesign.net/water/storage/) are often used in new large cooling system applications in conjunction with cogeneration and/or district energy systems. Water-ice storage is the most common cooling storage in smaller applications. Because latent heat storage (phase change between water and ice) has a smaller volume, it is often chosen for retrofit applications with limited space. In general, the buildings that offer the highest potential are offices, retail, and medical facilities. The Dallas Veterans Affairs Medical Center installed a 24,628 ton-hours chilled water TES that resulted in a reduction in demand of 2,934 kW and a reduction in annual electricity cost of $223,650. The local utility provided $500,000 of the total cost of $2.2 million required for design and installation. Savings resulting from installation of the thermal storage technology will allow the VA to recoup its investment within 7 years.

Performance/Costs

Thermal energy storage systems are installed for two major reasons: lower initial project costs and lower operating costs. Initial cost may be lower because distribution temperatures are lower and equipment and pipe sizes can be reduced. Operating costs may be lower due to smaller compressors and pumps as well as reduced time-of-day or peak demand utility costs. The economics of thermal storage is very site and system-specific. A feasibility study is generally required to determine the optimum design for a specific application. Several examples exist of effective TES systems that were installed for less cost than conventional alternatives and that also provided significant energy and energy cost reductions. TES projects often profit from unexpected benefits that are secondary to the primary reason for an action. For example, a well designed TES air conditioning application may experience reduced chiller energy consumption, lower pump horsepower, smaller pipes, high reliability, better system balancing and control, and lower maintenance costs.

Determining electrical cost savings from shifting chiller operation from daytime to night-time (or off-peak operation) can be complicated, depending upon the local utility rate structure. The utility may have time-of-day peak rates as well as differing peak demand rates. Without thermal storage, a chiller will typically operate during times of peak electrical demand, and thus be included in the peak monthly demand charge. The greatest savings will occur when you shift chiller operation to off-peak times.

MAGNETIC ENERGY STORAGE

Superconducting Magnetic Energy Storage (SMES)

Superconducting Magnetic Energy Storage systems store energy in the magnetic field created by the flow of direct current in a superconducting coil which has been cryogenically cooled to a temperature below its superconducting critical temperature.

A typical SMES system includes three parts: superconducting coil, power conditioning system and cryogenically cooled refrigerator. Once the superconducting coil is charged the current will not decay and the magnetic energy can be stored indefinitely (http://en.wikipedia.org/wiki/Superconducting_magnetic_energy_storage).

The stored energy can be released back to the network by discharging the coil. The power conditioning system uses an inverter/rectifier to transform alternating current (AC) power to direct current or convert DC back to AC power. The inverter/rectifier accounts for about 2-3% energy loss in each direction. SMES loses the least amount of electricity in the energy storage process compared to other methods of storing energy. SMES systems are highly efficient; the round-trip efficiency is greater than 95%.

Due to the energy requirements of refrigeration and the high cost of superconducting wire, SMES is currently used for short duration energy storage. Therefore, SMES is most commonly devoted to improving power quality. If SMES were to be used for utilities it would be a diurnal storage device, charged from baseload power at night and meeting peak loads during the day.

Characteristics of SMES

- SMES systems store energy in a magnetic field created by the flow of direct current in a coil of superconducting material that has been cryogenically cooled
- Principle: At low-temperatures, electric currents encounter almost no resistance Stores energy in the magnetic field Environmental friendly and highly efficient

Magnetic Energy Storage Efforts in Japan : A Case Study

Integrating energy storage into an electric power system has long been recognized as a way to maximize a utility's generation and/or transmission capacity. Electric power can be stored during off-peak periods and then recovered during high-peak conditions to offset the need for larger generation or expanded transmission capacity. In Japan, load-leveling or diurnal usage of stored energy is currently accomplished at pumped-storage installations, which are considered to be fairly inefficient, having only ~70% turn-around efficiency. Also, Japan's river system, highly dense settlement, and expensive real estate do not favor construction of additional pumped-storage facilities. The Japanese have thus been exploring alternative storage technologies, including SMES and flywheels (http://www.wtec.org/loyola/scpa/02_06.htm). As discussed earlier, SMES research in Japan has been underway since the early 1970s, with many prototypes built and tested under actual "utility" conditions.

Japan's International Superconductivity Technology Center (ISTEC) conducted a three-year feasibility study starting in 1988 on electric power apparatus, including SMES, under a program sponsored by MITI's Agency of Natural Resources and Energy. As part of this study, the Subcommittee on Energy Storage recommended in 1989 the detailed design using available technology of a small-scale SMES, with either a solenoid or toroidal field configuration that would be consistent with future R&D efforts. This SMES program, much like Super-GM, did not mandate using HTS materials; thus,

LTS conductors such as Nb-Ti and Nb3Sn were the primary choice. Demonstration of a small-scale SMES, whose size is closely related to that needed for power system stabilization, would also address many major technical issues facing the large-scale diurnal storage SMES, such as ac losses, power conditioning, and refrigeration. ISTEC's initial SMES effort was followed by a six-year program started in 1991 to implement the construction and test of a small-scale SMES pilot plant at a 100 kWh/20 MW rating. This ISTEC program, also sponsored by MITI's Agency of Natural Resources and Energy, involves Toshiba as the primary magnet manufacturer, the Electric Power Development Corporation providing power conditioning, and various utilities led by Chubu Electric with additional support from Tohoko and Kyushu Electric Power Companies (Fig. 4.3).

A hybrid electric vehicle (HEV) is a vehicle which combines a conventional propulsion system with an onboard rechargeable energy storage system (RESS) to achieve better fuel economy than a conventional vehicle without being hampered by range from a charging unit like a battery electric vehicle, which uses batteries charged by an external source. The different propulsion power systems may have common subsystems or components

Regular HEVs most commonly use an internal combustion engine (ICE) and electric batteries to power electric motors. Modern mass produced HEVs

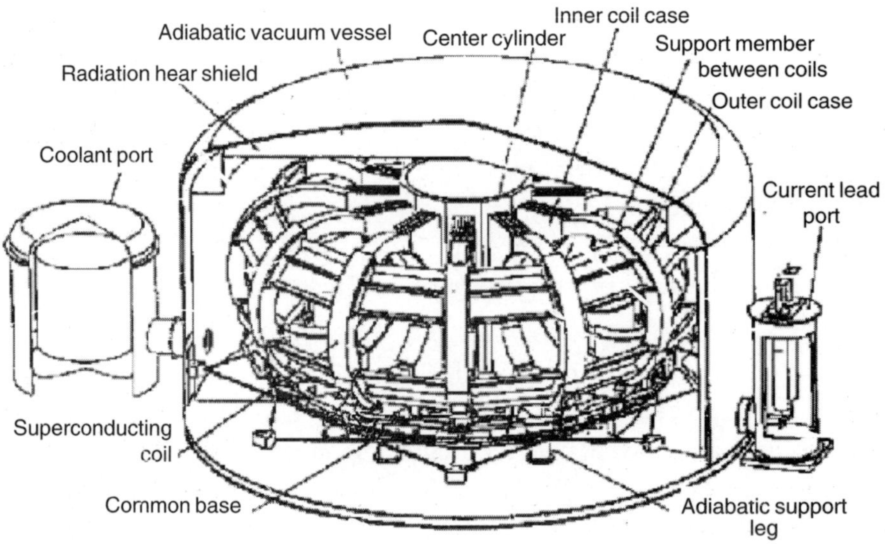

Figure 4.3: The conceptual design of an SMES system developed in Japan:
http://www.wtec.org/ioyola/scpa/02 06. htm

prolong the charge on their batteries by capturing kinetic energy via regenerative braking, and some HEVs can use the combustion engine to generate electricity by spinning an electrical generator (often a motor-generator) to either recharge the battery or directly feed power to an electric motor that drives the vehicle. Many HEVs reduce idle emissions by shutting down the ICE at idle and restarting it when needed. An HEVs engine is smaller and may be run at various speeds, providing more efficiency. HEVs became widely available to the public in the late 1990s with the introduction of the Honda Insight and Toyota Prius. HEVs are viewed by some automakers as a core segment of the next future automotive market.

There are several commercially viable energy storage systems that are being developed for hybrid electric vehicles (HEV's) on the market today. Major advances are being made on almost a daily basis. The reason for this is the fact that the government is subsidizing a large amount of the alternative fuel research going on by many U.S. as well as foreign manufacturers. The types of devices that hold the most promise to solve the energy storage problems are batteries, flywheels, and ultracapacitors. As shown in the plot below (Fig.4.4), both gasoline and hydrogen have a higher specific energy than the rest of these electrical storage devices. An advantage of HEV's is that they can use the high specific energy of liquid or gaseous fuels to provide the vehicle with long-range capabilities. Conversely, the HEV can use the high specific power of electrical energy storage to provide the peak power requirements.

Tidal Storage System

The increasing use of intermittent renewable energy presents a problem to balancing power on electricity grids. The wind does not always blow when electricity is needed. This can mean a physical lack of power and a missed opportunity to sell renewable power at the most financially attractive time.

Large-scale energy storage can adjust the time at which power is delivered, thus balancing the grid and providing better returns to the renewable energy provider. Among the many ways to store energy, water is a clean, safe method that can operate at large scale.

Tidal power is among the oldest sources of energy and its principles of operation, including enhancement by pumping, are well documented (http://tidalenergystoragesystem.com/).

These images are taken from a 3D model of a dual-lagoon system that can smooth intermittent renewable energy to a continuous flow independent of

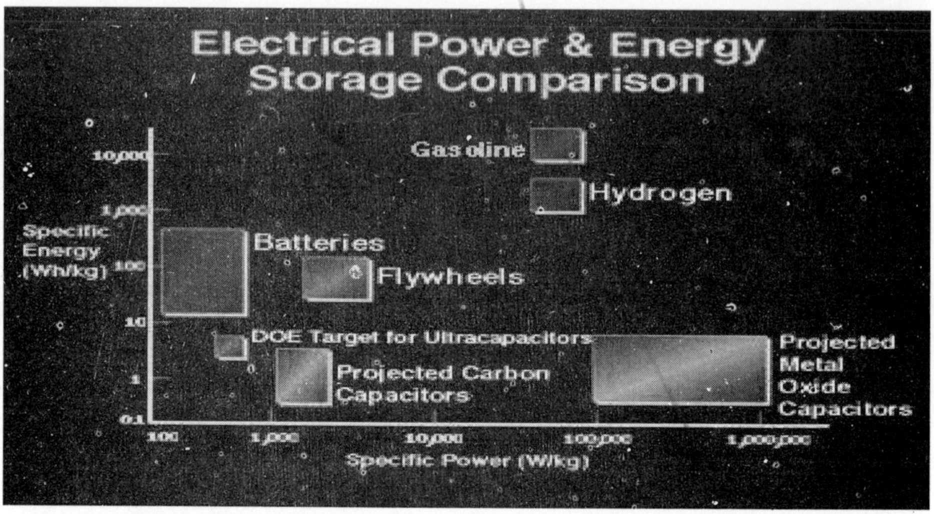

Fig. 4.4: Plot of Energy versus Power for various Energy Storage Devices:
http://en.wikipedia.org/wiki/Hybrid_electric_vehicle

the tide state. The wind turbines indicate the possibility to integrate with offshore wind, but are not an essential part of the design.

The full potency of the energetics, but not the economics, of enhancement through pumping is described in a brief note by Prof. David MacKay of Cambridge University Physics Department - Enhancing Electrical Supply by Pumped Storage in Tidal Lagoons. An informal consortium has been created around this work and an economic model, using cost estimates from an analysis by AEA Technology of a scheme developed by Tidal Electric Ltd, suggests that in spite of the substantial infrastructure costs, the optimization transforms the economic viability for the better. The consortium is actively pursuing participation and funding to improve the modelling work and undertake physical verification.

High-performance Energy Storage

North Carolina State University (NCSU) physicists have recently deduced a way to improve high-energy-density capacitors so that they can store up to seven times as much energy per unit- volume than the common capacitor.

High performance capacitors would enable hybrid and electric cars with much greater acceleration, better and faster steering of rockets and spacecraft, better regeneration of electricity when using brakes in electric cars, and improved lasers, among many other electrical applications. A capacitor is an energy storage device. Electrical energy is stored by a difference in charge between two metal surfaces. Unlike a battery, capacitors are designed to release their energy very quickly. They are used in electric power systems, hybrid cars, and all kinds of electronics. The amount of energy that a capacitor can store depends on the insulating material in between the metal surfaces, called a dielectric. A polymer called PVDF has interested physicists as a possible high-performance dielectric. It exists in two forms, polarized or unpolarized. In either case, its structure is mostly frozen-in and changes only slightly when a capacitor is charged up. Mixing a second polymer called CTFE with PVDF results in a material with regions that can change their structure, enabling it to store and release unprecedented amounts of energy.

Emerging New Electrical Storage Technologies

Several electricity storage technologies are emerging. These range from large-scale sodium-sulfur (Na/S) batteries (5-10 MW, 30-80 MWh) to medium-scale flowing electrolyte batteries (100-500 kW, 2 MWh), to short-duration, high-power systems (flywheels and electrochemical capacitors).

Larger-scale systems are designed for peak shaving in utility or surety Microgrid applications. NGK Insulators Inc., of Japan, has manufactured Na/S batteries that can deliver rated power output for six to 10 hours and over 150 MWh of them are operational. American Electric Power is installing a 1.2-MW, 7.2-MWh system in West Virginia that will operate near the load and will defer for six years the upgrade of the substation.

Several companies are developing battery systems where the electrolyte is stored in tanks and pumped through a reaction cell. The advantage here is that the energy storage rating and power rating are decoupled. To gain additional storage capacity, one simply increases the volume of the associated storage tank.

In early 2004, PacifiCorp installed a 250-kW, eight-hour discharge vanadium redox battery system in Castle Rock, UT, to stabilize a long rural distribution line that was suffering voltage stability problems due to load growth. This state-of-the-art system was manufactured by the Vancouver, BC-based VRB Power Systems Inc.

ZBB Energy Corp., of Menomonee Falls, WI, manufactures zinc-bromine (Zn/Br) battery energy storage systems and is currently certifying a 2-MWh system for a substation upgrade deferral application for Pacific Gas & Electric. The project is funded by the California Energy Commission (CEC) and the US Department of Energy (DOE).

High-power, short-duration products are also coming into the marketplace in the form of supercapacitors and flywheels. San Diego-based Maxwell Technologies Inc. and several other manufacturers produce electrochemical capacitors that combine the high power output of traditional capacitors with significantly higher energy storage capacities.

Maxwell, with DOE and CEC funding, is installing a Supercapacitor energy storage system in a Microgrid to stabilize output from a wind turbine and a hydroelectric plant and to provide bridging power to the utility.

Finally, in the arena of flywheels, Beacon Power Corp., located in Wilmington, MA, is demonstrating seven flywheels in a small-scale frequency stabilization system. Beacon also intends to develop a 20-MW system for frequency regulation services. Active Power Inc., of Austin, TX, is commercially successful in selling flywheels for power quality applications, both as stand-alone systems and as an integral part of one Caterpillar product line.

Ensuring Readiness in Microgrid System

There is much additional work needed to fully incorporate the various storage devices, especially advanced ones, into surety Microgrid systems. A number of problem areas exist.

First, methods for optimizing the storage components (fuel, thermal, and electric) and tying them to the surety metrics have not been developed. Questions remain about how much of the various kinds of storage should be included in a surety Microgrid to meet certain surety requirements. The problem is compounded by difficulties in quantifying some of the surety elements. Sandia National Laboratories is teaming with the Army's Construction Engineering Research Lab, New Mexico State University, and the University of New Mexico to address this challenge.

Second, the best methods for controlling the storage devices on the surety Microgrid are not known with certainty. A CEC-sponsored consortium including the University of Wisconsin, Sandia National Laboratories, and American Electric Power have created basic Microgrid control systems to maintain reliable operation in a reasonably controlled environment.

However, SANDIA believe that additional control system sophistication is needed to apply advanced generation storage devices effectively within a surety Microgrid concerned with five fundamental surety elements.

SANDIA envisions that an energy surety Microgrid should be capable of dynamically changing its operational features while serving loads. Properly controlled storage devices are an essential feature to maintain power stability on a surety Microgrid.

Third, technical, economic, and regulatory challenges remain. Many regulatory systems do not have provisions for including energy storage in a utility's rate base, preventing utilities from installing energy storage systems on a distribution system where it could benefit an energy surety Microgrid.

Fourth, while fuel and thermal storage is relatively inexpensive, electrical storage costs remain relatively high. Research and development in both the private and the government sectors is striving to improve the performance of storage and Microgrid products and bring down the capital and operating costs to allow more market penetration to occur.

Finally, with the exception of tanks that store fuel and lower-temperature thermal liquids, as well as ordinary batteries used mostly for motive power, advanced energy storage systems lack the extensive field experience needed to secure the confidence of surety Microgrid designers.

Advanced thermal technologies, such as molten salt, have only been demonstrated in limited settings. New electric storage technologies are also lacking in the number of systems successfully demonstrated.

The DOE Energy Storage Systems (ESS) program is currently investing in these areas but is severely limited in its discretionary budget. The DOE ESS program estimates that a $20 million-per-year budget would significantly change the nature of energy storage systems within a period of five years.

Today's grid is an evolutionary artifact that has worked reasonably well for more than half a century. However, rapidly changing economic conditions in the US are requiring a more robust system, one that meets all of the energy surety elements. By applying the Energy Surety Methodology to the existing system, the weaknesses become clearer.

The Energy Surety Microgrid under development at Sandia has the potential to improve the overall level of surety in the system. Nevertheless, the concept is highly dependent on storage to realize its full potential (John Boyes and Dave Menicucci, 2007J

While there are sufficient existing storage technologies available to begin implementation, there are many technological challenges that lie ahead. The most important research needs include reducing the cost and size of electrical storage systems, improving the component and system capability and reliability, and demonstrating these improvements. As these research needs are met in the lab and the results rolled out to the field in the form of energy surety Microgrids, levels of surety in our power generation systems will steadily rise.

Strategic Energy Plan for Energy Security

Developing a strategic energy plan helps prepare the facility for its energy future by factoring in some of the most important business decisions that directly affects the bottom line of business.

Here are 10 steps that every business can take to keep its facilities competitive in today's marketplace and provide a return on investment in the Energy sector.

1. Energy Forecasting

The first step in energy management is identifying where your businessl energy costs are headed. A long-range (up to 20-year) energy and fuel forecast should incorporate local, regional, national, and international influences on availability, reliability, and the cost of electricity, natural gas, and fuel oil. This will provide with the opportunity to examine the consumption on both a macro and micro level. Forecasting on a regional level should include talking to the local utility company to better understand the make-up of the power source. Let us discuss how they are planning to grow their fuel sources over the next few decades. Appreciating the fuel split ratio and its usage will help any consumer better anticipate current and future energy prices.

Another key to energy forecasting is looking at expenditures from an international perspective. Today, we live in a global economy where it is crucial to understand what our neighbors across the world are doing. For example, world electricity demand from 2003 to 2030 is expected to double, with 70 percent of this growth coming from non-Organization for Economic Cooperation and Development (OECD) countries, including China, India, Africa, Central and South America, and the Middle East (Fig. 4.5). This future demand for energy will be a major factor in the escalation of international and, ultimately, U.S. power costs.

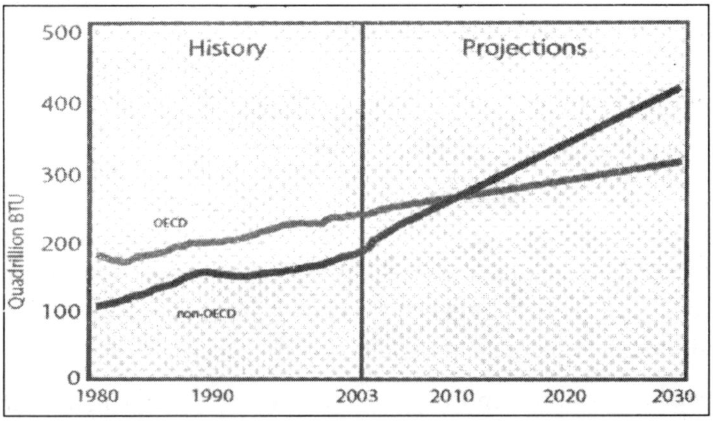

Sources: History; Energy Information Administration (EIA), Intl. Energy Annual 2003 (May-July 2005), Website (www.EIA.Gov/IEAL. Projections: EIA, System for the Analysis of Global Energy Markets (2006).

Figure 4.5. Geographic Growth Projection of Energy Markets

Fortunately, many organizations, like the U.S. Department of Energy (DOE), can make forecasting easier with annual energy reports that project international, national, and regional energy escalation and market analysis.

2. Environmental Compliance

An analysis of current, short-term, and expected future environmental compliance issues, including local, state, and federal regulations for all environmental media (air, water, solid waste, noise, etc.) is critical to formulating any facility's strategic energy plan.

Internationally, the Kyoto Protocol has been adopted by the United Nations and 165 other countries (the United States is not one of them) that have committed to reducing six greenhouse-gas emissions, including carbon dioxide, by at least 5 percent from 1990 levels between 2008 and 2012.

California is one of several states that recently adopted portions of this protocol. Under California's *Assembly Bill 32*, utilities, industry, and large businesses are required to go back and "clean up" existing operations by adding renewable resources to their portfolio. Electric utilities will be forced to raise the price of power to recover this investment.

In this case, there is a clear need to carry out research at regional, national, and international regulations to find out how they will affect the facility and thc bottom line. The EPA's *Plain English Guide to The Clean Air Act* walks through present and pending environmental regulations.

3. Financial Incentives

While the federal government authors most of the energy regulations existing today, state governments offer more of the financial incentives that make the edicts easier for big businesses to swallow. (Federal incentives are typically offered for research and development projects, or when a technology is first introduced to the market.) However, federal tax credits and low-interest money are available for some renewable energy projects.

One needs to conduct thorough research to determine all available state, federal, and utility rebates, incentives, and tax credits, as they can save as much as 50 percent of the initial cost of employing alternative technology systems.

4. Energy-Conservation Measures

A list of building-specific energy-conservation measures, or areas prime for building operation and reliability improvement, can be compiled on an initial walkthrough of each facility's energy system.

Some potential areas to examine may include (but are not limited to) lighting, energy-management systems, electrical-distribution systems, building scheduling, load shedding, mini central chiller plants, thermal energy storage, utility sub-metering, the building envelope, retro-commissioning, daylighting, ventilation, waste-heat recovery, swimming pool measures, water conservation, and behavioral-modification training. An owner will typically pick the low-hanging fruit first, like lighting retrofits, which can offer easy and immediate energy and dollar savings with minimum expenditure.

5. Renewable Technologies

Every thorough energy plan will consider renewable technologies, including biomass, geothermal, hydrogen fuel cells, solar, biodiesel, and wind technologies, as potential power sources. However, determining whether any of these options is technically feasible, operationally reliable, and/or cost effective can be complicated.

Renewable technologies are site specific and utilize the natural constraints of the facility's surroundings to produce energy. Today, one common renewable technology found suitable for the average facility is a photovoltaic (PV) system, which turns solar radiation into electrical energy, typically adding high performance value to a facility because of the sun's great accessibility.

However, as the costs of conventional energy continue to soar, they will eventually collide with the cost of renewable technologies. At that point, the market independence that renewable technologies offer will become more of a reality for the average building. The U.S. DOE's Energy Efficiency and Renewable Energy (EERE) website can offer background information on all of the technologies available.

6. Energy Procurement

Analysis of current procurement options means evaluating the use of natural gas to see if purchasing on the open market is a good idea for your facility.

Today, many large consumers procure their own natural gas on the open market instead of going through their local gas company. Buying from an independent supplier, these businesses pay only the cost of the energy and its transportation, avoiding other charges associated with a bundled service and saving as much as 5 to 7 percent.

Electric deregulation in the United States has occurred in several states with varying levels of success. One should monitor public utility commission activities and pending legislation to determine the right choice for your facilities. One also needs to review the electric rate structure of your facility to verify that it is optimum for your business' needs. A variety of rate structures are available from local electric companies, including time-of-day rates, which often have more latitude.

7. Energy Source Diversification

Energy source diversification is one way that one can play the energy-management exercise effectively.

Enter energy source diversification: One way to do this is to use a gas-fired chiller rather than an electric chiller during peak hours. This will shave off expensive peak-demand kW usage and typically offer significant savings to the bottom line.

Energy source diversification can also help mitigate the long-term financial operating risks associated with unexpected price increases, energy-market volatility, domestic and international politics, terrorism, supply availability, and reliability.

8. Distributed Cogeneration

Employing a cogeneration expert to perform a high-level screening analysis of distributed cogeneration options (including combustion, steam, and micro- turbines; reciprocating engines; and fuel cells) will help to determine which of these strategies, if any, are appropriate for the facility.

To make cogeneration a viable option, a building must have a constant electrical and waste heat thermal load. Typically, a minimum of 4,000 hours per year of operation are needed to make the economics attractive. An additional factor called "spark spread," which represents a price gap between the cost of power and natural gas, is also required.

If all these are present, distributed cogeneration can be an extremely energy-efficient alternative. A typical facility using electric utility operates at about 30- to 32-percent efficiency. When incorporating cogeneration, a plant can reach overall efficiencies in the 75- to 85-percent range.

9. Unplanned Utility Outage

Buildings with mission-critical operations that cannot afford any unplanned downtime have had on-site, standby emergency power (plus UPS) for years. Today, the financial loss associated with unplanned utility outages and/or utility "brownout" conditions has left more consumers looking into on-site standby power generation systems.

A facility owner who wants to include this as part of a strategic energy plan should conduct a preliminary evaluation of measures needed to maintain business operations in the event of an outage. From here, the economic impact of this standby power can be balanced against the potential effect of an unplanned utility outage to determine if it is the right solution.

10. Key Performance Indicators

Key performance indicators (KPIs), measured in MMBTU (1 million BTUs) per square foot per year, or dollars per square foot per year, are, simply put, baseline energy-consumption measurements.

Monitoring a facility's KPIs over its lifetime gives owners a way to track building performance relative to a baseline. KPIs can serve as a score card to continually benchmark against other facilities, determining the potential for efficiency improvements and to track progress of the overall energy reduction portion of the plan.

Building owners who wish to participate in a nationally based program to see how their facility's energy consumption compares to other buildings can participate in the federal government's ENERGY STAR® program.

The 10 steps provided here to form a strategic energy plan one needs to make sound utility infrastructure decisions. This dynamic process should be revisited at a minimum of every 5 years, or when major regulatory, political, and sociological events warrant (http://www.marketingreprints.com/).

STRATEGIC PETROLUM RESERVE AND STORAGE POLICY

Global Strategic Petroleum Reserves ("GSPR") refer to crude oil inventories (or stockpiles) held by the government of a particular country, as well as private industry, for the purpose of providing economic and national security during an energy crisis. According to the United States Energy Information Administration, approximately 4.1 billion barrels (650,000,000 m^3) of oil are held in strategic reserves, of which 1.4 billion is government-controlled. The remainder is held by private industry. At the moment the US Strategic Petroleum Reserve is one of the largest strategic reserves, with much of the remainder held by the other 26 members of the International Energy Agency. Recently, other non-IEA countries have begun creating their own strategic petroleum reserves, with China being the largest of these new reserves (http://en.wikipedia.org/wiki/Strategic_Petroleum_Reserve).

Basic Facts about the Strategic Petroleum Reserve : An Overview

The Strategic Petroleum Reserve (SPR) is an emergency supply of federally-owned crude oil stored in deep underground salt caverns along the Gulf Coast. The SPR is widely viewed as a useful asset for improving the nation's energy and economic security because it provides a potentially valuable buffer against short-term oil supply disruptions. Indeed, permanent authority to continue operation of the Reserve was among the uncontroversial provisions included in proposed national energy legislation in 2003. Within that context of broad support, debate has instead focused on: (a) how much oil should be stored in the SPR (b) what specific rules should govern future withdrawals and (c) what should the international community be doing in terms of establishing similar emergency reserves. In particular, there is disagreement about whether and when releases from the SPR should be used to dampen the macroeconomic impacts of high oil prices, even in the absence of an actual supply emergency. Questions have also been raised about recent government purchases to fill the SPR at a time when oil prices are high. The purpose of this paper is to provide a brief background of the SPR in an effort to clarify and provide perspective on the important economic and security issues that surround its establishment and use.

Details of the Strategic Petroleum Reserve

Provisions for the SPR were included in the Energy Policy and Conservation Act (EPCA) of 1975 of the USA with the intent of protecting the nation against supply disruptions of the kind created by the 1973 oil embargo. Today, the SPR holds roughly 660 million barrels of oil (with the capacity to hold 700 million barrels) and is the largest emergency stockpile of oil in the world. The capacity of the SPR is adequate to meet total U.S. oil demand for about 35 days and to offset nearly 53 days of oil imports from foreign suppliers. It takes 13 days for oil from the SPR to enter the market once a presidential order for a withdrawal is given. Oil can be withdrawn from the reserve at a rate of 4.3 million barrels per day.

The SPR is located at four sites along the Gulf Coast in Texas and Louisiana (Bryan Mound, Big Hill, West Hackberry, and Bayou Choctaw) where massive salts exist.

According to the EPCA, the Department of Energy (DOE) is also allowed to exchange oil with private companies for the purpose of "acquiring additional oil for the stockpile." In other words, these exchanges are allowed only where the SPR receives more oil in return than the amount that is released.

What conditions justify withdrawals from the Reserve has been a contentious issue since the SPR was established. Debate usually centers on whether or not the SPR should be used to dampen or moderate minor price spikes. Some argue that early intervention during a minor supply shortage will help calm markets and therefore prevent a major disruption. Others argue that the Reserve should only be used during emergency situations and suggest that early intervention will only discourage "private sector initiatives for preparedness or investment in contingency inventories." Inevitably, politics sometimes enters the debate, particularly during an election year.

Current Debate/Recommendations:

The current debate surrounding the SPR seems to be almost entirely focused on whether oil in the Reserve should be used at times when there is no supply emergency to mitigate the impacts of high oil prices on the economy. A closely related debate concerns the question of whether government should be adding to the Reserve at a time of high oil prices, thereby contributing to higher domestic demand and upward price pressures. The general consensus is that diverting oil from the SPR would likely lower oil prices in the short term. The longer-term effects of such a policy, however, are less certain.

Those who favor filling the Reserve to capacity argue that the amount of oil diverted for this purpose in the context of overall U.S. demand is so miniscule that it would not affect oil prices at all. John Felmy, the chief economist for the American Petroleum Institute (API), has said that while the Reserve is "absolutely an important insurance policy," "you have to be realistic, if we had some negative scenarios, about what kind of role it could play." An analysis by the Petroleum Industry Research Foundation (PIRINC) has concluded that diverting oil from the SPR would impact the oil prices seen by consumers by no more than about 1 cent per gallon. There is even concern that oil diverted from the U.S. Reserve could instead find its way to other markets, such as China. Finally, proponents of filling the Reserve to

capacity argue that current oil prices, if adjusted for inflation, are actually not at record highs and do not signal a supply emergency (which is what the Reserve is intended for). Those who argue for using the Reserve to respond to current market stresses, by contrast, generally argue that at a time of tight supply and high demand, even a small change in demand resulting from a suspension of purchases for filling the Reserve can have a substantial impact on prices.

International Energy Agency (IEA) Reserves

According to a March 2001 Agreement, all 26 members of the International Energy Agency must have a strategic petroleum reserve equal to 90 days of oil imports for their respective country. Only net-exporter members of the IEA are exempt from the reserve requirement. The exempt countries are Canada, Denmark, Norway, and the United Kingdom. However, Denmark and the UK have both recently created strategic reserves due to their requirements as European Union members.

Emergency Oil-sharing Agreements

In addition to maintaining a domestic stockpile of petroleum, several countries also have agreements to share their stockpiles in the event of an emergency.

The Japan, New Zealand and South Korea Agreement

In mid-2007 Japan announced a program to share its strategic reserve with other countries in its region. Negotiations are currently underway with New Zealand on an emergency oil-sharing program whereby Japan would make available for purchase its strategic reserves. In an emergency New Zealand would pay the market price plus negotiated option fees for the amount of oil previously held for them by Japan.

South Korea and Japan have also agreed to share their oil reserves in case of an emergency.

The United States and Israel Agreement

According to the 1975 Second Sinai withdrawal document signed by the United States and Israel, in an emergency the U.S. is obligated to make oil available for sale to Israel for up to 5 years.

The France, Germany, and Italy Agreement

France, Germany and Italy have an oil-sharing agreement to allow each other to purchase their strategic reserves in the event of an emergency.

Africa

South Africa has an SPR. It is managed by PetroSA and the primary facility is the Saldanha Bay oil storage facility, which is a major transit point for oil shipping. Saldanha Bay's six in-ground concrete storage tanks give the facility a storage capacity of 45 million barrels.

Malawi is considering creating a 21-day reserve of fuel, which is an expansion from the current five day reserve. The government has begun planning for storage facilities in the provinces of Chipoka and Mchinji as well as Kamuzu International Airport.

Asia

China

In 2007 China announced an expansion of their crude reserves into a two part system. Chinese reserves would consist of a government-controlled strategic reserve complemented by mandated commercial reserves. This new joint government/enterprise strategic reserve plan is the follow-up to a March 2007 announcement on the construction of a second strategic reserve with an additional 209.44 million barrels.

China's Reserve Structure

- Government Reserves; **101.9 million barrel** strategic reserve
  - ❑ Central government, National Development and Reform Commission(NDRC)
    - — Dalian, Liaoning Province. Approximate planned capacity 19 million barrels (3,000,000 m^3), planned completion 2008.
    - — Qingdao, Shandong Province. Approximate planned capacity 19 million barrels (3,000,000 m^3), planned completion 2008.
    - — Zhenhai, Zhejiang Province. 52 storage tanks with a capacity of 33 million barrels (5,200,000 m^3), filled as of December 2007.
    - — Zhoushan, Zhejiang Province. Approximate planned capacity 33 million barrels (5,200,000 m^3), 7.6 million barrels (1,210,000 m^3) filled as of June 2007.
  - ❑ Oil reserve base controlled by local governments
    - — Guangdong Province has begun plans for a reserve.
    - — Hainan Province has begun plans for a reserve.
- Enterprise Reserves; 209.44 million barrel strategic reserve
  - ❑ Commercial oil reserves by major Chinese oil companies, PetroChina, Sinopec and CNOOC
    - — PetroChina facility, Shanshan County, Xinjiang Uygur Autonomous Region. Planned capacity of 50.9 million barrels (8,090,000 m^3).
    - — PetroChina facility, Tieling, Liaoning Province. 8 storage tanks with a capacity of 5.03 million barrels (800,000 m^3), completion October 2008

- — Sinopec facility, Shanghai, under construction
- — Sinopec facility, Ningbo, under construction
- — Sinopec facility, Zhanjiang, under construction
- — Sinopec facility, Caofeidian, under construction
- — Sinochem facility, under construction
- — Unknown company, Heilongjiang Province
- — Unknown company, Gansu Province

❑ Oil storage reserves by medium and small Chinese oil companies

India

India has begun the development of a **strategic crude oil reserve** sized at **37.4 million barrels**, enough for two weeks of consumption. Petroleum stocks have been transferred from the Indian Oil Corporation (IndianOil) to the Oil Industry Development Board (OIDB). The OIDB then created the Indian Strategic Petroleum Reserves Ltd (ISPRL) to serve as the controlling government agency for the strategic reserve.

The current facilities, inter alia, include:

- Mangalore, State of Karnataka. Capacity of 11.22 million barrels (1,784,000 m^3).
- Padur village, Udipi in the state of Karnataka. Capacity of 18.7 million barrels (2,970,000 m^3).
- Visakhapatnam, State of Andhra Pradesh. Capacity of 7.48 million barrels (1,189,000 m^3).

Japan

As of 2003, Japan has an SPR composed of the following three types of stockpiles:

- State controlled reserves of petroleum at ten different locations totaling 320 million barrels.
- Tomakomai Eastern Oil Reserve Storage Base, 55 storage tanks, total capacity 34 million barrels (5,400,000 m^3).
- Mutsu-Ogawara Storage Base, 53 storage tanks, total capacity 31 million barrels (4,900,000 m^3).
- Kuji Storage Base, 3 storage tanks, total capacity 10.5 million barrels (1,670,000 m^3).

- Akita Storage Base, 15 storage tanks, total capacity 23.4 million barrels (3,720,000 m^3).
- Fukui Storage Base, 27 storage tanks, total capacity 17.9 million barrels (2,850,000 m^3).
- Kikuma Underground Petroleum Storage Facility, 8 storage tanks, total capacity 8.9 million barrels (1,410,000 m^3).
- Shirashima Storage Facility, 8 tankers (4.4 million barrels each), total capacity 35.2 million barrels (5,600,000 m^3).
- Kamigotou Storage Base, 7 storage tanks, total capacity 21.45 million barrels (3,410,000 m^3).
- Kushikino Storage Base, 3 storage tanks, total capacity 10.5 million barrels (1,670,000 m^3).
- Shibushi Storage Base, 40 storage tanks, total capacity 27.6 million barrels (4,390,000 m^3).
    - Privately held reserves of petroleum held "in accordance with the Petroleum Stockpiling Law" of 129 million barrels.
    - Privately held reserves of petroleum products for another 130 million barrels.

The state stockpile equals about 92 days of consumption and the privately held stockpiles equal another 77 days of consumption for a total of 169 days or 579 million barrels. The Japanese SPR is run by the Japan Oil, Gas and Metals National Corporation.

Others

Russia has begun plans for a strategic petroleum reserve. Analysts estimate the size of the Russian SPR would be around **78 million barrels**.

Singapore has an SPR composed of 31.8 million barrels (5,060,000 m^3) of crude oil with an additional 64.5 million barrels (10,250,000 m^3) of oil products for a total of **96.3 million barrels**.

South Korea has an SPR composed of 76 million barrels, equal to about 57 days of consumption. They recently announced plans to increase their SPR to around **141 million barrels** by 2010.

Taiwan has an SPR with a 1999 reported size of **13 million barrels**.

Thailand has recently increased the size of its SPR from 60 days to **70 days of consumption**.

EUROPE

In the European Union, according to a Council Directive 68/414/EEC of 20 December 1968, all 27 members must have strategic petroleum within the territory of the E.U. equal to at least **90 days average daily internal consumption**.

The Czech Republic has a four tank SPR facility in Nelahozeves run by the company CR Mero. The Czech SPR is equal to 100 days of consumption or **2.03 million barrels**.

Denmark has recently created a strategic reserve, the size is unknown. Finland has an SPR with an approximate size of **62.4 million barrels**.

France has an SPR with an approximate size of **65 million barrels**. France is also the only country in the world to hold strategic stocks of jet fuel. As of 2000 jet fuel stocks were required for at least 55 days of consumption, with half of those stocks controlled by the *Société Anonyme de Gestion des Stocks de Sécuritié* (SAGESS) and the other half controlled by producers.

Germany created the Federal Oil Reserve in 1970, stored in the Etzel salt caverns near Wilhelmshaven in northern Germany, with an initial size of 70 million barrels (11,000,000 m^3). The current German Federal Oil Reserve and the Erdolbevorratungsverband (EBV) (the German stockholding company) mandates those refiners must keep 90 days of stock on hand, giving Germany an approximate reserve size of **250 million barrels** as of 1997. The German SPR is the largest in Europe.

Hungary has an SPR with approximately 90 days of consumption or **11.88 million barrels**.

Poland has an SPR with approximately **70 days of consumption**. Another facility holding 20 additional days of consumption is scheduled to be completed in 2008.

Portugal has an SPR with an approximate size of **22.44 million barrels**.

Slovakia has an SPR with an approximate size of **748,000 barrels**.

Spain has an SPR with an approximate size of **120 million barrels**.

Sweden has an SPR with an approximate size of **13.29 million barrels**.

The United Kingdom has recently created a strategic reserve, the size is unknown.

MIDDLE-EAST

Iran

In April 2006 the Fars News Agency reported that Iran has begun plans to create an SPR. The National Iranian Oil Company (NIOC) has begun construction of 15 crude oil storage tanks with a planned capacity of **10 million barrels**. The planned facilities are:

- Ahwaz. 4 storage tanks, total capacity 2 million barrels (320,000m^3).
- Omidiyeh. 3 storage tanks, total capacity 3 million barrels (480,000m^3).
- Goureh. 6 storage tanks, total capacity 4 million barrels (640,000m^3).
- Sirri Island. 1 storage tank, total capacity 500,000 barrels (79,000m^3).
- Bahregansar. 1 storage tank, total capacity 500,000 barrels (79,000m^3).

Others

As of 1975 Israel is believed to have a strategic oil reserve equal to **270 days** of consumption.

Jordan has strategic oil reserves equal to **60 days** of consumption or **6.24 million barrels**.

North America

The United States has the largest reported Strategic Petroleum Reserve with a total capacity of **727 million barrels**. If completely filled, the US SPR could theoretically replace about **60 days** of oil imports. The U.S. facilities are:

- Bryan Mound - located near Freeport, Texas. Capacity of 226 million barrels (36,000,000 m^3).
- Big Hill - located near Winnie, Texas. Capacity of 160 million barrels (25,000,000 m^3).
- West Hackberry - located near Lake Charles, Louisiana. Capacity of 219 million barrels (35,000,000 m^3).
- Bayou Choctaw - located near Baton Rouge, Louisiana. Capacity of 72 million barrels (11,000,000 m^3).
- Richton, Mississippi. A new facility the capacity is unknown.

India to Build Strategic Crude Oil Storages as Insurance

India will begin construction on strategic crude oil storages this year as insurance against disruptions during wars and other emergencies.

Of the three sites selected to hold 5 million tons a year of crude oil reserves, equivalent to country's 15 days requirement, Visakhapatnam in Andhra Pradesh would be the first site with Hindustan Construction Co. emerging as the lowest bidder, official sources said.

Contract is likely to be awarded this week. Visakhapatnam will have underground caverns to hold 1.33 million tons of crude oil that will be managed by Indian Strategic Petroleum Reserves Ltd, a subsidiary of oil Industry Development Board.

Two other sites identified for the construction of crude storage facilities are Mangalore (1.5 million tons) and Podur (2.5 million tons), some 40-km from Mangalore.

India has said it eventually wants to double the overall strategic reserve capacity to 73.3 million barrels, twice the 15 days cover planned currently, but this is yet to be approved by the central cabinet.

Sources said Vizag site has already secured environment clearance and land acquisition is almost complete. The Vizag project envisages storage of high sulphur and low sulphur crude oil in the ratio of 70 per cent and 30 per cent respectively in two caverns.

Government set up Indian Strategic Petroleum Reserves Ltd in 2006 to build and operate the storage facilities. A total investment of Rs 112, 67 crore for the strategic reserves project had been approved with an annual operating cost of 20 million dollars.

INDIAN STRATEGIC PETROLEUM RESERVES

Energy security has become a growing concern for all the developing countries like India who are import dependent for its development energy needs. To ensure energy security at all times, the Government of India has decided to set up 5 million metric tones (MMT) strategic crude oil storages at various locations in the country [Mangalore (1.5 MMT), Vizag (1.0 MMT) and Padur near Udipi (2.5 MMT)]. This strategic storage would be in addition to the existing storages of crude oil and petroleum products with the oil companies and would provide an emergency response mechanism in case of short-term supply disruptions. The construction of the proposed strategic storage facilities is being managed by Indian Strategic Petroleum Reserves Limited (ISPRL), a Special Purpose Vehicle, owned by Oil Industry Development Board (OIDB).

The proposed storage sites are located near the coast line of both East and West so that they are readily accessible to refining sector and are ideally adapted to marine distribution.

The proposed Strategic Crude Oil Storages would be in underground rock caverns/concrete structures and are projected to come in a period of 54 months. The estimates cost of the project is around Rs.2400 crore. In addition, the cost of crude oil would be around INR.9000 crore @ $ 55/bbl crude price.

Engineers India Limited (EIL) has been appointed as Project Management Consultant and the field related activities are in advanced stage for Visakhapatnam site. Ministry of Environment and Forest has given environmental clearance for the project at Visakhapatnam and transfer of land from Visakhapatnam Port Trust (VPT) is in advanced stage. MOU to be signed between ISPRL and Eastern Navel Command for using Navy land at Visakhapatnam is in the final stages of approval at Ministry of Defence.

Land acquisition at Mangalore from Mangalore Special Economic Zone Ltd. is also in the advanced stage and cadastral pipeline route survey at Padur is nearing completion.

The overall position with regard to strategic oil reserves, as far as Indian oil industries are concerned, are summarized below (http//www.indiastat.com/india/showdata):

Petroleum Reserves Scenario at a Glance

- Exploratory and Development Drilling of Wells in India (1970-1971, 1975-1976, 1980-81, 1990-91, 1995-1996 and 2000-2001 to 2006-07)
- Number of Wells and Metreage Drilled in India (1980-1981, 1990-1991, 1995-1996 to 2006-07)
- Oil and Gas Reserves in India (1980, 1990, 1995 to 2007)
- Refinery-wise Capacity Addition Of Petroleum in India (2002-2003 to 2006-2007)
- Refining Capacity Addition of Petroleum in India (2001 -2002 to 2006-2007)
- Selected State/Basin-wise Area of Oil and Natural Gas Exploration

Blocks under New Exploration Licensing Policy (NEPL-VI) in India (As on March, 2007)

- Selected State/Basin-wise Number of Oil and Gas Fields in India (As on 01.04.2006 and As on 01.04.2007)
- Selected State/Basin-wise Number of Oil and Gas Fields in India (As on 01.04.2006 and As on 01.04.2007)
- Selected State-wise Exploration Inputs and Discoveries Made (Oil and Gas Reserves) by Private Companies/Joint Ventures in India (As on 31.03.2006 and 31.03.2007)
- Area-wise Deployment of Deep Drilling Rigs, Wells, Metreage Drilled by ONGC and OIL in India (1970-1971, 1975-1976 and 1980-1981 to 2005-2006)
- Basin/State-wise Number of Wells and Metreage Drilled in India (Since Inception Upto 31.03.2002 to 31.03.2006)
- Reserves of Crude Oil in India (1966, 1970, 1975, 1980, 1985, 1990, 1995 to 2006)
- Selected State-wise Exploratory Inputs Expended by ONGC, OIL and Private/JV Companies in India (Upto September, 2006)
- Selected State/Basin-wise Oil and Gas Fields in India (As on 01.04.2002, 01.04.2004 and 01.04.2005)
- Selected State-wise Number of Oil Wells Explored in India (2002-2003 to 2004-2005)
- Selected State-wise Reserves of Natural Gas in India (1966, 1970, 1975, 1980, 1985, 1990 and 1995 to 2005)
- Status of Wells of AOC, OIL and ONGC in India {(As on 1st April of each Year) (1975, 1980, 1985 and 1990 to 2005)}
- Expected Investment under New Exploration Licensing Policy (NELP) in India (Upto March 2004)
- Investment in Exploration Blocks under NELP in India (31.3.2004)
- Oil and Gas Reserves in India (As on 01.04.2004)
- Selected State/Region/Basin-wise Number of Wells and Meterage Drilled by ONGC in India (2003-2004)
- Selected State-wise in-Place Accretion of Gas Reserves by ONGC, OIL and Private/Joint Venture Companies in India (2001-2002 to 2003-2004)

- Total Investment under New Exploration Licensing Policy (NELP) in India (Upto March 2004)
- Exploratory and Development Drilling by ONGC and OIL (1970-1971, 1975-1976 and 1980-1981 to 2002-2003)
- State/Basin/Region-wise Number of Wells and Meterage Drilled by ONGC in India (2001-2002 and 2002-2003)
- Contracts Signed by the Governments for Onland Field in India (23.2.2001)
- Countrywise Petrol Benzene Content (As on 01.01.2001)
- Location-wise Hydrocarbon Finds by OIL, ONGC and Private/Joint Venture Companies in India (During 1999 to 2001)
- Petrol Lead Content in Different Countries (As on 01.01.2001)
- State-wise/Basin-wise Oil and Gas Fields in India (As on 01.04.2001)
- State-wise/Basin-wise Oil and Gas Fields in India (As on 01.04.2000)
- BID Response for the Blocks Offered under the First Round of CBM (CBM-I)
- Blocks Awarded at International Bidding under New Exploration Licensing Policy in India, 1999
- Blocks Awarded under New Exploration Licensing Policy -I in India
- Blocks Awarded under New Exploration Licensing Policy - II in India
- Exploration Blocks on Offer Under New Exploration Licensing Policy in India - Third Round (NELP-III)
- Exploratory and Development Drilling in India (Petroleum and Natural Gas)
- Number of Blocks Put up for International Bidding under New Exploration Licensing Policy in India, 1999
- Operating Refineries
- Seismic Surveys in India (Petroleum and Natural Gas)

The following table provides summarized information on the Oil stockpiling position in APEC with IEA Membership:

Oil Stockpiling in APEC: IEA Members

Countries	*Days of stockpile*	*Actual or Target*	*Time*
USA (Net Import)	53 clays (Govt) 100 days- (Industry)	Actual	March 2004
Japan (Net Import)	92 days (Govt) 81 days (Industry)	Actual	March 2004
Korea (Net Import)	51 days (Govt) 55 days (Industry)	Actual	End 2003
Germany (Consumption)	90 days (Govt)	Actual	End 2003
China (Net Import)	90 days (Govt)	Plan	By 2010

India Major Oil companies are presently concentrating on expanding the strategic buffer storage capacity of oil reserves to meet future eventualities of insecure supply of oil to support domestic industries, mainly in the energy sector (Fig. 4.6)

Type of Storage Systems

The various types of strategic storage structures built by the India Oil Companies broadly fall under 5 different categories:

Tankage with Oil Cos.

Crude	7.5 MMT
Prod.	7.0 MMT

	Import Basis	*Demand Basis*
Crude	34	23
Prod.	54	37
Total	88	60

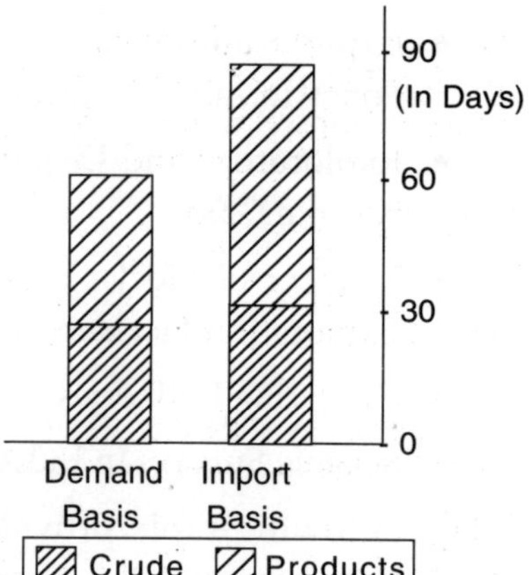

#Basic Data: 2004-05 in MMT.

Fig. 4.6: Existing Storage Available With Indian Oil Companies

- Surface Tanks
- Underground Concrete Tanks
- Underground Salt Cavern
- Underground Rock Cavern
- Floating Tanks

Consideration of Strategic Site Selection

The broad criteria chosen for site selection of strategic reserves are the following:

- Strategic and safe locations
- Proximity of supply source to Refineries.
- The cluster of refineries to be supplied crude oil.

Strategic Petroleum Reserve Storage Sites in the USA

SPR Storage Sites—A Case

The illustration presented here (Fig. 4.7) shows that an Emergency crude oil is stored in the Strategic Petroleum Reserve in salt caverns along Texas-Louisiana coastline. Created deep within the massive salt deposits that underlie most of the Texas and Louisiana coastline, the caverns offer the best security and are the most affordable means of storage, costing up to 10 times

Fig. 4.7: SPR Storage Sites

less than aboveground tanks and 20 times less than hard rock mines.

Storage locations along the Gulf Coast are selected because they provide the most flexible means for connecting to the Nation's commercial oil transport network. Strategic Reserve oil can be distributed through interstate pipelines to nearly half of the Nation's oil refineries or loaded into ships or barges for transport to other refineries.

Strategic Petroleum Reserve caverns range in size from 6 to 35 million barrels in capacity; a typical cavern holds 10 million barrels and cylindrical in shape with a diameter of 200 feet and a height of 2,000 feet. One storage cavern is large enough for Chicago's Sears Tower to fit inside with room to spare. The Reserve contains 62 of these huge underground caverns (STRATEGIC STORAGE\DOE - Fossil Energy The Strategic Petroleum Reserve Storage Sites.htm).

How the SPR Storage Sites Were Created

Salt caverns along the Gulf Coast have been used for storage for many years by the petrochemical industry. When the U.S. Government decided to create the Strategic Petroleum Reserve in the mid-1970s, it acquired previously created salt caverns to store the first 250 million barrels of crude oil. This was the most rapid way to begin securing an emergency supply of crude oil following the oil shocks of the 1970s. To stockpile oil beyond the first 250 million barrels, the Department of Energy created additional caverns.

Salt caverns are carved out of underground salt domes by a process called "solution mining." Essentially, the process involves drilling a well into a salt formation, then injecting massive amounts of fresh water. The water dissolves the salt. In creating the SPR caverns, the dissolved salt was removed as brine and either reinjected into disposal wells or more commonly, piped several miles offshore into the Gulf of Mexico. By carefully controlling the freshwater injection process, salt caverns of very precise dimensions can be created. For every barrel of crude oil to be stored in the SPR's salt caverns, it took 7 barrels of water to create the storage space.

Besides being the lowest cost way to store oil for long periods of time, the use of deep salt caverns is also one of the most environmentally secure. At depths ranging from 2000 to 4000 feet, the salt walls of the storage caverns are "self-healing." The extreme geologic pressures make the salt walls rock hard, and should any cracks develop in the walls, they would be almost instantly closed.

An added benefit of deep salt cavern storage is the natural temperature difference between the top of the caverns and the bottom? -a distance of around 2,000 feet. The temperature differential keeps the crude oil continuously circulating in the caverns, maintaining the oil at a consistent quality.

The fact that oil floats on water is the underlying mechanism used to move oil in and out of the SPR caverns. To withdraw crude oil, fresh water is pumped into the bottom of a cavern. The water displaces the crude oil to the surface. After the oil is removed from the SPR caverns, pipelines send it to various terminals and refineries around the nation.

The rationale for selection of unlinked Rock Caverns is primarily as follows:

Selection of Unlined Rock Cavern

- Availability of Competent Rock at relatively shallow depths to ensure a stable *caveirn* configuration.
- High permanent Ground Water Table above top of cavern to ensure water flow always into cavern.
- Economical for large capacities.

Strategic Storages: Surface Vs Underground

A comparative scenario analysis of the surface vis-a-vis underground strategic storage structures of Petroleum reserves is given below:

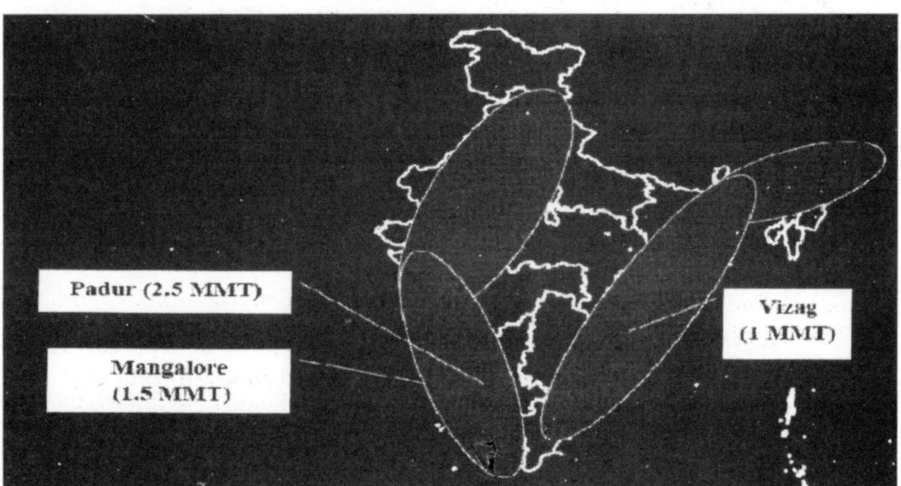

Figure 4.8: Location of Proposed Strategic Oil Reserve in India

Surface :	*Underground :*
• Do not meet safety requirements to withstand enemy attacks during wars.	• Have inbuilt safety to withstand attacks during wars
• Vulnerable to fire hazards, natural disasters and accidents	• Resistant to fire hazards & natural disasters.
• Occupy large tracts of valuable land	• Effective use of land

Refineries Covered by Strategic Storage

The following table 4.1 gives an update on the spread of Refineries covered under Strategic Storage in India.

Table 4.1: Spread of Refineries under Strategic Storage in India

Total Capacity : 5.0 Million Tonnes

Sl. No.	*Sites*	*Type Of Storage*	*Mainly Catering to*	*Capacity (in MMT)*
1.	Mangalore, Karnataka	Underground Rock Caverns	MRPL, KRL, BPCL (Mumbai) and HPCL (Mumbai)	1.5
2.	Visakhapatnam, Andhra Pradesh	Underground Rock Caverns	HPCL-VIZAG, CPCL, BRPL and IOCL Refineries at Haldia & Barauni	1.0
3.	Padur, Karnataka	Underground Rock Caverns	IOCL Refineries at Koyali, Mathura & Panipat and RPL, ESSAR and BORL	2.5

Areas of Cooperation

For setting up of Strategic Storage of Crude oil at various strategic locations the following nature of cooperation at the domestic and international level is being explored and worked upon:

- Government of India is in the process of setting up Strategic Storage of Crude Oil at various locations (up to 15 MMT in phases).
- There exists scope for mutual co-operation and exchange of information on technology transfer with respect to Strategic Reserves.

- Co-operation in areas of construction, operation and maintenance of Underground Rock Cavern and other Storages.
- Opportunity for participation of EU Construction Companies in storage projects.

Management Structure of Strategic Oil Reserve

- Indian Strategic Petroleum Reserves Ltd (ISPRL), a SPV created under Oil Industry Development Board (OIDB), Ministry of Petroleum & Natural Gas to have ownership and control of the crude oil inventories and to coordinate the release and replenishment of crude oil stock with "Empowered Committee" to be constituted by the Government.

Source: OIDB, ISPRI, 2007

How long will the Indian Petroleum Reserves last?

The Indian government is these days giving lots of attention to the conservation of petroleum products in view of the need to reduce ever increasing gap between demand for and indigenous supply of crude oil and petroleum products.

In the mechanized and the fast-moving world of today, the consumption of petroleum products has become an important yardstick of a country's prosperity.

Despite the discovery of new sources of unconventional energy, petroleum remains the primary energy source in India, and even more so, all over the world. The consumption of petroleum in the world, which started as a few tonnes a year around 140 years ago, has reached over 3000 Million metric tonnes (MMT) per year!

Even in India, it is increasing at a very steep rate from 3.5 MMT in 1950-51 to 74.7 MMT in 9596. This is expected to reach 130 MMT in 2001-02 and 175 MMT in 2006-07.

Out of the known reserves, only a part may be technically economically feasible to explore. This fact, coupled with the present and expected consumption rates implies that these reserves may not last beyond the next 30 years.

For India, the situation could be even more difficult. Given our limited reserves, our present known stocks may not last even 10 years at the current consumption rate. Our present indigenous production is only 30.86 MMT and is less than 50 percent of our annual requirement.

Therefore, the need of the hour is to conserve petroleum by its judicious use, substituting it by other resources wherever feasible and restricting its use only to the essential needs. Petroleum Conservation, then becomes our joint responsibility be it the industries, individual citizens, organizations, Oil Companies or the Government. Each one of us has specific and significant roles to play.

Overall Strategy of Promoting Oil Conservation

The Indian government has initiated various steps to promote conservation of petroleum products in the transport, industrial, agricultural and domestic sectors.

These include adoption of measures and practices which are conducive to increase fuel efficiency and training programme in the transport sector; modernization of boilers, furnaces and other oil operated equipments with efficient ones and promotion of fuel efficient practices and equipment in the industrial sector; standardization of fuel efficient irrigator pump sets and rectification of existing pump sets to make them more energy efficient in the agricultural sector and development as well as promotion of the use of fuel efficient equipment and appliances like kerosene and LPG stoves in the household sector.

These activities are promoted and coordinated by the Petroleum Conservation Research Association (PCRA) and Oil Marketing Companies under the guidance and supervision of Ministry of Petroleum & Natural Gas.

The Impact of Additions to Strategic Petroleum Reserves on World Oil Demand

"Three countries have publicly expressed plans to build and fill SPR's - China, Russia and India. These SPR's will be filled in addition to those that already exist in the 26 member IEA. A look at the numbers to fill the proposed Strategic Reserves in any reasonable time frame shows that this act of filling the reserves will be a significant demand on world oil production.

First, a background note on Strategic Petroleum Reserves worldwide is presented here. The EIA states that the US has 50% of the world's Strategic Reserves of oil at approximately 700 million barrels. This would leave about

700 million barrels for the rest of the world—currently the 25 other nations (besides the US) of the IEA, including the European Union, Japan, South Korea and Canada This is to be noted here that there is evidence that certain countries may have far more Strategic Reserves than the EIA's estimate. For example, an article in the China Daily asserts that Japan has Strategic Reserves for 169 days of domestic consumption - which would amount to 980 million barrels at current consumption rates

Note also, other countries, including the US (possible plans to increase the SPR by an additional 300 million barrels), Australia, Asia and the EU may be drawing up plans to increase the size of their SPR's.

Putting aside planned increased to SPR's in countries with existing SPR's for now, this analysis will go through the numbers on the planned increases in China, India and Russia:

India

India has stated that they have targeted a SPR of 40 million barrels initially. At a fill rate of 100,000 barrels per day (bpd) - the same rate that the US used from Nov 2001 onward for its SPR — this would require 400 days to achieve.

China

China has stated that they want a SR of 100 million barrels. At a fill rate of 100,000 bpd, this would require 1000 days · over 2.5 years. At 100 million barrels, the SPR would only supply China's petroleum needs for 20 days. A fill rate of 200,000 bpd would require 1.25 years to fill 100 million barrels.

Russia

Russia has not stated the size of their reserves, but at a daily consumption of oil of 2.6 million bpd, a SPR sufficient for 30 day consumption would equal 78 million barrels. At a rate of 100,000 bpd, this would require 2.1 years to achieve.

Note that once a country commits to build facilities for Strategic Petroleum Reserves, it does not make economic sense to keep them empty. Strategic Petroleum Reserves are kept in very large tankers (for example, as in Japan and in China) or underground storage tanks, which are both expensive to maintain - although underground storage facilities are significantly less expensive to maintain. Cost estimates per barrel of stored oil average $3.00 in Japan and $1.60 in the European Union, and $0.20 for the US—(demonstrating the clear cost benefit of underground storage, if it is feasible) (it is unclear whether these costs are one-time or annual).

The desire to have large reserves, particularly in Asian countries stems not only from the ability to "cushion" impacts of temporary shortages, made more severe by a lack of domestic oil production, but also a desire to influence the price of oil.

The increase planned SRP's worldwide may also be related to the increase in US dollar reserves worldwide. Economist Brad Setser estimates that increases worldwide in reserves of US dollars may have hit $700Bn this year.

The cost of the facilities, the increase in US dollar reserves, and the economic/political desire of having sizable SPR's mean that the plans will very likely go through in the corning years.

All in all, it appears that oil demand will be increased by 300,000 bpd —if India, China and Russia fill at 100,000 bpd respectively—to as high as 1,000,000 - if India, China and Russia fill at 200,000 bpd and the US, the EU and other Africa, Latin America fill at 100,000 barrels per day. Or possibly the numbers can go higher, if other countries, such as African or other Latin American countries, decide to build and fill SPR's, or, alternatively (or at the same time) the EIA countries decide to increase the size of their SPR's. These demand numbers to fill SPR's worldwide are not insignificant in a tight oil market.

America's Strategic Petroleum Reserve:
Energy Security for the Future

In his State of the Union message, President Bush announced his intention to increase the Strategic Petroleum Reserve (SPR) - the world's largest supply of emergency crude oil - to 1.5 billion barrels by 2027. SPR oil is stored in huge underground salt caverns along the coastline of the Gulf of Mexico. At the present time, the reserve holds about 700 million barrels of crude oil. The Minerals Management Service (MMS) and the Department of Energy work together to fill and maintain the SPR.

Oil from MMS's Royalty-in-Kind (RIK) program - by which royalties from oil production are accepted in-kind (oil) rather than in-value (cash) - is used to fill the reserve. The President's fiscal year 2008 budget includes a request in the Department of Energy budget for $18 million to expand the SPR. This spring, the government will begin buying 100,000 barrels of oil a day to fill the stockpile to its current capacity of 727 million barrels. Congress established the emergency reserve in 1975 after the Middle East oil embargo, to make up for global supply disruptions. The U.S. tapped the stockpile in 1991 after Iraq invaded Kuwait and in 2005 after Hurricanes

Katrina and Rita disrupted pipelines, refineries, and Gulf of Mexico production. MMS manages offshore oil and gas exploration as well as renewable and alternative energy sources such as wind, wave, and solar on 1.76 billion acres of the Outer Continental Shelf while protecting the human, marine, and coastal environments. MMS also collects, accounts for, and disburses mineral revenues from Federal and American Indian lands, sharing revenues with states, American Indians and individual lease holders, and the U.S. Treasury. The revenues are also contributed to the Land and Water Conservation Fund and other special use funds. In Fiscal Year 2006, disbursements were made of approximately $12.8 billion, totaling nearly $164.9 billion since 1982.

Grid Integration and Storage Strategies for Renewable Energy

Fuel costs, environmental regulations, renewable portfolio standard mandates, and customer demand is increasing the amount of energy utilities must obtain from renewable resources. However, many technical obstacles stand in the way, including issues with integrating renewable energy generation technologies with existing transmission networks, intermittency of resources, and difficulty in dispatching energy when and where it is needed. For utilities, renewable energy technology companies and advocates, effective RE storage is a "holy grail" that could potentially help solve all these problems. This webinar examines trends and developments related to grid integration and RE storage and how these opportunities may help facilitate the adoption of renewable energy technologies.

This webinar is designed to provide information on grid interconnection and RE storage to systems planners, technical staff, procurement groups, and other utility personnel who are responsible for obtaining energy from renewable resources and ensuring that it reaches the end user in the most cost-effective and efficient manner possible. The information provided will also be of interest to independent power producers, technology providers, government agencies that deal with RE issues and renewable energy advocates.

Carbon Capture and Storage (CCS): A New Zealand Experience

Background

Carbon capture and storage (CCS) is an engineering system involving the capture of carbon dioxide (CO_2) instead of its release to the atmosphere. Once captured, the CO_2 is then condensed, transported to the injection site (if not co-located with the extraction point) and then injected into a geological formation for indefinite storage. The intention behind developing CCS technology is to make a substantial global decrease in the amount of CO_2 being released into the atmosphere from large point sources (such as thermal power stations or gas and oil production facilities).

Internationally, CCS is considered a useful transition mechanism to more "environmentally friendly" technology for economies which are currently reliant on fossil fuels (primarily coal) for electricity generation. This means that CCS projects under the current regulatory regime would be subject to standard Resource Management Act (RMA) requirements, but that no other existing legislation either specifically enables or prohibits CCS activities. The International Energy Agency (IEA), together with the Carbon Sequestration Leadership Forum (CSLF) recently strongly recommended that governments take action to put in place appropriate regulatory frameworks for CCS.

The Ministry of Economic Development of the Government of New Zealand is facilitating a whole-of-government approach to CCS through the New Zealand CCS Policy Group and is coordinating a review of existing legislation of relevance to CCS, as well as monitoring international CCS developments. The policy group has set a timeframe for addressing regulatory gaps in the management of potential CCS activities. The Foundation for Research, Science and Technology-led NZ CCS Research Steering Group is a joint government/industry initiative. This group has contracted GNS Science to evaluate storage capacity in Taranaki and Waikato, while private interests are addressing storage capacity in Southland, where the bulk of New Zealand's substantial lignite deposits lie.

Timeframes for Deploying CCS as a Widespread Climate Change Mitigation Option

International timeframes for CCS

Internationally, CCS is viewed as a potentially useful addition to the growing collection of climate change mitigation mechanisms, particularly for economies with substantial reliance on fossil fuels. There are many CCS projects deployed for demonstration and research purposes, but few with immediate commercial applications.

Technology

The core processes of CCS have been practised for some time. CO_2 has been captured, transported and injected as part of enhanced oil and gas recovery projects for more than 20 years. This does not necessarily translate into a basis for widespread deployment of CCS for climate change mitigation purposes.

A recent IEA/CSLF report entitled "Near Term Opportunities for Carbon Capture and Storage" estimated the mitigation potential of CCS would amount to 6.0 cubic giga tonnes of captured CO_2 by 2050. The largest commercial CCS project is Sleipner in Norway, which stores about 1 million tonnes of carbon each year. It would take more than 6,000 Sleipner-sized CCS projects to meet the IEA's suggested 2050 capacity.

CCS technology is unproven at the scale and cost that would be required should CCS uptake in the global electricity generation sector meet its potential to significantly mitigate CO_2 emission levels. Some recent developments include that the European Union (EU) has indicated its intention that all new coal-based electricity generation will be required to incorporate CCS by 2020. This policy is conditional on the establishment of at least twelve CCS demonstration plants throughout the EU, to test CCS in different contexts. Meanwhile, last year British Columbia put in place requirements for CCS for all new coal-based electricity plants, and the federal Canadian Government is currently considering following suit.

At a global scale, there are multiple demonstration projects in the planning, construction or operational phases. A significant demonstration project in which New Zealand is involved (through the New Zealand CCS R&D group) is CO_2 CRC's Otway Basin Project in south-west Victoria, Australia. The injection phase of the research and demonstration project is scheduled to begin in early April 2008.

Current Commercial Applications

Two categories of existing commercial application of CCS exist. The first is where CCS is being used in association with oil or gas extraction, for example at Weyburn in Canada. In these circumstances, the oil/gas extraction process already requires the separation of CO_2. This reduces the overall cost of the CCS process, as the capture component is otherwise considered to be the most expensive phase, while injecting the CO_2 allows for greater recovery of the remaining oil or gas resource. The Algerian In Salah gas production facility includes a demonstration of CCS, but, as the European gas market requires a minimal CO_2 content, the CO_2 must already be stripped from the natural gas stream. There is therefore a strong commercial rationale for separating the CO_2 even without CCS.

The second form of existing commercial application for CCS is where a carbon price is securely in place. There are two noteworthy projects in operation at present, both in Norway (where a carbon tax has been in place since 1991) - the aforementioned Sleipner (1.0 million tonnes CO_2 stored per year) and Snehvit (0.7 million tonnes CO_2 stored per year). The Norwegian examples, however, are both associated with gas fields, and as such the capture of CO_2 is also a pre-existing component of standard operational models.

In their very recent joint report, the IEA and CSLF estimate that the high cost of CO_2 capture will limit pre-2025 deployment to points which already capture CO_2 for other ends or for whom capture is relatively cheap. At In Salah, for example, the CCS component adds around US\$6/CO_2 tonne, whereas the Intergovernmental Panel on Climate Change (IPCC) estimates that retrofitting existing coal fired power plants could add around US\$25-50/CO_2 tonne.

The IEA/CSLF report notes that CCS will only fulfil its potential as a climate change mitigation mechanism if it is technologically and commercially viable for deployment purely as an emission mitigation mechanism. Notwithstanding the effect that an increasing price for carbon internationally could have on CCS, the IEA considers that to precipitate useful CCS deployment, the following four actions need to be pursued:

- a diverse portfolio of at least 20 fully integrated industrial scale demonstration plants (larger than 2 mega tonne/year) by 2010;
- significant international investment in CCS projects, including in developing countries through Kyoto Protocol-sanctioned Clean Development Mechanisms;
- a robust regulatory framework that provides for safe storage, and is clear about liability for fugitive emissions;
- higher public awareness and education, to support CCS deployment.

While some jurisdictions are already beginning consultation on CCS regulatory options, there appear to be no specific regulatory frameworks in place for enabling CCS. The IEA/CSLF report highlights as a priority the need to ensure appropriate regulatory frameworks are in place by 2010: "By 2010 it is essential that governments have established the appropriate legal and regulatory frameworks that are needed for safe, large scale storage of CO_2".

Strategic Gas Reserve and EU Energy Security

Energy security is back at top of the political agenda of the European Union. Prime reasons are tighter energy markets in general, high capacity utilization in OPEC oil production and a volatile Middle East. As European demand for natural gas is rapidly growing, the European gas market may eventually become tight. When the market is liberalized, prices will react more directly than before with regard to whether or not there will be sufficient supplies to meet demand growth. It is of significant interest how a potential disruption of supply from one source, possibly Norway, Algeria or Russia, or another, caused by nature, military, political or economic reasons, could be dealt with among consuming European countries, as addressed in EU (2002).

To improve security-of-supply in the long-run it is necessary for the EU to develop regulation and market structures in ways that mitigate price volatility and keep them at sufficient levels, in order to make producers invest in long-term, huge and costly field developments and infrastructure. One problem that market liberalization creates is that the lower prices resulting in the short and medium term are not providing enough incentive for long-term investments. The lead-times between when decisions are made and the project actually is on stream are especially long when the fields are huge and a long distance from the market, as is the case for Europe. Lack of investments in the short and medium term creates shortages and higher prices in the long-term. It is thus a conflict between short and long-term interests also for the consumer.

In an emergency situation the establishment of Strategic Gas Reserves (SGR) is a means of mitigating prices, together with short-term arrangements that can move gas demand to other energy sources. The pure existence and possible use of SGRs also have the potential of working as insurance against price spikes ever to take place. This is parallel to how the Strategic Petroleum Reserves (SPR) and the International Energy Agency's (TEA) crisis program should work under an oil crisis.

STRATEGIC GAS STORAGE IN US

As of May 2004, there was roughly 8 Tcf of gas storage capacity in the US, with about 4 Tcf needed to always remain in storage as base gas. Base gas is needed in order to provide enough pressure for gas to be withdrawn on demand. Therefore, total working storage capacity is about 4 Tcf. This is equal to approximately 17% of annual consumption.

Most gas storage is in depleted gas or oil fields, with the second largest storage capacity being in aquifers, and the smallest in salt caverns. Depleted gas or oil fields are the cheapest to commission, as they take advantage of existing wells, internal distribution systems, and pipeline connections. They are also widely available. Aquifers are suitable for gas storage if the water-bearing sedimentary rock is overlaid with impermeable caprock. The use of aquifers requires more base gas than does depleted gas or oil fields. Last, salt caverns provide high withdrawal and injection rates, and have low base gas requirements. The commissioning of cavern storage is more expensive than depleted field conversions, but this type of storage allows several withdrawal-injection cycles per year.

Gas storage is heavily clustered in the consuming Northeast/Midwest, with most of the depleted field storage in Pennsylvania, West Virginia, Ohio, and Wisconsin, and most of the aquifer storage in Illinois and Indiana. Storage is also clustered in the producing Southwest, where there is mainly depleted field storage, but also a growing amount of salt cavern storage (primarily in coastal areas). Typically, gas storage reaches its peak volume in about October, and gas is drawn down throughout the heating season. About March, gas stocks reach their low point, after which the buildup for winter begins. Last, many salt formation and other high deliverability sites have been developed by independent storage service providers, who cater to customers that require quick response times, such as electricity generators and gas marketers. The seasonal role that storage plays can be clearly seen in the graph

Total Natural Gas in Storage in the US

New storage facilities are continuously being constructed. As of May 2006, FERC lists 130 Bcf of new storage projects that are on the horizon (projects where a permit has not yet been requested of FERC) (FERC, 2006).

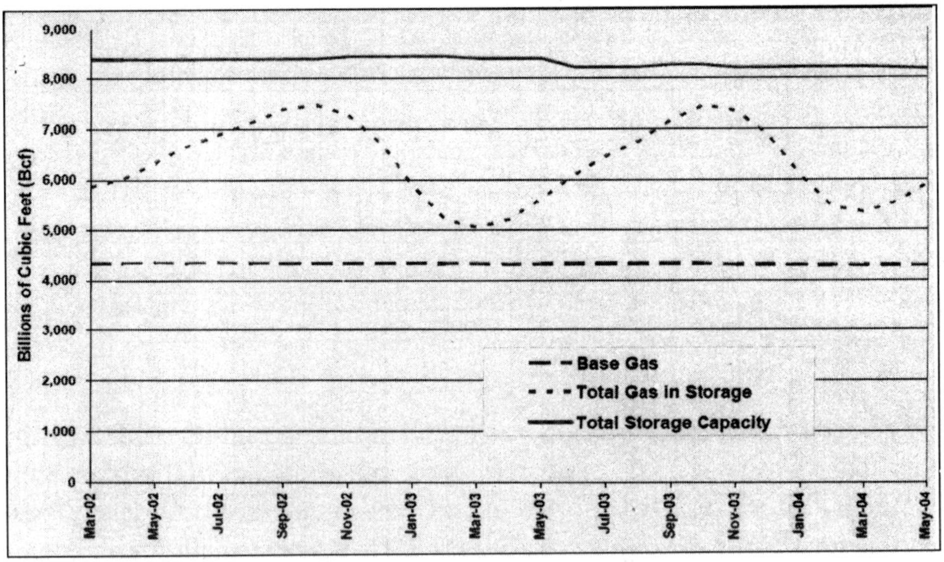

Source: *EIA, Natural Gas Monthly*, May 2002–July 2004.

Figure 4.9: Strategic Storage Capacities of Natural Gas

Transmission

The largest capacity pipeline route is from Gulf Coast production (onshore Louisiana and Texas, as well as offshore Gulf of Mexico) to the Midwest and Northeast. The Western part of the country uses much less gas than does the East. It is served, however, by multiple sources - namely, by pipelines from the Southwest (connecting into Southern California), pipelines from Canada, and pipelines from the Rocky Mountain gas fields.

Pipelines from gas-producing western Canada connect to the Northwestern, Central, Midwestern, and Northeastern parts of the US. A small amount of gas is exported to Mexico. The current US interstate natural gas pipeline consists of over 200,000 miles of transmission lines with an estimated daily delivery capacity of about 119 Bcf (billion cubic feet) (Tobin 2001). The average daily consumption rate in 2000 was half this amount. This results in a capacity utilization factor of roughly 50%.

International Connections/Imports

Pipelines from gas-producing western Canada connect to the Northwest with a capacity of about 4.6 Bcf/day (billion cubic feet per day), to the Central part of the US with a capacity of 4.2 Bcf/day, to the US Midwest with 4.3 Bcf/

day capacity, and into New England with about 3.5 Bcf/day capacity. The US Southwest has 15 interconnections with Mexico, with an aggregate export capacity of 3.6 Bcf/day. In 2004, net imports to the US were 3.4 Tcf, which is a 4.3% increase over the previous year, but below the 2001 volume of 3.6 Tcf. Net imports from Canada in 2004 were 3.2 Tcf. That same year, the US exported 0.4 Tcf to Mexico. Net LNG imports were about 0.6 Tcf. Given both the small size of the current and potential volume of imports at existing LNG facilities, we can consider North America essentially a closed system.

Impact of the 2005 Hurricane Season

Hurricanes Katrina and Rita caused about 800 Bcf of natural gas to be shut in (as of June 19, 2006), which is about 22% of annual Gulf production, or almost 4% of annual US natural gas consumption. Natural gas prices skyrocketed to over $15.00 per million Btu (MMBtu) in the aftermath of the hurricanes, and residential consumers paid record prices for natural gas heating in the winter. However, the market was successful in allocating the reduced production among consumers, and no shortages developed. The hurricane season was followed by a warmer than average winter. High gas prices combined with a mild winter resulted in below-normal consumption, which in turn resulted in the level of working gas in underground storage in the summer of 2006 exceeding the range of working gas in storage over the past five years, as shown in Figure 4.10 below.

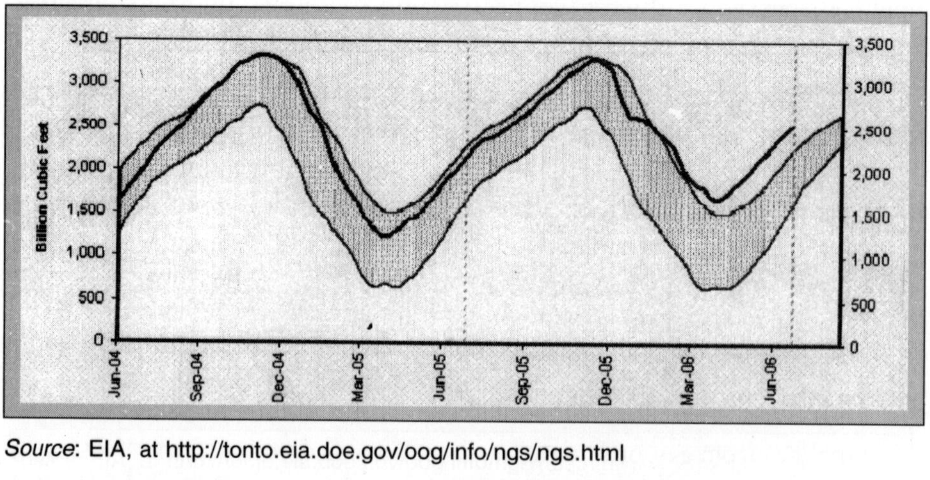

Source: EIA, at http://tonto.eia.doe.gov/oog/info/ngs/ngs.html

Fig. 4.10: Working Gas in Underground Storage (red line) Compared with 5-Year Range (Grey area—showing minimum and maximum storage volumes at the same time of year for 2001 to 2005)

However, perhaps we should plan for a more severe test of nature than the 2005 hurricane season followed by a mild winter brought. If we could determine whether the system could continue to function in the face of, say, a couple of 2005 hurricane seasons back-to-back, with a couple of harsh winters following them, then we would be more confident in judging whether a strategic reserve would be needed or not. It is with this test in mind that a model was created, which will be described below.

Model and Scenario Description

In order to better understand the dynamics involved and the effect a strategic natural gas reserve would have on the system, an aggregate model of natural gas storage, supply, and demand was created. The model is used to examine the effects a series of natural disasters would have on the natural gas infrastructure and the benefits of a strategic natural gas reserve. The natural gas system is modeled at an aggregate national level and neglects regional effects, such as natural gas transfers between regions. The model is an aggregate model of the natural gas system at the national level.

Production from all regions feeds into a single storage area from which national sector aggregated demand is removed. The model was balanced with data by sector residential, commercial, industrial, and power generation from the Energy Information Administration. The data used is a four (2001 to 2004) or five year average (2000 to 2004), depending on availability. Data from 2005 onward is not used due to the influence of hurricanes Katrina and Rita (http://www. systemdynamics.org/conferences/2007/proceed/papers/ELLIS216.pdf).

A Model Overview

For the purposes of testing a strategic storage reserve, the model assumes that the reserve contains 75 Bcf of natural gas, is opened one month after the natural disaster and stays open for five months. During this time period, the reserve is used at a rate that matches the current amount of daily production being lost due to the disaster. The storage reserve is not refilled during the course of the model run. The pricing mechanism assumes that price adjusts as a factor of demand, production, and storage volumes. Price is used to adjust demand to keep the system in balance. A price increase causes a decrease in demand and a price decrease causes demand to increase. The elasticity of demand used is 0.1 for the commercial and residential sectors, 0.15 for the power generation sector, and 0.2 for the industrial sector. The algorithm

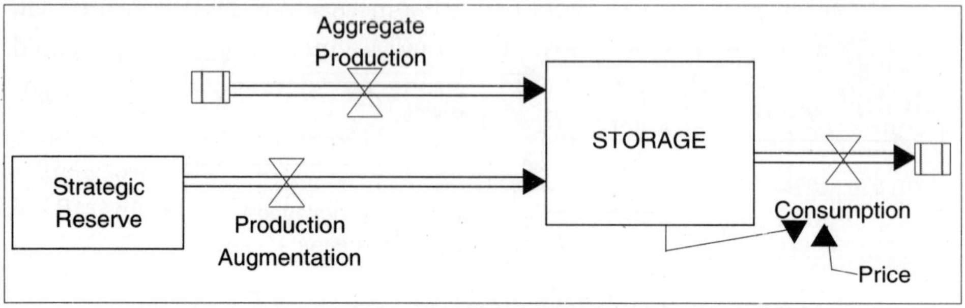

Fig. 4.11: A Model Plan Diagram Linking Strategic Reserve to Consumption Point

compares current demand and storage volumes with historic values for those numbers and current production with maximum production capacity and adjusts price to bring the system back into equilibrium. For example, if current volumes in storage are lower than what they have historically been for the current time of year, a reduction in demand is necessary to keep the system in balance, so the price increases. If volumes are higher than historic values, then a demand increase is necessary to keep the system in balance, and the price decreases (Fig. 4.11)

Production and storage are weighted as having a larger effect on the price than demand, with price adjusting in proportion to the ratio between current and maximum production and storage and as the square root of the ratio of current and historic demand. Price is adjusted with a 30 day delay to represent the time it takes to observe the information and make changes to the price.

Chapter 5

Energy Risk Management

Risk Management In Oil And Natural Gas Sector

Oil Stocks and Risk Management

Oil stocks are usually held by oil companies for operational purposes, and by countries and state utilities to provide a cushion against unexpected surges in demand and possible disruptions in imports. Oil companies usually hold stocks that account for 55–65 days of consumption. International Energy Agency members are required to hold emergency oil stocks equivalent to at least 90 days of net imports. The European Union requires its members—also IEA members—to hold stocks equivalent to at least 90 days of consumption. It is not easy to estimate oil stocks held by developing countries. Because of the cost, their stocks are relatively smaller than those of OECD countries, but can amount to 25–55 days of consumption, which is also typical for oil companies in these countries. Correspondingly, world oil stocks in 1997 were about 5,500 million barrels, equal to 70–80 days of average global consumption. This, at present, is adequate for unexpected transient shortages or temporary interruptions. With the continued growth of non-OECD oil consumption, oil stocks will function less effectively. Their size relative to the global oil market will decline, since most developing countries do not maintain emergency oil stocks. If this trend continues, vulnerability to sudden and substantial oil supply disruptions will increase.

Liberalization of Markets: Easing the flow of Oil

Another aspect of security is the liberalization of energy markets in importing countries. Liberalization and deregulation, coupled with the development of oil futures and forwards markets, mean easier and more secure flow2of oil from exporting to importing countries. Most oil producers are now inviting foreign companies to participate in oil development, which will significantly enhance the security of the oil market. And the strengthening of the World Trade Organization will add further to the security of the energy market. Although security in terms of flows of oil and gas to importing countries is improving, the security of supply to consumers faces new challenges. Liberalization, the withdrawal of government responsibility for supply, and competition among private suppliers are creating challenges in securing reliable supply to individual consumers.

Energy Treaties and Agreements: Enhancing Energy Security through Cooperation

In response to insecurity after the first oil shocks, OECD countries convened a conference in Washington, D.C., in 1974 that led to the establishment of the International Energy Programme (IEP), the founding charter of the International Energy Agency (IEA). To improve energy security, the participating countries pledged to hold oil stocks equivalent to 90 days of net imports. They also developed an integrated set of emergency response measures that included demand restraint, fuel switching, and surge oil production. These measures also included the important provision of stock drawdown and sharing of available supplies in the event of oil supply disruptions involving a loss of 7 percent or more for any member country or for the group (Martin, Imai, and Steeg, 1996).

In 1977 the IEA developed another set of coordinated emergency response measures that allow for a rapid and flexible response to an impending oil security crisis. Also in that year, IEA countries agreed to long-term energy policies and programmes aimed at diversifying resources, employing energy efficiency measures, and developing new energy technologies. And in response to changing circumstances, the IEA updated its policies in a statement of shared goals at its ministerial meeting in 1993.

In 1991, 51 countries signed the European Energy Charter to enhance energy security throughout the Eurasian continent and promote the creation of an open and non-discriminatory energy market. The signatories included the European Communities and their member states, the countries of Central and Eastern Europe, all the members of the Commonwealth of Independent States (CIS), and Australia, Canada, Japan, and the United States. By applying the principles of non-discrimination and market-oriented policies, the charter was aimed at improving energy security, increasing the efficiency of all links in the energy chain, enhancing safety, and minimizing environmental impacts.

Three years later, in 1994, all the signatories to the European Energy Charter (except Canada and the United States) signed the Energy Charter Treaty, along with a protocol on Energy Efficiency and Related Environmental Aspects, which entered into force in 1998. Japan and the Central Asian states have since signed the Charter Treaty and China is showing increasing interest in it, enhancing its geopolitical scope. The treaty applies to all economic activities related to a broadly defined energy sector. Its main purpose is to promote the creation of an open and non-discriminatory energy market throughout the Eurasian continent (Schuetterle, 1999). The Charter Treaty obligates signatories to encourage and create stable, equitable, and transparent conditions for foreign investors in their countries, stipulates that General Agreement on Tariffs and Trade (GATT) provisions will govern trade in energy materials and products, ensures the transit of energy exports through third countries, and sets out procedures for settling disputes relating to the treaty's provisions. Also serving to enhance energy security are interregional and intraregional agreements established to foster economic cooperation between member countries, such as Asia-Pacific Economic Cooperation (APEC), which involves 21 economies of Asia, Oceania, and the Americas. Enhancing energy security is one of the aims of APEC, which set up its own Energy Work Group and the Asia Pacific Energy Research Centre (APERC) for this purpose. No doubt the above-mentioned treaties and arrangements helped to foster energy investments and improve energy security—not only for their members, but also globally—by encouraging sustainable energy policies.

Oil in Transport: A special point of vulnerability

The transport sector accounts for half of global oil demand, with heating, electricity generation, industrial processes, and petrochemicals accounting for the rest. Demand for oil in transport is growing rapidly, particularly in aviation. Over the next 20 years demand for oil in transport is expected to grow by 2.3 percent a year, compared with growth in total demand for oil of around 1.9 percent a year. Most of this growth will occur in non-OECD countries, where it is expected to average 3.6 percent a year, with the highest growth projected for China and East and South Asia. Demand in OECD countries, which are already witnessing some saturation in vehicle ownership, is expected to grow at one-third that rate. In the near term there is no cheap and viable alternative to oil in transport, particularly in private vehicles and aviation (Douaud, 1999). Use of oil for mobility will increase in all countries, as the transport fleet grows and uses exceed improvements in transport efficiency. An interruption in oil supply, however temporary, could cause major disruption to the transport sector and to the world economy.

Oil Prices: A Source of Insecurity

The severe volatility of oil prices in the 1970s and early 1980s contributed to the insecurity in energy markets. The price of oil is the market leader for energy pricing. Gas and coal, because of competition, are priced accordingly. OPEC has the power to influence oil prices by allocating supply and monitoring and restricting production by its members. With the growing discipline in its ranks, this influence may increase in the future. Moreover, the depletion of non-OPEC oil and future growth in its marginal cost will increase oil prices in the medium and long term. Prices will be further increased by the development of the more expensive non-conventional oil, once crude oil supply peaks around 2010. Although short-term price volatility, like that in 1998–2000, cannot be ruled out because of the many factors explained above, oil prices are not expected to be as volatile as in the past. After 2010, gradual and moderate price increases are expected. Many recent predictions have been made of future oil prices. Such moderate price increases, along with continuous improvement in energy efficiency, mean that oil prices are unlikely to place a more serious burden on the global economy than they do now. Moreover, the expected improvements in the real price of oil will spur producing countries to enhance and expand their production and provide them with the badly needed financial resources to do so.

Income Security for Oil-exporting Countries

Some countries depend—for income and for development—on energy exports, particularly oil. This group is not limited to the Middle-East; it includes a few countries in Sub-Saharan Africa and Latin America. Nor is this dependence on oil export income restricted to exporting countries; the benefits of oil export income spread to other countries in the region through wage remittances and financial assistance. In the Gulf countries three-quarters of government revenue is derived from oil exports. Energy exports account for almost two-thirds of government revenue for other countries in the region, such as Algeria, the Islamic Republic of Iran, and Yemen. The dramatic drop in oil prices in 1998 and early 1999 led not only to budgetary problems in many energy-exporting countries, but also to unemployment and significant drops in incomes. Such economic problems were not only restricted to the oil exporters but were also experienced by their neighbours, which depend on revenues from exports of goods and services to the oil-rich countries and on remittances from workers in these countries. For energy-exporting countries, export security is becoming as important as energy import security is to resource-short countries. All this is enhancing the prospects for global energy security.

Dependence on oil exports has an additional implication for exporting countries. These countries, particularly OPEC members, are worried about the possible long-term impact on export demand of policies to mitigate environmental impacts, promote energy efficiency, and increase use of renewable energy sources. Although exaggerated in the short term, the potential impact could pose long-term problems for the countries, adversely affecting their economic and social development. Having met the needs of the global energy sector satisfactorily over the past 25 years, oil-exporting countries are asking for compensation if mitigation actions start to bite. This request is being reviewed in international negotiations. It may be many years before exporting countries' income is affected. Meantime, it is hoped that with international assistance and compensation, they will be able to diversify their income sources and reduce their dependence on oil exports.

Security of Natural Gas supply

Natural gas is slowly gaining importance in the energy market. Between 1987 and 1997 gas consumption increased from 1,756 giga cubic metres to 2,197, for an annual growth rate of 2.27 percent, compared with 1.47 percent for total primary commercial energy consumption. Over the period until 2020 natural gas demand is expected to grow still faster—at an annual rate of 2.6 percent, compared with 1.9 percent for oil. And natural gas supply, since it is starting from a much lower base than oil supply, is not expected to peak until well beyond 2020 (IEA, 1998).

Internationally traded natural gas accounted for 19 percent of gas consumption in 1997, compared with 44 percent for oil. So, just as for oil, though to a lesser extent, there is a mismatch between the location of gas supply and its consumption. Security of supply is therefore critical. But the physical characteristics of natural gas make ensuring security of supply for gas more complicated than for oil. Crude oil is an eminently fungible commodity, portable by ship, pipeline, road tanker, or even barrel. In contrast, gas requires expensive pipelines or LNG infrastructure. These delivery systems are relatively inflexible: pipelines cannot be moved or built overnight, and LNG, although somewhat portable, still requires an expensive receiving terminal. Crude oil and, more important, refined oil products can be transported to any location that can receive a ship or road tanker. Moreover, gas is difficult to store in significant quantities. The energy content per unit of volume is much lower for gas than for oil. Gas is simply more difficult to handle than liquid. Its storage often depends on the suitability of geological structures, while oil tank farms can be built relatively easily and cheaply. All these factors mean that the solutions used to ensure security of oil supply (storage, diversification of supplies) do not apply as easily to gas. At its simplest level, gas supply security can mean operational reliability—in other words, that gas flows to the consumer when it is required. In particular, this means meeting consumer needs on days of peak demand, usually in winter. The gas supply system must be configured to give the required flexibility. Security of supply also involves reducing strategic risk, namely, the risk of a major disruption to supplies caused by, for example, political factors or major technical failure, such as the failure of a high-pressure pipeline. This is an extension of operational security, but of a different order of magnitude. Strategic risk is growing in parallel with the growing share of gas in meeting countries' primary energy requirements. It can be reduced through:

Inter-connectivity, the degree of physical interconnection with other gas systems, an important factor in ensuring strategic security of supply. Interconnectivity is more than simply a guard against potential failure; it also encourages diversity of supply.

Diversity of supply, which is fundamental to security of supply because it spreads risk. All sources of supply are unlikely to fail at the same time. Countries have often explicitly diversified supply by contracting with several countries. France, for example, buys gas from Algeria, the Netherlands, Norway, and Russia. In recent years there have been a number of spot LNG sales into Europe from LNG suppliers using spare capacity. Security of supply also entails guarding against long-term risk—ensuring that consuming countries can secure future and additional supplies as their existing supplies are depleted. This represents a challenge, as the bulk of the world's gas reserves are in areas that are far from current markets and also often have a high level of country risk. Some gas-importing countries, such as France, use long-term strategic storage to guard against significant disruption of supply. Such storage can be in depleted oil or gas fields, aquifers, salt caverns, or other geological structures.

Political Risks to Gas supplies and Security of Interregional Grids

With the increase in internationally traded natural gas and LNG, political risk to gas supplies and cross-boundary networks will increase. One of the measures taken to reduce political risk is the Energy Charter Treaty, which attempts to provide a legal framework for the transit of hydrocarbons and electricity through pipelines and grids. The treaty prohibits contracting parties from imposing unreasonable charges for the transit of energy or taking unreasonable or discriminatory actions. Most important, in the event of a dispute over transit, transit states may not interrupt or reduce existing transit until the parties have had an opportunity to resolve the dispute using the treaty's dispute resolution mechanisms. As a further aid to international gas trade, the treaty prohibits countries from refusing new transit or new capacity to other treaty signatories solely on the basis of the origin, destination, or ownership of the energy being transported.

Political risk is also an issue for investment in the gas industry. Because of the capital intensity of the industry, a sound investment environment is needed to encourage companies to invest. This requires clear legal, fiscal, and contractual frameworks; transparent regulatory processes; and regulatory certainty. To improve the international investment environment for projects involving the transit of gas as well as oil and electricity across national boundaries, the Energy Charter Conference, an intergovernmental body made up of the 51 states that have signed the Energy Charter Treaty, began in 1999 to elaborate the Multilateral Transit Framework Agreement. The aim is to strengthen the international rule of law on transit issues by further developing the treaty's transit provisions.

With increasing utilization of gas, lengthy gas pipeline grids across countries and boundaries are becoming familiar. This raises concerns about political and security problems relating to the integrity of the pipeline and continuity of supply—because of possible regional disputes, disagreements among firms, or accidents or sabotage. One of the principal aims of the Energy Charter Treaty is to provide for such contingencies. But not all countries are signatories to the treaty, though the numbers are increasing. However, the treaty provides guidelines that non-member countries can incorporate in agreements relating to cross-boundary pipelines. Moreover, the increasing strength of markets, the World Trade Organization regulations, and the increasing interdependence of markets and countries enhance the security of supply from regional gas grids.

Natural gas is an ideal fuel for electricity generation. It is environmentally benign compared with coal and offers the potential for very high efficiencies in combined cycle plants. Like oil, natural gas resources are unevenly distributed across the world, but unlike oil, gas is not easily transportable or tradable. Expensive interregional gas grids are a solution as long as security is guaranteed, an aim of the Multilateral Transit Framework Agreement. Interregional grids provide benefits to all—suppliers, consumers, and transit countries. In addition, the increased security inherent in pipeline systems enhances cooperation among the countries involved. Satisfying the increasing energy demand in India and South and East Asia may require building a very large interregional pipeline from the Islamic Republic of Iran or the Gulf. This would require not only a huge investment but also a coordinated regional arrangement and guarantees. Such a pipeline could sustainably meet the increasing demand for electrification in parts of Asia that account for more than a third of the world's population and where electricity demand is growing at twice the world average.

Risks to Internal Security of Supply

In addition to the external risks, internal security risks are on the increase. These include the risk of electricity shortages due to increasing dependence on gas in electricity production. This increasing reliance on gas also raises supply security issues because of the possible domino effect in the event of gas supply problems. As a result of an interruption in gas supply to gas-fired power stations, a national grid could find itself short of capacity just as demand is peaking. Such security risks can be reduced, however, through coordination between the gas grid and the electric utilities, by switching combined cycle gas turbines (CCGT) to other fuels in the event of gas shortages, and by diversifying the energy sources for power generation (coal, nuclear, oil, gas, and hydro).

Diversity is more important than origin of supply. The mechanisms for securing diversity can be based on market instruments (payments for reserve capacity) or regulation (requirements for storing a certain number of days' worth of backup fuel supply). The U.S. gas market has shown how the price mechanism can enhance security of supply during less severe shortages. Many power stations burn both fuel oil and natural gas. As gas prices rise and the supply demand balance tightens, the generators switch to the cheaper fuel, freeing up supply for gas consumers who cannot switch.

RISK MANAGEMENT IN POWER SECTOR: CASE STUDY—US EXPERIENCE

Electric Power Risk Assessment

The security of electric power control networks represents a significant emerging risk to the electric power grid. This risk assessment is the result of a 6-month effort by the Information Assurance Task Force (IATF) of the National Security Telecommunications Advisory Committee (NSTAC), which included interviews and discussions with representatives throughout the electric power industry (IATF:http//www.ewaservices.com/)/(NSTAC:http/ /www.espionage info.com/MO-NR/National Security-Telecommunications-Advisory-Committee.html).

The electric power grid is a highly interconnected and dynamic system of over 3,000 public and private utilities and rural cooperatives. These utilities have incorporated a wide variety of information and telecommunications systems to automate the control of electric power generation, transmission, and distribution.

The electric power industry is undergoing significant change, fueled by marketplace forces and Federal legislative and regulatory activities. New players are entering the power generation and delivery market, and existing utilities are being required to offer open access to their transmission systems. The functions of power generation, transmission, and marketing which traditionally have been tightly integrated are now being separated within utilities and, in some cases, even spun off into new companies. Competition, aging proprietary systems, and reductions in staff and operating margins are leading utilities to rapidly expand their use of information systems and to interconnect previously isolated networks.

Physical destruction is still the greatest threat facing the electric power infrastructure. Compared to this, electronic intrusion represents an emerging, but still relatively minor, threat. Insiders are considered to be the primary threat to information systems. Downsizing, increased competition, and the shift to standard protocols will add to the potential sources of attacks, whether from inside, or outside, a utility.

Recent legislation increases the jurisdiction of Federal, state, and local law enforcement authorities over attacks on electric power control systems. However, the lack of effective reporting mechanisms, inconsistent use of logins, passwords, and warning banners, and a low probability of being detected, caught, and prosecuted hinder effective deterrence of potential attackers.

Substations represent the most significant information security vulnerability in the power grid. Many of the automated devices used to monitor and control equipment within transmission and distribution substations are poorly protected against intrusion. Interconnections between control centers and corporate data networks, widespread use of dial-up modems, and use of public networks (PN) are other sources of vulnerabilities.

Utilities use a variety of mechanisms to protect the electric power grid from disruption, including contingency analysis, redundant control centers, dial-back modems, and firewalls. However, few utilities have an information security function for their operational systems, and the lack of convincing evidence of a threat has led senior managers to minimize information security investments.

The recent U.S. western power outages left 2 million people without power for up to 6 hours on July 2, 1996, and 5.6 million people without power for up to 16 hours on August 10, 1996. A critical node analysis, combined with knowledge of weak protections on substation automation elements, could allow an electronic intruder to achieve similar effects. A major coordinated attack could disrupt activities at a national level.

The study found no evidence of a disruption of electric power caused by an electronic intrusion. Three trends, however, will increase the exposure of electric power control networks to attacks:

- The shift from proprietary mainframe control systems to open systems and standard protocols
- Increasing use of automation, outside contractors, and external connections to reduce staff and operating costs
- The requirement to provide open access to transmission system information dictated under FERC orders 888 and 889.

The probability of a nationwide disruption of electric power through electronic intrusion short of a major coordinated attack is extremely low, but the potential for short-term disruptions at the regional level is increasing.

The report closes with a number of recommendations for the President, the electric power industry, and the NSTAC. Of these, the most important recommendation is that the President should consider assigning to the appropriate Department or Agency the mission to develop and conduct an ongoing program within the electric power industry to identify the threat and increase the awareness of vulnerabilities and available or emerging solutions.

NASTAC Approach to Power/Energy Security

In January 1995, the Director of the National Security Agency briefed the National Security Telecommunications Advisory Committee (NSTAC) on threats to U.S. information systems and the need to improve the security of critical national infrastructures.

In May 1995, the NSTAC formed the Information Assurance Task Force (IATF) to work closely with the U.S. Government to identify critical national infrastructures and their importance to the national interest. Following several meetings with elements of the national security community, civil departments and agencies, and the private sector, the task force determined that electric power, financial services, and transportation were some of the most critical of the infrastructures. The task force determined that it would study these infrastructures to assess the extent to which their dependence on information and information systems puts them at increased risk to denial-of-service attacks.

This document is a report of the findings of the IATF's Electric Power Risk Assessment Subgroup's assessment of the risk that electronic intrusions pose to electric power distribution systems, specifically examining the vulnerability of the systems that manage and control generation, transmission, and distribution. This study represents a 6-month effort that included interviews with representatives from the operations, security, and information systems elements of eight utilities, one power pool association, the Utility Telecommunications Council (UTC), the North American Electric Reliability Council (NERC), the Electric Power Research Institute (EPRI), the Federal Energy Regulatory Committee (FERC), and a number of industry consultants. The utilities interviewed ranged in size and location and included both publicly held companies and government-owned and -operated power administrations.

During the course of the study, interview teams worked under the assumption that the risk to the electric power infrastructure was a function of four factors: threat, deterrence, vulnerabilities, and protection measures. In this model, a threat is any circumstance or event with the potential to cause harm to a system in the form of unauthorized destruction, disclosure, modification of data, or denial of service. A deterrent is an attempt to prevent or discourage an action before it is taken, thus mitigating a threat. Vulnerabilities are points of weakness within a given system and are mitigated by protection measures.

Interviews with the utilities and power pool were conducted in a nondisclosure/nonattribution environment, and utility staff was all forthcoming and helpful throughout the process. In addition, EPRI provided invaluable support to this study, undertaking its own survey of industry managers to assess their views on information security concerns. The UTC also assisted by arranging a meeting at its 1996 annual conference in Kansas City, Missouri, and identifying contacts in a number of utilities.

DERIVATIVES TO MINIMIZE RISK EXPOSURES

Derivatives: A Brief History

Following the introduction of swaps, in the mid-1980s, the energy derivatives market was valued in the year 2000 at $40-bil to $60-bil a year. The total exposure of US banks in energy swaps was conservatively estimated at $20-bil to $40-bil for long term deals. Energy derivatives include forwards, futures, options and swaps.

Swaps are becoming increasingly popular, with no hedging position to manage, no physical delivery and settlement by cash. Furthermore, swaps can be tailored to each individual company's needs.

Oil Swaps and Futures

Until relatively recently, future exchanges such as the New York Mercantile Exchange, the London International Petroleum Exchange, and the Singapore Monetary Exchange provided the main opportunities for oil traders to hedge their short, medium and long term risks.

The introduction of oil swaps in the mid 1980's changed the oil industry's view on hedging as swaps formed a new environment for risk management.

Besides future exchanges, the most widely used indices for pricing of oil swaps are the daily and weekly Platts crude oil and petroleum products assessments which cover Europe, the United States, Arab Gulf anf Far East markets.

As well as crude oil and petroleum products, Platts weekly petrochemical assessments are used as an index in the propane swaps market. As a result, Platts prices are regarded as an integral part of the swaps market as a means of determining price.

Financial institutions which are closely involved with the oil industry, e.g. providing letters of credit or financing long-term ventures use oil swaps in combination with other financial indices such as LIBOR rates in order to hedge their risks.

According to a survey of commodity risk management instruments published by the United Nations Conference on Trade and Development, three-quarters of all commodity swaps are petroleum-based.

Refinancing of loans could increasingly depend on evidence that countries are using risk management techniques. Mexico in a well-published risk management programme, successfully hedged its entire crude oil production on futures, cash and derivatives' markets for a six-month period during the Gulf War.

Extending forward months on the IPE and NYMEX has allowed swaps' players additional risk management. It is because of this additional risk management that future exchanges have seen a benefit through growth in swaps markets.

The opportunity to offset their swap positions on to the future exchanges by means of an Exchange for Swaps (EFS). This is similar in concept to Exchange for Physical (EFP) where two players offset their physical trade on to the exchange.

However the EFS mechanism is only valid where an IPE contract is the agreed pricing basis of the swap transaction e.g., a jet swap that is priced off a differential to the IPE's gasoil contract.

Energy Risk Management and Value-at-Risk (VAR) Modeling

The value of energy trades can change over time with market conditions and underlying price variables. The rise of competition and deregulation in energy markets has led to relatively free energy markets that are characterized by high price shifts. Within oil markets the volatile oil price environment after OPEC agreements in the 1970s requires a risk quantification." Value-at-risk" has become an essential tool for this end when quantifying market risk. There are various methods for calculating value-at-risk. The methods we introduced in this paper are Historical Simulation ARMA Forecasting and Variance–Covariance based on GARCH modeling approaches. The results show that among various approaches the HSAF methodology presents more efficient results, so that if the level of confidence is 99%, the value-at-risk calculated through HSAF methodology is greater than actual price changes in almost 97.6 percent of the forecasting period.

ENERGY RISK VALUATION: NERA MODEL

The growing complexity of energy markets has made risk management a critical issue for energy firms and market participants alike. Deregulation, volatile commodity prices, and shock events including the collapse of Enron, the California energy crisis, and most recently the "Blackout of 2003" are causing investors and shareholders to probe deeper into the risk management practices, analytics and controls in place at public energy companies. More than ever before, company management and its Board of Directors are being held accountable for performance deviations, lapses in risk control and other surprises, especially when they occur as a result of ineffective risk communication.

In this heightened state of shareholder and investor vigilance, effective risk management practices and clear communication are essential. In this regard NERA helps energy companies respond to the increasing demand for accountability by identifying, quantifying and prioritizing the risks they face, and then implementing strategic risk management programs such as hedging.

NERA' Focus in Energy Security Domain

NERA Economic Consulting is an international firm of economists who understand how markets work. NERA's clients include corporations, governments, law firms, regulatory agencies, trade associations and international agencies.

NERA's Energy Risk Management and Valuation Team includes more than 30 Ph.D. economists with commercial experience, committed to providing clear, independent advice on real world financial and risk management issues worldwide. Senior leaders in the Energy Practice are acknowledged experts and provide expertise on business issues confronting the energy industry, including energy market structure and regulation. In all, more than 500 professionals operate in 16 offices across North and South America, Europe, Asia and Australia. NERA economists devise practical solutions to highly complex business and legal issues arising from competition, regulation, public policy, strategy, finance and litigation. Founded in 1961 as National Economic Research Associates, our more than 40 years of practical experience creating strategies, studies, reports, expert testimony and policy recommendations reflects NERA specialization in industrial and financial economics. Because of NERA's commitment to deliver unbiased findings, we are widely recognized for our independence. NERA clients come to the clients expecting integrity; they understand this sometimes calls for their willingness to listen to unexpected or even unwelcome news.

NERA's Energy Risk Management and Valuation Team provides energy clients with independent, objective and credible advice on risk management, business strategy and corporate governance issues. NERA draw upon our industry "know-how," combining technical and quantitative expertise, market knowledge and trading experience with innovative thinking and creative approaches to meet our clients' needs.

NERA Energy

NERA is at the forefront of the continuing transformation of energy industries worldwide. NERA have pioneered in developing approaches for introducing competition in segments such as power generation where competition is workable and for improving the regulation of sectors where it is not. NERA works with companies and governmental bodies worldwide to design competitive power markets and to develop tariffs and rules of access for regulated transmission and distribution systems for electricity and gas and transport of oil and oil products. With industry restructuring, NERA also help companies develop strategies for exploring new opportunities and minimizing new risks, including issues related to climate change and other environmental initiatives. NERA helps its clients to develop new regulatory strategies and, when needed, support our clients with analysis and testimony before regulatory commissions, antitrust and competition policy agencies, and domestic and international courts. NERA helps clients to decide which lines of business to pursue; to divest assets no longer consistent with their strategy; to identify and evaluate opportunities for mergers, acquisitions and investment; and to develop bidding, trading, contracting, and marketing organizations and strategies. NERA's work also includes designing and conducting energy auctions, providing strategy and valuation, advice on mergers and acquisitions, the financing of energy companies and the financial restructuring of distressed companies.

NERA's Approach

In the last ten years, risk management has become integral to strategic planning at many energy companies. Driving this change are managers who have succeeded in stepping away from measuring and managing risks one at a time in order to better evaluate their firm's "risk landscape" in the aggregate. By examining risks in this holistic fashion, firms can realize enormous benefits in their capital structure, budgeting, capital allocation and other areas. With extensive experience in risk analysis and risk management techniques, NERA's experts are well versed in modeling, analyzing and communicating the effects of combined risks to energy companies. NERA then aggregated these risks across multiple risk factors and business units, taking into account correlations and diversification effects, to measure their combined effect on performance measures such as earnings-at-risk or cash-flow-at-risk.NERA also assists clients in measuring individual risk exposures on a consistent basis. By using NERA's portfolio approach to risk, a firm's risk analysis, management, communication, and strategy design can benefit from the hedges that already exist in the portfolio. Integrated risk modeling of NERA (NERA f-irm), cash flow at risk measurement (NERA c-far), and strategic planning services help their clients develop specific solutions to the portfolio of risks they face.

Risk management contributes to a company's bottom line in several ways. In addition to reducing the potential *financial* impact, risk management also *enhances firm value* by facilitating strategic decision making, reducing earnings and cash flow volatility, allowing for an optimal allocation of resources (including capital), and reinforcing shareholder confidence in company management. NERA's Strategic Planning for energy risk management entails the following steps:

Facilitate Decision-Making

- More effective cross-functional communication regarding risk.
- Better consideration of risks in the capital budgeting and strategic planning process.
- Improves performance measures and pricing by risk-adjusting results.

Risk management contributes to a company's bottom line in several ways:

Reduce Total Volatility of Cash Flow and Earnings

- Ensures sufficient internal funds for strategic investments
- Reduces likelihood of financial discomfort or distress and thus reduces the cost of financing
- Results in fewer surprises for shareholdersEnterprie Value Enhancement

Optimize the Allocation of Risk Management Resources and Operating Costs:

- Ensures cost-efficient risk mitigation
- Ensures cost-efficient risk transfer

Reinforce Stakeholder and Shareholder Confidence:

- Risks are better understood and managed
- Enhances the information flow to the board of directors

Effective risk management begins with an understanding of the nature of risks and their sources.

Risk Portfolio Diagnosis

Risk Identification

- Identification of financial & economic risk drivers
- Financial risk mapping

Risk Quantification

- Risk modeling
- Risk analysis

Risk Prioritization

- Risk comparison on a common basis
- Risk tolerance
- Ability to manage, hedge and mitigate

Risk Governance

- Risk guidance
- Designing risk strategy
- Setting risk management objectives
- Ensuring key risk management activities

Risk Management Structure and Design

- Risk policy, procedure, development and enhancement
- Setting risk limits and controls
- Risk monitoring
- Risk measurement

Risk Solutions

- Operational solutions
- Hedging solutions
- Analysis
- Development
- Implementation

Capital Market Solutions

- Deal design
- Deal evaluation
- Insurance

Internal and External Risk Communication

- Internal risk reporting enhancement
- Providing informative, actionable and timely information
- Ensuring risk transparency and consistency
- Risk disclosure

NERA's typical engagements focus on the following key aspects of a solid risk management program:

MANAGING RISK IN TODAY'S ENVIRONMENT

NERA Services on Portfolio Diagnosis: Risk Identification

Effective risk management begins with identifying the sources of risk, and defining the nature of those risks. Risks can be economic or financial, exogenous or endogenous, in addition to being driven by external and internal forces (including market, credit, operational and regulatory). In some cases, designing a proper categorization scheme to ensure that risks are being appropriately captured is the most difficult task. To further complicate matters, credit and operational risks can occur as a result of the same activity. But just because the credit risk and operational risk profiles increase jointly, the overall risk profile should not.

The Key Sources of Risk to Identify

Market Risk

- Price risks; Market liquidity risks; Basis risks

Credit Risk

- Counterparty risk; Doubtful accounts; Soverign risk (repatriation)

Performance Risk

- Earnings at risk; Cash flow at risk; Debt capacity; Funding risk

Treasury Risk

- Foreign exchange risk; Interest rate risk; Cost of capital; Liquidity risk
- Macroeconomic conditions
- Recession; Deflation

Other Risk

- Regulatory risk; Legal risk; Strategic risk; System risk.

Portfolio Diagnosis: Risk Quantification and Prioritization

Risk quantification determines whether a particular risk, or set of risks, merits further attention. By examining the correlation and diversification effects of the risk portfolio, NERA can use Earnings-at-Risk or Cash-flowat-Risk measurements to assess the relative contribution risks have on a company's overall exposure. By focusing on those risks that contribute most to the total risk profile, NERA can prioritize a company's risks and the company's efforts accordingly. This prioritization process also enables NERA to identify risks that require special risk management approaches.NERA also uses a portfolio approach to identify appropriate benchmarks that could be used in tracking or forecasting a company's aggregate risk exposure, and for use in hedging efforts and other risk transfer and risk financing strategies. NERA helps identify situations where risk management is being misapplied. For example, suppose that the company's foreign exchange risk naturally hedges some interest rate exposure. In this case, using financial contracts to hedge foreign exchange risk may prove to be costly and inefficient. NERA helps energy companies and other market participants evaluate their risk environment and bring their risk management practices in line with the risk profile of the company.

Risk Governance

Corporate risk governance includes not only the board and senior executive responsibilities, but also the policies, incentives and processes that enable companies to respond quickly and decisively to emerging risk. Risk governance also involves setting risk strategy, policy and procedural guidelines, as well as ensuring that the responsibilities and incentive structures of risk management personnel are aligned with risk management objectives. However, simply addressing these elements is only the beginning. Risk governance often sets the stage for developing risk culture; a "risk aware" organization should be the ultimate goal, with all involved understanding the importance of monitoring and managing risk. NERA can help a company create a fluid risk governance structure throughout its organization, beginning with the board and continuing all the way through the back office.

Hedging Strategy Design

Hedging strategies may involve structuring several different plans to obtain the right balance of flexibility and effective risk hedging. NERA experts offer hedging advice based on a thorough understanding of the underlying risks, relationships, and value drivers. NERA's hedging strategies incorporate our market insight, industry knowledge and analytical findings. Furthermore, NERA can identify counterparties, assess the total cost of hedging, and assist with implementation and performance measurement.

Hedging strategies of NERA give due consideration to certain parameters that include, but are not limited to:

- Available hedging markets: direct hedges vs. cross-hedges
- Physical, financial or synthetic opportunities

- Hedge durations, including seasonality where applicable
- Methods for evaluating hedge performance, such as using the Naïve Method or Regression Analyses
- Forward price behaviors, such as contango or backwardation
- Determining the expected margin needs (e.g., variation margin, collateral calls)
- Potential effect on cash flow volatility
- Evaluations of hedge effectiveness
- Hedge monitors
- Hedge adjustments (e.g., changes in risk exposure or hedging objectives, the hedging ratio, basis management, new information, and rolling the hedge)
- Evaluate the effectiveness of the hedging positions: ex ante vs. ex post facto.

Valuation

NERA experts provide accurate and independent valuation services for clients in our regulatory, litigation and risk advisory engagements.We specialize in the decomposition and valuation of complex energy assets and portfolios, generating units, regulated assets, stranded assets and retail customer portfolios. NERA's capabilities also extend to valuation of natural resources such as natural gas reserves, production sites, coal reserves and mining operations. For financial assets, NERA values portfolios of complex contracts, derivatives, securities, exchange-traded instruments, and complex components of structured notes.

ENERGY INFRASTRUCTURE RISK MANAGEMENT

Checklists for Small and Medium Sized Energy Facilities

Introduction

The security, economic prosperity, and social well being of the United States depend on a complex system of interdependent infrastructures. Key among these is the energy infrastructure, the electric power, oil, and natural gas production, transmission, storage, and distribution systems—large and small—that fuel and power the economy. Working through the states and with industry, the Department of Energy's Office of Energy Assurance (DOE/

OEA) is responsible for coordinating the federal government's effort to ensure a secure and reliable flow of energy to America's homes, industry, public service facilities, and the transportation system. As part of its multifaceted mission, OEA conducts analyses of physical and cyber vulnerabilities of the national energy infrastructure and develops scientific and technological solutions to correct or minimize system vulnerabilities (USDE, 2002).

To achieve the goal of protecting our nation's critical energy infrastructure, OEA is developing an integrated federal, state, local, and industry vulnerability mitigation and consequence management architecture. The purpose is to encourage each component of the energy infrastructure to implement a risk management program that starts with a vulnerability analysis and risk assessment, and results in the implementation of appropriate vulnerability mitigation measures. OEA's goal is to include all types and sizes of energy facilities that make up the U.S. energy infrastructure in this integrated risk management architecture. However, small and medium sized energy facilities (e.g., some municipal utilities, independent utilities, and rural cooperatives) without a large corporate parent company often do not have the human resources and financial means to implement a full risk management program.

The purpose of this document is to provide some general guidance and a starting point so that a smaller energy facility is able to identify its critical functions and assets, become aware of threats and vulnerabilities, evaluate and rank the threats in terms of the incidents they may cause, and initiate a security enhancement program, if appropriate. An asset of an energy facility is any person, equipment, material, information, installation, or activity that has a positive value to the facility. A threat is any indication, circumstance, or incident with the potential to damage disrupt an asset. An incident with the potential to cause the loss of or damage to an asset is referred to as an undesirable event. Undesirable events can be due to actions such as theft, compromise, destruction, sabotage, assault, assassination, and kidnapping or due to occurrences such as nonavailability or impaired operation of an asset. A vulnerability is any weaknesses that can be exploited by an adversary to initiate an undesirable event that damages or disrupts an asset.

Why Implement a Risk Management Program?

Risk is a measure of the potential for damage or loss of an asset that will adversely affect the ability of an organization to function properly or a mission to be carried out. The level of risk or risk rating of an asset is a function of two factors: (1) the value placed on the asset by its owner because of the consequences of a loss or disruption of that asset and (2) the likelihood that a specific vulnerability the asset will be exploited by a particular threat. The likelihood that a specific vulnerability will be exploited by a particular threat depends on the nature of the vulnerability and the level of the threat.

A risk management program provides a framework within which assets and their criticalities to an organization or mission are quantified, threats to these assets are characterized, and the vulnerabilities of the assets to the threats are analyzed. A full risk management program also provides a framework within which the resulting risks are assessed and ranked, possible mitigation options to reduce vulnerabilities (and thus risks) are identified, and appropriate options are selected and implemented to achieve and acceptable level of risk at an acceptable cost. Vulnerability analyses and risk assessments can assist in identifying the criticality of assets (or the impact of their loss) and existing threats and vulnerabilities. The tools of risk management also address the costs, benefits, and uncertainties associated with implementing recommendations involving security and vulnerability mitigation. Such information will aid in establishing priorities and developing a defensible plan of action.

Checklist Concept

Various approaches to the risk management process have been developed for various situations. DOE (USDE, 2002) has developed an initial step-by-step checklist approach to the risk management process for energy infrastructures and major energy companies. In this document, this checklist approach is adapted for use by small and medium sized energy facilities, such as some municipal utilities, independent utilities, and rural cooperatives. It includes an overview of a fairly standard, toplevel

approach to the concepts of vulnerability analyses and risk assessments and lists of questions and considerations for use during each major step of the overall risk management process. The purpose is to assist operators of small and medium sized energy facilities in identifying priorities for protecting their local individual portions of the nation's energy infrastructure. The appendix contains a list of definitions of key terms used in the risk management discipline and a list of nomenclature used in this document.

Risk Management Overview: Coordination of a Risk Management Program

Before the establishment of an energy infrastructure risk management program, the resources required to implement such a program should be identified, the present status of any existing infrastructure protection programs or procedures should be determined, and procedures to identify the critical assets of the infrastructures and to quantify risks associated with them should be established.

Along with a basic understanding and knowledge of the term risk and the risk management process, coordination is an important ingredient in a successful risk management program. An energy facility should work closely with industry associations (e.g., National Rural Electric Cooperative Association, American Public Gas Association) and with federal, state, and local governments and law enforcement agencies.

The energy facility should consider identifying the following to assist in coordination efforts:

- Existing help that is available from industry associations, larger energy companies, and federal, state, and local governments, regulating agencies, and law enforcement agencies for conducting an integrated vulnerability analysis and risk assessment of the energy facility;
- Protection and security assurance responsibilities at the federal, state, and local levels;
- Protection and response resources at the federal, state, and local levels that could be integrated with the resources of the first responders at the energy facility;
- Technical and resource needs available from federal, state, and local agencies and industry associations for supporting vulnerability analyses, risk assessments, risk management, consequence mitigation activities, and education and training;
- Common security requirements for energy systems (e.g., those adopted uniformly and onsistently throughout the united states) that might be available from industry associations;
- Information-distribution processes for sharing threat notifications, warnings, and alerts with neighboring energy facilities, energy associations, and local, state, and federal governments;

- Formal mutual assistance agreements at the federal, state, and local levels with government agencies and larger energy companies to support response, repair, and restoration activities if an energy facility is disrupted; and
- Processes to identify interdependencies among the infrastructures and assess the need for emergency or redundant backup systems.

Several of these items are complex and would require cooperation among the energy industry and all levels of government. Although energy facilities are responsible for their own risk management, local and state governments need to take a proactive role to help these facilities perform the needed risk assessments, adopt adequate and cost beneficial methodologies, and take actions to address the findings.

Through its Vulnerability Survey and Analysis Program, DOE has developed a risk management methodology along with lessons learned and best practices. Small and medium sized energy facilities, along with local governments and appropriate industry associations, can use an adaptation of this methodology as a starting point to help assess their current situation and develop action plans.

Before applying a risk management process to an energy facility or other organization, it is prudent to conduct a preliminary review of the facility or organization's mission and mission support documents and information. Relevant information about critical information, systems, and assets could include:

- Relative priorities or importance over time;
- Interrelationships and interdependencies with other infrastructures and organizations;
- Logical, physical, and functional network and system diagrams;
- Blueprints, user's manuals, and architectures of systems or assets;
- Purposes; and
- Concepts of operation (e.g., operations manuals or procedures).

Other information about the facility or organization that is germane to a risk assessment includes:

- Previous vulnerability analysis or risk assessment results and reports;
- Relevant policies and procedures (e.g., security or emergency preparedness procedures);

- Continuity of operations, contingency, disaster recovery, and backup plans or procedures;
- Dependence on other organizations or systems (e.g., supervisory control and data acquisition [scada] systems, telephone and fiber-optic line connectivity, utilities, government services).

The facility or organization should also consider preliminary information on the following:

- Its perception of the primary threats to critical mission and mission support information, systems, and assets;
- The types of threats, such as insider (by malicious act, espionage, or theft of property or sensitive information using their special access, knowledge, or privileges), terrorist (by bombing, kidnapping, or biological, chemical, or nuclear attacks), foreign or industrial intelligence (including hackers), environmental (from fires, storms, flood, tornados, or pollution), criminal (by theft, destruction or property, or violent acts against people with or without collusion with an insider), or military (using conventional, biological, chemical, or nuclear warfare); and
- the anticipated threat tactics, such as social engineering or collusion, stealth, brute force, physical attack and damage, open-source research, or third-party usage.

Outline of Risk Management Steps

This section presents an outline of the risk management process proposed for small and medium independent energy facilities which has been adapted from the initial DOE-developed step-bystep checklist approach to the full risk management process.

Step 1. Identify critical assets and the impacts of their loss

1.1. Identify the critical functions of the energy facility.

1.2. Determine which assets perform or support the critical functions.

1.3. Evaluate the consequences or impacts to the critical functions of the facility

1.4. From the disruption or loss of each of these critical assets.

Step 2. Identify what protects and supports the critical assets

2.1. Identify the components of the physical security system (e.g., perimeter barriers, building barriers, intrusion detection, access controls, and security forces) that protect each asset.

2.2. Identify the critical internal and external infrastructures (e.g., electric power, petroleum fuels, natural gas, telecommunications, transportation, water,emergency services, computer systems, air handling systems, fire systems,and SCADA systems) that support the critical operations of each asset.

2.3. Identify sensitive information about the energy facility and its operation thatmust be protected.

Step 3. Identify and characterize the threat

3.1 Gather threat information and identify threat categories and potentialadversaries.

3.2 Identify the types of threat-related undesirable events or incidents that might be initiated by each threat or adversary.

3.3 Estimate the frequency or likelihood of each threat-related undesirable event or incident based on historical information.

3.4 Estimate the degree of threat to each critical asset for each threat-related undesirable event or incident.

Step 4. Identify and analyze vulnerabilities

4.1. Identify the potential vulnerabilities of each asset to each threat or adversary.

4.2. Identify the existing measures intended to protect the critical assets and estimate their levels of effectiveness in reducing the vulnerabilities of each asset to each threat or adversary. (Step 2 provides a stating point for this activity.)

4.3. Estimate the degree of vulnerability of each critical asset for each threatrelated undesirable event or incident and thus each threat or adversary.

Step 5. Assess risk and determine priorities for asset protection

5.1. Estimate the effect on each critical asset from each threat or adversary taking into account existing protective measures and their levels of effectiveness.

5.2. Determine the relative degree of risk to the energy facility in terms of the expected effect on each critical asset (a function of the consequences or impacts to the critical functions of the facility from the disruption or loss of the critical asset, as evaluated in Step 1) and the likelihood of a successful attack (a function of the threat or adversary, as evaluated in Step 3, and the degree of vulnerability of the asset, as evaluated in Step 4).

5.3. Prioritize the risks based on the relative degrees of risk and the likelihoods of successful attacks using an integrated assessment.

Step 6. Identify mitigation options, costs, and trade-offs

6.1 Identify potential mitigation options to further reduce the vulnerabilities and thus the risks.

6.2 Identify the capabilities and effectiveness of these mitigation options.

6.3 Identify the costs of the mitigation options.

6.4 Conduct a cost-benefit and trade-off analyses for the various options.

6.5 Prioritize the alternatives for implementing the various options and prepare recommendations for decision makers.

CHECKLISTS FOR INITIATING A RISK MANAGEMENT PROCESS AT AN ENERGY FACILITY

The following sections describe the steps of the risk management process **outlined in Section 2.2 of the Document:**

> Where appropriate, the steps contain checklists of questions that could be used to guide the implementation of a risk management program for the energy facility, as detailed below:

Step 1. Identify Critical Assets and the Impacts of Their Loss

Estimates of the potential consequences, including economic implications, of not mitigating identified vulnerabilities or addressing security concerns are necessary to effectively apply risk management approaches to evaluate mitigation option and security recommendations. Outages because of security failures could degrade an energy facility's reputation and place the community served at risk to economic losses or even losses of property and life. In addition, the modern energy facility's telecommunication and computer network has many external connections to public and private networks. Such connections are used to communicate with customers and offer new electronic services, such as on-line billing and payment. Cyber security should be a primary concern, especially for utilities that operate in this interconnected environment. An information technology (IT) security architecture may need to be developed. Possible critical assets include people, equipment, material, information, installations, and activities that have a positive value to an organization or facility. People include energy facility executives and managers, security personnel, contractors and vendors, and field personnel. Equipment includes vehicles and other transportation equipment, maintenance equipment, operational equipment, security equipment, and IT equipment (computers and servers). Material includes tools, spare parts, and specialized supplies. Information includes employee records, security plans, asset lists, intellectual property, patents, engineering drawings and specifications, system capabilities and vulnerabilities, financial data, and operating, emergency, and contingency procedures. In addition to the operational installations that make up the energy infrastructure itself, installations include headquarters offices, field offices, training centers, contractor installations, and testing, research, and development laboratories. Activities include movement of personnel and property, training programs, communications and networking, negotiations, and technology research and development.

The energy facility, the local government, and energy industry associations have roles and responsibilities for identifying assets, effects of asset loss, vulnerabilities, threats, and risk mitigation options. Coordination among energy facilities; local, state, and federal agencies; and energy industry associations is crucial to this process.

Energy facilities need to identify the critical functions of the facility, and determine which physical and cyber assets perform or support the critical functions. The key assets identified should be related to the criticality of overall operations of the individual facilities. Potential assets include substations, transmission lines, pipelines, critical valve nests, power plants, pump stations, city gate stations, compressor stations, storage installations, interconnections, energy control centers, energy management systems (EMS), SCADA systems, remote monitoring and control units (remote terminal units [RTU]), communications systems linking RTUs and energy control centers, certain backup systems, and e-commerce capabilities. They should evaluate the consequences or impacts to the critical functions of the energy facility from the disruption or loss of each of these critical assets and prioritize the critical assets based on these.

Not all assets and activities warrant the same level of protection. The cost of reducing risk to an asset must be reasonable in relation to its overall value. The value, however, does not need to be expressed in dollars. A potential loss can be stated in terms of human lives or the impact on the local or state economy.

The first set of questions is designed to guide the process of identifying the critical functions of the energy facility and the assets that perform or support them, and evaluating the potential consequences of disruptions or loss of these critical assets.

Criticality Criteria (Functions and Assets)

- What critical mission activities take place at the energy facility or its remote sites?
- What critical or valuable equipment is present at the facility or its remote sites?
- Where are the critical assets located?
- Have people, installations, and operations been considered when assessing assets?
- Have cyber networks and system architectures (e.g., SCADA systems, business e-mail, and e- commerce) been documented fully?

Criticality Criteria (Impacts of Loss)

- What would the energy facility lose if an adversary obtained control of a specific asset?
- What affects would be expected if a specific asset were compromised?
- Is the asset still valuable to the energy facility once an adversary has it?
- What is the potential for immediate and significant local impacts due to the loss of the asset?
- What is the potential for loss of energy supply to civilian areas?
- What facility personnel, tenants, customers, and visitors could be affected by the loss of the asset?
- What would be the impact on people's lives and on national or local security due to the loss of the asset?

- What would be the financial impacts to the energy facility and the local community?

Criticality Criteria (Asset Value)

- Is there little or no redundant capacity or capability to mitigate the loss of the asset?
- What is the potential for cascading effects (e.g., to other interdependent infrastructures or industries) due to the loss of the asset?
- Do any special situations need to be considered regarding the loss of the asset, such as the status of hospitals, life support systems, or emergency services that depend on the energy infrastructure supported by the asset?
- What is the potential for catastrophic effects (weapons of mass destruction levels impact)?
- What did it cost to develop the asset?
- Would the energy facility need an extended period to make repairs to the asset?
- How does the need for protecting the asset compare with other assets also considered critical?

Once the assets critical to the operation of the energy facility have been identified and characterized, an impact assessment must be carried out to describe the consequences of losses if an undesirable event occurs. The degree of impact should be quantified by using a relative impact or criticality rating criteria and a consistent rating scale. (An example of a scale for rating criteria is presented in Step 5.) The assets are then ranked in terms of criticality.

Step 2. Identify What Protects and Supports the Critical Assets

The exiting protection of critical assets provided by the physical security system and the dependence of the critical assets on both external and internal infrastructures must be known to evaluate the vulnerabilities of the assets to threats or adversaries. In addition, operating procedures and other sensitive information, which if available to adversaries might jeopardize critical assets, must be identified as their availability can also affect the vulnerabilities of assets.

Physical Security Systems

Physical security systems are used to protect energy facilities and their assets from unauthorized individuals and outside attacks. Such systems usually include perimeter barriers, building barriers, intrusion detection, access controls, and security forces.

Infrastructure Interdependencies

Today's energy facilities depend on many different infrastructures to support their critical functions and assets. These infrastructure interdependencies must be identified and the adequacy of security measures that are in place to protect and back up these infrastructures must be evaluated. Typically, these supporting infrastructures include:

- Electric power supply and distribution;
- Petroleum fuels supply and storage;
- Natural gas supply;
- Telecommunications;
- Transportation (road, rail, air, and water);
- Water and wastewater;
- Emergency services (fire, police, and emergency medical);
- Computers and servers;
- Heating, ventilation, and air conditioning (hvac) systems;
- Fire suppression and fire fighting systems; and
- Scada systems.

The electric power supply and distribution infrastructure can include the local electrical distribution utility, facility-operated electric generation equipment, backup generators fueled by natural gas or petroleum fuels, uninterruptible power supplies (UPSs), and the associated switching and distribution hardware. The petroleum fuels supply and storage infrastructure includes on-site storage as well as local suppliers, storage terminals, and the entire petroleum industry. The telecommunications infrastructure includes commercial telephone, fiber optic, and satellite networks and facility-owned radio, telephone, microwave, and fiber-optic pathways.Computers and servers, HVAC systems, fire suppression and fire fighting systems, and SCADA systems tend to be operated by the energy facility and, in turn, depend on the other infrastructures such as telecommunication, electric power supply and distribution, petroleum fuels supply and storage, natural gas supply, water and wastewater, and emergency services.

Sensitive Information

Protecting operating procedures and other sensitive information, the release of which might jeopardize an energy facility and its assets, is the objective of operations security (OPSEC) programs. OPSEC programs utilize tools such as employee background checks, trash handling procedures, telephone policies, and IT (computer) security to protect against both industrial espionage and deliberate disruption of critical assets and functions.

The second set of questions is designed to guide the process of identifying the existing components of the physical security system that protect the critical assets, the critical infrastructure systems that support the critical assets, and the operating procedures and sensitive information that must be protected to avoid jeopardizing the critical assets.

Energy Facility and Critical Asset Protection (Physical Assets)

- What department or person has overall responsibility for security or is that responsibility spread over many departments or people with shared responsibilities for security along with their other responsibilities?
- What perimeter barriers (e.g., fences, gates, vehicle barriers) protect the energy facility as a whole and the individual critical assets and what levels of protection do they provide?
- What building barriers (e.g., walls, roof/ceiling, windows, doors, locks)?
- Protect each critical asset and what levels of protection do they provide?
- What is the status of the intrusion detection that protects each critical asset (e.g., intrusion sensors, alarm deployment, alarm assessment, alarm maintenance) and what level of protection does it provide?
- What is the status of the access control that is used at each critical asset (e.g., personnel access, vehicle access, contraband detection, access point illumination) and what level of protection does it provide?
- What is the nature of the security force (both the protective force and appropriate local law enforcement agencies) that protects each critical asset (e.g., number, training, armament, communications) and what level of protection does it provide?

- What types of undesirable events (e.g., surreptitious forced entry, technical implant, theft of sensitive information or materials) are protected against?
- During which hours of the day and under what conditions are the various components of the physical security system effective?
- Over what areas do the various components of the physical security system provide protection?
- What is the history of reported malfunctions of the various components of the physical security system?
- What is the correlation of the effectiveness of the various components of the physical security system to security incident reports that may indicate that the system was defeated?
- Have liaisons and working relationships been established with the local government and its departments, such as police, fire, emergency medical services, and public works?

Energy Facility and Critical Asset Protection (Infrastructure Interdependencies):

- Which infrastructures (both external and external) are essential for a specific critical asset to be able to carry out its critical functions?
- What external utility or internal department and equipment is the normal provider of each essential infrastructure for each critical asset and how is each infrastructure connected to each asset (e.g., the types and pathways of power lines, pipelines, and cables)?

Energy Facility and Critical Asset Protection (Infrastructure Interdependencies)

- What alternatives (e.g., redundant systems, alternative suppliers, backup systems established work-around plans) are available if the normal providers of the essential infrastructures are disrupted and how long can the alternatives support the critical functions of the assets?
- What is the potential for interdependency effects on external infrastructures (i.e., effects on the energy, telecommunications, transportation, water and wastewater, banking and finance, emergency services, and government services infrastructures)?

Energy Facility and Critical Asset Protection

- What types of information about the energy facility, its assets, and its operations should be considered critical or sensitive information?
- What are the methods and means by which sensitive information might fall in the wrong hands, such as via disgruntled employees; access to the facility by the public; outside construction, repair, and maintenance contractors; press contacts; briefings and presentations; public testimony; Internet information; paper and material waste; telecommunications system taps; and cyber (computer) intrusions?
- What are the existing policies and procedures that are used to protect sensitive information, such as employee background checks, disciplinary procedures, security training, trash handling procedures, paper waste handling procedures, salvage material handling procedures, dumpster control, telephone policies, and IT (computer) security.
- Once energy facilities have identified their existing physical protective measures, they should coordinate with their respective local governments and law enforcement agencies to ensure that the level of protection and response that they expect will be forthcoming. They should also coordinate with the critical external infrastructure providers to ensure that the robustness and redundancy that they depend on will continue to be provided. The objective of these coordination efforts is to ensure that roles for response and recovery from a disruption are understood by all so that quick and effective measures can be taken when problems occur.
- In addition, local and state governments can assist energy facilities in infrastructure restoration activities. Potential support can come in many areas, such as maintaining critical spare parts, assisting with special equipment, working with the emergency telecommunications spectrum, securing easy access to the site of the disruption for repair crews and needed equipment, working out mutual assistance programs with other energy providers, and supplying temporary staffing. The energy facility should also check with local and state governments to ensure that critical information about their facility, its assets, and its operations will not be released to the general public in any future additions to public Internet sites, press releases, or public hearings.

Step 3. Identify and Characterize the Threat

In order to put the information about the critical assets of the energy facility gathered above to use in a quantitative risk assessment, the potential threats and adversaries that may be expected must be identified and quantified. The set of questions provided in this section serves as guidance for evaluating the threat environment to which the energy facility could be exposed and establishing qualitative or quantitative threat ratings for each critical asset. The goals of the threat assessment are to understand, from the adversary's point of view, the adversary's capabilities and intent to collect critical information.

The federal agencies (e.g., DOE and the Federal Bureau of Investigation [FBI]), state governments, and energy industry associations each collect threat information. This information should be shared among these groups and with the local energy facilities in order to have the most comprehensive and updated threat information possible. In addition, threats to energy facilities could affect state and local assets. State and local governments have access to law enforcement and intelligence data. This information should be integrated and shared, together with any information that the energy industry associations and energy facilities collect. This third set of questions is to be used to identify and evaluate the threat environment to which an energy facility may be exposed.

Step 4. Identify and Analyze Vulnerabilities

In addition to identifying the critical assets of the energy facility, the impact of their disruption, the present protection provided, and the potential threats against them, the vulnerability of those assets to the potential threats must be quantified, at least to some extent, to determine the overall risk to the assets.

There are various types of vulnerabilities such as physical, technical/cyber, and operational. An energy facility, including perimeter barriers (fences, walls, gates, landscape, sewers, tunnels, parking areas, alarms), compound area surveillance (closed-circuit television, motion detectors, lighting), building perimeters (walls, roofs, windows, doors, shipping docks, locks, shielded enclosures, access control, alarms), and building interiors (doors, locks, safes, vents, intrusion sensors, motion sensors), is subject to physical vulnerabilities. Electronic equipment, such as acoustic equipment, secure telephones, computers and computer networks, and radio-frequency equipment, are subject to technical or cyber vulnerabilities. The guard force, personnel procedures, and operational procedures are subject to operational vulnerabilities. Various characteristics of assets, including any existing protection identified in Step 2, may affect their susceptibility to attacks and must be considered when identifying susceptibilities. Such asset characteristics include building design; equipment properties; personal behavior; locations of people, equipment, and buildings; and operational and personnel practices. Both energy facilities and local governments should be concerned with identifying and analyzing vulnerabilities. Energy facilities should analyze the vulnerabilities of their physical and cyber systems. Local governments should coordinate management of the vulnerabilities of the energy infrastructure, including individual energy facilities, that support government and community operations and assets.

This fourth set of questions is to be used to evaluate the vulnerability of the critical energy infrastructure assets to the potential threats and to establish qualitative or quantitative vulnerability ratings for each asset.

Energy Facility and Critical Asset Vulnerabilities

- How susceptible is each critical asset to physical attack if readily available weapons (guns, normal ammunition, vehicle, simple explosives) were used?
- How susceptible is each critical asset to physical attack if difficult-toacquire weapons (assault rifles, explosive ammunition, rocket launchers, biological or chemical agents, aircraft, sophisticated explosives) were used?
- How susceptible is each critical asset to physical attack from insiders?
- Are any of the critical assets unprotected? If so, describe them.
- Are any of the critical assets minimally protected? If so, describe them.
- How susceptible is each critical asset to cyber attack?

Step 5. Assess Risk and Determine Priorities for Asset Protection

Scales for the rating criteria identified in the first four steps (asset criticality in term of the impact of loss or disruption, threat characteristics, and asset vulnerability) must be developed. The concept of criteria development is presented below in the form of a generic example. Those that conduct an actual assessment should define rating scales that are appropriate to the specific assessment.

Using the individual rating values assigned to each combination of asset criticality, threat, and vulnerability, a relative degree of risk or a risk rating can be established for each asset for one or more postulated adverse events or consequences that could result from an attack by the identified adversary. Often a multiplicative approach involving the three rating criteria is used to obtain a risk rating:

Risk Rating = (Impact Rating) × (Threat Rating) × (Vulnerability Rating).

An additional scale must be developed to assign a qualitative overall risk level from the quantitative risk rating. The risk ratings or risk levels are used to prioritize the assets for the selection and implementation of security improvements to achieve an acceptable overall level of risk at an acceptable cost.

The following should be considered when developing and using rating criteria:

- Subject-matter expert opinions and perspectives should be documented. The team involved in the assessment should reflect a variety of different perspectives, and the team should work toward reaching a consensus regarding a set of priorities.
- Information should be presented in a usable format (e.g., table, matrix, or spreadsheet).
- Assumptions should be documented.

These or similar tables are used to establish qualitative or quantitative criticality, threat, and vulnerability ratings for each critical asset.

Asset Impact/Criticality Rating Criteria

Each critical asset that is identified in Step 1 of the risk management process is assigned an impact rating value that reflects the importance or criticality of a loss or disruption of that asset with regard to the continued operation of the energy facility or other organization need to be assessed.

In the example below, a quantitative criticality rating scale of 0 to 100% is used, which corresponds to qualitative criticality levels of critical, high, medium, and low.

Asset Impact/Criticality Rating Criteria
Criticality-Level Description-Rating Scale (%)

Critical Indicates that compromise of the asset would have grave consequences leading to loss of life or serious injury to people and disruption of the operation of the energy facility. It is also possible to assign a monetary value or some other measure of criticality.

75–100 High Indicates that compromise of the asset would have serious consequences that could impair continued operation of the energy facility.

50–75 Medium Indicates that compromise of the asset would have moderate consequences that would impair operation of the energy facility for a limited period.

25–50 Low Indicates little or no impact on human life or the continuation of the operation of the energy facility.

1–25 Low.

Threat Rating Criteria

The individual potential threats against the assets of the energy facility or other organization being assessed that are identified in Step 3 are assigned a threat rating value that reflects the magnitude of the threat. In the example below, a quantitative threat rating scale of 0 to 100% is used, which corresponds to qualitative threat levels of critical, high, medium, and low.

Threat-Level Description-Rating Scale (%)

Critical Indicates that a definite threat exists against the asset and that the adversary has both the capability and intent to launch an attack, and that the subject or similar assets are targeted on a frequently recurring basis.

75–100 High Indicates that a credible threat exists against the asset based on knowledge of the adversary's capability and intent to attack the asset and based on related incidents having taken place at similar assets or in similar situations.

50–75 Medium Indicates that there is a possible threat to the asset based on the adversary's desire to compromise the asset and the possibility that the adversary could obtain the capability through a third party who has demonstrated the capability in related incidents.

25–50 Low Indicates little or no credible evidence of capability or intent and no history of actual or planned threats against the asset

1–25 Low.

Vulnerability Rating Criteria

The vulnerabilities of the assets in terms of in-place measures to protect those assets that are identified in Step 2 are assigned a vulnerability rating value that reflects the extent to which the asset is protected against each threat identified in Step 3. In the example below, a quantitative vulnerability rating scale of 0 to 100% is used, which corresponds to qualitative vulnerability levels of critical, high, medium, and low.

Vulnerability-Level Description-Rating Scale (%)

Critical Indicates that there are no effective protective measures currently in place and adversaries would be capable of exploiting the critical asset.

75–100 High Indicates that although there are some protective measures in place, there are still multiple weaknesses through which adversaries would be capable of exploiting the asset.

50–75 Medium Indicates that there are effective protective measures in place; however, one weakness does exist that an adversaries would be capable of exploiting.

25–50 Low Indicates that multiple layers of effective protective measures exist and essentially no adversary would be capable of exploiting the asset.

1–25 Low.

Step 6. Identify Mitigation Options, Costs, and Trade-offs

The ultimate goal of a risk management process is to select and implement security improvements to achieve an acceptable overall risk at an acceptable cost. Step 5 of the risk management process prioritizes the combinations of assets and threats by the risk ratings or risk levels. This, in turn, helps to identify where protective measures against risk are most needed. In this step, potential measures to protect critical assets from recognized threats are identified, specific programs to assure that appropriate protective measures are put into place are established, and appropriate agencies and mechanisms needed to put protective measures in place are identified. Protective measures that can address more than one threat or undesirable event should be given special attention.

A variety of approaches to developing protective measures exist. Protective measures can reduce the likelihood of a failure due to an attack by adding physical security. Protective measures can also be implemented to prevent or limit the consequences of a failure or to speed the recovery following a failure, no matter what the cause of that failure.

Best practices and lessons learned from DOE's Vulnerability Survey and Analysis Program provide some general actions, activities, and recommendations that can help identify appropriate potential mitigations measures. Some of these are listed below.

- The trend in IT until very recently has been to outsource more and more functions. Since the events of September 11, 2001, outsourcing is becoming less popular again. If possible, cyber security should remain as an enterprise function and should not become a contractor function.
- Logging and reporting should be enabled on IT network routers and firewalls to gain a better understanding of user access and interactions with remote systems.
- Sensitive and confidential documents should not be placed on Web sites. Appropriate document review, classification, and access controls should be implemented. This practice should apply to documents and other information that is found in newsgroups, media sites, and other linked sites.
- Security measures, such as traffic filtering, authorized controls, encryption and access controls, minimizing or disabling of unnecessary services and commands, minimizing banner information, and e-mail filtering and virus control, should be implemented.
- A formal process for accessing relevant threat information and for contacting the proper government and law enforcement agencies should be instituted and reviewed and updated on a regular basis. The energy facility may need to work with government to obtain security clearances for appropriate personnel.
- Appropriate security measures (e.g., access controls, barriers, badges, intrusion detection devices, alarm reporting and display, closed-circuit television cameras, communication equipment, lighting, and security officers) should be implemented.

- Top management support is critical in ensuring a successful security program.
- Security training programs should be formalized.
- Procedures for escorting contractors and visitors into sensitive areas should be enhanced and enforced.
- Security should be incorporated in the company goals as well as in its corporate culture.
- The foundation for security is well-informed employees acting responsibly.
- A formal review process should be established for all information released to the public, particularly through the energy facility's Web site. A periodic review of "public" information should be performed to audit the effectiveness of information protection policies.
- The energy facility should be careful about disseminating sensitive information to the press or competitors. Only minimal information should be made available about personnel (especially executives).
- Security training and awareness should be provided to all employees on a regular basis.
- At a minimum, an annual audit of overall security should be conducted.
- Some illustrations specific to energy facilities, including large utilities not specifically considered in this report, are listed below as an example of specific protective measures that can be implemented. The examples are grouped by type.

Measures to Prevent Damage

- Harden key installations and equipment: protect critical equipment with walls or below-grade installations, physically separate key pieces of equipment, and toughen the equipment itself to resist damage.
- Install surveillance systems (e.g., video cameras, motion detectors) around key installations that is monitored and coupled with rapid-response forces.
- Maintain security guards at key installations.
- Improve communication with law enforcement agencies, especially local law enforcement agencies and the local FBI office) to obtain threat information and coordinate responses to emergencies.

Measures to Limit Consequences

- Improve emergency plans and procedures for continued operation during undesirable events and ensure that operators are trained to implement these contingency plans.
- Modify the physical system—improve control centers and protective devices, increase redundancy of key equipment, and increase reserve margins.

Measures to Speed Recovery

- Conduct contingency planning for restoration of service, including identification of potential spare parts and resolution of legal uncertainties.
- Clarify the legal and institutional framework for sharing reserve equipment.
- Stockpile critical equipment (e.g., transformers, pumps, compressors, regulators) or any specialized materials (e.g., cables, pipe sections) needed to manufacture critical equipment or make repairs.
- Assure availability of adequate transportation for stockpiles of very heavy equipment by maintaining a database of rail and barge equipment and adapting Schnabel railcars to fit all needed types of large pieces of equipment, if necessary.
- Monitor domestic manufacturing capability to assure adequate repair and manufacture of key equipment in times of emergency.
- Investigate mutual aid agreements with vendors, industry associations, or large near-by energy companies.
- Establish backup arrangements with contractors for emergency services and other emergency support.

General Mitigation Measures to Reduce Vulnerability

- Emphasize inherently less vulnerable technologies and designs when practical, such as using standardized equipment.
- Move toward an inherently less vulnerable bulk energy system (e.g., smaller generators near loads, local storage) as new installations are planned and constructed.
- As indicated earlier, local governments should coordinate energy facility activities related to risk management. The following

questions can help guide local and state governments through the risk management process.

Local and State Government's Role in the Risk Management Process

- Has the local or state government identified any critical issues or vulnerabilities regarding its energy infrastructure?
- If the local or state government has identified critical issues, what are they and why are they critical?
- Has the local or state government developed plans to counter these vulnerabilities?
- Has the local or state government coordinated information with other local energy facilities, local law enforcement agencies, and others concerning these vulnerabilities?

ENERGY DOWNSTREAM RISK MANAGEMENT STRATEGIES

The *Energy Downstream Strategies* research program assesses business trends and investment drivers in the downstream market, along with market forecasts of domain-specific technology. This program also covers a broad spectrum of technologies, such as those used in oil and gas transportation from the wellhead, gas processing, oil refining, energy trading and wholesaling, and transportation to the retail market. Energy Insights' forward-looking research, combined with fact-based analysis and best-practice case studies, helps energy downstream executives take advantage of current and future growth opportunities and provides actionable advice on maximizing the business value of technology investments in the downstream market.

Approach

This service develops unique analysis and comprehensive data through Energy Insights' proprietary research projects, along with ongoing communications with industry experts, oil and gas company staff, and vendors. With decades of experience in the downstream industry, our analysts leverage a broad spectrum of expertise and intellectual property from both IDC and Energy Insights.

To ensure relevance, analysts work with subscribers to identify and prioritize specific topics to be covered in research reports.

Topics Addressed

The *Energy Downstream Strategies* advisory service covers a broad range of issues, including:

- Meeting the challenge of maintaining reliability and availability of refineries (work and asset management)
- Mitigating risk and taking advantage of market conditions (energy trading and risk management)
- Preventing pipeline failures and their environmental and economic impact (condition monitoring, asset management, and regulatory reporting)
- Responding to the demands of the market for refined products and natural gas in near real time (supply chain management)

Key Questions to be Answered

Research addresses the following issues that are critical to your success:

- What are the key market trends and challenges facing the downstream business in the years ahead?
- How can technology be used to optimize production, reduce costs, and manage with fewer employees?
- How can return on existing technology investments be maximized and migration paths to new technologies be developed?

RISK ASSESSMENT OF A CROSS-COUNTRY PIPELINE TRANSPORTING HYDROCARBONS

A major oil company in India proposes to lay two 600mm dia pipelines for transporting hydrocarbon products like naphtha, motor spirit, high speed diesel and superior kerosene from a South Indian port to their storage terminal about 15 kms away. There are five major river crossings, three railway crossings and one NH crossing along the proposed route. It is proposed to transfer about 3000 m^3/hr of hydrocarbon product through each pipeline (Madhu, 2007). A booster pumping station is provided at an intermediate location to overcome the pressure drop and to provide sufficient pressure at the storage terminal end.

National and international codes and practices are usually followed while laying hydrocarbon pipelines. The welded joints would be radiographically tested and cathodic protection would be given to the pipeline to minimize the effects of corrosion. The pipeline will be mostly laid underground except at the booster pumping station. It is proposed to incorporate advanced instrumentation and communication system based on supervisory control and data acquisition (SCADA).

Inspite of all the safety standards and practices, failure of pipeline resulting in release of hydrocarbons cannot be ruled out. The present paper discusses the result of a risk assessment study carried out for the pipeline system. As part of the study, the probable failure modes associated with different operational areas for the proposed facility were identified. The predominant causes of hydrocarbon release from the pipeline have been identified as failure due to external factors, corrosion, construction defects and human error.

Consequence analysis was carried out for the identified failure scenarios using empirical models. The impact distances for pool fires and explosion were estimated. The catastrophic failure of the pipeline at booster pumping station results in the maximum impact distances. An attempt has also been made in the study to assess the probability of failure of the pipeline. Based on the risk assessment study a few recommendations have been made for the safe operation of the piping system.

Introduction

Chemical process industries handle, store and process large quantities of hazardous chemicals and intermediates. These activities involve many different types of material, some of which can be potentially harmful if released into the environment, because of their toxic, flammable or explosive properties. The rapid growth in the use of hazardous chemicals in industry and trade has increased the risk to employees as well as the neighbouring community.

Under these circumstances, it is essential to apply modern approaches to safety based on good design, management and operational control (Wells, 1980). The major hazard units should try to achieve and maintain high standards of plant integrity with due regards to the probabilities of undesirable events. While assessing design and development proposals for plants which handle hazardous materials, it is essential to identify potential hazards. Risk assessment techniques have been recognized as an important tool for integrating and internalizing safety in plant operation and production sequencing (Hoffman, 1973). In India risk assessment is mandatory for all new projects in chemical process industries dealing with hazardous chemicals and severe operating conditions.

Risk assessment includes identification of hazard scenarios and consequence analysis. Scenario identification describes how an accident occurs, while consequence analysis describes the anticipated damage to environment, life and equipment. This paper presents the results of a risk assessment study carried out for a pipe line system proposed for the transportation of petroleum products.

Description of the Proposed Facilities

The proposed project involves laying of two 600 NB diameter pipelines for the transport of petroleum products from the tanker berth at a south Indian port to the marketing terminal of a major oil company which is located about 15 Km away from the port. One of these lines will be used for the transport for superior kerosene oil (SKO)/high speed diesel (HSD) and the other for naphtha / motor spirit (MS). About 3000 m^3/hr of each product available at the ship end at 10 kg/cm^2g pressure will be transferred through the pipelines. The pipeline will be laid as per the guide lines of Oil Industry Safety Directorate (OISD 141). There are five river crossings, three railway crossings and one national highway crossing along the proposed route. The pipes will be designed for an operating pressure of 15 kg/cm^2 as per ASME B31.4. The entire line will be hydrostatically tested at 1.5 times the operating pressure before commissioning.

(i) Facilities at the Port

At present, there are two tanker berths at the port ; berths I and II. It is proposed to install two new 300 NB unloading arms in berth I which will be connected to the 600 NB headers (existing) through one of the 250 NB branches provided on the header. An interconnection will be provided between the arm connected to a 250 NB nozzle on a 600 NB header and a second 250 NB nozzle on the other 600 NB header. The interconnection will facilitate use of both the arms simultaneously for transferring either of the fluid. The interconnection will be made in such a way that the chances of mixing of the fluids are eliminated. It is proposed to use only one of the two 600 NB headers each from the berth upto the existing exchange pit. A tapping of 600 NB each is taken from these 600 NB lines at the existing exchange pit area and they join the new 600 NB lines from berth II at the new exchange pit, and is led to the marketing terminal via the booster pumping station located in between. Motor operated valves will be provided to isolate the other 600 NB lines during the operation of the new facility.

(ii) Booster Pumping Station

A booster pumping station is envisaged as part of the system to overcome the pressure drop in the long line and to provide sufficient pressure required at the terminal end. At the booster pumping station one pump with a standby is planned for each fluid.

(iii) Marketing Terminal

The petroleum product from the proposed 600 NB lines will join an existing 600 NB header at the terminal end from where the hydrocarbons can be directed to any of the respective storage tanks.

(iv) Pigging Facility

A pigging facility to pig the pipe line is also envisaged in the system. A launcher at the port end and a pig receiving station at the terminal end will form part of the facility.

(v) Instrumentation

All valves in the 600 NB lines will be motor operated. All the first block valves in the new exchange pit and the main block valves in the main 600 NB line running to the terminal are motor operated with provision for remote and local operation. These valves can be operated just before starting pumping from the ship.

The main block valves in the 600 NB lines after the new exchange pit will be interlocked with the leak detection system so that the lines can be isolated from the control room by closing these valves. The main line at the port end will be provided with pressure indicators, temperature indicator, turbine type flow meter. The flow meter will have indicator, integrator and low and high flow alarms. The flow meters are provided as part of the leak detection system. Thermal relief valves will also be provided at various locations.

Provision to start or stop the booster pumps locally or from the control room will be made. A panel indicator, a turbine flow meter with indicator, integrator and low and high flow alarms will be provided in the discharge line of the pumps.

The storage terminal will also be provided with all the necessary instrumentation. The motor operated valve in the main line is provided with two wire control system with local and remote operation. The smooth and safe operation of the systems will be ensured by incorporating a computerized Supervisory Control and Data Acquisition (SCADA) system.

Safety Features of the Proposed Project

The safety features proposed to be incorporated in the pipeline project are outlined below:

1. The entire stretch of the pipelines is proposed to be buried underground except at the booster pumping station, which will be properly fenced, and the pumping station would be manned round the clock.
2. The lines are to be buried with a minimum cover of 1.2 m as against 1 m specified in the standards. At road crossings, the lines will be laid with a minimum cover of 1.5 m through hume pipe protection using horizontal boring/trenching technique.
3. At railway crossings, casing pipe protection as per the norms of Indian Railways will be provided. Minimum cover shall be 1.5 m. The casing pipe shall also be protected with anti corrosive coating. Pipeline insulators will be used to support the carrier pipe inside the casing pipe and electrically isolate the carrier pipe from the casing pipe.
4. River crossings shall be below the scour bed with a minimum cover of 4 m. Isolation valves with valve chamber shall be provided at upstream and downstream of major water crossings. Anti-buoyancy concrete weight coating will be provided on the pipelines in the water logged areas and river crossings to prevent lifting up of pipes due to buoyancy.
5. The buried lines will be protected with anticorrosive coal tar based coating and the entire section of the pipelines would be provided with cathodic protection.
6. All butt weld joints will be 100 % radiographically examined and fillet weld will be subjected to dye penetration test and ultrasonic inspection.
7. The entire lines will be tested hydrostatically at 1.25 times the design pressure. The sections for crossing road, rail and river shall be pre-tested before erection.

8. In all 16 numbers motor operated valves (MOV) shall be provided at critical locations along the pipeline some of which are connected to the interlock system. These valves can also be operated from remote location. This will ensure quick isolation of the pipeline during emergency.
9. The computerized SCADA to be incorporated in the system will ensure its safe operation. Any leakage in the pipeline will be immediately detected by the computer system and pumping of the fluid will be immediately cut off.
10. Communication between tanker berth, booster pumping station, and the marketing terminal is also achieved through SCADA. This will be in addition to telephones.

Identification of Failure Scenarios

A hazardous material either flammable or toxic is safe till it is fully contained and maintained at desired parameters during storage, operation and transportation. In the case of the proposed pipeline, the major causes of hydrocarbons from the pipe lines can be attributed to external factors like mechanical interference, material failure (corrosion) and other causes like construction defects, pipe material defects and human error.

The failure due to external factors generally caused by third party mechanical interference is a puncture or a gouge severely reducing the wall thickness of the pipeline or guillotine failure of the pipeline. The failure can be immediate or may occur sometime later by fatigue.

Pipeline failures by corrosion can be due to internal corrosion or external corrosion. External corrosion failures are due to moisture in the ground and salinity of the soil and can take two forms – small pin hole failures caused by pitting and more generalized corrosion leading to a reduction in pipe wall thickness over a plane area.

Pipe line can also fail for a variety of other causes like construction defects, pipe material defects and human error.

The following failure cases are identified as probable in the pipe line system under study by carrying out a preliminary hazard analysis and HAZOP study.

1. Unloading arm failure in HSD / SKO pipeline (port area)

2. Unloading arm failure in Naphtha / MS pipeline (port area)
3. Failure of 300 NB flange in each pipeline (port area)
4. Partial failure of booster pump discharge on each pipeline
5. Catastrophic failure of pipelines at booster pump discharge
6. Partial failure of 600 NB flange at the terminal on pipeline.

Consequence Analysis

Despite the universal acceptance of excellent codes of practice for design and operation of storage facility there have been instances of losses due to major accidents of varying degree of severity. The failure cases generally depend upon the availability of safety systems, instrumentation and their response time and the probability of human error. Thus, prior to identifying the failure scenarios for estimating the affected areas, the above mentioned safety systems have been studied in detail. Other parameters like material of construction and protection systems proposed to be provided at the facility have also been given adequate consideration.

In the present study, models for flash fire, pool fire and unconfined vapour cloud explosion (UVCE) and dispersion have been used for consequence analysis (World Bank, 1985). Source models have been used to quantify the release scenarios by estimating the discharge rate and extent of flash and evaporation from a liquid pool.

UVCE and flash fires occur when a large amount of volatile flammable material is rapidly dispersed to the atmosphere, forms a vapour cloud which disperses and meets a source of ignition before the cloud is diluted to below lower flammability limit (LFL). The main concern for a UVCE is the shock wave that causes damage whereas for a flash fire the main concerns are the thermal radiation effects (Gugan, 1979). It is believed that the transition from flash fire to UVCE cloud be a function of the flammable mass, presence of confinement obstacles, burning velocity of the material and other factors.

Pool/jet fires generally tend to be localized in effect and are of concern mainly in establishing the potential for domino effects and employee safety zones. Issues relating to spacing of critical equipments can be addressed on the basis of specific consequence analysis for a range of possible pool/jet fires. The effects of a pool/jet fire depends upon factors such as flammability, combustibility, amount of material released, temperature, humidity and flame length (Lees, 1996).

Dispersion modeling aims at estimating the distances likely to be affected due to release of certain quantity of flammable gas. Depending upon the properties of the material released and the release conditions, a dense gas dispersion or a buoyant gas release model is used for estimating the affected areas.

The following assumptions are made for estimating the impact distances for cloud dispersion, vapour cloud explosion and flash fires.

1. Simultaneous failure leading to more than one scenario is not considered.
2. Catastrophic failure of the pipelines is not generally considered in view of the high integrity of construction and safety measures that are proposed.
3. It is assumed that the ground surface is level and the roughness for a given surface is uniform.
4. It is assumed that the atmospheric conditions are constant for at least the time taken for the cloud to develop as a plume, to the lowest concentration of interest.
5. Concentration fluctuations within the cloud are ignored.
6. The flame speed through the cloud is constant.
7. Stoichiometric concentration of the cloud is uniform.

Damage Criteria

(a) Thermal Radiation

The flammable material released accidentally, from an orifice would form a vapour cloud. The cloud if encounters an ignition source would result in a jet fire. The cloud formed due to any failure, if finds an ignition source before reaching a concentration below lower flammable limit and the flammable mass in the cloud is less than 5 tonnes, a flash fire is likely to occur (Craven, 1976). The flame could also travel back to the source of leak. Any person caught in the flash fire is likely to suffer burns of varying degrees and at times could be fatal. Therefore, in consequence analysis, the estimated distance upto LFL value is usually taken to indicate the area which may be affected by the flash fire.

The damage effects of thermal radiation of varying intensity are shown in Table 5.1.

Table 5.1: Damage due to Incident Radiation Intensity

Incident Radiation Intensity (KW/m²)	*Type of Damage*
37.5	Damage to process equipment. 100% lethality in 1min. 1% lethality in 10sec.
25.0	Minimum energy to ignite wood at indefinitely long exposure without a flame. 100 % lethality in 1 min. Significant injury in 10sec.
12.5	Minimum energy to ignite wood with a flame; melts plastic tubing. 1% lethality in 1min. 1st degree burns in 10 sec.
4.5	Causes pain if duration is longer than 20 sec but blistering is unlikely.
1.6	Causes no discomfort for long exposure.

(b) Explosion Overpressure

Distances are estimated for unconfined vapour cloud explosion for overpressures of 14, 28 and 70 kg/cm^2. These overpressures are the peak pressures formed in excess of normal atmospheric pressure by blast and shock waves.

Table 5.2 gives damage levels at various overpressures for both property damage and human injury.

Table 5.2: Damage Effects of Blast Overpressures

Blast Overpressure (kg/cm2)	*Damage level*
70.0	Major structural damage
43.0	Storage tank failure
35.5	Eardrum damage
28.0	Pressure vessels remain intact, light structures collapse
7.0–14.0	Major window glass breakage, possibly causing some injuries
4.3	10% window glass breakage

Results of Consequence Analysis

The results of the consequence of the various failure scenarios are given in Tables 5.3 and 5.4.

Table 5.3: Consequence Analysis for the Pipeline carrying High speed Diesel/Kerosene

Scenario	*Weather Class*	*LFL distance (m)*	*Flash Fire Distance (m)*	*Impact distances for pool fires in meters*			*Impact distances for explosion in meters*		
				4 kW/m²	*12.5 kW/m²*	*37.5 kW/m²*	*4.3 kg/cm²*	*28.5 kg/cm²*	*70 kg/cm²*
Failure of unloading arm at port	F	2	3	6	4	3	Not likely	Not likely	Not likely
	D	4	6	6	4	3	Not likely	Not likely	Not likely
Failure of 300 NB flange at port	F	20	42	50	33	-	73	40	38
	D	31	27	65	40	-	50	29	26
Partial failure of booster pump discharge	F	40	35	53	35	-	76	40	37
	D	32	34	80	44	-	75	42	38
Catastrophic failure of booster pump discharge	F	55	315	362	220	-	240	108	100
	D	58	235	422	225	-	229	105	98
Partial failure of 600 NB pipeline at terminal	F	30	35	62	40	-	75	40	37
	D	29	32	70	38	-	70	40	38

Unloading Arm Failure at Port Area

The quantity of hydrocarbon released in this failure is very small due to the availability of emergency release system (ERS). ERS will automatically shut off the transfer when there is breakage of arm due to movement of the tanker. In case of any pool fire, the effects will be very localized and hence will not cause much damage. The quantity released is too small to qualify for any vapour cloud explosion.

Failure of 300 NB flange on each Pipeline

Under this scenario, radiation intensity of 4 kW/m^2 will be felt up to a distance of 72 m. The LFL distance is found to be 84 m from the point of leak. Under worst weather conditions, a late explosion distance of 279 m is observed in case of naphtha. This may result in wide spread damage in the port area. Therefore it is recommended to avoid any open flame in the port area during transfer operation. It is also recommended to have fogging arrangements at the jetty to avoid any formation of explosive mixture.

Table 5.4: Consequence Analysis for the Pipeline carrying Naphtha/Motor Spirit

Scenario	*Weather Class*	*LFL distance (m)*	*Flash Fire Distance (m)*	*Impact distances for pool fires in meters*			*Impact distances for explosion in meters*		
				4 kW/m²	*12.5 kW/m²*	*37.5 kW/m²*	*4.3 kg/cm²*	*28.5 kg/cm²*	*70 kg/cm²*
Failure of unloading arm at port	F	3	4	8	5	3	Not likely	Not likely	Not likely
	D	4	6	6	5	4	Not likely	Not likely	Not likely
Failure of 300 NB	F	85	155	50	30	-	282	142	126
flange at port	D	75	175	75	44	-	278	190	180
Partial failure of booster	F	75	190	55	35	-	325	230	225
pump discharge	D	80	200	75	40	-	260	150	140
Catastrophic failure of	F	780	775	300	180	-	950	885	875
booster pump discharge	D	832	825	310	186	-	980	860	840
Partial failure of 600 NB	F	85	87	52	40	-	280	185	175
pipeline at terminal	D	65	65	68	40	-	250	150	135

Partial Failure of Pipeline at Booster Pump Discharge

The impact distances for this scenario is comparable with the above scenario. Under this scenario, the radiation intensity of 4 kW/m^2 will be experienced up to a distance of 75 m, the LFL distance being 80 m from the point of leak. The late ignition explosion distance can extend up to 320 m in case of naphtha under worst weather conditions. This may cause wide spread damage in the booster pump station. Fogging arrangement may be provided at the booster pump station to avoid the formation of an explosive mixture as there will be many flanges and hence probability of failure is high.

Catastrophic Failure of Pipeline at Booster Pump Discharge

This is the worst possible scenario for the pipelines. However, the probability of a catastrophic failure of the pipeline is very small. In the unlikely event of catastrophic failure of naphtha pipeline, the impact of vapour cloud explosion could be felt up to a distance of around 1 Km. During such a failure, the population living in the down wind direction may have to be notified to minimize the chances of ignition sources.

Partial Failure of 600 NB Flange on Pipeline at the Terminal

The impact distances for this scenario inside the terminal is comparable with those of a partial failure of pipeline at booster pump discharge. However, the main concern will be the protection of large storage tanks in the terminal.

Probability of Failure of the Pipeline

The duration of pumping from the port to the terminal is estimated as 100 hours. The number of such pumping operations in a year will be approximately sixty. The probability of a oil pipeline rupture is reported in literature as 2.16×10^{-3}/year. Assuming that the probability of a source of ignition available is 1, the probability of failure of the pipeline under study is calculated as 1.48×10^{-3} per year.

Conclusions and Recommendations

The following are the conclusions and recommendations emerging out of the study.

- Regular patrolling of the pipelines should be carried out especially when the transfer operation is in progress. This will help in identifying any activity that have the potential to cause pipeline damage or to identify small leaks whose effects are too small to be detected by instruments.
- Pipeline failures due to third party activity can be reduced by ensuring that the members of the public, surrounding population, and the district administration are aware of the pipeline.
- The entire stretch of the underground pipeline is proposed to be cathodically protected. Regular readings of pipe to soil potentials should be taken to ensure that rapid corrosion is not taking place locally.
- Prior to the transfer of hydrocarbons from the port to the storage terminal, water draw off should be done to minimize internal corrosion.
- Positive blinding of the lines may be carried out by using spectacle blinds both at the port and the terminal.

- The unloading operation should be continuously manned and monitored.
- At locations where the pipelines/pipe racks are close to traffic movement, adequate crash guards may be provided.
- All unloading arms may be inspected by non-destructive testing methods annually. The pipelines should be subjected to hydrotest at least once in 5 years.

Chapter 6

Corporate Governance for Energy Security

The term "Corporate Governance" has come into sharp focus of the corporate world following recently highly-publicised corporate failures in the US and other developed countries. The concept of Corporate Governance made its formal entry into the corporate management culture only in 1992 with the publication of "Code of Best Practices" by the Cadbury Committee; whose main recommendations were in the sphere of composition, functioning, responsibility of a company's Board of Directors, financial aspect of corporate governance, audit, inspection and control, code of best practices, etc.

The Cadbury Committee was succeeded by the Greenbury Committee in 1995, and the Hampel Report in 1998, both in the U.K. Recommendations contained in these reports were subsequently incorporated into the combined code of the London Stock Exchange (LSE). Possibly, the most comprehensive principles of Corporate Governance are enshrined in the "Principles of Corporate Governance", published by the Organization of Economic Cooperation and Development (OECD) in 1999. Specifically, the OECD Principles focused on the following five distinctive features, relating to good governance:

- The rights of shareholders
- The equitable treatment of shareholders
- The role of stakeholder in corporate governance
- Disclosures and transparency norms
- Responsibilities of the Board

Recent times have witnessed several more of such initiatives, designed to further strengthen the ongoing corporate governance framework. These *inter alia* include: the enactment of the Sarbanes Oxley Act, the proposed modification in the listing guidelines of New York Stock Exchanges (NYSE) and NASDAQ (Takkar, 2003).

Corporate Governance: Concept, Relevance and Context

The concept of corporate governance is essentially an all-pervasive and dynamic one, which is gaining grounds and momentum because of several contributing factors, changing business principles, ethos, strategies and business environment. The emergence of European Union, economic reforms, banking reforms and integration of domestic economy with global economy, under the WTO regime, has accelerated and impacted the process.

The essential business ingredients of corporate governance hinges around transparency in reporting and accounting, effective accountability to all stakeholders, performance rating, auditing and accounting, business ethics through well-defined corporate strategy, constant strive for corporate excellence through management transformation and good governance of the human side of enterprise.

The concept of "Corporate Governance", as brought out by "The Hindu", in its publication on July 9, 1997 "Corporate Governance: Time for a Metamorphosis" underlines its basic principles the following way: "Corporate governance is not just corporate management; it is something much broader to include a fair, efficient and transparent administration to meet certain well-defined objectives. It is a system of structuring, operating and controlling a company with a view to achieve long-term strategic goals to satisfy shareholders, creditors, employees, customers and suppliers; and complying with the legal and regulatory requirements, apart from meeting environmental and local community needs. When it is practiced under a well-laid out system, it leads to the building of a legal, commercial and institutional framework and demarcates the boundaries within which these functions are performed". According to the Advisory Board of the National Association of Corporate Directors (NACD), New York "Corporate Governance ensures that long-term strategic objectives and plans are established and that the proper management structure (Organization, systems and people) is in place to achieve those objectives, while, at the same time, making sure that the structure functions to maintain the corporation's integrity, reputation and responsibility to its various constituencies" (Kumar, 2000). This falls in the line of thinking of Sir Adian Cadbury in his Cadbury Report; which, *inter alia* states as follows:

> "A code of corporate governance cannot be imported from outside; it has to be developed based on the country's experience. There cannot be any compulsion on the corporate sector to follow a particular code. Equilibrium should be struck so that corporate governance is not achieved at the cost of the growth of the corporate sector".
>
> —**Sir Adian Cadbury**

This paper chronicles the broad principles and essential features of participatory corporate governance, global and Indian experiences, with special reference to the energy sector. The paper also lays emphasis on building good organizational structure, culture, ethics and transparency in reporting systems, highlighting, **inter alia**, energy security aspects in selected energy sector companies. Learning experience derived thereof can be used as a milestone to frame and guide future strategy.

Components of Corporate Governance

By Corporate Governance- taking a cue from above perceptions, it is meant the all-encompassing field of learning and practices, related in the main, with the following subject matter areas:

- Ownership structure
- Company's Charter and bylaws
- Board of Directors, Trustees, and the allocation of control rights
- Managers' fiduciary duties towards owners, and the allocation of decision rights
- Creditors protective covenants
- Changes in the capital structure
- Conflicts of interest between managers, creditors and owners
- Accountability to stakeholders
- Tight budget constraints and short-termism
- Managers' performance and incentives
- Information production and disclosure to markets and stakeholders
- The role of gatekeepers
- National and international corporate law, regulations and law enforcement

Concomitant to above, the following critical remarks may be offered on the **inter-se** relationship of these cardinal features for developing a broader approach to corporate governance principles and policies of an organization:

(i) Everybody that is able to hold a claim on the company becomes a stakeholder: owners and creditors are the main stakeholders, followed by managers, employees, government (taxes and complaints), suppliers (bonding and trust), customers (quality and conveniences), and communities (labor development and environmental damages).

(ii) Gatekeepers are distinctive organizations that safeguard the interests and rights of different stakeholders: auditing and accountancy firms, investment banks, law firms, market regulators, institutional investors, creditors' trustees, NGOs (non-government organizations acting as watchdogs of corporations, markets, regulators) and credit-rating firms.

(iii) Corporate Governance seems an unfortunate misnomer because all organizations, by far, display a governance structure of one sort or another. Besides, government organizations exhibit complex governance features.

Ethical Concerns in Corporate Governance

In so far as business ethics are concerned, it is the individuals who make the difference. Some people are driven by goals (e.g. market share, business targets, profit etc.). Others are driven by values (e.g. tradition, culture etc.). Whereas, goals will keep changing, values are more steadfast and enduring. For the first group, when values conflict with goals, values are generally discarded, because the goal is paramount. For the other group, those driven by values, it may so happen - oftentimes the values themselves become goals. And, if the business objectives do not conform to these values, it is business objectives that get discarded. The more one is driven by values, the easier it is to make choice. Balancing business imperatives with ethical concerns is a challenge and the business managers must grapple with it throughout their career (Guzder, 1998).

According to Gilbert (1996), as summed-up in his book "Ethics through Corporate Strategy", business ethics is a "Corporate Social Responsibility" and even sometimes company's survival, to a large extent, could hinge upon possessing a business attitude called ethics. Such a belief could also be regarded as "Corporate Social Performance", in the context of corporate governance. Cultivating good code of conduct and balancing it with a good sense of business ethos leads to what can be termed as organizational/ company's culture: which, in effect, is the sum-total of company's way of working. Consequently, this organizational culture determines how the company fares in the market place (Chanda, 2000). It takes long years to develop corporate culture; but probably takes even longer to sustain it.

The real challenge confronted by business manager is not merely to induce a change in business environment but to sustain it perpetually down the line. Team-building, effective communication systems, developing organization culture, leadership developments; complemented by setting goals and standards, performance appraisal, generous rewards and recognition etc. are some of the important elements that can sustain a change in a non-reversible manner, and organizations can successfully combine the technical and human-side of change to create a more effective and lasting transformation (Galpin, 1996). Such transformations, can in turn, see through turnaround, which should be the mission for a professionally managed organization with good governance.

Corporate Governance: Indian Scenario in Statutory Context

The corporate governance in Indian context provides a broad contour and canvas for understanding its relevance to overall business management in government, public and private enterprises, including the financial institutions. Corporate governance became an "in-thing" for effective organizational management, subsequent upon the economic reforms and banking reforms initiated by the Government of India on the lines of recommendations contained in the Narasimham Committee on Financial Sector Reforms (1991). The operational and institution framework for effective implementation of corporate governance has been provided in a comprehensive manner in the Company's Bill, 1997 i.e. two years following the formal entry of India into WTO, as an active member. Coupled with this other policy-enabling regulatory instruments of the Government such as New Industrial Policy, Modified Exim Policy (1997-2002), FEMA Bill, Modified Income Tax Act, FERA/SEBI Regulations (1997) etc. have paved the way and created a new ambience for developing good corporate culture through good governance. For professionalization of corporate governance as a system the Institute of Company Secretaries of India (ICSI) has prepared a report on "Code of Corporate Governance"; which, *inter alia*, contains a voluntary code of good corporate practices. This report will, hopefully, open up a new vista of professionalized corporate governance in India. Accounting standards ¾ both Indian and International, are presently serving as an effective policy-cum-regulatory instrument for ensuring transparency in corporate governance.

For boosting export under WTO regime, the Government of India's Foreign Investment Promotion Board (FIPB) is playing a catalytic and proactive role for India's industrial sector. The Foreign Investment Promotion Board (FIPB) has been thoroughly revamped to ensure that decision-making is quicker and more transparent. The Foreign Investment Promotion Council (FIPC) has been set up to promote smooth inflow of foreign capital. The list of industries eligible for automatic approval has been further enlarged. Specific guidelines for foreign investment have been laid down for each industrial sector. The government is committed to achieve the goal of attracting least $10 billion a year as foreign direct investment in near future, for which a national strategy formulation is currently under active consideration of the government.

In India, the Accounting Standards Board (ASB) was constituted by the Institute of Chartered Accountants of India (ICAI) on April 21, 1977. Accounting standards are issued under the authority of the Council of the ICAI. The Central Board of Direct Taxes (CBDT) is a standard-setting authority in terms of Section 145 (2) of the Income tax Act, 1961. Now it is also proposed to set up a National Advisory Committee on Accounting Standards (NACAS). Internationally, the International Federation of Accountants (IFAC) formulates auditing guidelines through the International Accounting Practices Committee (IAPC). According to IAPC, International Accounting Standard is a brief, and as far as possible: (a) simple statement dealing with a particular aspect of financial statement, and (b) what minimum information should be disclosed. The standards prescribed are often quite detailed, and in several places, permit alternatives. International standards are structured to cater to a wide spectrum of countries from both the developed and developing world.

Indian Energy Sector: Need for Good Governance

With a population of around 1.1 billion, India is the world's second most populous country and ranks fifth in the world in terms of primary energy consumption, accounting for about 3.5 per cent of the world's commercial energy demand. With a GDP growth rate of around 8% during the Tenth Five Year Plan of the Government (2002-07), India is currently one of the fastest growing economies of the world. The future levels and patterns of energy use in India therefore have important implications – at the national level in terms of environmental impacts of energy use, issues of access and equity, and at the global level in terms of geopolitics of energy supply and GHG emissions related to the combustion of fossil fuels.

The Challenge of Growing Energy Demands

According to World Bank estimates, around 35% of the country's population subsists below the poverty line ($1/day, 2000 PPP) and does not have access to basic amenities and clean energy forms. Even by 2001, around 44% of house-holds did not have access to electricity (Census of India, 2001). The country continues to face electricity shortages, with an overall power shortage of 8.4% and a peaking power shortage of 12.3% in 2005/06.

Despite gradual urbanization, around 72% of the country's population resided in rural areas in 2001. The rural urban divide in India is manifest not only by the differences in the levels of energy requirement but also in the availability and choice of fuel and technologies to meet the same useful energy needs and services. On a per capita basis, India's energy consumption is still a fraction of that in developed countries. In 2003, India's primary energy consumption was 439 kgoe per capita, compared with 1090 in China, 7835 in the US and a world average of 1688.

Future Energy Needs

Various estimates indicate that India would need to increase its primary energy supply by at least 3 to 4 times and its electricity generation capacity by 5 to 6 times of the 2003/04 levels.

The Integrated Energy Policy report brought out by the Planning Commission estimates that under an 8% GDP growth scenario, India's total energy requirements would be in the range of 1536 mtoe to 1887 mtoe by 2031 under alter-native scenarios of fuel and technological diffusion. TERI's analysis based on the MARKAL model, indicates that under an 8% GDP growth scenario with current plans and policies of the Government, commercial energy needs would in-crease to 2108 mtoe by 2031/32. In reality, the Government of India would like to achieve a GDP growth of above 10% per annum ((Srivastava & Mathur, 2007).

Although India has considerable coal reserves, with the current coal production technology, it is estimated that India's domestic coal production could increase to a maximum level of around 600 MTPA. Oil production has stagnated at around 33 MT in the past few years and is not expected to increase significantly. Further, while natural gas has emerged as a relatively clean option in the past decade, there is uncertainty regarding the level of its indigenous availability. Accordingly, under a business-as-usual (BAU) scenario, the country is expected to increasingly become reliant on imports of all forms of commercial energy, with total energy import de-pendency increasing to around 80% by 2031. Although the country has been dependent on oil imports for several decades, imports of coal and gas have started during the last decade. By 2031, TERI estimates indicated a dependency of 78% for coal (over a billion tonnes), 93% for oil (~ 700 million tonnes) and 67% for gas (~ 93 BCM) with current estimates of future availability of indigenous energy. India's likely Energy Dependency (BAU scenario) terms of the large monetary outflows that the country would have to bear but also in terms of the infrastructural requirements for port development, handling and transportation of this energy- not to mention access to these resources in, and inputs on, global markets (Srivastava & Mathur, 2007).

Policy Initiatives in India

Given the bleak current energy scenario and the future prospects, the Government of India has put in place several measures that it hopes would lead to an easing of the shortages in the country and a more even distribution of access to energy. Some key initiatives along these lines are listed below:

Structural and Regulatory Reforms: The oil and gas sector was one of the first sectors in which the Government tried to introduce a much higher level of autonomy by allowing the public sec-tor enterprises to work as corporate entities with their own Boards of Directors that would man-age the companies at an arm's length distance from the Government. Private Sector participation in refineries was also introduced as a result of which the private sector body has a share of nearly 30% in India's refining capacities today. In the exploration and production areas, the Government has progressively refined its terms and conditions for sharing the benefits with the private sector under various rounds of the New Exploration Licensing Policies (NELP). The Government has also unbundled the functioning of erstwhile Oil Coordination Committee that was responsible for the complete supply planning and procurement of oil and gas in the country, into two entities – Petrofed which is a trade association for oil and gas and the Petroleum and Natural Gas Authority (PNAU) which is an independent regulator in the sector. Unfortunately, one of the weakest points of the regulator in this sector is the fact that it does not have a right to regulate the prices which continue to be in the domain on the Government.

In the case of power sector, reforms were introduced in the early 1990's and, through a process of learning; India has finally reached a stage where it has enacted the Energy Conservation Act in 2001 and the Electricity Act in 2003. The Energy Conservation Act requires the establishment of a Bureau of Energy Efficiency as a deemed statutory autonomous body that would work towards encouraging energy efficiency in the country. The broad objectives of BEE are to provide a policy framework and direction to national energy conservation and efficiency efforts and programs; to coordinate energy efficiency and conservation policies and programs and take it to the stakeholders; to establish systems and procedures to measure, monitor and verify energy efficiency results in individual sectors as well as at the macro level.

The Electricity Act- 2003 requires the functional unbundling of erstwhile vertically integrated state electricity boards and puts in lace regulatory commissions both at the federal and state level. These electricity regulatory commissions have significant powers and have the responsibility to determine not only the tariff structures in their areas of jurisdiction but also to satisfy quality of supply and service norms and create a competitive environment apart from several other functions. The coal sector, unfortunately, is one sector that has not made adequate progress on reforms.

Enhanced Private Sector Participation: Private sector interest in the oil and gas sector has built up and much more significantly than in the case of electricity sector because it got an early start and because distortions in the case of these sectors were not severe as in the case of electricity. Despite several efforts towards encouraging private sector participation in electricity generation and distribution the response from the private sector has been grossly inadequate. This has largely been because of the inability of the distribution business to generate adequate revenues to provide an adequate return or indeed comfort that the services would be paid for! Once again, learning from the past experiences and the need to quickly add significant capacities, the Government of India launched the Ultra Mega Power Project (UMPP) scheme that identified seven sites for setting up large-scale power plants with each site having a capacity of 4000 MW.

Universal Service

As far as electricity is concerned, the challenge of universal services remains daunting for nearly 400 million people having no access to electricity supply in the country. Under a scheme launched by the Government called the Rajiv Gandhi Gramin Vidyutikaran Yojana (RGGVY), the Government is facilitating the extension of electricity infrastructure to rural areas through a high capital subsidy but linked to the establishment of franchise distribution arrangement at the local level. This particular scheme takes advantage of a provision of the Electricity Act, 2003 that has delicensed generation and distribution of electricity in rural areas. The attractiveness of RGVVY schemes lies in its design where in the local level entrepreneur would be allowed to recover tariffs from its consumers on the basis of their ability to pay and require the distribution licensees to pro-vide electricity to such entrepreneurs at those prices. Any loss that the distribution licensee would incur for such supplies would be borne by the larger consumer's urban and industrial areas.

Transport Initiatives: Recognizing the growing role of the transport sector in energy demand, the Government of India has started another scheme JNNURM (Jawaharlal Nehru National Urban Renewal Mission) that is providing support to city bodies to plan their transportation and infrastructure in the most efficient manner taking into account size, density and spread of the city. A number of State Governments have now come up with proposals for integrated urban transport system that rely heavily on the development of public or mass transit systems.

India and the "Petersburg Declaration"

As it is apparent from the above discussion, India is almost completely in line with the core principles of the Petersburg action plan with a small differentiation in its approach to climate change and sustainable development. India is clearly pursuing aggressively the path of sustainable development which by itself has been well recognized both in the third and fourth Assessment reports of IPCC (Intergovernmental Panel on Climate Change) as having strong linkages with climate change.

India is also strongly aligned with the principle of open, transparent and competitive markets with the exception of coal sector. Competitive bidding processes have been introduced in all segments of the other energy sectors. However, a key weak point comes to the fore when such processes run into disputes. What is required in such instances is to have strong and independent dispute resolutions mechanisms. The Government cannot assume onto itself this role—especially when a large part of the energy sector continues to be in the public sector. In a similar fashion while the dialogue between the Government and the various stakeholders in energy developments have increased substantially as compared to a decade ago, the challenge of informing and educating consumers of energy products and services still remains daunting. This is apparent both in the public consultations held by the Electricity Regulatory Commissions as well those that are part of the Environment Impact Assessment processes in the country. One key principle of the Petersburg declaration that needs focused attention, relates to the safeguarding of critical energy infrastructure. While it is easy to identify such critical infrastructures on a point basis, India has not undertaken any exercise to identify and prioritize critical points along its networks.

Energy and Climate Change

Faced with the huge challenge of meeting its rapidly increasing energy demand, India is focusing sharply on both energy efficiency improvements as well as tying up energy resources at the global level – either through purchases on the international markets or through equity investments in global assets. India would also be keenly interested in acquiring clean and efficient energy technologies. However, it would have to be extremely sensitive to the costs of such technologies. The Indian consumers, specially the very large percentage that today do not have an access to electricity, are extremely price sensitive and the Government would need to take into account not only the ability of such people to pay for energy ser-vices but also to its own ability to absorb the costs of energy subsidies. Energy subsidies, especially for the deserving, are provided by almost every country in the world—developed or developing..

The option of using the clean development mechanism (CDM) also exists but has thus far been focused primarily on the "low hanging fruit". It would be interesting to look at the possibility of apply the public-private-partnership model to-wards the financing of clean technologies for a large scale energy production and consumption in the country.

The Indian Government has already undertaken or planned for several policies and initiatives that encourage sustainable energy growth – both in terms of improved efficiency of use and in terms of its environmental implications. Several policies and measures have for example focused on improving energy efficiency, enhancing renewable and clean energy forms, bringing about power sector reforms, promoting clean coal technologies, promoting cleaner and less carbon intensive fuels for transport, and addressing environmental quality. The Indian Government has actively been pursuing a multi-pronged strategy for the promotion of renewable energy sources. Against a target of 3,075 MW, the country added 4,613 MW capacity based on renewables during the Tenth Plan. During the Eleventh Plan period, the MNRE aims to have 10% of grid interactive power generation installed capacity and 4% of the electricity mix based on renewables. The study of alternative sources of fuels has become increasingly important in recent years. TERI's pioneering work in terms of exploring ***Jatropha curcas*** as a biodiesel plant and in associating with the National Mission on Biofuels to study the techno-commercial viability of biodiesel production from its seeds constitutes an important step in this area. As reflected in Figure 6.1, not only has there been considerable improvement in commercial energy intensity during 1986-2006, but the intensity is also likely to improve further if the current plans and policies of the Government are implemented, revealing the decoupling of energy and economic growth over time in the Indian economy.

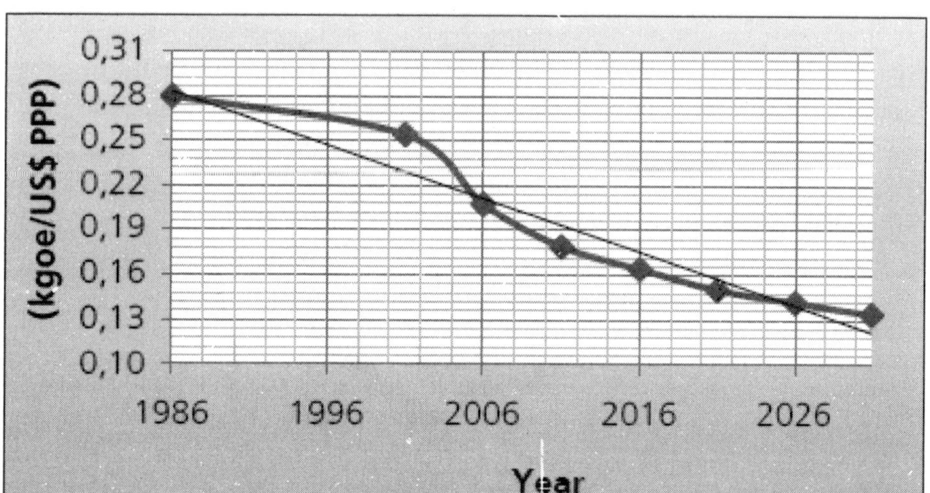

Figure 6.1: Energy intensity trends (Source: TERI analysis-2007)

CASE STUDIES

The following pages highlight some illustrative case studies- mostly from the developed economies- pertaining to the application of corporate governance principles in energy sector for attaining long-term sustainability and energy security on the strength of good corporate governance.

CASE I

The Impact of Corporate Governance Structures in the Development of the Nordic Energy Sector

Anders Sandoff (2002 a,b), School of Economics, Göteborg of Nordic Energy in Norway conducted a research study on the impact of corporate governance structures in the Development of the Nordic energy sector. As a group, the publicly owned energy companies occupy a place apart among the Nordic energy companies and are entitled to special interest. The stated research studies pinned downed the appropriateness of assuming a standard profit-maximizing model as a basis for understanding development in the stationary energy system. Results from a survey conducted by the School of Economics, Göteborg of Nordic Energy in Norway showed that there are important deviations from this assumption present for publicly owned energy companies. This type of ownership is better described as value-driven rather than profit-driven and therefore involves other challenges and opens up other kinds of possibilities. This implied that publicly-owned companies will not always invest in the most profitable technique and they will need larger economic incentives to seize lucrative opportunities that do not clearly enhance important owner values. In order to better understand these deviations Nordic Energy developed an extended framework for describing important drivers for initiating change in the stationary energy sector. The objective is to deepen the understanding of the values that are central to these organizations, and to elucidate the consequences of them in terms of how they operate their business. The framework suggests that one has to consider not only the values that these companies hold but also the fact that they are for profit organizations operating in an infrastructural industry. The condition for change in the stationary energy sector therefore would have to be dependent on an intricate balance between prevailing values, interpretation of financial demands and conception of the current and future business logic of the industry.

What Motivated Owners to have Stakes in Energy Companies?

This may seem a naive question, given the answer that the main purpose for a corporation is to make money, create shareholder value, or as Milton Friedman expressed it:"the business of business is business". Applying this perspective, the company's line of business or how it is carried out is therefore of less importance to the owner. Given the large confidence that policy makers show deregulations and market-based instruments, where maximal profitability is the principal guide for long-term actions, it is important to understand why it is convenient to assume profit to be the primary driver for investors as well as for the management of a corporation. Give below is a short account of the basic mechanisms governing this model by Nordic Energy.

The Basic Model of a Profit-maximizing Corporation

An investor who wants to maximize the value of an investment must at the same time minimize the risk in the investment. Typically this is done by spreading the invested capital between many different securities, which will include shares in several different companies. From the company's perspective it is difficult to attract capital (investors) to the company, if at the same time it means that the investor have to get involved in the management, or be a member of the board of directors. Both these explanations imply that it is favorable to separate ownership from the actual running of the company. However, if maximizing the value of the investment is the main motive, is the investor not worried that the invested capital will be used in ways not aiming at that? A separation of ownership and management will limit the investor's insight into the company. How can the investor safeguard his investment without sacrificing the need of disengagement? In other words, what are the stabilizing mechanisms in this construction? Here two types of mechanism, based on formal and informal control are important safeguards for unwanted behavior. Formal control is exercised by legal requirements that regulate conduct and the content of managerial activities. Much of this control is exercised through concentration of ownership, delegation of control in the boards of directors, and by accountants. More important though is probably the informal control stemming from the professionalization of management (socialization into code of conduct, culture, career, long training etc.) and by constant monitoring of company's performance.

Another way of exercising control is by aligning managerial interests with those of the investors through executive compensation programs. Having a diversified investment portfolio with a lot of companies to keep track of, preferably the investor relies on the monitoring (valuation) that takes place in the stock market. This was considered not only a safeguard protecting his own investment from serving other interests than maximizing the company's value, but also an important benchmark for assessing the valuation done by potential investors.

How well does the typical Nordic energy company fit this model?

Despite the fact that almost all of the Nordic energy producers these days are corporations and in many ways look like such, several of the institutional arrangements of these companies are not in line with the model outlined above. Given below are three examples of important differences.

First, these companies are typically owned and controlled by the state or municipalities. No matter how convincingly the owner states that such a corporation is run for profit, this kind of ownership can never be totally equivalent to that of a private one. Public ownership is inherently connected to public wants and needs. This has important implications for what the company can and cannot do. In many cases these restrictions are subtle and limit the actions by what the general public thinks such a company ought to do. *Second*, ownership is typically very concentrated, e.g. the largest owner controls more than 50 % of the capital. It is hard to see the financial logic behind such a poorly diversified portfolio. Usually the reason for a concentrated ownership is that the owner has certain goals for the company that go beyond short-term profit maximization.

Third, energy companies are to a large extent not listed and hence do not get their actions valued by the market. Owners have only limited references to what a competitive performance would be. This indicates that profit estimations are not very important for the owners of the company. Public owners do not trade shares as a mean of maximizing the value of the portfolio. Rather they hold on to their shares and if they sell, they typically sell the whole company or a large part of it to a single buyer.

To sum these observations up, one can conclude that judging from a couple of fundamental characteristics of corporate governance structures in the Nordic energy sector, these companies are not primarily set up to be moneymakers.

Framework for Initiating Change in the Stationary Energy Sector

The suggested framework points towards appropriateness of assuming standard profit maximizing as a basis for constructing policy instruments to facilitate investments in sustainable energy productions. It was clearly borne out from the study that there are important deviations from this assumption present for a large number of the energy companies. These findings have implications for how the stationary energy system will develop. It will also have an effect on the efficiency of the market-based policy instruments in use. It is clear that a diversion from value maximization as the primary goal of a company will lead to a decrease in effectiveness and efficiency of these instruments. Value-driven energy companies will not always invest in the most profitable techniques. Investments that don't enhance owner motives have to be accompanied with relatively larger economic incentives to be attractive. From a societal point of view it is relevant to consider if existing policy instruments ought to be supplemented with other methods of influencing energy companies owned by the public sector. Thus, one may conclude that one major difference between these companies and the model corporation outlined above is that they are driven by values rather than profits.

Influencing these values by a structured, coordinated and persistent use of; education, cooperation and standard-setting will likely have a significant impact on the values these organizations hold. In such an approach, it is of great importance to include owner representatives in the dialogue. The objective is to deepen the understanding of the values that are central to these organizations, and to elucidate the consequences of them in terms of how they operate their business. The business logic of publicly controlled utilities is fundamentally different from that of most other industries since it emphasizes the infrastructural purpose of the industry rather than traditional market forces. These companies can be said to have a triad-like foundation for explaining its long term commitments. The condition for change in the stationary energy sector is therefore dependent upon an intricate balance between prevailing values, interpretation of final demand and conception of the current and future business logic as shown below in Fig. 6.2:

What these three entities contain and how they should be handled in order to facilitate change is not only a very complex issue, but also of a fairly recent date. Conversion of municipal utilities into independent subsidiary corporations became popular in the nineties. At the same time the Nordic countries deregulated their electricity markets. That gives different practitioners (owner representatives, managers and policy makers) only a

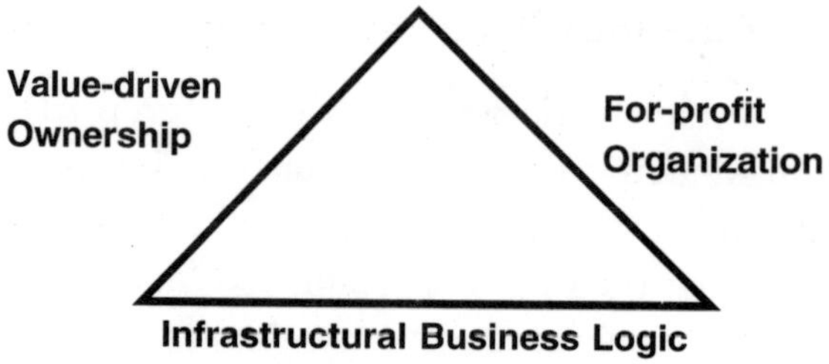

Figure 6.2: The Triad-like Foundation of Publicly owned Energy Companies

limited experience. They are still trying to understand the new situation how to balance these three entities. Little research has so far been done in order to bring clarity to the implications of this triad like foundation for publicly owned energy companies. As a group, the publicly owned energy companies occupy a place apart among the Nordic energy companies. The case study explored the importance of corporate governance structures in these companies for the development of the Nordic energy system. Value-driven ownership involves other challenges and opens up other kinds of possibilities. The discussion here indicates that the infrastructural nature of the stationary energy sector will make it dependent on much more interaction and hands on involvement than traditional industries in order to function properly.

CASE II

Corporate Governance through Policy Reforms in Russia's Oil Sector

According to a study conducted by Charles P. McPherson (2007), despite difficult circumstances, policy reform in Russia's oil sector has been impressive. Nevertheless, further reforms and investments in excess of $60 billion over the next 10 years will be needed to help the sector realize its potential.

USSIA'S OIL sector is critical to the country's overall economic recovery. Oil accounts for 5 percent of Russia's GDP, 20 percent of its foreign exchange earnings, and 10 percent of its fiscal revenues. Over the past five years, oil sector performance has fallen far below its potential. The world's largest oil producer in 1990, Russia has now slipped to third place, with production declining at annual rates of 7–14 percent. Investments on the order of $50 billion to $60 billion will be required over the next 10 years just to stabilize production, and even larger sums will be needed to bring about a recovery. Funding at these levels will not be forthcoming unless the private sector, both

Price reform	*Tax reform*	*Legal reform*	*Enterprise reform*	*Foreign direct investment*
President's office	President's office	President's office	President's office	President's office
Ministry of Fuel and Power	Ministry of Fuel and Power	Ministry of Fuel and Power	Ministry of Fuel and Power	Ministry of Fuel and Power
Ministry of Finance	Ministry of Finance	State Committee on Geology	Ministry of Economy	State Committee on Geology
Ministry of Economy	Ministry of Economy	Ministry of Environment and Natural Resources	State Property Agency	Regional government
Ministry of Foreign Economic Relations	Duma Economic Policy Committee	Duma Industry and Energy Committee	Regional government	Producers
Duma Economic Policy Committee	Regional government	Duma Ecology and Natural Resources Committee	Producers	World Bank and IMF
Regional government	Producers	Duma Economic Policy Committee	World Bank and IMF	Bilateral lenders
Producers	World Bank and IMF	Federation Control		
Consumers	Bilateral lenders	Regional Government		
World Bank and IMF		Producers		
Bilateral lenders		World Bank and IMF		
		Bilateral lenders		

Source: World Bank.

foreign and domestic, can be engaged. Private sector commitments will depend crucially on policy reform in the oil sector. Achieving policy reform in Russia has presented major challenges. Many reform concepts were entirely new to Russia four years ago, especially those based on market principles or the need for legal transparency. The number and range of participants involved has also made the reform process highly complex (see table). Against this background, Russia's achievements in the oil sector have been impressive. Not surprisingly, however, a number of critical issues are still outstanding.

Legislation

A legal framework setting out clearly the rights and duties of the government and contractors, and covering key issues such as ownership and taxation is a *sine qua non* for investment in the oil sector of any major oil-producing region. While some saw the urgency of establishing such a framework, many Russians, including leaders in the oil industry, did not at first recognize the importance of the necessary legislation. During the Soviet era, the industry had operated through administrative fiat and the lobbying of powerful contacts. Now, acceptable framework legislation is widely regarded as essential, but questions remain concerning what form the legislation should take:

- Should legislation cover all resources, or focus specifically on petroleum?
- Should the legal regime be license based, raising the specter of unilateral withdrawal or revision of licenses by the government, or should it be a contract based regime that is mutually binding on the government and the investor?
- Should the parliament approve all contracts and amendments, or should reasonable authority be delegated to the government?
- How should federal and regional interests and authority be balanced in such difficult areas as approving licenses and contracts, controlling operations, safeguarding the environment, and sharing tax revenues?
- What special privileges, if any, should be granted to foreign investors?

These conceptual issues and most of the standard provisions of petroleum legislation and contracts represented largely uncharted water for the Russian reformers. Not surprisingly, progress has come in fits and starts. Overlapping and sometimes competing legal drafting initiatives were common, as were serious inconsistencies and conflicts among the laws and drafts affecting petroleum operations. An omnibus law, the Law on Underground Resources, covering all natural resources was enacted in 1992, but it contained no specific provisions for petroleum and established a license-based, rather than a contract-based, regime.

During 1992–95, considerable effort was made to draft more than half a dozen laws or regulatory packages, involving several government ministries, parliamentary committees, and industry lobbies, and some coherence began to emerge. Over the same period, foreign and domestic investors made great strides in negotiating PSAs (Production Sharing Agreement) containing provisions that were standard internationally for the petroleum industry. The Law on PSAs, enacted in December 1995, represents a very important step toward an acceptable legal framework for major PSA investments in the oil sector.

Several key issues relating to assurances of a contract-based regime, contract stability, governing law, and arbitration, are still unresolved, but the government is working actively to address them, drafting clarifying regulations and, as required, legislative amendments.

Enterprise Reform

Viewed against the background of the legacy of central planning and a complete absence of accountability, transparency, and competition, Russia's achievements in the areas of institutional and enterprise reform in the oil sector have been considerable. Legislation and decrees have, with reasonable clarity, defined the roles of government at both the national (Moscow) and regional levels. The government has increasingly distanced itself from interference in the commercial operations of the oil industry and recently decided against the creation of a national oil company. As early as November 1992, presidential decree established a blueprint for enterprise reform: all oil enterprises were to be given independent legal (joint stock Company) status as quickly as possible; up to 12 vertically integrated oil companies would be formed; and the government's controlling shareholdings would be sold off in three years. These goals have all been largely met. It is generally accepted that with more careful management, and more openness and time, these sales could have realized much larger revenues for the government and attracted more experienced, market oriented investors.

With independent legal status and the prospect of privatization, enterprises have begun to restructure, to put their operations on a commercial basis. The need to gain access to international capital markets and to attract share capital has led most companies to conduct independent legal, financial, tax, and reserve audits, thereby promoting good corporate governance. Recent gains notwithstanding, tax arrears are a major, urgent problem for companies and the government alike. Finally, competition, supported by legislation, appears to be developing well at the producing level and even at the refining and distribution levels of the "oil chain." Local monopolies are likely to be short-lived. Natural monopolies in oil pipeline transport are still state-owned and will be subject to regulation of rates and rules of access. Given the difficult circumstances, Russian progress on oil sector reform has been substantial. Prices have risen from less than 5 percent of world levels to 70 percent; an acceptable tax package has been developed, which was negotiated in the context of PSAs; and the government has committed itself to seriously considering broader tax reform. The recently enacted Law on PSAs was a major achievement. A rational institutional framework for the oil sector now exists, with minimal state interference, and enterprises have rapidly become more commercial. Despite the fact that many Russians remain ambivalent about foreign investment in the oil sector, truly worlds-scale projects are now pending on a foreign joint-venture basis, and more are planned. These achievements notwithstanding, a number of critical obstacles to reform remain: export duties need to be abolished in order to complete price reform; PSA fiscal provisions should be further defined and confirmed by legislation; broader tax reform for the oil sector needs to be urgently addressed; regulations and legislative amendments will be required to complement the PSA law and unlock the billions of dollars in pending PSA investments; and further progress on commercialization, audits, and tax compliance is required to bring oil sector enterprises up to international standards.

CASE III

Enron: the Failure of Corporate Governance

The accounting drama that surrounded the collapse of Enron in the USA during the month of December 2001 will not be known for several years as investigations and lawsuits proliferate and remain embedded in the US legal system. Three issues are clear, however. First, the company had a corporate culture that encouraged its staff to influence public policy-makers on the deregulation or privatization of the US (and world) energy sector. Second, the company both instructed and led its accounting firm into 'dubious' financial transactions, which ultimately caused the collapse of Enron (Verma, 2003).

A detailed research study was conducted by Apreda Rodolfo (2000-a, b & 2000 a, b) and Apreda Rodolfo & Logan (2002) on "How Corporate Governance and Globalization can run afoul of the Law and Good practices in Business: The Enron's Disgraceful Affairs".

The purpose of these studies was to set out the Enron's demise into the perspective of Corporate and Global governance. To accomplish this target, the incremental cash- flow model was expanded to give room for governance issues. Simultaneously, a functional introduction to information sets is developed, including bounded rationality, asymmetric information, opportunistic behavior, transaction costs and agency problems. Then, corporate governance is linked to globalization by means of some recent approaches that go beyond a narrow economic mindset to encompass a far-reaching dynamics. Taking advantage of such background, the Enron's story was tracked down over a span of fifteen years since its starting day to its bankruptcy filing. Leading events are explained from corporate and global governance viewpoints, while an in-depth analysis is worked out on Enron's complex game of deception and breach of contracts: the outrageous affiliated limited partnerships, the lavish pay package to its executives, the involvement with global governance through the Indian affair and the Taliban connection. It was for the incremental cash-flow model to explain malfeasance with cash-flows from assets, and how cash flows to creditors were actually contrived. Furthermore, to highlight how cash flows were swindled from stockholders and, finally, how Enron made wheeling and dealing with cash flows on behalf of its managers. When linking corporate governance with global governance, complex and dangerous matters arise. In the Enron's tale, sleaze and political peddling were the vehicles chosen to back the managers 'pretense that the company was going to excel forever. Global agencies disbursed millions of dollars to enable Enron to expand all over the world in unsuccessful projects in contempt of law. At last, employees, pension funds, institutional investors, banks, emergent countries communities and their governments, all of them were unfairly called to foot the bill.

The main lesson to draw from this narrative lies on the accountability problem. Whereas Enron will have to face the music in several courts of justice, this disgraceful tale of malfeasance uncovered the ultimate actors that should be blamed for: the gatekeepers. They neglected their fiduciary role and damaged the credibility of many institutions and practice either in corporate or global governance. To raise the standards in accountability remains an unsettled issue and the task to address in the future on behalf of corporate life, democracy and stakeholders.

CASE IV

Corporate Governance and Climate Change: Ceres Commission Report

Douglas G. Cogan (2006) edited the Ceres Commissioned Report on Corporate Governance and Climate Change: Making the Connection from the Investor Responsibility Research Center (IRRC).

Ceres is a national coalition of investors, environmental groups and other public interest organizations working with companies to address sustainability challenges such as global climate change. Ceres directs the Investor Network on Climate Risk, a group of more than 50 institutional investors from the U.S. and Europe managing nearly $3 trillion in assets. IRRC is a research firm that has been a leading source of high quality, impartial information on corporate governance and social responsibility issues affecting investors and corporations since 1972. IRRC was acquired by Institutional Shareholder Services in August, 2005.

This report is the first comprehensive examination of how 100 of the world's largest corporations are positioning themselves to compete in a carbon-constrained world. With the launch of the Kyoto Protocoll in 2005, managing greenhouse gas emissions is now a routine part of doing business in key global trading markets. As the United States moves to join the international effort to combat global warming, climate governance practices will assume an increasingly central role in corporate and investment planning. Eventually, nothing short of an energy and technology revolution will be needed to stem rising greenhouse gas emissions across the globe.

Faced with record warmth, unprecedented hurricane activity and rapid shrinking of polar ice caps, industry opposition to confronting climate change is diminishing. Skeptics no longer question whether human activity is warming the globe, but how fast. Companies at the vanguard no longer question how much it will cost to reduce greenhouse gas emissions, but how much money they can make doing it. Financial markets are starting to reward companies that are moving ahead on climate change, while those lagging behind are being assigned more risk.

Ultimately, effective corporate responses to climate change must be built on well-functioning environmental management systems and properly focused governance practices. Shareholders and financial analysts will increasingly assign value to companies that prepare for and capitalize on business opportunities posed by climate change—whether from greenhouse gas (GHG) regulations, direct physical impacts or changes in corporate reputation.

This report is designed to be used as a benchmarking tool by institutional investors and corporations that are ready to seize on these trends. It employs a "Climate Change Governance Checklist" to evaluate how 76 U.S. companies and 24 non-U.S. companies are addressing climate change through board oversight, management execution, public disclosure, emissions accounting and strategic planning.

CASE V

ExxonMobil's Corporate Governance on Climate Change

This Report on "**ExxonMobil's Corporate Governance on Climate Change**" analyzes ExxonMobil's actions and new statements concerning climate change and renewable energy. It compares their actions and statements of competitors, as well as against basic standards put forth by investors concerned about climate change risks and the economic opportunities presented by a clean energy future. The report demonstrates the following points (Andrew Logan & David Grossman, 2006):

1. ExxonMobil's statements in its 2005 Corporate Citizenship Report (May 2006) and its 2006 Tomorrow's Energy (February 2006) report demonstrate a corporate plan and mindset unprepared for leadership in a carbon constrained world.
2. ExxonMobil's statements, plans, actions, and investments on climate change and clean energy lag behind competitors like BP, Royal Dutch Shell, Chevron and Total.
3. ExxonMobil's shareholders bear a substantial financial, competitive, and reputational risk as a result of the company's lack of strategic focus on R&D and deployment of clean, renewable energy technologies. ExxonMobil's energy outlook sees fossil fuels continuing to satisfy the vast majority of global energy demand through at least 2030, as these are "the only fuels with the scale and flexibility to meet the bulk of the world's vast energy needs over this period." The company predicts that oil and gas will continue to represent roughly 60% of overall energy sources in 2030 and that no large-scale alternative to oil as a transport fuel will arise in the

near-term. ExxonMobil expects wind power, solar power, and biofuels to supply about 2% of world energy by 2030, despite the fact that current calculations by the Renewable Energy Policy Network estimate that renewable energy already supplies roughly 4% of world power.3 Specifically, ExxonMobil forecasts that biofuels will grow from less than 1 million barrels per day in 2005 to more than 3 million in 2030. It predicts that wind and solar will grow about 11% per year "supported by subsidies and related mandates", despite the fact that grid-connected solar power grew by 60% per year from 2000 to 2004.

4. ExxonMobil's view is that alternative energy sources can have the greatest carbon-offsetting impact in the electricity sector, and that the world will continue to demand oil and gas for most of its primary energy needs for decades to come.

HIGHLIGHTS OF GOOD COOPERATE GOVERNANCE ACTIONS BY ENERGY SECTOR COMPANIES

Following is a summary of governance actions taken by the top-scoring companies in each of the 10 industries examined in this report:

BP (Oil & Gas): BP was the first major oil company to state publicly, in 1997, that the risks of climate change are serious and that precautionary action is justified. The company has cut its operational GHG emissions 10 percent below 1990 levels, and now aims to hold its emissions steady through 2012. In 2005, BP established an alternative energy business unit that plans to invest $8 billion in solar, wind, hydrogen and combined-cycle power generation technologies over the next decade.

AEP and Cinergy (Electric Power): In response to shareholder requests, the board of directors at these power companies agreed in 2004 to produce reports on their climate risk mitigation strategies. Both have targets to reduce GHG emissions and are pursuing development of integrated gasification combined cycle (IGCC) power plants. By gasifying coal to generate electricity and disposing of CO2 emissions underground, these companies believe it is possible to make coal an emissions-free generating source.

General Electric (Industrial Equipment): As part of the "eco-imagination" initiative announced in 2005, GE has pledged to achieve a 1 percent reduction in its GHG emissions from 2004 levels by 2012. GE plans to double its investments to $1.5 billion a year by 2010 in clean technologies, such as wind turbines, high efficiency gas turbines, IGCC power plants, and hybrid diesel-electric locomotives.

Rio Tinto (Coal and Minerals): Rio Tinto has a Climate Change Leadership Panel and a climate change executive to help coordinate GHG reduction efforts among its business groups. The company is developing "low emissions pathways" for its products to reduce the GHG emissions intensity in coal combustion, metals smelting and electricity use.

Climate Change Governance Checklist Scores of the major Oil Companies

A report commissioned by Ceres from the Investor Responsibility Research Center in March 2006 (Andrew Logan & David Grossman, 2006) evaluated companies in several industry sectors against a Climate Change Governance Checklist consisting of 14 governance steps in 5 categories that companies can take to proactively address climate change. The checklist topics include: Board Oversight, Management Execution, Public Disclosure, Emissions Accounting, and Emissions Management & Strategic Opportunities. Using a 100-point scoring system, ExxonMobil scored 35, compared to 90 for BP and 79 for Royal Dutch/Shell. These two prime competitors to ExxonMobil have set long-term GHG reduction goals and measure emissions from customer use of their products. They also have strong Board and Management involvement on climate issues, have made efforts to demonstrate carbon sequestration to enhance oil recovery, and have made major financial commitments to alternative energy sources like solar, wind, and hydrogen. The Climate Change Governance Checklist scores of the major oil companies clearly demonstrate the significant gap that exists between them as illustrated below (Table 6.1):

Table 6.1: Climate Change Governance Checklist Scores of the major Oil Companies

Company	*Board*	*Mgmt.*	*Disclosure*	*Emissions*	*Strategies*	*Total*
Maximum	12	18	14	24	32	100
BP	9	16	13	23	29	90
Royal Dutch/Shell	7	15	7	23	27	79
Total	6	15	12	13	16	62
Chevron	7	10	5	17	18	57
ExxonMobil	5	5	5	12	8	35

The differences in company focus among the major oil companies are clear:

BP was the first major oil company to state publicly, in 1997, that the risks of climate change are serious and that precautionary action is justified. Since then, its business planning and long-term strategy have been focused on the need to stabilize atmospheric GHG concentrations, even as global energy use continues to grow. BP set initial targets to reduce operational GHG emissions 10% below 1990 levels by 2010, which it achieved by 2001. BP now aims to hold its emissions steady through 2012 through additional energy efficiency gains and increased customer use of less carbon-intensive products. BP established BP Alternative Energy in 2005, which plans to invest $8 billion over 10 years in solar, wind, hydrogen, and combined-cycle generation technologies over the next decade, representing an annual expenditure equal to eighty times ExxonMobil's yearly GCEP expenditure.

- **Royal Dutch Shell has** invested more than $1 billion since 1998 to develop alternative energy technologies and has established Shell Renewable and Shell Hydrogen as business units. It has set a long-term target to hold its GHG emissions from its facilities at least 5% below 1990 levels through 2010. Shell has a climate change advisor and assigns personnel within each of its business groups to address climate-related issues. It has extensive experience with GHG emissions trading, first internally and now through several government programs. Shell reports extensively on its climate change and GHG control programs, and in 2004, it made an estimate of its carbon footprint.

- **Total has** set and exceeded goals to reduce the intensity rate of its GHG emissions from exploration and production activities relative to 1990 levels and new targets are under development for 2010. The company's R&D investments in new technologies evaluate the potential costs of GHG emissions. TOTAL is involved in solar, wind, and carbon sequestration technologies as emerging commercial businesses, and it is discussing biofuel production plants in Africa and South America.

- **Chevron incorporates** GHG assessments into its strategic planning process. Chevron set a target in 2004 to hold its GHG emissions flat, mainly through improvements in energy efficiency and reductions in flaring and venting of natural gas. In 2004, Chevron launched an expanded strategy to integrate renewable energy applications into its portfolio of energy products. Its strategy is focused mainly on wind and geothermal energy projects, though it is also evaluating opportunities in solar. With the acquisition of Unocal, Chevron has become the largest producer of geothermal energy in the world. It is also involved in gas-to-liquids production and carbon sequestration programs. Through Chevron Technology Ventures, it invests more than $100 million a year in low-carbon and carbon-free technologies.

• **ExxonMobil,** in contrast, has set no targets to control its GHG emissions and has no current investments in renewable energy businesses, saying it has a "responsibility to provide oil and gas supply" to meet future energy demand. Internally, the company has focused on increasing energy efficiency at its refineries and chemical plants, achieving a 35% reduction in energy and CO2 intensity rates of production since 1973; it has targeted a further 10% reduction in its intensity rates in 2002–2012.16 As noted, the company's recent reports highlight the uncertainties in climate science, and Exxon has invested little in clean energy technologies. ExxonMobil has also supported the work of some of the nation's leading skeptics on climate change, some of whom claim that fears of global warming are overblown.

BP, Royal Dutch Shell, Chevron and Total have shown leadership in promoting clean energy technologies, launching separate clean energy businesses with meaningful financing. ExxonMobil has exhibited no inclination to play a leadership role in a low-carbon world.

Corporate Regulatory Frameworks by ADB

ADB supports a number of mechanisms for creating an enabling environment for private sector growth. They include (http:// www.adb/ documents/TARS/IND/tav_ind_36323.pdf):

- strengthening forums for business-government interaction, such as deliberation councils;
- public enterprise reform and corporate governance; and
- upgrading the state's regulatory function.

Corporate governance is central to public enterprise reform. The key issues typically revolve around the process of corporatization and the establishment of the independent legal entity and selection of the agent to represent the government. In many transitional economies, the solution is to establish a semi-autonomous agency and to pursue management improvement through the selection and/or retraining of managers and the removal of non-performing managers. Efforts to establish performance contracts have had a mixed success, and greater effort must be devoted to improving the capability and performance of public enterprise boards.

Another promising area is ADB's potential role in strengthening financial and other regulatory institutions. Such institutions are active in a wide range of areas, including the promulgation and enforcement of commercial laws and directives, as well as in monitoring natural monopolies and financial markets. The procedures by which these laws are developed, enforced, and communicated are often inconsistent and non-transparent. The private sector needs to be involved in the drafting of these laws, perhaps in conjunction with deliberation councils. ADB extends help to its developing member countries, establish in building consistency and predictability in the operation of their commercial laws and regulations. Efforts are also being directed to ensure the availability of information, including relevant laws to ensure the accountability of companies to their shareholders. ADB's support to Power sector in selected countries in Asia with focus of on building built-in institutional mechanism of corporate governance is highlighted below:

Bangladesh: Power Sector Development Program

Supporting the Government's power sector reforms policy that was adopted in 1994 to improve governance and build long-term institutional capacity, improve efficiency, and promote private sector participation.

India: Assam Power Sector Development Program

Helping restructure Assam State Electricity Board (ASEB), a vertically-integrated utility, into independent companies and strengthen its policy and regulatory framework to implement reforms. (November 2003)

State Power Reform

Supporting comprehensive reform in State Electricity Boards that are not being considered for direct assistance by the Bank and World Bank, and which are undertaking comprehensive reforms.

Sri Lanka: Power Sector Development Program/Project

Establishing independent regulation and tariff setting mechanism; enhance efficiencies in the sector by introducing competition and commercialization through change in management practices; encourage private sector participation in the sector through the development of an enabling transparent business environment; and improve the quality and quantity of power supply.

Technical Assistance Program

Bangladesh: Corporatization of Dept. of Electric Supply Authority (DESA)

Assisting the Government to commercialize operations of DESA, to formalize them into corporatization, and to review and design an effective organizational structure.

People's Republic of China: Power Pricing Strategy: Tariff Setting and Regulation

Developing a power pricing strategy by preparing a reform action plan and focusing on tariff setting and tariff regulation (May 2003)

India: *Building the Capacity of Assam Electricity Regulatory Commission*

Assisting AERC to develop its operational standards and procedures and build up its institutional capacity to handle regulatory matters effectively and efficiently so as to promote the power sector reform of the state of Assam.(January 2003)

- Enabling Environment for and Restructuring of Asset Reconstruction of companies in India

Assisting in the creation of a specialized entity for handling problem loans to reduce non-performing assets in the Indian financial system, and accelerate the debt recovery process.

Summing-up

The section examined the historic evolution of the concept of corporate governance principles and its potentiality of applications in a various organizations- ranging from the Government and non-government organizations to industries, banking, socio-cultural organizations and civil societies. The status of implementation of corporate governance principles in the Indian energy sector was analyzed and it was found that there is a need to accelerate and integrate the ongoing reforms processes with corporate principles and practices. Concerted efforts should be made to evolve indigenous models in this respect which conforms to laid-down global standards that are replicable and sustainable on a long-term basis. The highlights of a selected number of case studies, covering a cross-section of lead energy sector companies have been presented to provide an eye-sight into Model approaches used by these companies- including company-wise governance performance ratings of the major energy sector companies. Since in the next decade India is going to be one of the major Asian players in the Global energy scene, it is high time that Indian companies formulate long-term strategies to embrace corporate governance principles for demonstrating grater transparency and accountability for achieving corporate excellence on a sustainable basis as a part of corporate social responsibility.

Bibliography

A

A. Hauer (2002), Thermal Energy Storage with Zeolite for Heating and Cooling, Proceedings of the 7th International Sorption Heat Pump Conference ISHPC '02, Shanghai, China, 24.-27. September 2002.

A. Hauer, Thermal Energy Storage with Zeolite for Heating and Cooling Applications.

A. Hauer, Thermal Energy Storage with Zeolite for Heating and Cooling Applications.

A.P.J. Abdul Kalam, "Address to the Nation on the Eve of the 59th Independence Day–2005," Rashtrapati Bhawan, New Delhi, August 14, 2005.

Adam, T., 2003. Why firms use non-linear hedging strategies, working paper, Hong Kong University of Science and Technology.

Ahmad, "Geopolitics of Oil," *Seminar* #555 (November 2005): 25.

Aiyar, "Energy Cooperation: India and Its Neighbours," p. 23.

Aiyar, "Interview," p. 59.

"Aiyar Laments India's lack of synergy in energy," *Platts Commodity News*, December 2, 2005, 04: 25.

Ajish Joy, "India's Energy Security: The Central Asian Odyssey" (www.observerindia.com/strategic/ st060403.htm).

Almeida, H., Campello, M., Weisbach, M.S., 2004. The cash flow sensitivity of cash, The Journal of Finance 59, 1777-1804.

al-Moneef, M. (2003). "Internal Challenges to OPEC and its Member States." Middle East Economic Survey 46 (November 17).

American Gas Association Rate Committee, 1987, Gas Rate Fundamentals,

Fourth Edition, American Gas Association, Arlington, VA.

American Wind Energy Association (2000) "Wind Energy Fact Sheet: Comparative Costs of Wind and Other Fuels" and "Global Wind Energy Market Report." URL: http://www.awea.org. [The American Wind Energy Association (AWEA) is a national trade association, representing wind power plant developers, wind turbine manufacturers, utilities, consultants, insurers, financiers, researchers, and others involved in the wind industry, that promotes wind energy as a clean source of electricity for consumers around the world.

Amit Bhandari and Cuckoo Paul, "PSU oilcos give Reliance a tough fight," *The Economic Times*, June 21, 2006.

"An Old School Oilman," *Business Today*, October 21, 2005.

Andreas Hauer (2007).Innovative Thermal Energy Storage Systems for Residential Use. Bavarian Centre for Applied Engineering Research Zae, Bayern.

Anil Agarwal, "Introductory Remarks," conference on "India's Energy Security: Major Challenges," National Conclave, Observer Research Foundation, New Delhi, February 14, 2006. (Agarwal is president of ASSOCHAM, a business association.)

Annath Chikkatur, "Comments on the *Draft Report of the Expert Committee on Integrated Energy Policy*," presentation at conference on "India's Energy Security: Major Challenges," National Conclave, Observer Research Foundation, New Delhi, India, February 15, 2006.

Article 1.4 of Ad Hoc Grouof Experts, *Report of Ad Hoc Grouof Experts on Empowerment of Central Public.*

ASEAN Competitiveness Study, McKinsey & Company, August 2003.

Asian Development Bank, *The Bank's Policy Initiatives for the Energy Sector—Energy Policy Issues* (www.adb.org/ Documents/Policies/Energy_Initiatives/ energy_ini322.as[July 1, 2006).

ASSOCHAM and IPCS, *Study on India's Energy Security* (New Delhi: IPCS and Assocham, 2004), p. 47.

B

"Bill to set uregulator for downstream petroleum gets RS nod," *The Press Trust of India*, March 2, 2006.

"Burnout: Oilcos lose $51m/day," *The Economic Times*, May 18, 2006.

Bani P. Banerjee, *Handbook of Energy and the Environment in India* (New Delhi: Oxford University Press, 2005), p. 175.

Barton, J., 2001. Does the use of financial derivatives affect earnings management decisions?

Benefits and savings of chiller replacement & various thermal storage projects U.S. Army case studies. http://www.cecer.army.mil/ul/gascool/storage.htm

Berger, P., Ofek, E., 1995. Diversification's effect on firm value. Journal of Financial Economics

Blum, J. (2005). National Oil Firms Take Bigger Role. Washington Post. Washington DC: D01.

Bohi, D.R., M. Russell, et al. (1978). Limiting oil imports: an economic history and analysis. Baltimore Published for Resources for the Future by the Johns Hopkins University Press.

BP, *BP Statistical Review of World Energy* (June 2005), p. 37.

BP, *BP Statistical Review*, p. 28.

BP, *BP Statistical Review*, p. 9.

Brown, G.W. and K.B. Toft, 2002. How firms should hedge, Review of Financial Studies 15, 1283-1324.

C

"Cairn Energy gets new exploration blocks in India," *Dow Jones International News*, July 26, 2005.

"Cairn Energy plans early oil production from North Indian fields," *BBC Monitoring South Asia*, July 8, 2005.

"Centre decides to form new entity for OIL," *The Press Trust of India*, November 27, 2005.

"China and India bid for PetroKazakhstan," *Greenwire*, August 16, 2005.

"Concern over environment degradation," *The Hindu*, January 2006: 3.

"Creating energy security priority area: Murli Deora," *Business Line*, January 30, 2006.

"Crude jolt: Oil import bill bloats 52% in '05-06," *The Economic Times*, May 11, 2006. Figures for India's total import bill are from Reserve Bank of India, "Balance of Payments (BoP) Developments in 2005–06," June 30, 2006 (www.rbi.org.in/scripts/BS_PressReleaseDisplay.aspx?prid=15001).

"Curtains for Raha; Sharma acting CMD of ONGC," *The Press Trust of India*, May 25, 2006.

Cairn Energy, *Cairn Energy PLC: Operations* (www.cairn-energy.plc.uk/operations/index.htm [July 1, 2006]).

Castaneda, C. J., Smith, C. M., 1996. Gas Pipelines and the Emergence of America's Regulatory

Charles Feinstein (2002); Economic Development, Climate Change, and Energy Security –The World Bank's Strategic Perspective, The Energy and Mining Sector Board, The World Bank Group.

Christopher C. Géczy (2007). The Use of Multiple Risk Management Strategies: Cleaner Production – Energy Efficiency Manual for GERIAP, UNEP, Bangkok prepared by National Productivity Council.Statistics have been drawn from BP Statistical Review of World Energy, June 2003, International Energy Outlook, March 2002, Energy Information administration, Office of integrated analysis and forecasting, US department of energy, Washington Indian Planning commission statistics

Cleaner Production – Energy Efficiency Manual for GERIAP, UNEP, Bangkok prepared by National Productivity Council.

Climator AB, Kylarv. 2, SE-54134 Skovde, Sweden, Telephone: +46 (0)500 48 23 50, Fax: +46.

Coal India Limited, "Functions & Responsibilities," May 23, 2006 (coal.nic.in/file1.html).

Comment, R., Jarrell, G. A., 1995. Corporate focus and stock returns. Journal of Financial Economics 37, 67-87.

Committee on Vision 2020, *Report of the Committee*, p. 69.

Cristopher C. Geczy. (2006). The use of multiple Risk Management Strategies: Evidence from the Natural Gas Industries. University of Pennsylvania.

Crude oil and Indian retail price data from Indian Petroleum Planning and Analysis Cell (pac.org.in/OPM/

Culp, C., 2001. The risk management process. John Wiley & Sons, Inc., New York.

Culp, C., Miller, M., 1995. Metallgesellschaft and the economics of synthetic storage, *Journal of Applied Corporate Finance* 7, 62-76.

D

Dadwal, Shebonti Ray (1999). India's Energy Security Policy: A Case for Nuclear Power, *Strategic Analysis: A Monthly Journal of the IDSA*, November 1999 (Vol. XXIII, No. 8)

Daniel Yergin, "The Katrina Crisis," *The Wall Street Journal*, September 2, 2005, p. A14.

Department of Energy (2002), Govt, of USA: Ref: Energy Infrastructure Risk Management-Checklists for Small and Medium Sized Energy Facilities.

Derivatives: A brief history, support@platts.com

Developing Asia and the World, Asian Development Bank, 2005, http://www.adb.org/Documents/Books/ADO/2004/update/part010000.asp

Dietl, "Gas Pipelines: Politics and Possibilities," in Khosla, "Energy Cooperation," p. 84.

Duke, R. D., and Kammen, D. M. (1999) "The Economics of Energy Market Transformation Initiatives", *The Energy Journal*, 20 (4): 15 – 64.[An economic analysis of market transformation programs for the energy sector, showing that such programs can potentially have attractive benefit to cost ratios once the effects of reducing technology costs are considered.

E

"Economic Benefits of Biomass Power" – U.S. Department of Energy; Solar, Thermal and Biomass Power Division. June 1995.

"Energy Committee set up," *EIU Viewswire* no. 301, July 21, 2005, p. 19.

EIU Data Services, *EIU Country Data.*

Emad Mekay, "Oil Hoarding Helps PumUPrices, say Analysts," *Inter Press Service*, September 3, 2004.

Encyclopedia of Energy – McGraw Hill Publication.

Energy Efficiency Fact-sheet (2007): Thermal Energy Storage, Washington State University, Energy Extension Unit, USA.

Energy Handbook, Von Nostrand Reinhold Company - Robert L. Loftness.

Energy Infrastructure Risk Management, Checklists for Small and Medium Sized Energy Facilities.U.S. Department of Energy, Office of Energy Assurance, August 19, 2002

Energy Risk Management & Valuation, NERA ECONOMIC Consulting, USA.

Energy Security, Institute of Global Energy Security; Ref.: info@iags.org

Energy Storage Breakthroughs: Ref: westernunion.com/billpayments1028_WUS0024Western Union Energy Biz3.5

Energy Storage: *U.S. Climate Change Technology Program – Technology Options for the Near and Long Term* August 2005, Page 1.3-11.

Energy Storage" of the ECES Implementing Agreement, can be ordered from: fredrik.

Eric Anderson, "GE Sees Potential in India's Energy Plans," *Times Union* 27, July 2005, p. E1.

Evidence from the Natural Gas Industry; University of Pennsylvania Expert Committee on Energy Policy, "*Draft Report*," p. 56.

Expert Committee on Energy Policy, *Draft Report of the Expert Committee on Integrated Energy Policy* (New Delhi: Planning Commission, 2005), p. 11. Also Debnath Shaw, *Securing India's Energy's Needs: The Regional Dimension* (Washington, DC: Center for Strategic and International Studies, 2004), p. 5.

Expert Committee on Energy Policy, *Draft Report of the Expert Committee on Integrated Energy Policy*, p. 73.

Expert Committee on Energy Policy, *Draft Report*, pp. 1, 11, 35, 39, 54, 63, 73, 76.

Export-Import Bank of India, *Performance Highlights 2005-06* (www.eximbankindia.com/ph.pdf [May 23, 2006]).

F

Fama, E., French, K., 1993. Common risk factors in the returns on stock and bonds, Journal of Financial Economics 33, 3-56.

Fama, E., French, K., 1997. Industry costs of equity. Journal of Financial Economics 43, 153-193.

Federal Energy Management Program (FEMP) New Technology Demonstration Program evaluates ice storage retrofit for rooftop air conditioning. http://www.eren.doe.gov/femp/prodtech/icesum.html © 2003, Washington State University Cooperative Extension Energy Program. This publication contains material written and produced for public distribution. You may reprint this written material, provided you do not use it to endorse a commercial product. Please reference by title and credit Washington State University Cooperative Extension Energy Program. WSUCEEP00-127

Final Report of Annex 17 "Phase Change Materials and Chemical Reactions for Thermal Financial Accounting Standards Board, 1994. Accounting for the effects of certain types of regulation, Statement of Financial Accounting Standards No. 71. FASB, Stamford.

Fitzgerald, J., Franke, G., Stapleton, R.C., Subrahmanyam, M.G., 1998, Who buys and who sells options: The role and pricing of options in an economy with background risk, Journal of Economic Theory 82, 89-109.

Froot, K.A., Scharfstein, D., Stein, J., 1993. Risk management: Coordinating corporate investment and financing policies. Journal of Finance 48, 1629-1658.

Fusaro, Peter, C. (2007). Energy Trading & Risk Management,www. utilpoint.com/utilpoint@ International, Inc., June, 2007

Future?" *Biomass and Bioenergy*, 15 (4/5): 357-367. [Article analyzing the future role of modern biomass energy systems as part of a sustainable global energy supply future using life-cycle analysis and evaluation of external costs.]

G

"Get professional," *Hindustan Times*, May 29, 2006.

"Govt loses by refusing to let ONGC acquire Nigeria oilfield," *The Press Trust of India*, April 28, 2006.

"Govt. in India Encourages Investment, Floats Notion of Strategic Partnershiwith South Korea," *Global Insight Daily Analysis*, August 8, 2005.

G. Ganesh, "The politics of disinvestment," *Business Line*, June 6, 2005, p. 8.

G. Madhu (2004). Risk Assessment of a Cross Country Pipeline Transporting Hydrocarbons, School of Engineering, Cochin University of Science and Technology, Cochin.

Gallis, Paul (2007), NATO and Energy Security : Order Code RS22409-Foreign Affairs, Defense, and Trade Division.

Géczy, C., Minton, B., Schrand, C., 1997. Why firms use currency derivatives. Journal of Finance 52, 1323-1354.

Girijesh Pant, "India and the Asian Energy Initiatives: Partnershiin Development," in Khosla, *Energy and Diplomacy*, p. 91.

Goldman Sachs, "Improving Energy Intensity Across the BRICs," *BRIC Layers*, Issue no. 06/02, February 14, 2006.

Green Peace Foundation, "Green Peace Says Soviets Admit Nuclear Dumping", Virginian Pilot, September 2, 1991.

Green Peace Foundation, "Green Peace Says Soviets Admit Nuclear Dumping", Virginian Pilot, September 2, 1991.

Gupta et al., "India's Energy Needs," p. 101.

H

H.N. Chanakya, "Bioenergy: From the margins to the mainstream," India's Energy Security: Major Challenges,

Hall, D.O. and Scrase, J.I. (1998) "Will Biomass be the Environmentally Friendly Fuel of the

Handbook of Energy Engineering , The Fairmont Press Inc – Albert Thumann

Hansen, L.P. Hodrick, R.J., 1980. Forward exchange rates as optimal predictors of future spot rates: An econometric analysis. *Journal of Political Economy* 88, 829-853.

Harford, J., 1999. Corporate cash reserves and acquisitions. Journal of Finance 54, 1969-1997.

Haushalter, G. D., 2000. Financing policy, basis risk, and corporate hedging: Evidence from oil and gas producers. Journal of Finance 55, 107-152.

Henderson, J. S., Guldmann, J. M., Hemphill, R. C., Lee, K., 1986. Natural gas rate design and transportation policy under deregulation and market uncertainty. Working paper 85-15. The National Regulatory Research Institute, Columbus.

Higher Global Oil Prices Implications for Asia in 2005, Asian Development Bank, 2005; http://www.adb.org/Documents/Books/ADO/2004/update/part030200.asp

Himangshu Watts, "India aims to team uwith China in oil asset race," *Reuters News*, February 1, 2005.

http://www.iea-eces.org/

http://www.pwi-energy.com/main/whitepapers/tsdereg.htm

Hubbard, R.G., Weiner, R., 1986. Regulation and long-term contracting in U.S. natural gas markets. Journal of Industrial Economics 35, 71-79.

"Hardly a regulator," *The Economic Times*, May 16, 2006.

"High oil prices to cut Asian economic growth. ADB," *Agence France Presse*, May 4, 2006.

"Hunt for new IOC chief takes off," *Indian Express*, November 22, 2004.

I

I.P. Khosla, "Introduction," in *Energy and Diplomacy*, edited by I. P. Khosla (New Delhi: Konark Publishers, 2005), p. 8.

IF Technology b.v., Frombergstraat 1, P.O. Box 605, 6800 EA Arnhem, The Netherlands, email:

IIASA/WEC (1995), Global Energy Perspectives to 2050 and Beyond, N. Nakicenovic and M. Jefferson (Laxenburg, Austria and London, UK). [A study conducted jointly by the International Institute for Applied Systems Analysis (IIASA) and the World Energy Council (WEC) looking into three cases of economic and energy developments encompassing six scenarios of energy supply alternatives extending until the end of the 21st century. The study takes account of world population prospects, economic growth, technological advance, financing requirements, and the future prospects of both fossil and nonfossil fuels and industries.]

Indian Planning commission statistics.

India's Energy Sector (2005-2010): Ref: http://www.researchandmarkets.com/

reports/307511/

India's Energy Sector (2005-2010):Ref: http://www.researchandmarkets.com/reports/307511/

Indrani Bagchi, "French N-tech Firms Eyeing India," *The Times of India*, May 18, 2006.

Indrani Dutta, "Capacity build-up in coal essential," *The Hindu*, May 22, 2006, p. 16.

International Energy Agency, *World Energy Outlook 2004* (Paris: OECD, 2004), pp. 498–99.

International Energy Agency, *World Energy Outlook 2004*, pp. 498–99.

International Energy Agency, *World Energy*, p. 106. At a conclave held in New Delhi in February 53.

International Energy Agency, *World Energy*, p. 82, 498.

International Peace Research Institute, Oslo (PRIO)

IPCC (Intergovernmental Panel on Climate Change), *Climate Change 1995: Scientific-TechnicalAnalyses of Impacts, Adaptations, and Mitigation of Climate Change*, Watson, Zinyowera, Moss (eds), Chapter 19, Cambridge University Press, Cambridge, 1996. [The Intergovernmental Panel on Climate Change (IPCC), established by the World Meteorological Organization and the United Nations Environment Programme, to assess available scientific information on climate change and the environmental and socioeconomic impacts, and to formulate response strategies. This is the Second Assessment Report of the IPCC Working Group II to assess the impacts and response options to climate change.]

"In national trend, state agency in India opens doors to green energy markets," *Renewable Energy Report* no. 85, July 25, 2005, p. 4.

"India as an energy hot spot," *Indian Express*, July 13, 2005.

"India central bank urges Govt to take oil price decision," *Reuters News*, May 3, 2006.

"India Energy Panel Advises against State Oil Companies Merger," *Dow Jones International News*, July 11, 2005.

"India eyes energy resources abroad and cooperation with China," *Gas Matters Today Asia*, August 8, 2005, p. 8.

"India Hints at Removing Energy Subsidy," UPI, May 22, 2006.

"India in global deal to emulate power of sun," *The Telegraph*, May 24, 2006.

"India is Planning to Invest $40bn in Nuclear Reactors," *Bloomberg*, May 20, 2006 (www.gulf-times.com/site/ topics/article.asp?cu_no=2&item_no=87386&version=1&template_id=48&parent_id=28 [May 23, 2006]).

"India May Build Gas Storage Facilities for Emergencies," *Dow Jones International News*, March 15, 2004.Aiyar, "Energy Cooperation: India and Its Neighbours," p. 36.

"India needs better relations with National Oil Companies," *Indian Express*, April 30, 2006.

"India Opens Green Energy Markets," *Energy Economist*, August 1, 2005, p. 29.

"India Pledges to HelModernize Nigerian Army" *People's Daily*, November 29, 2005.

"India private oil majors gain retail fuel oil market share," *Platt's Commodity News*, December 22, 2005.

"India to Double Power Production," *The Press Trust of India*, May 21, 2006.

"India to target Gulf for energy partnerships, says Power Minister," *Hindustan Times*, July 3, 2005.

"India to target Gulf for energy partnerships, says Power Minister."

"India, China Energy Deals with Iran 'raise concerns': US," *Asia Pulse*, July 28, 2005. Indeed, in OVL, *Corporate: Profile* (www.ongcvidesh.com/corp_profile.as[May 23, 2006]).

"India, Uzbekistan sign protocol for cooperation," *Business Line*, March 8, 2006.

"India's ONGC aims for 417% rise in foreign oil, gas output," *Platts Commodity News*, June 4, 2004.

"India's ONGC, Mittal team ufor energy projects," *AK&M Russia*, July 25, 2005.

"India's OVL Begins Drilling in Iranian Block," *Asia Pulse*, May 15, 2006.

"India's SPR To Offer 12–13 Days Of Cover—Oil Min," *Oster Dow Jones Commodity Wire*, September 15, 2004.

"India's State Energy Co. Announces New Oil, Gas Finds," *BBC Monitoring South Asia*, August 14, 2005.

J

Jandik T., and A.K. Makhija, 2005, Can diversification create value? Evidence from the electric utility industry. Financial Management 34, 61-93.

Jeffrey Jones, "India to invest $1-billion in oil sands," *Reuters News Agency*, February 1, 2006, p. B5.

Johansson, T.B., Kelly, H., Reddy, A.K.N., and Williams, R.H. (editors) (1993) *Renewable Energy: Sources for Fuels and Electricity* (Island Press: Washington, D.C.). [A comprehensive reference work on alternative energy providing information and documenting progress for a wide range of renewable energy options.]

John Larkin, "India's energy woes go deep," *The Wall Street Journal*, July 11, 2005, p. A11.

K

Kaminski, V., Managing Director and Head of Research for Enron Corp., 2001. Telephone interview by authors, July 25, Philadelphia.

Kartha, Sivan and Eric D. Larson, Bioenergy Primer: Modernised Biomass Energy for Sustainable Development, United Nations Development Programme, Energy and Atmosphere Programme, New York, 2000. [This report is designed to help facilitate the practical realization of sustainable modernized bioenergy activities, including the technical, policy, and institutional aspects, by presenting promising new biomass technologies, including in-depth analyses of their respective characteristics and their relationship to UNDP's sustainable development objectives.]

Khosla, *Energy and Diplomacy*, p. 8.

KPMG, *India Energy Outlook* (2006), p. 6.

KPMG, *India Energy*, p. 8.

L

Lagrasta, F., Kaminski, V., Prevatt, R., 1999. The natural gas market. In Managing energy price risk, 2nd Ed. Risk Books, London.

Lamont, O., 1997. Cash flow and investment: Evidence from the internal capital markets. Journal of Finance 52: 83-109.

Leslie K. McNew (2004). Credit Derivatives. Energy Finance and Credit Summit 2004:Risk Limited, Sungard and Deloitte (Sponsors).

Ligia Noronha, "The Problem," *Seminar #555* (November 2005): 12.

Loftner, Robert L. –Energy Handbook, Van Nostrand Reinhold Co., N.Y.

M

M. K. Dhar, "Iran and India's Energy Security," *Central Chronicle*, May 25, 2006.

M. K. Venu, "India, China pumuthe energy levels," *The Economic Times*, January 13, 2006.

M. Reuß, W. Schölkopf, Solar District Heating with Seasonal Storage in Attenkirchen,

M. Reuß. Solare Nahwärmeversorgung Attenkirchen, Proceedings of the 7. International

M.V. Ramana, "Nuclear Power: Expensive and Unsafe," *Electrical India 2005*, Annual Issue.

Madan, Tanvi (2006). The Brookings Energy Policy Studies. Energy Security Series on India, The Brooking Institute, November, 2006.

Mahajan, "Accessing Neighbourhood Energy" in Khosla, *Energy and Diplomacy*, p. 122.

Mahajan, "Accessing Neighbourhood Energy" in Khosla, *Energy and Diplomacy*, p. 125.

Major Challenges," National Conclave, Observer Research Foundation, New Delhi, February 14, 2006.

Mani Shankar Aiyar, "Energy Cooperation: India and Its Neighbours," in Khosla, *Energy and Diplomacy*, p. 37.

Mani Shankar Aiyar, "Interview," *Seminar #555* (November 2005): 59.

Manmohan Singh, prime minister of India, "Inaugural Address," at conference "Petrotech 2005" (New Delhi,India, January 16, 2005).

Marat Yermukanov, "Kazakhstan-India Relations: Partners or Distant Friends," *Eurasia Daily Monitor*, November 16, 2004 (www.jamestown.org/edm/article.php?article_id=2368860 [May 23, 2006]).

Margolis, R. and Kammen, D. M. (1999) "Underinvestment: The energy technology and R&D policy challenge", *Science*, 285: 690-692. [An analysis of R&D investment trends in the energy sector in comparison with other sectors of the economy.]

Masten, S. E., Crocker, K. J., 1985. Efficient adaptation in long-term contracts: Take-or-pay provisions for natural gas. American Economic Review 75, 1083-1093.

Maycock, P. (2000) "The World PV Market 2000: Shifting from Subsidy to 'Fully Economic'?",

Milind Raginwar, "Step on the gas," *Business Standard*, January 23, 2006.

Ministry of Commerce and Industry, *Industrial Policy Highlights* (eaindustry.nic.in/handbk/chap001.pdf [May 23, 2006]).

Ministry of Defence, *Uzbekistan Special Forces Training: 2006*, January 2, 2006 (pib.nic.in/release/release.asp?relid =14709 [May 23, 2006]).

Ministry of Power, Power Sector at a Glance, October 15, 2006 (powermin.nic.in/JSP_SERVLETS/

Montek Singh Ahluwalia, "Inaugural Address," to conference on "India's Energy Security: Major Challenges,"

Monthly Energy Review. 1978-1995. U.S. Dept. of Energy, Energy Information Administration, Washington, D.C.

Moschini, G., Lapan H., 1995. The hedging role of options and futures under joint price, basis and production risk, International Economic Review 36(4), 1025-1049.

"Myanmar to Support India's Energy Need," *The Press Trust of India* (www.ibnlive.com/news/myanmar-to-support- indias-energy-need/10336-7.html# [May 23, 2006]).

"Mysore firm to produce biodiesel," *Business Standard*, January 23, 2006, p. 5.

N

N.K. Singh, "Introduction to Conclave," presentation for conference on "India's Energy Security: Major Challenges," National Conclave, Observer Research Foundation, New Delhi, February 14, 2006. (N. K. Singh was a senior official in the Indian bureaucracy.)

N.K. Singh, "Introduction to Conclave."

Nance, Smith and Smithson, 1993, The determinants of corporate hedging. Journal of Finance, 267-284.

National Conclave, Observer Research Foundation, New Dehli, February 14, 2006.

National Science Foundation Forum on Global Change Modeling, U.S. Global Change Research Program (USGCRP): July 1995. "World Proven Recoverable Oil Reserves by Country" – World Resources Institute – 1991.

National Science Foundation Forum on Global Change Modeling, U.S. Global Change Research Program (USGCRP): July 1995.

NEERA Economic Consulting: Energy Risk Management and Valuation

Nevin John, "RIL to Invest Rs. 5000 cr in Methane Production," *Business Standard*, January 23, 2006, p. 14.

New York Mercantile Exchange, undated. Risk management with natural gas futures and options. NYMEX, New York.

Nuclear Power Corporation of India Limited, *Nuclear Power Plants in Operation* (www.npcil.nic.in/

"Negotiations on EU/India action plan continue while both partners steudialogue on energy," *Agence Europe*, July 5, 2005.

"New price policy for oil & gas to be declared," *Financial Express*, February 10, 2006.

"NTPC in search for gas for low-cost powergen," *International Gas Report*, no. 550 (June 2, 2006): 27.

"NTPC, Reliance Energy in Deal to Bid Abroad," *Dow Jones International News*, August 15, 2005.

O

"Oil Majors Go Slow on Retail Outlet Expansion," *Financial Express*, June 16, 2006, p. 11

"ONGC at Rs. 154.85 Bn net profit is India's most valuable corp," *The Press Trust of India*, April 16, 2006.

"ONGC loses one more Russian oil asset to China," *The Economic Times*, June 21, 2006.

"ONGC, Petroleum Ministry sign MoU," *Hindustan Times*, April 10, 2006.

"OVL to buy 15% stake in Brazilian oil field for $170 mln," *The Press Trust of India*, April 27, 2006.

OIL, *Our Company: Backdro*(oilindia.nic.in/ourcomp_backdrop.htm [May 23, 2006]).

OIL, *Strategic Alliance: Overseas Operations* (oilindia.nic.in/alliance_overseas.htm [May 23, 2006]).

OIL, *Strategic Alliance: Overseas Operations* (oilindia.nic.in/alliance_overseas.htm [May 23, 2006]).

ONGC, *"ONGC first Indian company with 2-digit rank in Fortune global companies by profit,"* August , 2005 (www.ongcindia.com featart1.asp?fold=feature_article&file= feature_ article168. txt [May 23, 2006]).

ONGC, *Distribution of Shareholding* (www.ongcindia.com/download/jan18_06_company.htm [May 26, 2006]).

ONGC, *Distribution of Shareholding.*

ONGC, *Our Company: History* (www.ongcindia.com/history.as[May 23, 2006]).

ONGCNews, "Shell and ONGC Join Hands," January 19, 2006 (www.ongcindia.com/ongcnews1.asp?fold=ongcnews&file=ongcnews283.txt [May 23, 2006]).

Opler, T., Pinkowitz, L., Stulz, R., Williamson, R., 1999. The determinants and implications of corporate cash holdings. Journal of Financial Economics 52, 3-46.

OVL, "Shell, Petrobras and ONGC announce changes in BC-10 holdings and the entry of OVL," April28, 2006

OVL, *OVL Assets* (www.ongcvidesh.com/ovl_assets.as[May 23, 2006]).

OVL, OVL Assets (www.ongcvidesh.com/ovl_assets.as[May 23, 2006]).

P

"Panel to guide India's energy policy," *Hindustan Times*, July 13, 2005.

"Parliament okays bill to set uPetroleum Regulatory Board," *The Press Trust of India*, March 21, 2006.

"Petroleum, gas regulator to boost competition," *Financial Express*, February 27, 2006.

"Plan for Strategic Oil Reserves Revived," *Business Standard*, May 22, 2002, p. 1.

"PM Stresses Need for India to Diversify Energy Supplies," *BBC Monitoring South*

Asia, August 6, 2005.

"Pursuit of Power," *Economist Intelligence Unit—Business Asia*, June 26, 2006: 1.

Pachauri, "Oil in India's Energy Future," p. 54-56.

Parikh, "Valedictory Address."

PCAST Energy R&D Panel (1997) *Federal Energy Research and Development for the Challenges of the Twenty-First Century*, Report of the Energy Research and Development Panel of the President's Committee of Advisors on Science and Technology, November. [Review of the current national energy R&D portfolio and strategy on how to ensure that the United States has a program that addresses its energy and environmental needs for the 21st century.]

Peter C. Fusaro (2007). Energy Trading and Risk Management *Ref.: ©2007 UtiliPoint ® International, Inc. www.utilipoint.com*

Petersen, M. A., Thiagarajan, S. R., 2000, Risk measurement and hedging: With and without derivatives, Financial Management 29, 5-29.

PFC - Financing of Power Sector in India, Power Scenario, Power Finance Corporation Limited.

Planning Commission (2006), Integrated Energy Policy-Report of the Expert Committee, Govt. of India

Planning Commission of India, *8th Five Year Plan*. (planningcommission.nic.in/plans/planrel/fiveyr/8th/vol2/8v2ch8.htm [July 1, 2006]).

PlantsInOperation.asp [May 23, 2006]).

Pokalsky, J. T., 1995. The Natural Gas Market. In Managing Energy Price Risk, Risk Publications, London.

Pradeep Chaturvedi (2006), Draft Report of the Expert Committee on Integrated Energy Policy – Planning Commission, Government of India, December 2005; World Energy in 2006, WEC.

Prem Shankar Jha, "The Perils of Populism," *The Deccan Herald*, May 3, 2006.

Price_revision_other_cities_MS.htm and http://ppac.org.in/ppac_0506/international_price_0506.htm)

Price_revision_other_cities_MS.htmand http://ppac.org.in/ppac_0506/international_price_0506.htm); US retail price data from EIA, "Retail Gasoline Historical Prices" (http://www.eia.doe.gov/oil_gas/petroleum/data_publications/wrgp/mogas_history.html).

PriceWaterhouseCoopers, *Oil and Gas* (Gurgaon, India: India Brand Equity Foundation, 2006), "The Brookings Foreign Policy Studies Energy Security Series: India 92

PRIO Report 2006 Energy Security in Asia: China, India, Oil and Peace

Proceedings of the 2nd International Heat Powered Cycles Conference, Paris, France, 5.-7.

Proceedings of the 3rd Workshop of Annex 17 ECES IA / IEA, Tokyo, Japan, 1.-2. Oktober.

Proceedings of the ISES International Solar World Congress in Gothenburg, Sweden, 14.

Pumped Hydo: Image provided by Wikimedia - http://en.wikipedia.org/wiki/Pumped-storage_hydroelectricity

R

R. Abdullayev, "India Takes Interest in Purchase of Azeri Oil," *Trend News Agency*, August 16, 2005.

R.K. Pachauri, "Oil in India's Energy Future," *Seminar #555* (November 2005): 54.

R.K. Pachauri, "Securing India's Energy Future," *Indian Express*, August 4, 2005.

R.P. Sinha – Personal Communication, Syncrude (Canada) Ltd. (1975) Virginia Pilot – May, 1988.

R.P. Sinha – Personal Communication, Syncrude (Canada) Ltd. (1975)

Rajat Gupta et al., "Securing India's Energy Needs," *The McKinsey Quarterly* (2005): 92.

Rajgopal, S., Pincus, M., 2002. The interaction of accounting policy choice and hedging: Evidence from oil and gas firms. The Accounting Review 77, 127-161.

Rajiv Kumar, "Energy Pipelines," in Khosla, *Energy and Diplomacy*, p. 69.

Recycling of Nuclear Fuel (2007); US Department of Energy's Department of Nuclear Energy

Redfork nergy Limited. Energy Risk Management. www.redforkenergy.com.au

Renewable Energy World, 3 (4): 59-73. [A recent review of developments in the global PV market, including global and regional sales figures and future cost projections.]

Report to the Norwegian Ministry of Foreign Affairs.

Rick Wilkinson, "GAIL, Arrow Plan Joint Coalbed Methane Work," *Oil & Gas Journal*, April 17, 2006.

Risk Management Duke Energy's Code of Business Ethics, Duke Energy.

Risk Management Strategy Key to Budget Control. webmaster@food-management.com

Rolfo, J., 1980. Optimal hedging under price and quantity uncertainty: The case

of a cocoa producer, Journal of Political Economy 88(1), 100-116.
"Regulator in the Pipeline," *Business Line*, March 27, 2006, p. 8.
"Reliance cements Ras Issa refinery stake," *Middle East Economic Digest*, May 19, 2006.
"Reliance to acquire stake in Colombian oil block," *The Press Trust of India*, February 5, 2006.
"RIL, Essar Too Seek Oil Bonds," *The Economic Times*, June 19, 2006, p. 7.
"Romania, India seek cooperation in energy, IT sector," *BBC Monitoring Europe*, July 5, 2005.

S

S.V. Narasimhan, "Removing Price & Market Distortions to Enhance Fuel Choices," presentation at conference on "India's Energy Security: Major Challenges," National Conclave, Observer Research Foundation, New Delhi, February 14, 2006.
Sajal Ghosh, et al., *Energy Security Issues–India* (New Delhi: Confederation of Indian Industry: 2003), p. 3.
Salman Haidar, "Energy Security," *The Statesman*, August 2, 2005.
Sanjay Jog, "Mandatory Ethanol Blending from Oct Likely," *Financial Express*, May 9, 2006.
See ITER, "The ITER Project" (www.iter.org/ [July 1, 2006]).
Shaw, *India's Energy's Needs: Regional*, p. 8.
Shebonti Ray Dadwal, "Politics of the Iran-Pakistan-India Gas Pipeline Project," in Khosla, *Energy and Diplomacy*,p.133.
Shell Petroleum (2000) "Global Scenarios: 1998-2020", Summary Brochure. [Shell Petroleum's scenario forecast of major fuel sources for electricity production for the OECD through 2020.]
Shin, H., Stulz, R., 1998, Are internal capital markets efficient? The Quarterly Journal of Economics 113, 531-552.
Siddharth Varadarajan, "India and China: Rivals or Partners?" in Khosla, *Energy and Diplomacy*, p. 152.
Siddharth Varadarajan, "India, China and the Asian axis of oil," *The Hindu*, January 24, 2006.
Siddharth Zarabi, "Work on Oil Reserve to Start Next Year," *Business Standard*, June 22, 2006.
Sinha, R. P. – "Economics of the Production and Productivity of Coal in the United States, DOE-CMTC. Report No.: SCM-79-1. (1979)
Sinha, R. P. – "Economics of the Production and Productivity of Coal in the

United States, DOE-CMTC. Report No.: SCM-79-1. (1979)

Sinha, R. P. – "Public Opinion and Nuclear Energy Policies and their Impact on Alternative Energy Planning", World Resources Review, Volume 4, No. 4. pp. 519-527. (1993).

Soumya Kanti Mitra, "Energy Synergy," *The Economic Times*, April 9, 2006.

Sri Jegarajah, "Indian Oil Min Says Reserves Brimming, Facilities Secure," *Dow Jones Energy Service*, May 28,2002.

Srinivasan, "Energy Cooperation," p. 48.

State: A History of Panhandle Eastern Corporation, 1928–93. Cambridge University Press, New York.

Statistics have been drawn from BP Statistical Review of World Energy, June 2003, International Energy Outlook, March 2002, Energy Information administration, Office of integrated analysis and forecasting, US department of energy, Washington.

Statistics of Interstate Natural Gas Pipeline Companies. 1978-95. U.S. Dept. of Energy, Energy Information Administration. Washington D.C.

Stein Tønnesson and Åshild Kolås (2006), Energy Security in Asia: China, India, Oil and Peace

Steven Knell, "India Views Partnerships Abroad to Service Soaring Energy Needs," *Global Insight*

Strengthening Global Alliances: Enhancing National Energy Security and International Relationships Source: U.S. Department of Energy, Energy Information Administration, USA

Stulz, R., 1996. Rethinking risk management. Journal of Applied Corporate Finance 9, 8-24.

Stulz, René, 2002, *Risk management and derivatives*, South-Western Publishing, Cincinnati, OH.

Subir Raha, "Energy Tomorrow," *Seminar #555* (November 2005): 18.

Sudha Mahalingam, "Accessing Neighbourhood Energy: Thinking out of the Box," in Khosla, *Energy andDiplomacy*, p. 120.

Sudha Mahalingam, "In pursuit of energy security," *The Hindu*, February 1, 2005, p. 10.

SunGard's Energy Risk Thought Leadership - Risk Information http// www.sungard.com/Energy/default

Switch it Off, The Asia Section, The Straits Times, June 2, 2005.

Symposium for Solar Energy SOLAR 2004 (8.-12.09.2004) in Gleisdorf, Austria, S. 111 – 120.

T

"The Perils of Populism, *DNA India*, May 7, 2006. (www.dnaindia.com/report.asp?NewsID=1028247& CatID=19).

T.N.R. Rao, "Involve Private Players," *Seminar* #555 (November 2005): 44.

TERI, "New Exploration."

TERI, *New Exploration Licensing Policy: Will It Strike Oil?* (static.teriin.org/energy/nelp.htm [May 23, 2006]).

TESS: Tidal Energy Storage System: Ref. TESS - Tidal Energy Storage System.htm

The Accounting Review 76, 1-26.

The BG Group, *BG Country Operations: India* (www.bg-groucom/international/int-india.htm [July 1, 2006]).

The Boston Consulting Group (2007)- Integrated Value and Risk in Portfolio Strategy for Energy Companies. www.bcg.com

The Brookings Foreign Policy Studies Energy Security Series: India 87-89, 91, 93.

The Committee on Vision 2020, *Report of the Committee on India Vision 2020* (New Delhi: Planning Commission,December 2002), p. 73.

THE ECONOMY MIRROR: A weekly Snapshot by Corporate Planning & Economic Studies Department.IOC (Focus: Solar Energy)

The Energy and Resources Institute (TERI) www.bp.com/centres/energy www.eia.doe.gov www.epa.org

The title of his chapter on India. See Robert A. Manning, *The Asian Energy Factor* (New York: Palgrave, 2000), p.119.

The World Bank, World Development Indicators, 2005 (devdata.worldbank.org/wdi2005/Table2_5.htm).

Thermal Energy Storage at a Federal Facility: Describes the benefits of a project in which the Dallas Veterans Administration Medical Center and Texas Utilities Electric Company join in an unprecedented partnership to lower energy costs.http://www.eren.doe.gov/femp/financing/fed_facility_439.html

Thermal Energy Storage. http://www.energyusernews.com/buyers.htm

Thermal storage and deregulation:From a paper published in the April 1998 ASHRAE Journal.

Thornton, D., Welker, M., 1999. Impact of market risk disclosures on stock price sensitivity to oil and gas prices. Working paper. Queen's University.

Tidal Energy Storage System; Energy Security\TESS - Tidal Energy Storage System.htm

Tidal Energy Storage System; Energy Security\TESS - Tidal Energy Storage System.htm

Tufano, P., 1996. Who manages risk? An empirical examination of risk management practices in he gold mining industry. Journal of Finance 51, 1097-1137.

Tufano, P., 1998. The determinants of stock price exposure: Financial engineering and the gold mining industry. Journal of Finance 53, 1015-1052.

U

"US Joins India, Australia, China, Japan, S Korea in Energy Pact," *The Press Trust of India*, July 28, 2005.

U.S. Department of Energy (1997) *Renewable Energy Technology Characterizations*, Topical Report Prepared by U.S. DOE Office of Utility Technologies and EPRI, TR-109496, December. [A comprehensive assessment of renewable energy technologies, including technical descriptions, potential applications, and cost assessments and forecasts.]

U.S. Department of Energy (2000), *Annual Energy Outlook 2000*, DOE/EIA-0383(00), Energy Information Administration, Washington, D. C., December. [U.S. Department of Energy's annual report which presents midterm forecasts of energy supply, demand, and prices through 2020 prepared by the Energy Information Administration (EIA). The projections are based on results from EIA's National Energy Modeling System (NEMS).]

UNEP (2007). Financial Risk Management Instruments of Renewable Energy Projects, UNEP- Division of Technology, Industry & Economics, United Nations.

United Nations ESCAP, *Urban Environmental Governance: For Sustainable Development in Asia and the Pacific* (New York: United Nations, 2005), p. 65. From data derived by analyst Gerald Walsh using data from the Central Statistical Organization. EIU Data Services, EIU Country Data, (eiu.bvdecom/cgi/template.dll?product=101 [May 23, 2006]).

V

Videocon Industries, *Videocon: Oil & Gas* (www.videoconworld.com/oil-gas/index.ph[July 1, 2006]).

Virginia Pilot – May, 1988.

W

Wikipedia (2006), Energy Management Systems, Ref: Energy Security\Energy_management_system-Wilipedia.htm

Wikipedia: Energy Policy of India; Energy Security\Energy_ policy_of_India.htm

Williams, J., 1986. The Economic Function of Futures Markets. Cambridge University Press, New York.

Working, H., 1962, New concepts concerning futures markets and prices, American Economic Review 52, 431-459.

World & Climatic Change: Ref- *World Energy Council (KNI-WEC).*

World Economic Forum (2006: The New Energy Security Paradigm, WEF in Collaboration with Cambridge Energy Research Associates (CERA), 2006; Ref. Christoph.frei.weforum.org 37, 39-65.

World Energy Assessment (WEA) (2000), *Energy and the Challenge of Sustainability*, Report Prepared by United Nations Development Programme, Chapter 5 and 7,United Nations Department of Economic and Social Affairs and World Energy Council, September (United Nations Publications, New York, NY). [This report analyses the social, economic, environmental, and security issues linked to energy supply and use, and assesses options for sustainability in each area.]

World Energy Council (2007). Business Action for Energy- Working for Sustainable Solutions, WEC Ref: www.businessaction.org

World Energy Demand & Supply (2007); Ref: Energy Security\energy_outlook_outlooksector.aspx.htm; EXONMOBIL

World Energy Demand & supply Projections-2050; jp/en/republication/a2004/04kiban03.pdf

Worldwatch Institute (1999) Vital Signs 1999: The Environmental Trends that are Shaping our Future, (W.W. Norton & Co., London). [Worldwatch Institute's annual documentation of the key global trends for 1999, includes charts, tables and analysis of topics ranging from nuclear power generating capacity to the proliferation of genetically modified crops.]

"Will India Skid on Oil Prices?" *Business Line*, May 3, 2006, p.10.

"World Proven Recoverable Oil Reserves by Country" – World Resources Institute – 1991.

www.eia.doe.gov; www.epa.org

www.nuclear.energy.gov

Z

ZaiNet -Advanced Portfolio and Risk Management

Zee News, *Nonconventional sources can help generate 15,000 mw power*, June 1, 2006 (www.zeenews.com/znnew/ articles.asp?rep=2&aid=297398&ssid-50&sid=BUS).

Index